Transnational Environmental Liability and Insurance

The International Bar Association Series
Other titles in this series:

Arab Comparative and Commercial Law — The International Approach. Volumes 1 and 2
Volume 1 ISBN: 0 86010 977 1
Volume 2 ISBN: 0 86010 978 X
Civil Appeal Procedures Wordwide, (Editor, C. Platto)
ISBN: 1 85333 725 0
Developing Global Securities Market, (Editor, F.W. Neate)
ISBN: 0 86010 979 8
Due Diligence, Disclosures and Warranties in the Corporate Acquisitions Practice.
ISBN: 1 85333 086 8
Due Diligence. Disclosures and Warranties in the Corporate Acquisitions Practice.
2nd edn. (Editors, D. Baker and R. Jillson)
ISBN: 1 85333 633 5
Energy and Resources Law 92, (Section on Energy & Natural Resources Law)
ISBN: 1 85333 759 5
Energy Law 88, (Section on Energy & Natural Resources Law)
ISBN: 1 85333 097 3
Energy Law 90, (Section on Energy & Natural Resources Law)
ISBN: 1 85333 477 4
Enforcement of Foreign Judgments Worldwide, (Editor, C. Platto)
ISBN: 1 85333 315 8
Environmental Liability, (Editor, P. Thomas)
ISBN: 1 85333 561 4
Legal Opinions in International Transactions — Foreign Lawyers' Response to US Opinion Requests, (2nd ed.) (M. Gruson, S. Hutter, M.Kutschera)
ISBN: 1 85333 192 9
Life After Big Bang, (Editor, S. macLachlan)
ISBN: 0 86010 982 8
Nuclear Energy Law After Chernobyl, (Editors, P. Cameron, L. Hancher, W. Kuhn)
ISBN: 1 85333 110 4
Obtaining Evidence in Another Jurisdiction in Business Disputes, (Editor, C. Platto)
ISBN: 1 85333 082 5
Pre-Trial and Pre-Hearing Procedures Worldwide, (Editor, C. Platto)
ISBN: 1 85333 458 8
The Impact of the Freeze of Kuwaiti and Iraqi Assets — on Financial Institutions and Financial Transactions, (Editors, B. Campbell and D. Newcomb)
ISBN: 1 85333 558 4
Trial and Court Procedures Worldwide, (Editor, C. Platto)
ISBN: 1 85333 608 4
Using Set-Off as Security — A Comparative Survey for Practitioners, (Editor, F.W. Neate)
ISBN: 1 85333 363 8
Water Pollution—Law and Liability, (Editor, P. Thomas)
ISBN: 1 85333 874 5

International Bar Association Series

Transnational Environmental Liability and Insurance

Chairman
Ralph P. Kröner

Conference Committee
R.P. Kröner
D.P. Reichenbach
J.H. Wansink

Graham & Trotman
A member of Wolters Kluwer Academic Publishers
LONDON/DORDRECHT/BOSTON

and

International Bar Association

Graham & Trotman
Sterling House
66 Wilton Road
London SW1V 1DE
UK

Kluwer Academic Publishers Group
101 Philip Drive
Assinippi Park
Norwell, MA 02061
USA

International Bar Association
2 Harewood Place
Hanover Square
London W1R 1DE
UK

First published 1993

British Library Cataloguing in Publication Data

Transnational Environmental Liability and
Insurance – (International Bar Association Series)
I. Kröner, Ralph P. II Series 341.762
ISBN 1–85333–778–1

Library of Congress Cataloging-in-Publication Data

Transnational environmental liability and insurance/ editor, Ralph P. Kroner.
p. cm. — (International Bar Association series)
ISBN 1-85333-778-1
1. Liability for environmental damages—Europe—Congresses.
2. Insurance, Pollution liability—Europe—Congresses. 3. Liability for environmental damages—United States—Congresses. 4. Insurance, Pollution liability—United States—Congresses. I. Kröner, Ralph P. II Series.
K955.A55 1992
346.03'8—dc20
[342.638] 92-32774
CIP

Typeset in 10/11pt Times by Expo Holdings, Malaysia
Printed and bound in Great Britain by Hartnolls Ltd, Bodmin, Cornwall

Contents

About the IBA, the Section on Business Law, and Committee H (Insurance)

The International Bar Association (IBA) is the world's foremost international association of lawyers, with a membership of over 15,000 individual lawyers in 147 countries as well as 139 Bar Associations and Law Societies. Its principal aims and objectives are:

— to encourage the discussion of problems relating to professional organisation and status:
— to promote an exchange of information between legal associations world-wide:
— to support the independence of the judiciary and the right of lawyers to practise their profession without interference:
— to keep abreast of developments in the law, and to help in improving and making new laws.

Above all, it provides a forum for the dissemination of specialist knowledge on all areas of law as well as promoting contact and interchange between lawyers throughout the world.

Sections and Committees

The IBA has three Sections: the Section on Business Law, the Section on General Practice, and the Section on Energy & Natural Resources Law.

The Section on Business Law is the largest Section with over 11,500 members. It aims to promote exchange of information and views amongst members as to laws, practices, and procedures affecting business, financial, and commercial activities throughout the world.

The Section operates through 28 specialist Committees, of which Committee H (Insurance) is one of the larger with over 750 members.

Committee H (Insurance)

Committee H aims to provide its members, and the Section on Business Law as a whole, with up-to-date information about developments in insurance law throughout the world, as well as with specialist knowledge to assist in the efficient solution of practical insurance problems.

As insurance is present in every facet of commercial, industrial, and private life, lawyers practising in many different fields inevitably encounter insurance and its problems. Thus, lawyers can greatly benefit from the knowledge which membership of this Committee provides in order to help solve them.

The Committee has created a Subcommittee on Professional Indemnity which aims to study national laws in this field with a view to improved exchange of information and discussion of new developments.

The Committee and its Subcommittee meet annually at IBA or Section Conferences to present one or two day programmes.

For further details, please contact the International Bar Association, 2 Harewood Place, Hanover Square, London W1R 9HB, England. Tel: +44 (0) 71 629 1206 Fax: +44 (0) 71 409 0456

List of Contributors

Ralph P. Kröner
Trenité Van Doorne, Rotterdam, The Netherlands

Carlo Ripa di Meana
European Commissioner for Environmental Affairs

A. Kosto
State Secretary for Justice for the Netherlands

Professor Dr. J.H. Wansink
Erasmus University of Rotterdam, The Netherlands

Professor Robert Force
Tulane University Law School, New Orleans, USA

Michael J. Harrigan
Alexander & Alexander, New York, USA

Hans-Dieter Sellschopp
Munich Reinsurance Company, Munich, Germany

Jan C.P. Ekering
Loeff Claeys Verbeke, Rotterdam, The Netherlands

Colin de la Rue
Ince & Co, London, U.K.

Fred J. Rutgers
Trenité Van Doorne, Rotterdam, The Netherlands

W.J. Ouwerkerk
Koninklieke Nederlandse Shell, The Hague
The Netherlands

Charles S. Donavan
Walsh, Donavan, Lindh & Keech
San Francisco, USA

Elizabeth M. Miller
Walsh, Donovan, Lindh & Keech
San Francisco, USA

Dr. W. Pfennigstorf
New Hamburg, Germany

Anthony J.E. Fitzsimmons
Ince & Co., London, U.K.

Robert A. Lewis
McCutchen, Doyle, Brown & Enersen
San Francisco, U.S.A.

Sonia F. Saul
McCutchen, Doyle, Brown & Enersen
San Francisco, U.S.A.

Vianney Bollier
Faugère & Jutheau S.A., Paris, France

Professor Robert Cleton
Erasmus University, Rotterdam
The Netherlands

Gerd Jan van der Ziel
Nedloyd Lines B.V.
Rotterdam, The Netherlands

Peter F. Morgan
Council of Bureaux
London, U.K.

Geoffrey Brice, Q.C.
London, U.K.

Gordon Humphreys
Davies Arnold Cooper
Brussels, Belgium

Carl Martin Roos
Folksam Insurance Group
Stockholm, Sweden

Preface

On 8th and 9th May 1992, Committee H of the Section on Business Law of the International Bar Association held a seminar on "Transnational Environmental Liability and Insurance". Lawyers (both experienced practitioners and scholars from the academic world) from at least eight different countries and jurisdictions presented contributions relating to a field of law which is currently of interest.

Over the last two decades an acute awareness of the environmental damage which may be caused by accidents involving oil, chemicals, or other hazardous goods has developed. This has resulted in a flood of new legislative initiatives to promote environmental protection.

In many regimes there has been a move towards strict liability in these legislative initiatives. The consequence has been a growing need for insurance. Insurance, however, calls for limitation of liabilities. This theme and various related subjects (e.g. unlimited liability, multiple tortfeasors and collective responsibility, damage assessment, reinsurance and pooling) are discussed in this work. The contributions were extremely well received at the seminar and the Committee was encouraged to edit them into a suitable form.

The Committee wishes to express its gratitude to the authors for their assistance in reviewing the various papers produced at the seminar. The Committee would also like to thank the staff at the IBA headquarters in London and, last but not least, the publishers, Graham & Trotman Limited, for their support, assistance and enthusiasm for the project. Out of all the people who have worked to make this seminar a success I would like especially to thank my colleague at Trenité Van Doorne, Dorianne Broekman, who cheerfully helped to put this book together and Barbara Wiggers who was a great help during the seminar.

The Dutch DES case has been mentioned further on in this book. The Supreme Court of The Netherlands passed a judgment on 9 October 1992 (no. 14.667), whereby each and every producer of the medicine DES is liable towards the victims irrespective of the question of whether the victim has used the product of that particular DES producer if and so far as it is proven that the distribution of the product DES constitutes a tortious act. Therefore, in The Netherlands, the theory of alternative causation has been accepted and the theory of market share liability has been refuted. Each producer may be held liable for the whole of the loss. As my firm Trenité Van Doorne acted for plaintiffs, I refrain from further comments.

At the present time there are two developments to note concerning the EC's plans to establish a harmonized system of environmental liability law throughout Europe. One is the continuing lack of any progress concerning the EC Commission's draft Green Paper on this subject (intended consultation paper). There is no clear idea when the Green Paper might surface in finished form and no high-level Commission discussions have been scheduled. Further, the current draft is said not to be substantially changed from the draft that was initially circulated informally. A commission officially responsible for this matter had earlier stated that major redrafting was planned in order to focus and elaborate on the Commission's liability thinking.

Secondly, the Council of Europe ("COE") draft Convention on liability for damage resulting from activities dangerous to the environment (latest text dated July 1992) may take centre stage in the European environmental liability debate. The COE's legal department has revealed that the Convention may become the legal instrument of preference of the COE member countries who are also EC Member States. These countries' experts have been actively negotiating the drafting of the Convention for several years, so the current text is seen to represent the "best" that these countries can agree on at this time in this field. It may be questionable, therefore, whether the EC Member States would support the initiation of a whole new EC-focussed discussion on the same subject matter (based on the Green Paper), or to agree anything substantively other than what is already set forth in the Convention. Also, the Convention may sit more comfortably with the EC Member States' subsidiarity concerns.

The COE Convention may consequently undercut the EC Commission's Green Paper initiative. Further, if, beyond the present scope of the COE Convention, the COE eventually addresses the notion of "compensation funds" (to deal, *inter alia*, with historic contamination), the "integrated liability system" as foreseen in the draft version of the Green Paper would finally offer very little, if anything, new to the environmental liability discussion. The current text of the Convention is scheduled to be finalised this December, approved by the COE Council in Spring 1993 and then opened, probably in June 1993, for signature and ratification by the COE Member States.

Ensuring that a book of this nature is up to date as at the time of publication as far as every technical detail of the law is concerned in every jurisdiction is almost impossible. We are reasonably confident that we have represented the position correctly as at February 1992. The Committee trusts that the reader will benefit from reading this work.

Ralph P. Kröner
Chairman, Committee (Insurance Law)
of the International Bar Association's
Section on Business Law
Partner, Trenité van Doorne
"Plaza", Weena 666, Rotterdam

16 October 1992

Conference Committee:
R.P Kröner
D.P. Reichenbach
J.H. Wansink

Opening Speech

Carlo Ripa di Meana

Mr President, Ladies and Gentlemen,
I profoundly regret that this opening address has to be read to you by the organisers and that I cannot be with you this morning. Indeed, urgent and unforeseen obligations within the Commission make it impossible for me to attend this conference. I know that this brings a particular sadness to my colleague Mr Janssen Van Raay whom I had told that I would attend. And I beg his understanding for my absence.

Your conference addresses a very important subject and it does so at a timely moment. Indeed, as we are faced with considerable problems of environmental pollution and the damage and impairment which it causes. It becomes more and more relevant to ask who shall bear the cost of environmental restoration : who shall, under which circumstances and conditions, pay compensation; and how should a liability system be organised? When the Commission started to take a closer look into questions of this kind, it found that more than 20 international treaties either adopted or in preparation were dealing with questions of environmental liability. At a time when the EEC is trying to achieve its single European Market, and when national frontiers are no longer economic frontiers, this proliferation of legal approaches, which are often different and even contradictory, is likely to create and gradually increase difficulties within this single European Market. The Commission has therefore started to prepare a green book on questions of environmental liability. Contrary to what many might believe, this green book has not yet been adopted by the Commission and any document which is in circulation is no more than an internal draft, which has been leaked to the public.

I therefore have no intention of going into details of our present line of thinking, all the more so since any formal proposal for a legislative initiative would be, in view of the available time for the discussion of the greenbook, made in 1993 rather than in 1992. I only want to underline the importance of the subject of this conference for the EEC.

As regards the substance of the subject which you will be considering, it is becoming more and more evident that we cannot continue to privatize the profits from emitting pollutants into the water, the soil or the air, while socialising the costs of cleanup measures and letting the taxpayer pay for these measures — or refraining from introducing financial liability for environmental pollution altogether. In the long run such a system cannot work, and I am very pleased to see that the Dutch Government and the Dutch Legislature have started to take several very important steps to ensure that in future pollution no longer pays, but that the polluter shall be bound to pay for impairment and damage caused by him. Also, the City of Rotterdam has contributed, and is contributing, to the effort of ensuring that responsibility is assumed where contamination has occurred.

Problems of environmental liability are far from being solved and it is obvious that insurance questions are a very relevant aspect of this problem. I therefore congratulate the organisers on the choice of topic and wish you all useful discussions, good entertainment and a lot of fun during the conference. Again, I regret and apologise for not being with you.

Welcoming Speech

A. Kosto

Mr Chairman, ladies and gentlemen.

I was delighted to accept the invitation from the organisers of this seminar to speak to you here today. I should first of all like to welcome you to the Netherlands and, more especially, to Rotterdam. I regard it as a great honour that the International Bar Association elected to hold its business law seminar here in Rotterdam. This city, with its unique location at the mouth of two great rivers — the Rhine and the Maas — has long been an important centre of international trade and shipping. After the Second World War, the petrochemical industry established itself in a big way in Rotterdam, and this has had an enormous effect on the city's infrastructure, making it one of the world's biggest ports. The Dutch always refer to it as the biggest port in the world; it is at any rate the principal commercial gateway to Europe.

However, there is another side to Rotterdam's unique geographical position. The Rhine and the Maas carry pollution downstream to Rotterdam. I recall a number of cases brought by market gardeners in the Rotterdam delta area concerning damage they had suffered as a result of salts discharged into the Rhine by the French potash mines. These cases set an important international legal precedent on transboundary environmental pollution. But the many activities carried out in the port area itself involving the processing, storage and transportation of polluting and hazardous substances also constitute a major threat to people, property and the environment. This area is therefore a constant focus of attention for Dutch environmental policy, including that on liability for damage.

Mr Chairman, numerous international organisations have undertaken initiatives on liability for environmental pollution and many treaties, directives and recommendations are in the pipeline. I would draw your attention to the activities being undertaken under the auspices of the UN specialised agencies, including UNEP, ECE and IMO, and of the OECD, the Council of Europe and the European Community. The general trend is towards replacing general liability with strict liability, which is limited in some cases and linked to an insurance obligation. This worldwide focus on environmental problems is of course a welcome development, but I find myself wondering whether all these regulations will be sufficiently harmonised. We must make sure that we are not confronted in a few years with overlapping international regulations which only give rise to legal complications. Indeed, many of the regulations pertaining to liability are complex enough, even without such complications. Another problem could lie in the extent to which it is possible to insure against these new liability risks. Developments on the international insurance market show that there is a limit to the cover which insurers can provide for major new risks. It is at any rate clear that insurance cannot be provided against every type of risk.

It is clear that in the future there will be no shortage of work for lawyers in informing and advising industry on new developments in the field of environmental liability law. The subject of your seminar is therefore topical and well-chosen. It is also important that legal practitioners have a hand in developing new regulations, which should be drawn up on the basis of dialogue between government and those who will be involved in their practical implementation.

Mr Chairman, as State Secretary for Justice, I am also responsible for the legal profession. From this point of view, too, I am delighted that the International Bar Association chose the Netherlands to host this important seminar. The Dutch bar is also increasingly focusing its attention on the situation abroad and is fully aware of the need for cooperation with its foreign counterparts. Many law firms either have offices abroad or have entered into cooperative agreements with firms in other countries. This has become essential in order for them to offer their clients a good service.

Finally, I should like to express my hope that over the next few days, the participants of this seminar will not only concentrate on environmental problems, but will also have the opportunity of getting to know the Netherlands and its people a little better. This is a small and densely-populated country, but it has many beautiful areas. I wish you all a pleasant and productive stay in the Netherlands.

Thank you.

Environmental Liability Insurance: Tour d'Horizon in Europe[1]

John H. Wansink

In many European countries the government has recently introduced or is preparing new rules to be introduced in the near future relating to strict liability to compensate pollution damage, (e.g. Sweden, Germany and The Netherlands).[2] These developments will effect the insurance industry because in practice the impact of any liability system depends on a pass-through mechanism provided by the insurance and reinsurance industries. Generally speaking the insurance industry shows a willingness to support such legislation initiatives by setting up new insurance schemes provided some conditions are met. It is interesting to look at these new schemes in more detail and to mention items which they have more or less in common.

1. Pooling

First of all, there is a tendency to form non-exclusive pools to underwrite new, relatively unknown pollution risks under a well-controlled regime of environmental legislation. Pools have been set up in France (Garpol 1978, replaced by Assurpol in 1989), Italy (ANIA in 1979), The Netherlands (MAS in 1985) and very recently Denmark (1992).

Special pollution policies and endorsements are offered in Denmark, Finland, Germany, Italy, Sweden, the U.K. (the American International Underwriters (U.K.) Limited, AIU policy) and The Netherlands.

[1] Parts of this paper are based on material collected for the special study XIV of the AIDA Working Partly on Pollution and Insurance, directed by Werner Pfenningstorf in co-operation with James Morrow and John H. Wansink.

[2] The Swedish Environmental Damage Act (1986), the German Environmental Liability Act (1990) and the Dutch Bill on Environmental Liability book 6 New Civil Code (1989).

2. Overall Coverage for Pollution Risks, Both Sudden and Gradual

There is a tendency to extend coverage to gradual pollution risks: the old dogma that one should abstain from any coverage for non-accidental risks, has vanished, that is to say, in the new environmental liability insurance schemes. I will refer to the insurance markets in France, the Netherlands, Sweden, Denmark, Germany, the U.K. and Italy. In some policies the coverage for non-accidental risk is explicitly mentioned:

ASSURPOL (France)

> "This cover applies to the pecuniary consequences of the Insured's liability arising from bodily injury, material damage and consequential loss suffered by third parties after accidental or non-accidental environmental impairment provided that such impairment has been caused fortuitously in direct or indirect connection with the Insured's activities inside his own premises, as described in the Special Conditions."

Environmental Liability Model (Germany)

> "Within the range of the risks insured under no. 2 the coverage includes — in partial deviation from sect. 4, no. 15 AHB — statutory liability claims on account of property damage caused by gradual action of temperature, gases, vapors, humidity, precipitation (smoke, soot, dust and the like...)."

The two largest insurance companies in Sweden displayed a very unique attitude when very recently they decided to delete the traditional exclusion clause for gradual pollution from their new general liability insurance policies (CGL) for middle- and small-sized industries: a decision based on experience: the polluting industries have done much to improve their cleaning techniques and industrial processes are no longer the major pollution problem.

Nonetheless it is clear an extended coverage for gradual pollution is not realistic without some restrictions. First of all the insured's liability is very often only covered insofar as the damage is the result of an emission directly from a site specified in the policy (e.g. the French ASSURPOL policy, the Dutch MAS policy, the Italian ANIA policy, the Danish policy, the English AIU policy and the German Model). The reason for this geography restriction is clear. It limits the coverage to risks linked to activities whereon the insurer has some grip by means of risk surveys and — dependent on the outcome — the requirement that certain preventive measures be taken. It also enables the insurer to make sound ratings based on the nature of the environment in which the insured carries out its activities (sand, clay, water extraction areas, agriculture, nurseries, residential areas).

Secondly, a lot of policies explicitly exclude the expected and accepted consequences of normal operations and/or the consequences of wilful neglect in the maintenance of installations designed to prevent or minimize pollution.

ASSURPOL (§ 3 under 10 and 11)

"Being always excluded:
10. Damage which the insurer may prove to be the inevitable and foreseeable consequence for the insured of operating methods such as prescribed or effected by the insured or, where the insured is a corporate body, by the management of the firm;
11. Damage which the insurer may prove that they have been caused or aggravated by the poor state, inadequacy or defective maintenance of installations intended to prevent environmental impairment and that such poor state, inadequacy or defective maintenance was known or could not be ignored by the insured or, where the insured is a corporate body, by the management of the firm."

Denmark (§ 3 under m and o)

"This insurance shall not provide cover for:
m. injury or damage occasioned by the negligent maintenance of installations primarily intended for the purpose of preventing, stopping or limiting the extent of environmental impairment caused by the activities of the Policyholder.
o. injury or damage occurred and arising out of the ordinary operation of the business and/or which has been approved or is tolerated by the authorities."

German Model (§ 6 under 1, 2 and 7)

"Not insured are:
1. Claims on account of damage resulting from substances hazardous to water which in the course of handling are spilled, or drip, run off, evaporate, or otherwise get into the ground or into a body of water. This shall not apply if events of this kind are caused by a disruption of operations.
2. Claims on account of damage resulting from effects on the environment which due to the operation are unavoidable, necessary or accepted.

This shall not apply if the policyholder proves that given the state of technology at the time of the effect on the environment causing the damage considering the circumstances of the individual case, he did not need to know the possibility of such damage.
7. Claims against persons (policyholder or any insured person) who caused damage by consciously failing to observe the guidelines or instructions provided by the manufacturer or to be observed according to the state of technology for use, regular test, inspections or service, or to make necessary repairs."

As the non-accidental risk is so much linked to the ordinary conduct of business, one may wonder whether particularly the last-mentioned category of exclusion clause does not set aside the coverage to a substantial extent. It looks like the main practical impact of the extended coverage will be the elimination of the distinction between sudden and non-sudden as the decisive factor for granting coverage (see under 6).

Two other restrictions on an extended coverage for gradual pollution are worth mentioning. First, some policies explicitly exclude pollution due to *acid rain or acid deposition*. One of the features is that acid deposition on a certain part of the soil cannot generally be attributed to a specific source of emission.

Traffic, domestic and foreign industries as well as farming are collectively responsible. Insurers do not want to cover this collective responsibility, even if the law of liability based on individual responsibility offered any prospect of recovery of damages. However, the Dutch MAS policy provides a limited coverage if and insofar as the insured proves the damage results from acid deposition caused by him only and from one insured site.

MAS (§ 2 under 5)

"The insurance shall not cover the insured's liability for damage resulting from acid deposition not caused by the insured alone from one site. Acid deposition shall be the deposition from the air of materials which have a direct of indirect effect upon the pH value."

Denmark (§ 3 under n)

"This insurance shall not provide cover for:
injury or damage occurred and arising out of acid rain and the discharge of nutritive salts and other similar kinds of environmental impairment the hazardous effect of which is due to the aggregate impact of discharges from several pollution sources."

AIU policy (UK)

"This insurance does not apply to loss arising from pollution conditions based upon or attributable to acid rain conditions."

The second restriction refers to clauses excluding *specified installations or activities* (nuclear risks, oil well, port and offshore activities) or covering these risks with a high gradual polluting potential subject to special conditions (underground tanks). See for these risks (with the exception of nuclear risks) the following clauses.

ASSURPOL (§ 3 under 7)

"Being always excluded from the cover:
Damage caused by any engine or installation for research, drilling, storage and exploitation of oil at sea."

MAS (§ 1 under 4)

"The following provisions apply for environmental impairment in respect of subsoil tanks:

1. *Subsoil tanks*

Subsoil tanks shall be understood to mean tanks completely or partially under ground. This includes the underground supply and waste pipes.

2. *Tanks for heating purposes (diesel, gas or heating oil)*

The insurance covers damage in connection with subsoil tanks if at the moment the damage arises

— the tank is younger than 15 years and
— the tank has not been out of use for more than 18 months at a stretch

This condition does not have to be complied with if it appears from an official certificate that the tank was approved by KIWA or by a KIWA acknowledged fitter two years before at most.
3. *Other tanks*
The insurer covers damage in connection with subsoil tanks other than described above, if the insured proves in connection with a claim that the tanks have been checked frequently by standards laid down in CPR 9-1 and/or CPR 9-4 by a KIWA acknowledged fitter and approved by him."

Denmark (§ 3 under h)

"This insurance shall not provide cover for:
injury or damage occurred and arising out of the application of machines or installations used for the exploration, drilling and extraction of oil or gas."

AIU policy (§ IV under 3 and 19)

"This policy does not apply to loss:
3. arising from the ownership or operation of any offshore facility, nor shall there be any coverage for liability resulting from emissions of drilling fluid, oil, gas or other fluids from any oil, gas, mineral, water or geothermal well of any nature whatsoever;
19. arising from pollution conditions emanating from any underground storage tank and associated piping until satisfactory integrity test results are received, approved and on file with the Company, such test(s) having been carried out in a form approved by the Company. Coverage will only be provided for those tanks specifically approved and scheduled on to the policy by endorsement.

An underground storage tank is any tank, including associated underground piping connected to the tanks, that has at least ten (10) percent of its volume below ground."

A lot of these clauses (e.g. regarding nuclear and marine activities) are also found in the CGL policies, while the same caution is shown by the fact that the extended coverage of the Swedish CGL policy as mentioned hereabove does not apply to the large and hazardous industrial operations. Also the new German Model coverage is divided in separate blocks for different risks.

3. Unlawful Emissions, Initiated at Management Level

One of the major problems in fighting pollution is that, from a financial point of view, it is often cheaper for companies to discharge noxious substances illegally instead of neutralizing them or disposing of them in a lawful way. Granting cover for such actions would not be justifiable towards the collectivity of bona fide insureds.

To exclude this risk, one cannot always successfully invoke the classic exclusion clause for damage deliberately caused, as according to the wording of the policy it is not merely sufficient for the claims-causing act (i.e. the discharge) to have been performed deliberately, but, instead, the damage itself must be the intended result of this act. In those cases an additional explicit exclusion clause may solve the problem, excluding the financial consequences of wilful violation of laws or regulations, as the following clauses may illustrate.

ASSURPOL (§ 3 under 11)

"Being always excluded:
11. Damage which the insurer may prove that it has been caused or aggravated by non-compliance with legal texts mentioned in the special conditions or any other text having substituted them and with standards and regulations enacted by competent authorities in application thereof and that such non-compliance was known or could not be ignored by the insured or, where the insured is a corporate body, by the management of the firm."

MAS (§ 2 under 3)

"The insurance shall not cover the liability for damage resulting from actions or omissions in defiance of any State regulation with regard to the environment, if such action or omission occurred by order of or with the approval of the policyholder or any of the insureds mentioned in the schedule.

If the policyholder or the insured meant in the previous paragraph is a body corporate, the policyholder or insured shall, for the purpose of this exclusion, be considered to be a member of the board of management as well as any staff member employed by the policyholder or insured charged by the management with the special responsibility of observing the above regulations."

Denmark (§ 3 under d)

"This insurance shall not provide cover for:
injury or damage occurred and arising out of actions or omissions in violation of public regulations for the protection of the environment, where such actions or omissions occur as a result of an order from, or with the approval of, the Policyholder and where such violations may be characterized as intentional or grossly negligent.

If the Policyholder is a body corporate or any other kind of legal person, for the purpose of the present exclusion of cover the policyholder shall be considered to be all members of the board and management of the policyholder's business as well any persons in the employment of the Policyholder whom the management or the board have charged with the responsibility of supervising compliance with the above provisions."

German Model (§ 6 under 6)

"Not insured are:
6. Claims against persons (policyholder or any insured person) who cause damage by wilfully deviating from statues, regulations or orders directed to the policyholder by public authorities."

AIU policy (§ IV under 15, jo II under A)

"This insurance does not apply to loss:
15. arising from pollution conditions based upon or attributable to the insured's intentional, wilful or deliberate non-compliance with any Stature, Act, Bye-law, Statutory Instrument, Order or Regulation, or with any Notice, order or Instruction of any Ministry or other Governmental or Statutory body or agency or of any local authority, or any like organization;

Insured means the policyholder and any director, officer, partner (where the policyholder is a partnership) or employee thereof while acting within the scope of his/her duties as such."

Particularly the French, Danish and Dutch policies explicitly show that where the insured is a corporate body, the knowledge and attitude of the management of the company is decisive. It looks like the same applies to Finish and Swedish policies, as is the contrary in the English AIU policy.[3]

The majority underlines in my opinion the basic philosophy that casual misbehaviour of lower-ranked employees without any consent or knowledge of the management should be considered as a fortuitous event which does not suspend coverage on behalf of the insured company.

4. An Extended Concept of Loss Insured

Apart from bodily injury the classic General Liability Policy covers property damage, but only if it concerns physical damage to, destruction or loss of, tangible property. This concept of property damage is too restricted in view of an adequate environmental impairment liability cover. In a number of cases of environmental pollution there would be no cover at all for damage that can well be imagined. Think of damage as a result of the loss of use of a hotel or an industrial plant because of excessive stench or toxious air pollution in the immediate neighbourhood, while the hotel or the plant itself is not physically damaged.

A lot of new insurance schemes fill this gap. The Dutch MAS policy and the English AIU policy provide an extended coverage for loss of economic use of tangible property not physically damaged, etc., including any consequent loss. The same applies to the ASSURPOL policy, which covers "any pecuniary loss resulting from the loss of use of a right, the interruption of a service rendered by a person or by movables or immovables", and — within a more limited scope — to the new German Model, which covers economic loss resulting from violation of appropriation rights (fishing, etc.), the right not to have one's business disrupted and water use rights.

To date there is no trace of any extended coverage for ecological damage which is not linked to loss of economic use or damage to individually owned property.

5. Time-limits and the Legacy of the Past

It is characteristic of environmental risks that it can take many years before the disposal of chemical waste in the ground or the release of toxic material into the

[3] See the following Finnish clause: "the insurance does not cover any injury, loss or damage resulting from action which is against the law, acts or statutes or against regulations or directives issued by competent authorities regarding product safety, of which action the company management has, or should have been aware."

air or the water eventually results in noticeable damage to people or property. The actual exposure to pollution often has a gradual and invisible character, especially if the release of harmful substances is the continuous and repeated result of normal and regular plant operation. This also implies that it is often very difficult to establish exactly when the damage arose in the event of gradual pollution.

As the General Liability Policies generally apply the loss occurrence principle to limit the coverage by time, there is a tendency to adopt a "claims made" system for the specific environmental liability cover. Basically, there are three variants. According to the first one the decisive factor is the receipt of the claim by the *insurer*.

ASSURPOL (§ 5)

"The cover of this contract as described under article 2 will apply to claims notified to Insurers between the date of inception and the normal date of expiry or anticipated date of cancellation of this contract excepting claims relating to circumstances or events for which Insurers may prove that the Insured was aware before the date of inception of this contract that the related cover would apply to them".

MAS (§ 1)

"The insurance provides cover for the liability of insureds for damage as a result of an environmental impairment occurring direct the site(s) mentioned in the schedule, provided the claim for indemnification of damage and expenses has been received by the company during the period of insurance."

This variant makes the system less susceptible to fraud than the second one wherein the receipt of the claim by *the insured* prevails.

Denmark (§ 5)

"The insurance shall cover liability for claims made against the Insured by public authorities or third parties duri.ng the insurance period.

Cover shall not be provided for claims notified to the Insurers later than 3 months after the expiry of the insurance period."

ANIA (Italy)

"The coverage is granted for claims made for the first time during the period of insurance."

The third variant is a combination of the two other ones, providing coverage for claims first made against the insured and reported to the insurer during the policy period (see AIU policy).

The majority of policies provide an explicit regulation in respect of the application of the time-limits to serial claims. Generally speaking a claim in a series is deemed to have been made/received when the first claim was made/received. There will be coverage for all subsequent claims in the series, that is to say insofar as they are actually made/received during the policy period of the run-off-period, if applicable. It seems only the Italian ANIA policy and the Danish policy provide a more generous cover in this respect.

MAS (§ 1 under 3 and 4 under 3)

"If one single environmental impairment results in more than one claim, these claims — as far as they have actually been received by the company during the period of insurance — shall be regarded as one claim and shall be deemed to have been received by the company at the time the first claim was received.

For the application of the amount mentioned in the schedule for each claim, the run-off period is deemed to be part of the period of contract of the cancelled insurance."

Denmark (§ 6)

"Claims made against the insured under § 5, injury or damage occurred and arising from the same liability-entailing conduct shall be considered one single insurance event (claim series).

A claim in a claim series shall be deemed to have been made at the point in time when the first of such claims is made, cf § 5 above.

Whenever just one claim in a claim series relates to environmental impairment arising from actions or omissions which occurred prior to the inception of this the present insurance policy, no cover shall be provided for any of the claims in the series.

No cover shall be provided for claims in a claim series which are made later than 5 years after the expiry of this the present insurance policy.

ANIA

"In cases with more than one claim arising from the same polluting source, the day of the first claim will be considered the day of all further claims, even if they are made after termination of the insurance.

The choice of a "claims made"-system instead of the loss occurrence system does not confront the insurer with the ambiguity of the notion "occurrence" and the inherent problems, well known from the asbestosis cases.

An alternative way of avoiding this ambiguity shows the German Model: it maintains the loss occurrence principle and it looks as if the insurers are trying to solve the inherent problems mentioned above by introducing a new definition of loss occurrence, i.e. "the verifiable first discovery of the bodily injury or property damage by the injured person or a third person".

One cannot deny that a "claims made"-system basically ignores the interests of the insured. He instantly loses any coverage at the time of expiry of the policy, even with respect to losses which occurred during the term of the insurance contract and which may give rise to a claim in the future. It is clear that no insurer is prepared to protect the insured for any actual subsequent claim under a new insurance contract.

To mitigate the consequences of this abrupt cut-off of the coverage, almost all policies provide a type of "run-off" cover in case of the expiry of the policy for reasons other than the insured's bad faith.

ASSURPOL (§ 5)

"In case of the Insured's cessation of activities, both parties may agree that against payment of an extra premium, the cover will still apply to damage occurred during the period of validity of the contract and notified to Insurers within a lapse of time to be precise after the normal date of expiry or the anticipated cancellation. In any case, the maximum available commitment will be as set under article 6 hereunder for a full year of insurance."

MAS (§ 4)

"If the policy is cancelled due to one of the following cases, the company shall offer the policyholder to cover the run-off risk for a period of twelve months from the date the insurance is cancelled:

— cancellation by the policyholder in accordance with article 8.2 of section A (revision of premium and conditions);
— cancellation by the company as per contract or premium renewal date or after a claim for reasons other than the deliberate supply of incorrect details (article 8.1 and 8.3 of section A);
— cancellation by the company in accordance with article 1.6.2 or 1.6.3 if this section (aggravation of risk)

If the policyholder has accepted this offer in writing within the period mentioned above, and at the same time has paid within 30 days from receipt of the notice of cancellation the annual premium due for this section, the cover in accordance with this section shall remain in force in respect of:

1. *claims*
claims for the indemnification of losses received by the company and insofar as they concern;

— bodily injury or impairment of health either or not resulting in death,
— damage, destruction or loss of material objects belonging to anyone other than the policyholder, including pollution or contamination thereof,
— the pollution or contamination of any surface water, including the subsequent damage, or
— impairment of the economic useful value of the material objects belonging to anyone other than insureds, other than by damage to, or destruction or loss of these objects, arisen during the period of contract of the cancelled insurance, but prior to the inception of the agreed run-off period;

2. *salvage cost*
claims for the compensation of salvage cost received by the company during the run-off period and insofar as they relate to measures taken during the period of contract of the cancelled insurance, but prior to the inception date of the agreed run-off period.

For the application of the amount mentioned in the schedule for each claim, the run-off period is deemed to be part of the period of contract of the cancelled insurance.

For the application of the indemnity limit per insurance year mentioned in the schedule all claims for the determination and compensation of damage and expenses actually received by the company during the run-off period, unless an earlier year of insurance is applicable in accordance with the provision in articles 1.3 and 1.3.2."

AIU-policy (§ V)

"The policyholder shall be entitled to purchase an Extended Discovery Period upon termination of coverage as defined herein except in the event of non-payment of premium.

(a) The Company shall issue an Extended Discovery Period of 12 months for all covered locations or any specific location listed in Item 5 of the Schedule if the policy holder:
1. makes a written request for it which the Company receives within 30 days after termination of coverage as defined herein;
2. properly pays the additional premium when due. If that additional premium is paid when due, the Extended Discovery Period may not be cancelled, provided that all other terms and conditions of the policy are met.

(b) A claim first made and reported within the Extended Discovery Period will be deemed to have been made on the last day of the policy period, provided that the claim arises from pollution conditions that commenced before the end of the policy period.

(c) Termination of coverage means:
1. cancellation or non-renewal of this policy by the policyholder or by the Company; or
2. deletion of a covered location from this policy by the Company.

(d) The Extended Discovery Period is available to the policyholder for not more than 100% of the policy premium."

German Model (§ 8)

"If the insurance relationship is terminated by complete or permanent absence of the insured risk, or by notice given by the insurer or the policyholder, the coverage shall continue for damage that occurred while the contract was in effect but had not been discovered when the contract expired, provided that:

— the coverage shall exist for three years counting from the time when the insurance relationship expired.
— the coverage exists for the entire extension period within the scope of coverage applicable at the time of expiration, and within the limits of the unused part of the amount of coverage agreed for the last year prior to expiration."

If the policy provides an aggregate limit as an ultimate limit per insurance year, it is necessary to impute claims made during the run-off cover to a particular period of insurance. Mostly the insurer does not offer the insured a separate limit for the run-off cover. All claims are imputed to the last year prior to expiration (see MAS, German Model, AIU policy). The exception is the French ASSURPOL policy.

An alternative solution to mitigate the consequences of an abrupt cut-off of the coverage is provided in the Danish policy by introducing elements of the occurrence principle in the definition of claims made:

"A claim shall be deemed to have been made at the earliest of the following points in time:

(a) the point in time when the insured receive(s) the first written notification relating to an injury or damage and containing a claim for compensation,

(b) the point in time when the Policyholder or any person in charge of the operations of the business on his/her behalf for the first time obtains information of the occurrence of a case of environmental impairment which may lead to the submission of a claim for compensation."

A claims-made system in principle fully exposes the insurer to the so-called "run-in-risk" and thereby to the threat of being manôeuvred into the position of paying the bill for pollution caused in the past: pollution caused when society permitted us to live at home and in industry under the motto of "every man for himself and the environment for all of us". As mentioned above the risks of the past are a time-bomb, the extent of which is even now hard to estimate. In the French ASSURPOL policy protection against this legacy from the past is secured by the operative clause (§ 5), as mentioned hereabove.

A lot of policies prefer an alternative solution by way of an explicit exclusion clause for pollution from the past.

MAS (§ 2)

"The insurance shall not cover the liability for damage as a result of an environmental impairment caused by the insured's acts or omissions which took place prior to the inception of the insurance."

Denmark (§ 5)

"Cover shall not be provided for liability for injury or damage arising out of environmental impairment caused by actions or omissions which occurred prior to the inception of this the present insurance policy.

German Model (§ 6 under 3)

"The following are not insured:
Claims on account of damage that had already occurred when the contract became effective.

There shall be no coverage for claims on account of damage caused by events for which coverage exists or could have been obtained in accordance with previous insurance contracts."

It appears the English AIU policy (§ IV under 1) applies a less strict exclusion clause for pollution from the past as it requires actual or constructive knowledge at management level that pollution conditions existing prior to the inception of the policy could have been expected to give rise to a claim.

"This insurance does not apply to loss:
1. arising from pollution conditions existing prior to the inception of this policy, if any employee of the policyholder responsible for environmental affairs, control or compliance or any officer, director or partner of the policyholder knew or could have reasonably foreseen that such pollution conditions could have been expected to give rise to a claim."

So far we have focused on new insurance schemes, but what about the classic General Liability policies? In the past these policies very often provided coverage on a so-called "act committed" basis: the liability of the insured is covered, provided the liability is based upon an act or omission committed during the period of insurance. The use of that system of limitation of coverage by time, together with the absence of any particular pollution clause, implies that even a cancelled policy still provides coverage of liability for pollution damage which occurred afterwards during the full period of limitation, provided that this liability stems from an act or omission committed before cancellation of the policy.

Nowadays the current system for limitation of coverage by time in the General Liability Policies cuts off the above-mentioned "run-off" risk, as the coverage is restricted to liability for pollution damage as a result of bodily injury or property damage which occurred during the period of insurance ("loss occurrence" principle). However, at the same time it fully exposes the insurer to the so-called "run-in" risk, referring to claims based on unlawful acts and omissions with regard to past environment management. As the time-bomb effect is largely linked to non-accidental (gradual) discharge of noxious substances, the insurance industry has to rely for protection primarily on the restriction of coverage of the General Liability Policy to the *accidental* pollution risk only.

6. The Boundaries of the "Accidental" Pollution Risk

To be fully protected the distinction between accidental and gradual pollution should be well defined in policy text. The less strict and clear the wording of the policy, the likelier the chance of an excessive interpretation by the courts to establish coverage on behalf of the innocent victims of pollution.

It is beyond doubt the insurers' aim to eliminate from coverage, pollution damage as a result of normal business as well as damage caused by deliberate acts of pollution, ordered or authorized for economical reasons by the policy making management. As I mentioned before, it is reasonable to an insured company and in full accordance with the basic principles of fortuity and public policy to grant coverage in those cases where casual misbehaviour of employees at a lower level causes an expected and intended polluting event. In other words the sudden, unintended and unexpected nature of the polluting incident as generally required for coverage in the policy wordings, should be determinated from the standpoint of the policymaking management.

This view is most clearly expressed in a Belgian policy, defining the concept of accident as "a sudden event which is involuntary and unforeseen as regards the policyholder, his board of management or leading staff members". It is also the key statement in the Dutch CGL policy-clause:

> "The insurance shall not cover the liability for damage in connection with an environmental impairment, unless this environmental impairment is a sudden and

accidental event and this occurrence is not the direct cause of a slow and gradual process."

The experience in the United States shows the eroding effect of policy-wordings in which the requirement of sudden, unexpected and unintended was not linked to the polluting event itself (i.e. the release of polluting substances) but (partly) to the resultant damage to third parties. The coverage focused on an accident, including continuous and repeated exposure to conditions, which results in bodily injury or property damage neither expected nor intended from the standpoint of the insured. This coverage even included intentional pollution insofar as it was uncertain and/or unexpected whether a third party would be injured or a third party's property would be damaged and/or what the nature and extent of the injury or property damage would be. For that reason it is preferable to emphasize the sudden, unexpected and unintended nature of the polluting event, as is done in the Dutch CGL policy clause and the following two English clauses:

"This policy excludes all liability in respect of pollution or contamination other than caused by a sudden identifiable unintended and unexpected incident which takes place in its entirety at a specific time and place during the period of Insurance.
This insurance does not cover any liability for:
1. Personal injury or bodily injury or loss of, damage to, or loss of use of property directly or indirectly caused by seepage, pollution or contamination, provided always that this paragraph (1) shall not apply to liability for personal injury or bodily injury or loss of or physical damage to or destruction of tangible property, or loss of use of such property damaged or destroyed, where such seepage, pollution or contamination is caused by a sudden, unintended and unexpected happening during the period of this Insurance."

7. Salvage Costs/Clean-up of the Insured Site

An essential part of any environmental impairment liability policy is the coverage of clean-up expenses and other costs needed to avert or minimize pollution damage. Basically one can divide these costs into three categories:

(a) costs claimed by third parties as a financial loss, sustained as a result of measures initiated by themselves to clean up or to avert or otherwise minimize pollution damage;
(b) expenses claimed by public authorities as a financial loss, sustained as a result of measures carried out by them to fulfil an explicit or implicit obligation to clean up;
(c) expenses incurred by the insured/polluter as a result of preventive measures taken by or on behalf of himself.

Generally speaking, the costs mentioned under (a) and (b) are covered in as far as they fall within the scope of the concept of damage covered under the policy, and, secondly, if the insured can be held legally liable for these costs.

In some countries the coverage of expenses incurred by the insured himself as mentioned under (c) is based upon a general rule of insurance law. This applies to Germany (§ 62 VVG), Belgium (§ 17. Com. C.), the Netherlands (§ 283 Com. C.), Italy (§ 1914, 1932 Av.C.) and Denmark (§ 52, 53 Ins. Law). All legal provisions mentioned above have more or less in common that they refer to costs incurred for measures taken by or on behalf of the insured, which are reasonably required to avert *the imminent danger* of third parties suffering damage for which, on the occurrence thereof, the insured would be responsible and for which the insurance provides cover, or, if the damage has materialized, to limit such damage as much as possible.

The presence of "imminent danger" as a condition precedent to coverage particularly in cases wherein an insured event has not yet occurred is to set aside the not-covered costs linked to the general obligation of the insured towards the insurer to take reasonable care to prevent accidents.

Usually the coverage of salvage costs is elaborated in a special policy clause like the one in the German Model (§ 5).

5. *Expenses incurred prior to occurrence of insured event*
5.1. The insurer will, even if no insured event has occurred, reimburse the policyholder for expenses incurred for measures taken after a disruption of the operation of an insured installation or in compliance with an order issued by a public authority to avert or minimize personal injury or property damage which would otherwise unavoidably occur. Sentence 1 shall also apply provided that there may be recourse claims of the owner of an installation against the policyholder and that such claims are insured. The order of the public authority or the discovery of the disruption of operation, whichever is earlier, must occur while the insurance is in effect.

The policyholder is obligated,

— to notify the insurer without delay of the discovery of a disruption of operations or issuance of an order by the public authority;

— to do everything necessary to limit expenses to what is necessary and objectively suitable for averting the occurrence or minimize the extent of the damage;

— upon the insurer's request, to file in time for review of administration orders.

If the policyholder does not meet these obligations, expenses will be reimbursed only to the extent they were necessary and objectively suitable for averting the occurrence or minimizing the extend of the damage.

If the policyholder and the insurer have agreed on the measures, the cost of such measures will be reimbursed.

If under the circumstances of the individual case there is not time for an agreement, the insured will reimburse the expenses that the policyholder could under the circumstances regard as appropriate.

Expenses will be reimbursed, within the agreed amount of coverage, up to an aggregate amount of DM … for each disruption of operations or administrative order, but not more than DM … for each insurance year.

Of the expenses, the policyholder shall bear …% himself.

If a loss occurs despite the measures taken, the expenses reimbursed by the insurer shall be counted toward the amount of coverage.

5.2. Expenses incurred in compliance with administrative orders as specified in no. 5.1 will be reimbursed irrespective of whether the measures are taken by the policyholder or by the public authority.

5.3 In no case will there be any reimbursement for expenses — even if they overlap with expenses under 5.1 — for maintaining, repairing, renovating, refitting, securing or rehabilitating facilities, premises or personal property owned (or rented, or leased) by the policyholder; including property formerly owned or possessed by the policyholder.

There will be reimbursement, however, for expenses caused by the necessity to impair, for the purpose of averting or minimizing personal injury or property damage that would otherwise unavoidable occur, facilities, premises or personal property of the policyholder not affected by an effect on the environment. Resulting increases in value are to be deducted."

Two aspects are particularly interesting in this German Clause. First of all the *expenses incurred in compliance with administrative orders*. These costs are explicitly covered, even if the measures are taken by the public authority itself. Thus an extensive coverage in this respect, as it looks like the scope of the concept of property damage covered under the policy is not decisive.

Secondly, *the costs of clean-up at the insured's premises*. The German Model explicitly excludes reimbursement of any expenses for repairs on the insured's premises, except where uncontaminated property had to be sacrificed to avert or minimize damage to third parties. In that case, however, any resultant increases in value will be deducted . It looks like the Dutch MAS policy and the Danish special EIL policy provide a wider coverage: costs of clean-up at the insured site are covered insofar as the measures were reasonably required to *avert* the imminent danger of environmental impairment outside the insured site causing losses covered by the policy.

MAS (§ 2 sub. g)

"The insurance shall not compensate expenses, by whoever incurred, so as to limit or undo the environmental impairment on and the consequences thereof for the insured location itself, except if the insured proves that these expenses are salvage costs at the same time."

Denmark (§ 2 sub. 3)

"Cover shall also be provided under the rules applying to damage to property for any reasonable expenses incurred for the purpose of preventing a polluting substance from spreading beyond the insured premises or further on from there, however only insofar as the Insured has been under an obligation to undertake such preventive measures."[4]

Consequently, there will generally be no coverage for the expenses incurred; just for the restoration and reconstruction of the insured's operating equipment including the plant site: this is in line with the ASSURPOL policy, which explicitly excludes these expenses. Moreover, at least in the Netherlands, it is argued that the insurer is entitled to a deduction of the payment of clean-up costs due to an increase of value of his own premises, not covered.

No coverage at all for clean-up costs at the insured site is provided by the English AIU policy (§ II): "Clean-up cost means expenses incurred in the removal or remediation of pollution conditions but does not include such

[4] I refer to the comments of George Lett on "Conditions for EIL-insurance", 14 February 1992.

expenses incurred in the removal or remediation of pollution conditions on the property of the insured. The pollution conditions must have emanated from the locations described in Item 5 of the Schedule."

8. Limits to Indemnity

Characteristic of environmental risk is that *one* emission may result in noxious effects at various places and for many people. In addition, non-accidental industrial discharge often implies a chain of emissions, all having the same or similar causes. This creates a serious danger of cumulation which, without special precautions, is considered non-insurable.

These facts, linked to the limited financial capacity available for environmental impairment liability insurance, explain why most insurers apply the same strict system to limit their financial responsibility.

Generally speaking, all "claims made"-policies apply a scheme based upon *a limit per claim*. This establishes the maximum amount of money the insurer will pay in respect of one impairment (emission) or imminent impairment of the environment as to all claims including interest, legal expenses, and costs of court proceedings, as well as to all claims for salvage costs for the account of the insured.

Additionally, *a serial claims provision* is added to the definition of "claim", saying a claim comprises any single claim or any series of claims from one or multiple claimants resulting from the same isolated, repeated or continuing environmental impairment.

Finally, There is an ultimate limit per insurance year (an aggregate limit), setting a maximum to be paid in respect of all claims (initially) reported by third parties or the insured (for salvage costs) in the same period (year) of insurance.

MAS (§ 1 sub. 3)

"The following provisions shall apply with regard to the indemnity limit:

1. More claims

If one single environmental impairment results in more than one claim, these claims — as far as they have actually been received by the company during the period of insurance — shall be regarded as one claim and shall be deemed to have been received by the company at the time the first claim was received.

2. More claims/salvage costs

All claims for the compensation of salvage costs will, if resulting from one single imminent environmental impairment, be regarded as one claim and will be deemed to have been received by the company as such as soon as the insured started to take salvage measures.

3 Indemnity limit per claim

The indemnity limit per event mentioned in the schedule shall be the aggregate limit due by the company with regard to one single imminent environmental impairment, in respect of:

— all claims for indemnification including the legal rate of interest and the expenses as described in part 5 of this article;

— all claims for indemnification of salvage cost.

4. Indemnity limit per insurance year
The indemnity limit per insurance year mentioned in the schedule shall be the aggregate maximum due by the company in respect of:
— all claims for indemnification received by the company in the course of such year, including the legal rate of interest and the expenses and described in part 5 of this article, but subject to the provisions in article 1.3.1. and
— all claims for the compensation of salvage cost which, in accordance with the provision in article 1.3.2. shall be deemed to have been received by the company in the course of such year.
5. Excess
The excess per occurrence mentioned in the schedule shall not apply if the compensation concerns only expenses as described in part 5 of this article.
6. Sequence of environmental impairments
Environmental impairment shall also be an interrupted or uninterrupted sequence of environmental impairments with the same or similar cause.

ASSURPOL (§ 6)

"Limits of cover in amount
(A) the third party liability cover under article 2-1 applies up to the respective amounts provided in the Special Conditions
- per loss as defined under article 1-6, (only single claim or series of claims resulting from one and the same environmental impairment)
- to all claims notified to insurers during one and the same year of insurance.

(B) the cover of costs and expenses for reducing and preventing damage provided under article 2-II applies within above liability limits up to sub-limits set in the Special Conditions:
- to all expenses related with operations necessitated by one and the same environmental impairment;
- to all expenses related with operations undertaken during one and the same insurance period.

In terms of maximum commitments for covers described under paras. A and B above, year of insurance means period between two annual dates when premiums fall due. However, wherever the inception date of the contract is different from the date of payment, 'year of insurance', means the period between that date and the next date of payment. If the contract expires between two annual dates of payment, the last year of insurance means the period between the last annual date of payment and the date of expiry of the contract.

Unless stipulated to the contrary in the contract, there is no reinstatement of cover per insurance year. Consequently, after any provisional or final settlement or loss, the maximum commitment will be reduced by this settlement up to the next anniversary date of the contract."

Denmark (§ 6 and 7)

"Claims Series
Claims made against the Insured under § 5 for injury or damage occurred and arising out of the same liability-entailing conduct shall be considered as one single insurance event (claim series).

Indemnity Limits
The indemnity limits specified in the policy shall be the maximum limits for the Insurer's commitment to pay compensation for claims made against the Insured (§ 5) within the individual insurance years.

An insurance year shall be defined as the period between two principle premium payment days (or, in case of yearly premiums, the period between two premium payment days — hereinafter referred to as principal payment days).

If the inception date of the insurance policy differs from the principal payment day, the first insurance year shall run from the inception date to the first principal payment day. If the expiry day, the last insurance year shall run from the last principal payment day to the expiry date.

German Model (§ 7)

"Amounts of coverage/maxima/serial claims/deductible
The amount of coverage for each insured event and also for insured events of one insurance year shall be, for personal injuries (however, not more than DM .... for each person) and for property damage, DM ...
1. The amounts of coverage specified in the policy shall be the maximum limit of the insurer's liability for each insured event. This shall also apply if the coverage extends to several liable persons.
2. Several insured events occurring while the insurance is in effect as a result
— of the same effect on the environment
— of several effects on the environment resulting directly from the same cause or directly from like causes, if between the like causes there is an intrinsic, especially substantive and temporal, connection

shall be deemed, regardless of their actual occurrence, one insured event, which is deemed to have occurred at the time of the first of such insured events."

AIU policy (§VI)

"The policy is to pay 100% of any loss in excess of the retention amount stated in Item 4 of the Schedule. The retention amount is to be borne by the insured and is not to be insured. All loss arising out of the same or related pollution conditions at any one location shall be considered a single loss, and the limit of liability shown in Item 3 of the Schedule as applicable to 'each loss' shall apply.

The total liability of the Company for:
1. Claims arising out of the same, interrelated, associated, repeated or continuous acts or omissions; and
2. Claims arising out of the same, interrelated, associated, repeated or continuous exposure to substantially the same general conditions;

shall be considered a single loss subject to the applicable limits of liability and shall be deemed first reported to the Company during the policy period in which the initial claim was first reported to the Company.

Subject to the foregoing, the Company's total liability for all losses from claims first made against the insured and reported in writing to the Company during the policy period and including the extended discovery period, if applicable, shall not exceed the limit of liability in Item 3 of the Schedule as applicable to the 'total for all losses'."

8. Compulsory Insurance

Finally, some remark about compulsory insurance. In the context described above, it is not appropriate to introduce compulsory insurance for environmental impairment liability risks and most governments seem to realise this. Besides some rather tricky questions should be answered first. Does compulsory insurance imply that an industrial operation has to be discontinued if the insurers decline the risk? How could the problem of "anonymous or uninsured pollution" be solved? The most obvious solution is to set up a guarantee fund, subsidised by the collectivity of potential polluters. Particularly in cases of "uninsured pollution" this system demands solidarity of the individual bona fide enterprise and the collectivity of *mala fide* enterprises with the innocent pollution victim. A solidarity which seems to be acceptable only in a society in which activities with a high pollution exposure are well controlled by an effective enforcement of a comprehensive environmental legislation scheme. It looks as if the Swedes have already been successful in this respect, insofar as, on 1 July 1989 a new insurance scheme came into force, financed on a compulsory basis by all enterprises with environmentally dangerous activities which provides coverage directly to any natural person who suffers pollution damage in case the actual polluter is insolvent or cannot be identified or the right to indemnity under the Environmental Damage Act is statute-barred. However, according to Swedish sources in the insurance industry the practical impact up to now is disappointing, amongst other things due to the very restrictive coverage.

This illustrates once again that, above all, top priority should be given to the creation of a society which is aware of its environmental responsibilities.

Insurance and Liability for Pollution in the United States

Robert Force

Introduction

In the beginning there was liability based on fault and in many circumstances this liability was subject to limitation. Then came strict liability which, in many circumstances, was also subject to limitation. Most recently the Oil Pollution Act of 1990 has created the realistic prospect of absolute liability, and, perhaps, in many circumstances, no right to limit liability. Initially liability for pollution in the United States was based on the traditional common law and maritime law tort doctrines of negligence and nuisance.[1] As such some element of fault was required to impose liability and various defences were available. In the case of marine pollution, a vessel owner might avail itself of the Limitation of Liability laws.[2] In the last 30 years, however, environmental liability in the United States and its consequent effect on insurance has been driven increasingly by statutory regimes.

Today three major federal statutes are controlling, to wit, the Clean Water Act (33 U.S.C.A.§ 1321) (CWA) as amended by the Federal Water Pollution Control Act (hereinafter FWPCA), the Comprehensive Environmental Response, Compensation and Liability Act (42 U.S.C.A. §§ 9601 *et seq.*) (hereinafter CERCLA) as amended by the Superfund Amendments and Reauthorization Act of 1986 (SARA) and the Oil Pollution Act of 1990 (33 U.S.C.A. §§ 2701 *et seq.*) (hereinafter OPA). These statutes, enacted at different times, have established a trend in which the defences available to a party against whom claims have been made for the discharge of oil or hazardous substance have been narrowly cir-

1 W. Rodgers, *Environmental Law* (2nd edn., West Pub. Co., 1986) § 4.37, pp. 548–551.
2 46 App. U.S.C.A. §§ 183 *et seq.*

cumscribed, limitation amounts have been increased, the circumstances in which limitation of liability is permitted have decreased, and the right to recover damages and the amounts recoverable in damages have increased substantially.[3]

Today there are five major characteristics that emerge from these statutes.

1. Imposition of "strict" or "absolute" liability with only limited defences available imposed on persons made legally "responsible" for pollution from oil and other hazardous substances for:
   (a) removal (clean up) costs, and
   (b) damages for injury to or destruction of natural resources, private property, and other economic interests of governmental and private parties.
2. Limitation of the amount of the responsible party's liability and enumeration of circumstances in which the right to limit is not available.
3. Duty on those who may be held legally responsible for pollution to provide proof of financial responsibility, such as by insurance, to cover their exposure to liability, and direct action against those who provide financial responsibility for legally responsible persons.
4. The establishment of various governmentally administered "Funds" to pay removal costs and damages when they are not immediately forthcoming from the person legally responsible.
5. Parallel, but not necessarily identical, regulatory and liability regimes at both the federal (national) and state levels.

The Clean Water Act which by amendment has become the Federal Water Pollution Control Act in Section 311 (33 U.S.C.A. § 1321) specifically provides for "Oil and Hazardous Substance Liability". As will be explained subsequently, some provisions of the FWPCA have been superseded or modified by OPA. As to pollution from hazardous substances other than oil, the FWPCA, has been supplemented by CERCLA. The latter, however, did not expressly repeal or supersede the former. It would seem reasonable to suggest that removal costs and damages could be recovered only once and that double recovery should not be permitted.

In addition to these federal statutory sources of law, two other sources merit consideration. An action may be brought to impose liability for removal costs and damages resulting from an oil or hazardous substance discharge based on state law, either under common law principles or under special legislation enacted in some states.[4] Also the negligent discharge of oil or hazardous substance on navigable waters which results in damage to others is a maritime tort

[3] Several of these statutes are discussed in Rodgers, *Environmental Law*, § 4.37. Various statutory actions are succinctly summarized in Bagwell, "Liability under United States Law for Spills of Oil or Chemicals from Vessels" (1987) *Lloyd's Mar. & Comm. L.Q.* 496.

[4] Rodgers, *Environmental Law*, 558–560; Liples "State Control of Oil Pollution: Legislating in the Twilight Zone" (1976) 1 *Harv. Envt'l. L. Rev.* 431.

and supports an action for damages against the tortfeasor. A nuisance theory might also be available. Such actions can be brought in a federal district court under the court's admiralty jurisdiction (28 U.S.C.A. § 1333). Suit also can be brought in a state court under the "saving to" suitors provision.[5] The enactment of the Clean Water Act and its amendment by the Federal Water Pollution Act had raised issues in regard to the possible pre-emption of common law and admiralty remedies,[6] but these doubts have been resolved in favour of state and maritime remedies by specific provisions in CERCLA and OPA. These statutes are discussed below.

Section 311 of the FWPCA (33 U.S.C.A. § 1321) contains provisions which deal with the discharge of oil and hazardous substances. However, the discharge of oil in or on navigable waters, adjoining shorelines, and the exclusive economic zone is now controlled by the Oil Pollution Act of 1990. This includes the provisions that are crucial to liability. Nevertheless, some of the provisions of the FWPCA are still relevant to oil spills, and although Section 311 has been modified, many of its provisions remain applicable to discharges of oil. Section 311 is composed of 18 subsections.

Subsection (b) (3) of the FWPCA declares that: "The discharge of oil or hazardous substances (i) into or upon the navigable waters of the United States, adjoining shorelines, or into or upon the waters of the contiguous zone,[7]... in

[5] Rodgers, *Environmental Law*, 549–551; Glickstein, "Federal Preemption and Private Legal Remedies for Pollution" (1985) 134 *U. Pa. L. Rev.* 121; Guss, "Interaction of the Federal Water Pollution Control Act with the Limitation of Liability Act and the General Maritime Law" (1981) 6 *Mar. Law* 199; Duncan, "Liability of Third Parties for Oil Spill Cleanup Costs under the Federal Water Pollution Art and under General Maritime Law" (1985) 10 ibid. 25; Note, "Slick Maneuvering: The Fifth Circuit Finds Liability for Oil Pollution Exists Outside of the Federal Water Pollution Control Act — United States v. M/V Big Sam" (1983) 8 ibid. 171; Murray, "United States v. M/V Big Sam: Preserving a Niche for the Federal Common Law of Maritime Tort of Oil Pollution" (1984) 51 *Ins. Couns. J.* 325; Note, "Oil Spills and Cleanup Bills: Federal Recovery of Oil Spill Cleanup Costs" (1979–80) 93 *Harv. L. Rev.* 1761; Roady, "Remedies in Admiralty for Oil Pollution" (1977) 5 *Fla. State U. L. Rev.* 361; Post, "A Solution to the Problem of Private Compensation in Oil Discharge Situations" (1973–4) 28 *U. Miami L. Rev.* 526.

[6] *Middlesex County Sewerage Authority* v. *National Sea Clammers Ass'n.* 453 U.S. 1 (1980); *Conner* v. *Aerovox*, 730 F. 2d 835 (1st. Cir. 1884), *cert. denied*, 469 U.S 1015 (1985); In re *Oswego Barge Corp.*, 664 F. 2d 327 (2nd. Cir. 1981); *State of Louisiana* v. *M/V Testbank*, 752 F. 2d 1019 (5th. Cir. 1985) (*en banc*), cert. denied, sub nom. White v. M/V Testbank, 477 U.S. 903 (1986); Glickstein, "Federal Preemption and Private Legal Remedies for Pollution", supra n 5; Jarman, "Marine Pollution: Injury Without a Remedy" (1987) 24 San Diego L. Rev. 603; Comment (1983 – 4) 28 *N.Y.L.S. L. Rev.* 195; "The Demise of the Federal Common Law of Water Pollution" (1982) *Wis. L. Rev.* 627.

[7] The Act also applies: "(ii) in connection with activities under the Outer Continental Shelf Lands Act or the Deepwater Port Act of 1974, or which may affect natural resources belonging to, appertaining to, or under the exclusive management authority of the United States (including resources under the Magnuson Fishery Conservation and Management Act [16 U.S.C.A. § 1801 *et seg.*] . . .".

such quantities as may be harmful as determined by the President ... is prohibited[8]...". This provision remains in effect.

Subsection (b) (4) of the FWPCA provides that "the President shall by regulation determine for the purposes of this section those quantities of oil or any hazardous substances the discharge of which may be harmful to the public health or welfare of the United States, including but not limited to fish, shellfish, wildlife, and public and private property. shoreline, and beaches." The President has delegated this function to the Administrator of the Environmental Protection Agency.

> "The President through the Environmental Protection Agency has determined by regulation that oil discharges in harmful quantities include, with a few minor exceptions, all those that violate water quality standards or cause a film or sheen upon or discoloration of the surface of the water or adjoining shorelines or cause a sludge or emulsion to be deposited beneath the surface of the water or upon adjoining shorelines."[9]

This provision and its administrative implementation remain in effect.

Under § 1321 (b) (5) of the FWPCA "any person in charge of a vessel or of an onshore facility or an offshore facility shall, as soon as he has knowledge of any discharge of oil or a hazardous substance from such vessel or facility in violation of paragraph 3 of this section, immediately notify the appropriate agency of the United States of such discharge." This provision remains in effect.

CERCLA like the FWPCA imposes a duty on the part of any person in charge of a vessel or an offshore or onshore facility immediately to notify the National Response Center under the Clean Water Act (33 U.S.C.A. § 1521) as soon as he has knowledge of any release of a hazardous substance from such vessel or facility in quantities equal or greater than those specified in section 9602 of CERCLA. It is the responsibility of the National Response Center to notify all appropriate government agencies.

Subsection (c) of the FWPCA provides that "whenever oil or a hazardous substance is discharged or there is a substantial threat of discharge into or upon the navigable waters of the United States, adjoining shorelines, or into or upon the contiguous zone,[10]... the President is authorized to act to remove or arrange for the removal of such oil or substance at any time, unless he determines such

[8] The Act provides for several exceptions: (A) in case of such discharges into the waters of the contiguous zone or which may affect natural resources . . . [as aforesaid], where permitted under the Protocol of 1978 Relating to the International Convention for the Prevention of Pollution from Ships, 1973, and (B) where "the President by regulation determines that specified discharges are not harmful."

[9] Rodgers, *Environmental Law*, 513, citing 10 CFR § 110.3(b) (1985).

[10] ". . . or in connection with activities under the Outer Continental Shelf Lands Act or the Deepwater Port Act of 1974, or which may affect the natural resources belonging to, appertaining to or under the exclusive management authority of the United States."

removal will be done properly by the owner or operator of the vessel, onshore facility, or offshore facility from which the discharge occurs."

This provision has been amended to reflect the enactment of OPA and to reorganise the provisions relating to federal authority over removal activities. As amended it remains in effect. It is now entitled "Federal Removal Authority" and delegates to the President the responsibility of effectively and immediately removing discharges of oil or hazardous substances from the navigable waters of the United States, adjoining shorelines, waters of the exclusive economic zone or from an area where natural resources belonging to or under the management and authority of the United States may be affected. Such action shall be taken in accordance with the National Contingency Plan and any appropriate Area Contingency Plan which is now provided for in subsection (d).

CERCLA contains a similar provision. Whenever a hazardous substance is released or there is a substantial threat of such a release into the environment or there is a release or substantial threat of release into the environment of any pollutant or contaminant[11] which may present an imminent and substantial danger to the public health or welfare, the President is authorized to act, consistent with the National Contingency Plan, to remove or arrange for the removal of and to provide for remedial action or take any other response measure consistent with the National Contingency Plan which is deemed necessary to protect the public health or welfare or the environment. The Act not only authorizes the President to remove hazardous substances or to prevent their release but specifies steps which shall be taken.[12] There is broad power in the President to institute abatement actions.[13]

Subsection (d) provides that

> "whenever a marine disaster in or upon the navigable waters of the United States has created a substantial threat of a pollution hazard to the public health or welfare of the United States, including but not limited to, fish, shellfish, and wildlife and public and private shorelines and beaches of the United States, because of a discharge or an imminent discharge of large quantities of oil or of a hazardous substance from a vessel, the United States may (A) coordinate and direct all public and private efforts directed at the removal or elimination of such threat and (B) summarily remove, and, if necessary, destroy any such vessel...".

This provision has been amended so that the authority to remove pollution threats, including the destruction of vessels is now provided for in subsection (c). Subsection (d) now delegates to the President the duty of preparing a National Contingency Plan for the removal of oil and hazardous substances. In this regard, subsection (d) sets out the various matters which should be included in the Plan. This had previously been included in subsection (c).

[11] These terms are defined *infra*.
[12] 42 U.S.C.A. § 9604.
[13] 42 U.S.C.A. § 9506.

Subsection (e) authorises the President to require a U.S. attorney to initiate action in a court to secure judicial relief against "imminent and substantial threat to the public health or welfare of the United States" presented by actual or threatened discharges of oil or hazardous substance. This subsection remains in effect.

Subsection (h) provides that the liability imposed by Section 311 (33 U.S.C.A. § 1321) does not affect any rights the owner or operator of a vessel or facility or the United States might have against a third party who caused or contributed to the discharge.

Subsection (k) established a revolving fund to carry out the provisions of subsections (c) (d) (i) & (l). This provision has been repealed and superseded with respect to discharges of oil by provisions establishing the Oil Spill Liability Trust Fund, 26 U.S.C.A. § 9509 and with respect hazardous substances by the Hazardous Substance Liability Trust Fund, (Superfund) 26 U.S.C.A. § 9507. There are complex procedures for presenting claims to the respective Funds. These procedures are not discussed in this paper.

Liability for Pollution

1. Scope

Section 2702 (a) ot OPA provides:

> "Notwithstanding any other provision or rule of law, ... each responsible party for a vessel or a facility from which oil is discharged, or which poses the substantial threat of a discharge of oil, into or upon the navigable waters or adjoining shorelines or the exclusive economic zone is liable for the removal costs and damages as specified in subsection (b) [§ 2702 (b)] that result from that incident."[14]

The Act defines a "discharge" as "any emission ... and includes, but is not limited to, spilling, leaking, pumping, pouring, emitting, emptying, or dumping."

In contrast to OPA, CERCLA applies to all hazardous substances other than oil. CERCLA provides that:

> "Notwithstanding any other provision or rule of law,
> (1) the owner or operator of a vessel or a facility,
> (2) any person who at the time of the disposal of hazardous substances owned or operated any facility at which such hazardous substances were disposed of,
> (3) (omitted),
> (4) (omitted), from which there is a release, ... of a hazardous substance, shall be liable for ...".[15]

[14] The term "incident" is defined as "any occurrence or series of occurrences having the same origin, involving one or more vessels, facilities, or any combination thereof, resulting in the discharge or substantial threat of discharge of oil . . .". 33 U.S.C.A. § 2701 (14).

[15] 42 U.S.C.A. § 9601 (a).

CERCLA applies to hazardous substances which are defined as any substance so designated under 33 U.S.C.A. § 1321 (b) (2) (A) of the FWPCA, any element or compound, etc., designated under § 9602 of CERCLA, any hazardous waste having the characteristics or listed pursuant to 42 U.S.C.A. § 6921, to any toxic pollutant listed in 33 U.S.C.A. § 1317(a), to any hazardous air pollutant listed in 42 U.S.C.A. § 7412 of the Clean Air Act and any "imminently hazardous chemical substance or mixture with respect to which the Administrator has taken action pursuant to section 2606 of Title 15. The stature specifically excludes petroleum, including crude oil. The term "pollutant or contaminant" is defined in 42 U.S.C.A. § 9601(33) and generally includes substances that represent a threat to living organisms. Again, oil is specifically excluded from the definition.

The term "release" means any spilling, leaking, pumping, pouring, emitting, emptying, discharging, injecting, escaping, leaching, dumping, or disposing into the environment.[16]

(a) Geographic Application

OPA applies to discharges of oil into or upon the navigable waters of the United States (including the territorial sea), the adjoining shoreline and the exclusive economic zone.[17]

It also applies to discharges of oil in or on the territorial sea, internal waters or adjacent shoreline of a foreign country[18], but only if the discharge is from:

1. a facility on the Outer Continental Shelf or a deepwater port;
2. a vessel in the navigable waters of the United States;
3. a vessel carrying oil as a cargo between two places in the United States;
4. a tanker that has received oil at the terminal of the pipeline constructed under the Trans-Alaska Pipeline Authorization Act for transportation to a place in the United States, and the discharge occurs prior to delivery of the oil to that place.

For a foreign claimant to recover the discharge must occur in United States waters or on the Outer Continental Shelf except under the Trans-Alaska Pipeline situations where a spill might occur in the waters of Canada or the former U.S.S.R. Thus, discharges in the exclusive economic zone or in international waters which drift into the territorial sea, inland waters or shoreline of a foreign country are not within the Act. However, because of the difference of the wording of § 2702 (a) as compared with § 2707 (b), a discharge in foreign or international waters that drifts into United States waters or its exclusive economic zone might be covered depending on the scope given to the term "discharge".

[16] Ibid. § 9601 (22).
[17] 33 U.S.C.A. § 2702(a). The terms "navigable waters" and "exclusive economic zone" are defined Ibid § 2701 (21) and (8) respectively.
[18] Ibid. § 2707 (b).

It should be noted with respect to foreign claimants that the Act does not apply to discharges which occur in the exclusive economic zone of the United States; it does not include removal costs and damages that a foreign country or its citizens may incur from discharges in the exclusive economic zone of that foreign country.

Also a foreign claimant must show that (1) it has not otherwise been compensated and that (2) recovery is authorised by statute or executive order or that the Secretary of State in consultation with the Attorney General and other officials has certified that the claimant's country provides U.S. citizens with a comparable remedy.[19]

CERCLA through its definition of the term "environment", applies not only to navigable waters, the waters of the contiguous zone, and to ocean waters of which the natural resources are under the exclusive management authority of the United States under the Magnuson Fishery Conservation and Management Act (16 U.S.C.A. § 1801) but also to surface, ground and drinking waters, to land surfaces and subsurface strata, or ambient air within the United States or under the jurisdiction of the United States.[20]

(b) Activities Covered

OPA applies to a vessel or facility from which oil is discharged.

"Facility" is defined as "any structure or group of structures, equipment, or device which is used for one or more of the following purposes: exploring for, drilling for, producing, storing, handling, transferring, processing, or transporting oil."

The term "vessel" is defined broadly as has been customary, to include "every description of watercraft or other artificial contrivance used or capable of being used, as a means of transportation on water, other than a public vessel." A "public vessel" is a vessel owned or bareboat chartered and operated by the United States, or by a State ... or by a foreign nation, except when the vessel is engaged in commerce.

It is important to note that the term "vessel" is not restricted to vessels that carry oil as cargo, that is, tankers, it includes all vessels that have oil on board whether as cargo or bunkers.

CERCLA applies to vessels and onshore and offshore facilities from which hazardous substances have been released.[21] The definition of vessel is the same as that used in OPA. "The term 'facility' means (A) any building, structure, installation, equipment, pipe or pipeline ... well, pit, pond, lagoon, impoundment, ditch, landfill, storage container, motor vehicle, rolling stock, or aircraft, or (B) any site or area where a hazardous substance has been deposited, stored, disposed of, or placed, or otherwise come to be located; ...". 42 U.S.C.A. § 9601 (9).

[19] Ibid. (a).

[20] 42 U.S.C.A. § 9601 (8).

[21] Ibid (17) (18) (28); § 9603; § 9607.

2. *Liability*

(a) Persons Liable

Under OPA there are three groups of persons who may be liable: responsible parties, guarantors and third parties.

RESPONSIBLE PARTY

A "responsible party" includes the owner and operator of a vessel, onshore and offshore facility, deepwater port and pipeline. In the case of a vessel, the term "responsible party" also includes a demise charterer.

GUARANTOR

A "guarantor" is "any person other than the responsible party, who provides evidence of financial responsibility for a responsible party ...".

THIRD PARTIES

A third party is a person other than the responsible party or its agents or employees, or the agents or employees of its independent contractors, or a guarantor whose conduct is the sole cause of a discharge of oil.

It is very important to note that liability falls on the owner or operator of a vessel or facility only. OPA does not impose liability on the owner of the oil. Thus, in the case of a discharge of oil from a vessel, liability would fall on the vessel or its owner or bareboat charterer but not on the owner of the cargo.

Under CERCLA liability is imposed on owners and operators of vessels and facilities.[22] The terms "owner" and "operator" mean:[23]

(i) in the case of a vessel, any person owning, operating, or chartering by demise, such vessel;
(ii) in the case of an onshore facility or an offshore facility, any person owning or operating a facility.

The term "owner" does not include a person who, without participating in the management of a vessel or facility, holds indicia of ownership primarily to protect a security interest.

There are also special definitions of the terms "owner" and "operator" with regard to hazardous substances which have been accepted for transportation or delivered by a carrier to a disposal or treatment facility.[24] Furthermore, there are special provisions which, in effect impose liability on successors in interest as well be explained in the discussion of the third-party defence.

CERCLA, like OPA, authorizes a direct action against the person who provides a guaranty of financial responsibility. Thus, liability extends to that person.

[22] 42 U.S.C.A. § 9607 (A).
[23] Ibid. § 9601 (20 A).
[24] Ibid. (20 B & C).

(b) Basis for Liability

As provided in § 2702 (a) OPA *supra*, the liability imposed is *strict liability*. If oil is discharged from a vessel or from a facility, the responsible party, subject to very limited exceptions,[25] is liable. Liability is imposed by the very fact of the discharge and is not predicated on the fault of the responsible party. The same is true under CERCLA[26] and the FWPCA.[27] Therefore, it is unnecessary for the claimant to show negligence or other fault of the owner or operator.

This view of strict liability is reinforced by provisions in both OPA and CERCLA which provide that a person who is liable for a discharge of oil or a release of a hazardous substance may not avoid liability because of an indemnification, or similar agreement.[28] These provisions do not prohibit any agreement to insure, or indemnify a party from such agreement from and against any liability under this Act. The respective Acts do not bar any right of subrogation that might otherwise exist.[29]

(c) Removal Costs

As under prior legislation, a major feature of OPA is the provision for the recovery of removal costs. The term "removal means containment and removal of oil from the water or shorelines or the taking of other actions as may be necessary to minimize or mitigate damage to the public health or welfare, including but not limited to, fish, shellfish, wildlife, and public and private property, shorelines, and beaches."[30] Subsection 2707 (a) makes a responsible party liable for removal costs. "Removal costs" are defined as "the costs of removal that are incurred after a discharge of oil has occurred or, in any case in which there is a substantial threat of a discharge of oil, the costs to prevent, minimize, or mitigate oil pollution from such incident."[31] Removal costs are recoverable by the United States, a State or an Indian tribe under 33 U.S.C.A. § 1321 (c) (d) (e) or (1), under the Intervention on the High Seas Act or under State law.

They are also recoverable when incurred by any person for acts taken by that person that are consistent with the National Contingency Plan. A responsible party may recover removal costs incurred by it from the Oil Spill Liability Trust

[25] Subsection 2702(c) provides for exceptions to the liability of a vessel for discharges:
"(1) which are authorized by a permit issue under Federal, state of local law;
"(2) from a public vessel, that is, a vessel owned or bareboat chartered and operated by a government, except when the vessel is engaged in commerce."
There is another exception that relates to onshore discharges from facilities subject to the Trans-Alaskan Pipeline Authorization Act.

[26] 42 U.S.C.A. § 9607 (a).

[27] 33 U.S.C.A. § 1321 (f).

[28] Ibid. § 2710 (b) (OPA); 42 U.S.C.A. § 9607 (e) (1) (CERCLA).

[29] 33 U.S.C.A. § 2710 (a) (OPA); 42 U.S.C.A. § 9607 (e) (2) (CERCLA).

[30] 33 U.S.C.A. § 2701 (30).

[31] Ibid. (31).

Fund under circumstances where it is entitled to a complete defence.[32] Where it is entitled to limit its liability under the Act[33] it may recover amounts expended for removal which exceed the limitation amount.[34] Under § 2707 (a) (1), a foreign claimant may recover removal costs.

Subsection 9607(a) of CERCLA deals with liability. In the pertinent part, it states that the owner and operator of a vessel or facility from which there is a release or a threatened release of a hazardous substance which causes the incurrence of response costs shall be liable for:

(A) All costs of removal or remedial action incurred by the United States government or a state or an Indian tribe not inconsistent with the national contingency plan;

(B) Any necessary costs of response incurred by any other person consistent with the national contingency plan;

...

(D) The costs of any health assessment or health defects study carried out under section 9604(i) of the Act.

(d) Damages

Section 311(f) (33 U.S.C.A. § 1321(f)) provided not only for the recovery of removal costs, but also for the expenses of replacing and restoring natural resources that had been damaged or destroyed. It did not otherwise expressly provide for a right to recover damages for persons whose property was damaged or who otherwise suffered economic losses due to the discharge of oil. Efforts were made through litigation to persuade the courts to imply such an action or to recognize one under the aegis of federal common law. These efforts were unsuccessful.[35]

[32] Defences under the Act are discussed *infra*. Under subsection (i) of the FWPCA where the owner or operator of a vessel which had discharged oil or a hazardous substance removes the oil or substance, the owner or operator is entitled to recover reasonable costs incurred in such removal upon establishing such entitlement, in a suit brought against the U.S. government in the U.S. Claims Court. It is entitled to reimbursement when it proves a defence under subsection (f). The same right is not available under this subsection where liability was established pursuant to the Outer Continental Shelf Lands Act or the Deepwater Port Act of 1974. This subsection has been superseded with respect to oil discharges by § 2708 of the OPA.

[33] Limitation of liability under the Act is discussed *infra*.

[34] 33 U.S.C.A. § 2708.

[35] *Middlesex County Sewerage Authority* v. *National Sea Clammers Ass'n.*, 453 U.S. 1 (1980); *Conner* v. *Aerovox*, 730 F.2d 835 (1st. Cir.1884), *cert. denied*, 469 U.S. 1015 (1985); In re *Oswego Barge Corp.*, 664 F.2d 327 (2nd. Cir. 1981); *State of Louisiana* v. *M/V Testbank*, 752 F.2d 1019 (5th. Cir. 1985) (*en banc*), *cert. denied, sub nom. White* v. *M/V Testbank*, 477 U.S. 903 (1986); Glickstein, "Federal Preemption and Private Legal Remedies for Pollution", *supra*, n 5; Jarman, "Marine Pollution: Injury Without a Remedy" (1987) 24 San Diego L. Rev. 603; Comment (1983 – 4) 28 N.Y.L.S. L. Rev. 195; "The Demise of the Federal Common Law of Water Pollution", 1982 Wis. L. Rev. 627.

i. Damages Recoverable by Governments and Agencies and Instrumentalities of Governments

(1) NATURAL RESOURCES[36]

Under OPA a governmental entity may recover "damages for injury to, destruction of, loss of, or loss of use of, natural resources, including the reasonable costs of assessing the damage" which may be recovered by government appointed trustees[37] including a trustee appointed by a foreign country.[38]

"Natural resources includes land, fish, wildlife, biota, air, water, ground water, drinking water supplies, and other such resources belonging to, managed by, held in trust by, appertaining to, or otherwise controlled by the United States (including the resources of the exclusive economic zone), any state or local government or Indian tribe, or any foreign government."[39] Subsection 2706(d) provides that the measure of damages is:

"(A) the cost of restoring, rehabilitating, replacing, or acquiring the equivalent of, the damaged natural resources;
(B) the diminution of those natural resources pending restoration; plus
(C) the reasonable cost of assessing those damages."

Funds recovered by a trustee may be used only to pay costs incurred with respect to the damaged natural resources.[40]

CERCLA in Section 9607(a) also provides for damages for injury to natural resources as follows: "(C) Damages for injuries to, destruction of, or loss of natural resources, including the reasonable cost of assessing such injury, destruction, or loss resulting from such a release." Furthermore, Section 9607(f) authorizes the recovery of damages where there has been injury to, destruction of, or loss of natural resources by the United States, any state and Indian tribe. Damages recovered may only be used to restore, replace or acquire the equivalent of the damage to natural resources. The Act provides for the federal government and the respective states to designate trustees for natural resources.

As stated, the scheme of legislation which had been in effect prior to the enactment of OPA provided for the recovery of "clean-up" costs and for injury to natural resources, but, except for several statues of limited applicability, did not create a private action for damages caused by oil spills. A major innovation introduced by OPA is the provision for the recovery for a wide range of damages by governmental entities and private persons.[41]

[36] 33 U.S.C.A. § 2702 (2) (A). Comment: "The Recovery of Restoration Costs: Analytical Synthesis of Common-Law Property Damages, Restitution, and Natural Resource Damages Under CERCLA" (1991) 5 *Tul. Envt'l. L.J.* 255.

[37] See 33 U.S.C.A. § 2706.

[38] A foreign trustee may be designated by the head of a foreign government. § 2706(b) (5).

[39] 33 U.S.C.A. § 2701 (20).

[40] Ibid. § 2706 (f).

[41] Ibid. § 2702 (b) (2).

(2) REVENUES
OPA permits the United States, a state and a political subdivision to recover "damages equal to the net loss of taxes, royalties, rents, fees, or net profit shares due to the injury, destruction, or loss of real property, personal property, or natural resources ...".[42]

(3) PUBLIC SERVICE
OPA authorizes a state and a political subdivision to recover "damages for net costs of providing increased or additional public services during or after removal activities, including protection from fire, safety, or health hazards, caused by a discharge of oil ...".[43]

ii. Damages Recoverable by Governmental Entities and Private Persons

(4) REAL OR PERSONAL PROPERTY (IMMOVABLE AND MOVABLE PROPERTY)
Under OPA any person may recover "damages for injury to, or economic losses resulting from the destruction of, real [immovables] or personal [movables] property which shall be recoverable by a claimant who owns or leases that property."[44]

(5) SUBSISTENCE USE
OPA allows any person who uses natural resources which have been injured, destroyed, or lost to recover damages for loss of subsistence use of natural resources, without regard to the ownership or management of the resources.[45]

(6) PROFITS AND EARNING CAPACITY
OPA provides that any person may recover "damages equal to the loss of profits or impairment of earning capacity due to the injury, destruction, or loss of real property [immovables], personal property [movables], or natural resources ...".[46]

The scope of damages that can be recovered under OPA is greater than is currently permitted under admiralty tort law and the tort law of many states. As a general proposition, except where specifically authorized by statute, so-called "economic loss", that is, indirect economic loss sustained by a person because of a tortfeasor's physical injury or destruction of property, may be recovered only by the owner of the property and not by a mere user or others. In a classic case, *Robbins Dry Dock & Repair Co.* v. *Flint*,[47] a ship repairer negligently damaged the propeller of a time-chartered vessel during routine maintenance. The United States Supreme Court speaking through Justice Holmes held that the charterer, because he was not the owner of the damaged vessel had no other property

[42] Ibid. (D).
[43] Ibid. (F).
[44] Ibid. (B).
[45] Ibid. (C).
[46] Ibid. (E).
[47] 275 U.S. (1927).

interest in the vessel, and could not recover his economic loss attributable to his inability to use the vessel during a period of two weeks while a new propeller was installed and while the vessel was off-hire.

In a more recent case, *Louisiana ex rel. Guste* v. *M/V Testbank*,[48] the United States Court of Appeals for the Fifth Circuit held that restaurant owners, owners of fishing-bait shops, and others involved in providing tourist services in a resort area[49], could not recover their lost profits when, because of a collision, hazardous chemicals were discharged into the Mississippi River outlet and impaired the use of the waters thereby destroying the tourist season. Damages were denied because the defendant did not injure the plaintiffs' property. The plaintiffs did not own the waters or the fish therein and could not show physical damage to their property. The court did recognize an exception to the rule in favour of fishermen who were allowed to recover for loss of their livelihood despite the fact that they did not own the fish that had been killed or tainted by the chemical.

Subsection 2702 (b) (E) provides for the recovery of loss of profits and earning capacity by any claimant due to the injury, destruction or loss of real or personal property or natural resources. It is clear from the legislative history of this provision that Congress intended legislatively to overrule *Robbins Dry Dock rule* in oil pollution cases.[50]

Another feature of OPA relates to pre-trial interest. Although the rule in admiralty cases has been to award pre-trial interest, this has not been the rule in non-admiralty cases. Section 2705 provides that interest begins to run on a claim 30 days after it has been presented to the responsible party or its guarantor. The limitation of liability provisions of the Act are not applicable to amounts recoverable as interest.[51]

CERCLA originally did not expressly create an action for damages for private persons except, under certain circumstances, for removal costs. However, Subsection 9607(h) was amended and now provides that the owner or operator of a vessel shall be liable under maritime tort law and as provided under section 9614 of the Act (recovery under state law) notwithstanding any provision of 46 U.S.C. 183 (limitation of liability) or the absence of any physical damage to the proprietary interest of the claimant. There appears to be no judicial construction of this provision. On its face, it appears not only to create a private right of action for damage to property but also to overrule the *Testbank*, *supra*, decision. There is some support for this view of the amended Subsection 9607(h). Senator

48 752 F.2d 1019 (5th Cir. 1985) (*en banc*), *cert. denied*, 477 U.S. 903 (1986).

49 The unsuccessful plaintiffs included: shipping interests, marina and rental boat operators, wholesale and retail seafood enterprises not actually engaged in fishing, seafood restaurants, tackle and bait shops and recreational fishermen.

50 Wilkinson, Pittman and Dye, "Slick Work: An Analysis of the Oil Pollution Act of 1990", citing H. Rep. No. 653, 101st Cong., 2d Sess. at p.103. Paper presented at the Tenth New Orleans Maritime Seminar (10 January 1990), 40. P.L. Seminar papers are available in the law library of the Tulane Law School.

51 33 U.S.C.A. § 2705 (b) (5).

Bentsen, speaking to the various amendments to CERCLA in the proposed Superfund Improvements Act of 1985, stated

> "There is a strong demand, interest and concern that there be clear liability for third-party damages as well as cleanup costs. So this amendment, as prepared, is a change to the Ocean Dumping Act that removes these barriers to third-party claims. It clarifies the congressional intent in that regard, allowing claims for third-party damages under other applicable Federal and State Law.
> Additionally, I have clarified that under CERCLA and maritime tort law third parties may recover for economic loss due to the release of hazardous substances even though there is no direct physical damage. Thus, for example, down in our part of the country commercial fishermen in the gulf injured by a release from an incineration vessel can recover their damages in that regard."[52]

Although Senator Bentsen referred to the Ocean Dumping Act and to incineration vessels, there is nothing to that effect in amended Subsection (h), and, therefore, nothing that limits the clear and unqualified language therein contained.

3. *Defences*

Subsection 2703(a) of OPA provides for so-called "complete defences". It states that a responsible party is not liable if the responsible party shows by a preponderance of the evidence that:

> "The discharge and resulting damage or removal costs "were caused solely by:
> (1) an act of God;
> (2) an act of war;
> (3) an act or omission of a third party: other than an employee or agent of the responsible party or a third party whose act or omission occurs in connection with any contractual relationship with the responsible party ... But a 'third party' defense is available only if the responsible party establishes by a preponderance of the evidence that it:
> A. exercise due care with respect to the oil concerned, taking into consideration the characteristics of the oil and in light of all relevant facts and circumstances; and
> B. took precautions against foreseeable acts or omissions of any such third party and the foreseeable consequences of those acts or omissions.
> (4) any combination of the above."

The "third party" defence in § 2703(a) seems to be reinforced by § 2702(d) (1) (A) which deals with the liability of third parties. The latter subsection provides that in any case in which a responsible party establishes that a discharge and the resulting removal costs and damages were caused solely by an act or omission of one or more third parties described in § 2703(a) (3), the third party shall be treated as the responsible party for the purpose of determining liability under OPA.

52 Cong. Rec. Sept. 23, 1985, pp. S11918–S11920; S11926–S11956, 101 Cong. 2d Sess., also contained in *A Legislative History of the Superfund Amendments and Reauthorization Act of*

However, the protection ostensibly given to a responsible party under the "liability of third parties" provision § 2702 (d) (1) (A) and the "third party" defence provided in § 2703 (a) (3) may be illusory. Although these provisions may relieve a responsible party from being held ultimately liable where the third party at fault is solvent or where a claimant elects to proceed directly against a third party at fault, § 2702 (d) (1) (B) (i) & (ii) state that where "the responsible party alleges that the discharge . . . was caused solely by an act or omission of a third party, the responsible party in accordance with section 2713 . . . shall pay removal costs and damages to any claimant; and shall be entitled by subrogation to all rights of the United States Government and the claimant to recover removal costs and damages from the third party or the Fund paid under this subsection."[53] Furthermore, § 2713 provides that generally and to the extent possible all claims for removal costs or damages shall be presented first to the responsible party or its guarantor.[54]

However, under § 2703(c) even these very limited defences are not available where the responsible party fails or refuses:

> "3. to report the incident as required by law if the responsible party knows or has reason to know of the incident;
> 2. to provide all reasonable cooperation and assistance requested by a responsible official in connection with the removal activities; or
> 3. without sufficient cause, to comply with an order issued under subsection (c) or (e) of section 1321 ... or the Intervention on the High Seas Act."

Thus, a "third party" defence might be difficult to establish for several reasons. First, the responsible party must prove by a preponderance of evidence not only that the conduct of the third party was the *sole* cause of the discharge but also that it, the responsible party, exercised due care and, furthermore, that it took reasonable precautions against foreseeable acts of third parties. Nevertheless, the responsible party may not use the defence when the act or omission which caused the discharge was that of its agents or employees or the act or omission of someone with whom it has a contractual relationship. The latter provision means that if an employee of an independent contractor with whom a responsible party has contracted, negligently causes a discharge, the "third party" defence is not available to the responsible party. Finally the requirements in § 2703(c) that the responsible party must report, cooperate and comply with orders are very unclear and a responsible party may lose its defence through inadvertence or ignorance.

[51] 33 U.S.C.A. § 2705 (b) (5).

[52] Cong. Rec. Sept. 23, 1985, pp. S11918–S11920; S11926–S11956, 101 Cong. 2d Sess., also contained in *A Legislative History of the Superfund Amendments and Reauthorization Act of 1986* (Public Law 99–499), Vol. 2, p. 1180.

[53] Wilkinson, Pittman and Dye, "Slick Work", 43–44.

[54] Under § 2714(c) when the President receives information about a discharge of oil, he should designate the source of that discharge and notify the responsible party and its guarantor. The Act provides for making this information available to potential claimants who are directed by § 2713 to submit their claims to the responsible party or its guarantor.

[55] 33 U.S.C.A. § 2703 (b).

There is also a defence as to the claim of a particular claimant to the extent that the incident was caused by the gross negligence or wilful misconduct of the claimant.[55]

It should be noted that even where a responsible party does not have a "complete defence" it may proceed against a third party for contribution in case the discharge was caused at least in part by the third party[56] or for indemnity.[57]

The FWPCA also provides for a "third-party" defence and for third party liability.[58]

Likewise, CERCLA in Section 9607(b) provides for defences. It imposes the burden on a person who would otherwise be liable to establish by a preponderance of the evidence that the release or threat of release and the damages resulting therefrom were caused solely by:

(1) An Act of God;
(2) An act of war;
(3) An act or omission of a third party other than an employee or agent of the defendant or other than one whose act or omission occurs in connection with a contractual relationship existing directly or indirectly with the defendant, if a defendant establishes that:
    (a) he exercised due care with respect to the hazardous substance concerned, taking into consideration the characteristics of such hazardous substance, in light of all relevant facts and circumstances, and
    (b) he took precautions against foreseeable acts or omissions of any such third party and the consequences that could foreseeably result from such acts or omissions; or
(4) Any combination of the above.

The "third-party" defence specified in Subsection 9607 (b) (3) is much more limited than would appear. Such a defence is not available where the actions of the "third party" occur "in connection with a contractual relationship existing directly or indirectly with the defendant ...". This, in effect, may impose liability on successor owners such as persons who purchase contaminated property or lending institutions which foreclose on such property. It should be noted that Subsection 9601 (35)A which was added as part of the Superfund Amendments and Reauthorization Act of 1986(SARA) states:

[55] 33 U.S.C.A. § 2703 (b).

[56] Ibid. § 2709.

[57] Ibid. § 2710.

[58] Subsection (f) of the FWPCA also provides for defences. The only defences available are when the discharge was caused by:

(A) act of God;
(B) act of war;
(C) negligence on the part of the United States Government; or
(D) act or omission of a third party regardless of whether such act or omission was negligent;

"The term 'contractual relationship' for the purpose of section 9606(b) (3) … includes, but is not limited to, land contracts, deeds or other instruments transferring title or possession, unless the real property on which the facility concerned is located was acquired by the defendant after the disposal or placement of the hazardous substance on, in or at the facility, and one or more of the circumstances described in clause (i), (ii) or (iii) is also established by the defendant by a preponderance of the evidence:

(i) At the time the defendant acquired the facility the defendant did not know and had no reason to know that any hazardous substance which is the subject of the release … was disposed of on, in or at the facility.
(ii) The defendant is a governmental entity, etc.
(iii) The defendant acquired the facility by inheritance or bequest."

Under Subsection 9601(35)B a defendant establishes that it had no reason to know of the presence of a hazardous substance at the facility only if the defendant has undertaken at the time of acquisition all appropriate inquiry into the previous ownership and uses of the property consistent with good commercial or customary practice in an effort to minimize liability. In this respect the court should take into account any specialized knowledge or experience on the part of the defendant, the relationship of the purchase to the value of the property if uncontaminated, commonly known or reasonably ascertainable information about the property, the obviousness of the presence or likely presence of contamination at the property, and the ability to detect such contamination by appropriate inspection.

Where an owner or operator has actual knowledge of a release of a hazardous substance at the facility and subsequently transfers the property to another person without disclosing that information, the former owner or operator will be liable and has no defence under Subsection 9607(b) (3). Likewise a defendant who causes or contributes to a release remains liable.

The substance of these provisions essentially result in a form or successor liability and, in effect, impose a duty of environmental inspection on a purchaser of property.[59]

4. *Limitation of Liability*

One important feature of OPA is that actions for removal costs and damages are not subject to the general Limitation of Liability Act.[60] Instead OPA provides for its own limits of liability. Section 2704 establishes the following limits:

[59] Chase, "The Lender Liability Paradox: A Fresh Approach" (1991) 5 *Tul. Envt'l. L.J.* 1; James, "Financial Institutions and Hazardous Waste Litigation: Limiting the Exposure to Superfund Liability" (1988) 28 Nat. Res. J. 329; Rashby, United States v. Maryland Bank & Trust Co.: Lender Liability Under CERCLA (1987) 14 *Ecology L.Q* 569. In the last article the author describes the case of *United States* v. *Maryland Bank & Trust Co.*, 632 F. Supp. 573 (D. Md. 1986). In that case, "the United States District Court for the District of Maryland was presented with the question of whether a mortgagee that had foreclosed on a hazardous waste site could be liable as an owner under CERCLA for the Environmental Protection Agency's (EPA) costs of cleaning up the site. In granting summary judgment for the United States, the court held that the mortgagee-turned owner could be liable for costs." 14 *Ecology L.Q.* at 571. Cf. United States v. Mirabile, 84-2480 E.D. Pa., 15 *Envtl. L. Rep.* (Envtl. L. Inst.) 20992 (1985).

[60] 46 U.S.C.A. §§ 183 *et seq.*

"(1) For a tank vessel, the *greater* of -
(A) $1200 per gross ton; or
(B) (i) in the case of a vessel greater than 3,000 gross tons $10,000,000; or(ii) in the case of a vessel of 3,000 tons or less, $2,000,000."

A tank vessel is defined as "a vessel that is constructed or adapted to carry or that carries oil or hazardous material in bulk as cargo or cargo residue, and that:

(A) is a vessel of the United States;
(B) operates on the navigable waters [of the United States]; or
(C) transfers oil ... in a place subject to the jurisidiction of the United States."[61]

"(2) For any other vessel, $600 per gross ton or $500,000, whichever is greater;
(3) for an offshore facility ... the total of removal costs plus $75,000,000;
(4) for any onshore facility and a deepwater port, $350,000,000.

A mobile offshore drilling unit which is being used as an offshore facility is considered to be a tank vessel, however, if damages and removal costs exceed the limits placed on such a structure as a vessel, the limits applicable to offshore facilities will be applied to the excess."[62]

The changes in limitation amounts[63] introduced by OPA have received some comment. For example, in their article "The Oil Pollution Act of 1990", Rodriguez and Jaffe point out that:

"The Oil Pollution Act contains liability limits which are significantly higher than the limits contained in the Clean Water Act [FWPCA] and other previous legislation. For instance, a tank vessel's liability is now $1200 per gross ton or $10,000,000 for a vessel over 3,000 tons (or $2,000,000 for a smaller vessel), whichever is greater. By contrast, under the Clean Water Act the limit was $150 per gross ton or $250,000, whichever was greater. Although considerably higher, the new limits are dwarfed by the actual amount spent by Exxon following the spill from the Exxon Valdez which is reported to be in excess of $2,000,000,000."[64]

Also Healy, Paulsen and Marion have noted that:

The enormous increase in a shipowner's potential liability can be illustrated by using a 100,000 gross ton oil tanker as an example. Under the FWPCA, a vessel of this size would have been liable for a maximum of $15,000,000 in cleanup and removal costs

[61] § 2701 (34).
[62] 33 U.S.C.A. § 2704 (b).
[63] Under subsection (f) of the FWPCA liability was limited to:
In the case of an inland barge to $125 per gross ton or $125,000 whichever is greater, "In the case of all other vessels $150 per gross ton of such vessel (or, for a vessel carrying oil or hazardous substances as cargo, $250,000), whichever is greater . . .".
The right to limit ones liability is not available when the discharge was the result of wilful negligence or wilful misconduct within the privity and knowledge of the owner in which case the owner or operator is liable to the government for the actual amount of the removal costs.
Subsections (f) (2) & (3) contain similar provisions with respect onshore and offshore facilities respectively with the limitation amounts set at $50 million. Under subsection (q) the President may reduce this to an amount not less than $8 million.
[64] Rodriguez and Jaffe, "The Oil Pollution Act of 1990" (1990) 15 *Tul. Mar. L.J.* 1, 16.

(100,000 g.t. × $150), assuming that the responsible party had not been guilty of willful negligence or willful misconduct, and that no statutory defenses applied. Under the new law, the vessel would now be liable for federal cleanup costs up to $120,000,000 (100,000 g.t. × $1200) for a comparable spill.[65]

In addition to higher limitation amounts, there is a serious question as to whether or not this provision for limitation of liability carries any realistic protection for vessel owners. Under § 1321(f) of the FWPCA, which formerly contained the defences available to an owner and also limited the amount of its liability to $150 per gross ton, the right to limit liability was lost only where "the United States can show that such discharge was the result of wilful negligence or wilful misconduct *within the privity and knowledge of such owner* . . .". OPA, however, provides in § 2704(c) (1) that a responsible party has no right to limit its liability under the Act where "the incident was proximately caused by":

"(A) the gross negligence or willful misconduct of, or
(B) the violation of an applicable Federal safety, construction or operating regulation by, '*the responsible party, an agent or employee of the responsible party, or a person acting pursuant to a contractual relationship with the responsible party* . . . "Thus, on the face of the statute, it would seem that gross negligence of a low level employee that results in a discharge of oil denies the responsible party the right to limit its liability under the Act because there is no requirement that such conduct be within the privity or knowledge of the owner."

Likewise under § 2704(c), the responsible party is not entitled to limit its liability if its "fails or refuses":

"(A) to report the incident as required by law and the responsible party knows or has reason to know of the incident;
(B) to provide all reasonable cooperation and assistance requested by a responsible official in connection with removal activities; or
(C) without sufficient cause, to comply with an order issued under subsection (c) or (e) of section 1321 of this title or the Intervention on the High Seas Act."

As stated in the discussion of defences, the language used in this subsection, § 2704 (c), is far from clear. Applied literally, an innocent mistake, misunderstanding or oversight could result in the loss of the right to limit liability under the Act.

There is also no right to limit liability with regard to removal costs incurred by the United States, any state or local governmental unit with respect to discharges from a facility on the Outer Continental Shelf or from a vessel carrying oil from such a facility.[66]

CERCLA also contains provisions on limitation of liability in Section 9607(c). (1) Except as provided in paragraph (2), the liability of an owner or

[65] Healy, Paulsen and Marion, "The United States Oil Pollution Act of 1990" (1991 93 *IL Dirittimo* 244, 246.
[66] 33 U.S.C.A. § 2704 (c) (3).

operator or other responsible person for each release of a hazardous substance or incident involving release of a hazardous substance shall not exceeds:

"(A) For any vessel, other than an incineration vessel, which carries any hazardous substance as cargo or residue, \$300 per gross ton, or \$5,000,000, whichever is greater;

(B) For any other vessel, other than an incineration vessel, \$300 per gross ton, or \$500,000, whichever is greater;. . .

(D) For any incineration vessel or any facility other than those specified in subparagraph (C) [motor vehicle, aircraft, pipeline], the total of all costs of response plus \$50,000,000 for any damages under this subchapter.

(2) The right to limit liability is lost and the full costs of response and damages will be imposed if:

(A)(i) the release or thereat of release was a result of willful misconduct or willful negligence within the privity or knowledge of such person or,

(ii) the primary cause of the release was a violation within the privity or knowledge of such person of applicable safety, construction, or operating standards or regulations; or

(B) Such person fails or refuses to provide all reasonable cooperation and assistance requested by a responsible public official in connection with response activities under the National contingency Plan."

This subsection also authorizes the imposition of punitive damages if a person who is liable for a release fails without sufficient cause properly to provide removal or remedial action upon order of the President in an amount at least equal to and not more than three times the amount of costs incurred as a result of the failure to take proper action.

CERCLA offers a better opportunity for an owner or operator to retain the benefits of limitation because the right to limit is not lost by the mere application of *respondent superior*. On the other hand, like OPA, the right to limit is lost if the defendant fails to co-operate or provide assistance to public officials. But the co-operation and assistance requested must be in connection with response activities under the National Contingency Plan.

5. *Financial Responsibility*

Section 2716(a) is one of the most important provisions of OPA in that it requires responsible parties, that is, owners and operators of vessels and oil production facilities, to provide evidence of financial responsibility.[67] Operation

[67] Ibid. § 2716 (a) sets the requirement for vessels and subsection (c) sets the requirements for offshore facilities and deepwater ports.

The FWPCA also required evidence of financial responsibility. Subsection (p), which has been repealed by OPA and is now superseded by 33 U.S.C.A. § 2716, required any vessel over 300 gross tons, including barges except those that were not self-propelled and did not carry oil or hazardous susbstances as cargo or fuel, to establish and maintain evidence of financial responsibility to meet its liability to the United States in the following amounts:

In the case of an inland barge \$125 per gross ton or \$125,000 whichever was greater, "In the case of all other vessels \$150 per gross ton of such vessel (or, for a vessel carrying oil or hazardous substances as cargo, \$250,000), whichever was greater . . .".

of a vessel without having provided the required evidence of financial responsibility subjects a vessel to the denial of clearance or entry, to seizure by the Government[68] and also to other penalties.[69] With regard to vessels, the financial responsibility requirement applies "(1) to any vessel over 300 gross tons (except a non-self-propelled vessel that does not carry oil as cargo of fuel) using any place subject to the jurisdiction of the United States", or "(2) any vessel using the waters of the exclusive economic zone to transship or lighter oil destined for a place subject to the jurisdiction of the United States."

Although there is some ambiguity in the wording of the provision setting the amount of financial responsibility, the most reasonable interpretation of § 2716 is that the amount of financial responsibility must be sufficient to meet the maximum amount of liability to which, in the case of a vessel owner, the responsible party would be subjected in a case where it would be entitled to limit its liability under § 2704(a) and (d)[70] of the Act. Where a responsible party owns or operates more than one vessel, then evidence of financial responsibility need only be in an amount sufficient to satisfy the maximum liability applicable to the vessel having the greatest exposure to liability.

The financial responsibility requirement may be satisfied by evidence of insurance, surety bond, guarantee, letter of credit, qualification as a self-insurer, etc.[71]

Any claim for removal costs or damages authorized under the Act may be brought *directly* against the guarantor who provides the evidence of financial responsibility for a responsible party. A guarantor may assert against a claimant "all rights and defenses which would be available to a responsible party" and also "the defense that the incident was caused by the willful misconduct of the responsible party."[72] But there is an important limitation on the defences that may be asserted by a guarantor. Unlike the FWPCA, " the guarantor may not invoke any other defense that might be available in proceedings brought by the responsible party against the guarantor."[73] Thus, a guarantor may not defend against a claim even where, for example, the responsible party has obtained insurance through fraud or misrepresentation. A guarantor, however, cannot be held liable for damages in an amount that exceeds "the amount of financial responsibility required under this chapter which that guarantor has provided for a responsible party."[74]

[68] Ibid. (b).

[69] Ibid. (a).

[70] Ibid. § 2704 (d) provides, *inter alia*, that the President of the United States may not less often that every 3 years adjust the limits of liability provided in § 2704 (a) to reflect significant increases in the Consumer Price Index.

[71] Ibid. § 2716 (e).

[72] Ibid. (f).

[73] Ibid.

[74] Ibid. (g).

CERCLA in Section 9608 requires proof of financial responsibility. It requires the owner or operator of a vessel (except a non-self-propelled barge that does not carry hazardous substances as cargo) over 300 gross tons that uses any port or place in the United States or the navigable waters or any offshore facilities to establish and maintain in accordance with the regulations promulgated by the President, evidence of financial responsibility of $300 per gross ton (or for a vessel carrying hazardous substances as cargo, or $5,000,000, whichever is greater) to cover liability under section 9607 of the Act. Where an owner or operator owns, operates, or charters more than one vessel, evidence of financial responsibility need be established only to meet the maximum liability of the largest vessel. With respect to facilities, the Act directs the President to formulate the amounts of financial responsibility. Financial responsibility may be established by insurance, guarantee, surety bond, or qualification as a self-insured.

Subsection (c) of section 9608 authorizes a direct action against any guarantor providing evidence of financial responsibility for a vessel. In defending such a claim, the guarantor may invoke all rights and defences which would be available to the owner or operator. The guarantor may also invoke the defence that the incident was caused by the wilful misconduct of the owner or operator. Like OPA and unlike FWPCA the guarantor may not invoke any other defence that the guarantor might have been entitled to invoke in a proceeding brought by the owner or operator against it. There is a similar provision applicable to those who act as guarantors for facilities.

Under subsection 9608(d), a guarantor's liability is limited to the amounts of its insurance policy, guarantee, surety bond, etc. However, this statute is not intended to limit any other state or federal statutory, contractual, or common law liability of a guarantor, including liability for bad faith in negotiating or failing to negotiate the settlement of a claim.

Where an owner of operator fails to comply with the financial responsibility requirement the Secretary of the Treasury shall withhold or revoke the clearance required by 46 U.S.C.A. § 91. Furthermore, the Secretary of Transportation shall deny entry to any port or place or navigable waters in the U.S. or detain a vessel which is about to depart.

Jurisdiction and Procedure

OPA has very far-reaching implications for it has created a federal right in favour of persons and governments who have been financially injured because of an oil spill. Furthermore, the Act confers jurisdiction over actions brought to recover damages under the Act in the United States District Courts.[75] The Act permits such actions to be brought in state courts as long as the state has authorised its courts to hear pollution damage claims. In creating a Federal

[75] Ibid. § 2717 (b).

statutory right and conferring jurisdiction in the District Courts, it is likely that plaintiffs who bring such actions will be able to do so under 28 U.S.C.A. § 1331 (federal question jurisdiction) and thereby invoke the right to trial by jury. Additionally, the statute expressly states that it does not affect admiralty and maritime law or the jurisdiction of the District Courts in maritime action.[76] Presumably then, Supplemental Rules B, C & F of the Federal Rules of Civil Procedure would apply to actions commenced as admiralty attachments and to actions brought *in rem*.

Under section 9613 of CERCLA, the United States District Courts have exclusive original jurisdiction without regard to citizenship of the parties or the amount in controversy. Also Subsection 9607(h) as amended, maritime tort remedies against owners and operators of vessels are provided.

6. *State Legislation*

One of the objectives of those who, prior to the enactment of OPA, campaigned for adoption of the Civil Liability Convention and the 1984 Protocol was to have a single exclusive national (federal) liability regime, that is to have a federal law that would pre-empt state laws. Not only was the effort to adopt the Convention unsuccessful, but also the goal of a single liability regime was not achieved. OPA expressly preserves the authority liability of states and their political subdivisions to impose additional liability and requirements where oil has been discharged within a state and removal activities in connection therewith.[77] Also states may establish their own funds to pay for costs and damages resulting from oil spills and require persons to contribute to such funds.[78] Furthermore, neither the limitation of liability provisions set forth in § 2704(a) of OPA or the general Limitation of Liability laws[79] are applicable to such state liability or penalty regimes. States may enact legislation that imposes *unlimited liability* on the owners of vessels from which oil has been discharged. Some states have already responded to this "invitation" in OPA and have enacted oil pollution regulation and liability provisions.

CERCLA in Section 9614 likewise provides that nothing in this chapter shall be construed or interpreted as pre-empting any state from imposing any additional liability or requirements with respect to the release of hazardous substances within a state. Double recovery, however, is precluded. Furthermore, no persons may be required to contribute to any fund, the purpose of which is to pay compensation for claims for any costs of response or damages or claims which may be compensated under this Act. However, states may use general revenues or impose taxes or fees on any person or substance to purchase hazardous substance response equipment.

[76] Ibid. § 2751 (e).
[77] Ibid. § 2718 (a).
[78] Ibid. (b).
[79] 46 U.S.C.A. §§ 183 *et seq.*

Subsection 9614 (d), however, states that no owner or operator of a vessel or facility who establishes and maintains evidence of financial responsibility under this Act shall be required under any State of local law to establish or maintain any other evidence of financial responsibility in connection with liability for the release of a hazardous substance from such vessel or facility. Evidence of compliance with the financial responsibility requirements of the Act shall be accepted by a State in lieu of any requirement of financial responsibility imposed by a State in connection with liability for the release of a hazardous substance from a vessel or facility.

Recently enacted state statutes reveal that the states are approaching oil spill liability in different ways. The Louisiana Oil Spill Prevention Response Act,[80] essentially tracks OPA with respect to the basis for liability, removal cost and damages and limitation of liability amounts. It does not require a certificate of financial responsibility if one is provided under OPA. Texas also relies on the certificates of financial responsibility required under the Federal Act. The limitation of liability amounts for a vessel exceeding 8,000 gross tons are $600 per gross ton not to exceed $50,000,000 for removal costs and a similar amount with respect to damages other than natural resource damages. Liability for natural resource damage is unlimited.[81] Defences are similar to that provided under OPA.

Florida has amended its statute[82] so that the liability limits are similar to OPA, but the statute is more favourable to vessel owners than Federal law because limitation is denied only for wilful or gross negligence within the privity or knowledge of the owner, operator or agent.

California's Oil Spill Prevention and Response Act, however, goes much further than other states. Vessels or owners of oil are required to obtain state certificates of financial responsibility commencing on 1 January 1992 in the amount of $500,000,000, rising to $750,000,000 in 1995 and 1 billion dollars in the year 2000. The "responsible party" is defined as including the owner or transporter of oil. The Act imposes absolute liability and a "third party" defence is not available unless the conduct of the third party constitutes a criminal act. The damages recoverable are more extensive than those allowed under OPA. Finally, the California statute does not appear to include a limitation of liability provision, and, thus, it appears to impose unlimited liability.[83]

OPA — Absolute and Unlimited Liability?

Under OPA carriers of oil may face the prospect of unpredictable and possibly unlimited liability. This is so for several reasons. First, as stated earlier in this

[80] L.S.A. R.S. 30: 745, *et seq.* (First Extraordinary Session 1991, Wests Session Law Service 1991).

[81] Vernons Texas Statutes Annotated, Natural Resources Code § 40.202 (Session Law Service 1991).

[82] Fla. Stat. Ann. § 376.12 (Session Law Service 1991).

[83] Deering's Cal. Codes Ann., Government Code § 8670.1, *et seq.* (1992 Supp.).

chapter, the so-called "complete defences" are somewhat illusory. Second, the limitation protection extended by § 2714(a) is compromised by subsection (c) whereby limitation may be lost by the wilful misconduct or violation of a safety regulation by any employee of the responsible party or by an independent contractor performing services for the responsible party. Third, the limitation protection is further compromised because limitation may be denied where a responsible party fails to report, co-operate and assist or comply with an order even though, in any given situation, these requirements as stated in §2704(c) (2) may be far from clear. Fourth, it is not clear as to how courts will interpret and apply the newly created damage provisions especially those relating to loss of profits and earning capacity, loss of governmental revenues, costs of providing governmental services, and damage to natural resources. Finally, there is the as yet unknown role of state legislation. As noted above the states are free to enact their own liability legislation without providing for limitation of liability.

Some Concepts of Collective Responsibility in U.S. Products Liability and Environmental Situations

Michael J. Harrigan

An essential element for recovery in any products liability claim is the causal relationship between the defective product and the claimed injury. Essential to the causal link is the identification of the party responsible for the product (designer, maker, seller). There are, however, occasions when identification of a specific party is impossible but where the injury is such that only a particular product could have caused the harm. This is especially true in that class of product liability cases generally referred to as "toxic torts". Toxics (and within this catch-all category are included asbestos, pesticides, herbicides, insecticides, household cleaning agents, drugs, solvents, fungicides, petroleum distillates, and chemicals in general) are frequently fungible and untraceable back to a specific manufacturer. There is often a latency period between exposure to the toxin and onset of symptomatology. In DES and asbestos cases, the gap is measured in decades. The ability of plaintiffs to make that vital link between injury and a particular defendant is, in the context of toxic torts, frequently too difficult a burden to bear.

Some American courts have found ways of abolishing the plaintiff's need to prove causality in order to further what is believed to be the more societally valuable objective of compensating the injured without regard to who is actually at fault. What essentially happens is that the burden of proof shifts to the defendants in those cases where "Collective Responsibility" applies.

"Alternative Liability" applies in those few products liability cases where a plaintiff cannot identify the correct wrongdoer but can identify a set of all possible wrongdoers. In its simplest form it goes back to the "two hunters" situation (*Summers* v. *Tice*, 33 Cal. 2d 80, 199 P. 2d 1 [1948]) where the plaintiff was unable to specify which of two hunters had fired the shotgun that injured him.

The court shifted the burden to the defendants to extricate themselves and upon their failure to do so found them jointly and severally liable. The rationale is understandable and informs all of the related decisions in these kinds of cases: a helpless plaintiff should not be left without remedy because of an inability to specify which, of a number of defendants who *must* have caused the harm, was actually responsible. The drawback of the Alternative Liability Theory is that 100% of the responsible parties must be identified and sued. This has proven to be limiting and in time more creative approaches have been adopted.

One of these was "enterprise liability" where the court held that a group of manufacturers which comprised virtually the whole of the industry were jointly and severally liable if the plaintiff could establish that they had joint awareness of the risk and joint capacity to reduce the risk. It is akin to "concert of action" and almost smacks of conspiracy theories (*Hall* v. *DuPont*, 345 F. Supp. [E.D.N.Y. 1972]; *Bichler* v. *Lilly*, 55 N.Y. 2d 521 [1982]). The problem with enterprise liability is that all or "virtually" all of the industrial entities had to be before the court and the industry had to be a small one. Application of the theory was unreasonable with a large, decentralized industry.

"Market share liability" developed to deal with this problem. It was first articulated in *Sindell* v. *Abbott* (26 Cal. 3rd 588, *cert. denied*, 449 U.S. 912 [1980]). Faced with a class of innocent DES daughters, an industry where over 200 manufacturers of DES had existed, and five defendants who collectively had made 90% of the product, the court held that as long as the plaintiff had sued a sufficient number of manufacturers to constitute a "substantial share" of the market, then each defendant could be held responsible for a proportion of the judgment based upon its market share unless it could exculpate itself. The liability, a subsequent case held, was several, not joint; each defendant was liable only to the extent of its market share (*Brown* v. *Superior Court*, 44 Cal. 3rd 1049 [1988]).

Market Share Liability has not found universal favour within the U.S. It has been specifically rejected in Louisiana (Federal court; asbestos), Kentucky (Federal court; tetracycline), South Carolina (Federal court; DES), Florida (State court; asbestos), Missouri (State court; DES), Ohio (State court; asbestos), California (State court; asbestos and polio vaccine).

Some courts have modified the approach, accepting the concept of collective liability with something less than wholeheartedness or finding specific reasons why the particular case at bar would not qualify entirely.

Some have found market share liability inadequate. Wisconsin adopted a theory whereby each manufacturer who contributed to the *risk* of injury ("risk share liability") could be held responsible. Under this theory the plaintiff has to sue only one defendant. It then becomes that defendant's responsibility to identify and bring into the case other possibly responsible parties or bear the exposure alone (*Collins* v. *Squibb*, Wis. 2d 166, *cert. denied*, 469 U.S. 826 [1984]).

New York went perhaps farthest, adopting a kind of synergy of risk-share and market-share liability theories in a DES case (*Hymowitz* v. *Lilly*). In that case, liability was determined by the "overall culpability" of each manufacturer measured by the risk it created to the public at large; each defendant's proportionate share was based on its percentage of the national market (and limited to that — there is only several liability); but *there is no exculpation.* Even if a defendant can prove it had nothing to do with the product responsible for the injury, if anybody pays — everybody pays.

Certain kinds of pollution injuries have proof problems similar to those of toxic torts. Those who are adjacent to hazardous waste dumps where hundreds of chemicals have been deposited over time and who have been harmed when chemicals leach out of the containment area have the same difficulty tracing the damage back to its ultimate cause. One would think that the above theories of collective responsibility would serve as attractive solutions in these cases, and some of the principles are discernible in the way Federal and State regulatory agencies deal with the clean-up (remediation) of hazardous waste sites and this in turn guides the pragmatic approaches to the resolution of private tort actions.

In 1980 the Federal government adopted the Comprehensive Environmental Response, Compensation and Liability Act ("CERCLA", also known as the Superfund Act). This authorises the Environmental Protection Administration to investigate and clean up sites which are releasing, or threatening to release, hazardous substances. The states have adopted similar regulations since that time, some of them more restrictive in their classification of "hazardous substance" (they cannot be less restrictive). A site need not be a land fill or lagoon containing hazardous *wastes* to be subject to Superfund clean-up; EPA can act if the site contains hazardous *substances* (a much broader category than hazardous wastes). The law allows the government to clean up the site and charge the cost to the owners, transporters, and generators of the hazardous substances. As a practical matter, the government tries to identify all "potentially responsible parties" ("PRP's") and get them to clean up the site themselves. As a practical matter, PRP's prefer it that way because anything the government does tends to cost double or triple what the private sector could achieve.

A PRP who is liable under CERCLA is strictly liable, it is no defence that the company was not negligent or that it complied with all applicable state and Federal laws. The amount of material shipped or found is immaterial for liability purposes. Joint and several liability applies. Nor is it material that *the* hazardous substance shipped to the site by a PRP is not being (or likely to be) released. All parties who disposed of *any* hazardous substance are liable. PRPs are permitted (in fact encouraged) to identify other PRPs. This statutory/regulatory approach more than faintly echoes (it practically shouts in your ear) the *Collins* Risk Share theory where merely contributing to the *risk* of harm can render one liable for all the harm.

The government and most PRPs are more interested in settling than in litigating and most responsible parties settle for a "volumetric" share, that is, they contribute to the cost of remediation a percentage based upon the ratio of the volume of the substance they shipped to the total volume of all hazardous substances on the site. Typically, PRP's split up into groups: a *de minimus* group (say those who each contributed less than 1% of the total volume); a median group (those, perhaps, with between 1% and 10%); and a group of major generators (more than 10%, for example). It is possible for a PRP to exculpate itself by proving that it never shipped anything to the site, but those in the *de minimus* group seldom bother anymore since it is often many times more costly to do so than to pay what the government is willing to accept as a per share contribution. (The government usually assesses the *de minimus* group a flat amount per "head".) Those in other groups expend a lot of effort and cost trying to establish that they are responsible for smaller volumetric shares. Most of the defence effort is directed towards arriving at a remediation scheme that will achieve the objective of cleaning up the site at a reasonable cost; what the British would, I believe, refer to as the Best Practical Method.

What we see here in this pragmatic approach is analogous to "Market Share" where "volumetric" is substituted for "market".

Despite grumblings from PRPs about "extortionate" government behaviour, this settlement methodology works (not rapidly, but it does work). Consequently, it is the usual way of dealing with personal injury and property damage claims brought by those adjacent to Superfund sites. Frequently numbering in the hundreds, occasionally in the thousands, per site these claims can allege anything from diminution of property values to actual physical injury to fear of contracting a future disease. By concentrating the defence effort towards minimising the scope of the claims (rather than by wasting time and money trying to exculpate a particular defendant) quicker, more reasonable, settlements have been obtained.

Because pollution-related matters have a high profile and because the systems that have evolved to deal with these problems seems to be working, it would appear that a concept of collective responsibility is becoming entrenched in the U.S. How it develops for the future, however, is anybody's guess.

Multiple Tort Feasors/Combined Polluter Theories, Causality and Assumption of Proof/Statistical Proof, Technical Insurance Aspects

Hans-Dieter Sellschopp

The city of Rotterdam is an appropriate place to talk about multiple causation and transnational pollution. The port, in its "end-of-pipe position", gets the sediment of industrial effluents from four highly industrialised countries. Dutch law gives the city of Rotterdam the right to file civil charges for damages against the polluters, but not without having first attempted to negotiate a reduction in toxic discharges with the polluters. In 1985 the city launched its Rhine Study Project, which identified the polluters along the entire length of the river by listing discharges of cadmium, chrome, copper, lead, and zinc into the Rhine. If negotiations with polluters fail, however, the city does not hesitate to use the options provided under Dutch civil law, as we have seen in its suit against French potassium mines at the end of 1990.[1]

But the Rhine is only one of many polluted rivers. And river pollution is by no means the only kind of transnational pollution. Air pollution that damages forests can spread halfway across the continent, whereas the effects of CFC emissions on the ozone layer are global.

In the following pages I would like to give you a condensed account of how liability insurance is affected by the liability law concepts of "the proof of causation" and "multiple liability". There are four aspects I wish to touch upon. One effect of expanding pollution liability on insurance is the increase in the number of potentially liable parties. This increase involves not only manufac-

[1] Van Dunné (ed.), *Transboundary Pollution and Liability: The Case of the River Rhine* (Rotterdam, 1990), pp. 1–34.

turers but also shippers, users, waste site operators, and others. This multiple liability with cumulative effects has a bearing on liability insurers' considerations with regard to accumulation control — and hence to the policy they adopt in accepting risks and ceding them to reinsurers. In this connection it is worth mentioning the growing importance of risk evaluation also in a technical sense by inspection of sites and soil as a precondition of insurance.

Secondly, the number of potential claimants also multiplies. Statistical methods of producing evidence (epidemiological statistics on the effects of mineral fibres on workers, and public or regional statistics) make liabilities towards entire population groups conceivable. The procedural handling of such cases is facilitated by collecting claims, and this can be done either by the state and public bodies, or by pressure groups and class actions or through recourse by social and health insurers. For instance, claims for medical costs caused by increased lead levels verified by regional statistics can be made against identifiable polluters by health insurers on the basis of subrogation. This possibility means a new dimension in calculating the cost of personal injury in particular.

Thirdly, there is the influence of geographical aspects on the scope of coverage. Transnational pollution can be dealt with in terms of liability law. The covers provided by liability insurers are becoming more and more international. In domestic covers, "domestic loss events" can also include "loss events in other countries that are generated domestically". Also, more and more insurers are offering cover for foreign risks.

Finally, pollution is often if not mostly long term, which forces liability insurers to take the temporal aspects into account when making their calculations and drafting clauses.

The Tortfeasors

Causation has both a factual, scientific side and a legal, philosophical side. The legal concept of adequate or proximate causation can be dependent on non-legal values which are continuously changing. It is quite possible now to believe, for instance, that the depletion of the ozone layer is a "proximate" result of CFC production. With the criterion of negligence becoming less significant, causation is increasingly becoming the only standard by which liability is judged.[2]

And in this regard the new environmental laws even go one step further. Such laws as the Environmental Liability Act in Germany and the EC Draft Directive on Civil Liability for Damage caused by Waste go so far as to replace scientific proof of causation with the broader concept of "general capability" to cause damage which reverses the onus of proof of causation.

[2] Fenyvess and Weyers (eds.), *Multikausale Shäden in modernen Haftungsrechten* (Frankfurt, 1988).

The trend towards easing the proof of causation coupled with trends towards joint and several liability and market-share solutions[3] will lead to liability insurers being involved in a growing number of law suits. Insurers and reinsurers alike will have to review their assessments of potential accumulations. The complexity of the liability questions involved in these suits will make them expensive and time-consuming affairs. Inherent in the German Environmental Liability Act for instance is the certainty of a running battle between expert witnesses, which will be fought in various phases of these cases.

I do not have time to elaborate on the law itself which establishes strict liability without the state-of-the-art defence also for normal business operations as permitted by authorities. These risks are also included in the new insurance concept if the insured can prove that according to the technical state-of-the-art at the time of production he could not foresee the possibility of damage resulting therefrom.

The coverage issues are therefore just as complex as the liability issues, and coverage disputes may follow. Court costs will be a factor that insurers will have to include in their premiums, while the calculation of adequate reserves will require some new thought, too. Liability insurers will have to include statistical material in their calculations even though in given cases the statistics may be inconclusive. For example, a statistically larger number of leukemia cases recorded in the vicinity of a nuclear power station - at present, at least in Europe, far from being grounds for a successful liability claim - must be given due consideration in the calculation of liability insurance premiums. Each risk factor has a price. Recoveries for Cancerphobia recognized in the U.S. give claimants compensation if they have been exposed to carcinogens and can prove they have a statistically higher risk of cancer. As with asbestos cases, the large number of plaintiffs and defendants in pollution cases creates an administrative nightmare for insurers. Setting reserves for such claims is a particularly difficult task.

All this means that an insurer has to collect an enormous amount of information to arrive at a fair evaluation of the risk — as far as this is possible at all.

The discussion of multiple causation and joint tortfeasors in environmental liability law centres on those cases in which various polluters make various contributions to one and the same loss or series of losses.[4] One classic case of joint and several liability is less often discussed, however, and that is the case in which several parties at various levels - such as manufacturer, user and waste site operator - may be jointly liable for a single environmentally harmful contribution - such as a toxic waste product.

When the EC products liability standards were defined after long years of discussion, the environmental aspect was generally ignored. When the German

[3] Snijder, "Van market share liability naar pollution share liability?" *TMA/Environmental Liability Law Review* (Rotterdam), 6 (1990), 141–150.

[4] Köndgen, "Multiple Causation and Joint Tortfeasors in Pollution Cases according to German Law," in Dunné *Transboundary Pollution*, n. 1 *Supra*, pp. 199–106.

Environmental Liability Act was drawn up, in discussions that also lasted for years, the question of product liability was likewise largely ignored. The EC standards on liability for damage caused by waste, on the other hand, will overlap to a certain extent with the products liability laws and, in Germany, also with liability as defined by the Environmental Liability Act. We are dealing here with different legal systems that have developed in the course of time, and how they are co-ordinated in the handling of environmental losses remains to be seen.

The same goes for insurance, too. The specific concepts of cover for environmental damage in the Anglo-American markets or the pool covers in the Netherlands, France, and Italy are public liability covers. The various environmental clauses, for example restricting coverage for gradual pollution, relate in part only to public liability, in part also to products liability.

Certain types of environmental losses excluded from public liability insurance may be covered within the framework of products liability. There is a situation in which, as we say in Germany, the devil that has just been shown out through one door comes in through the other. If, on the other hand, environmental clauses apply to products liability, too, this will lead to major problems of interpretation. For example, should the destruction of agricultural crops by defective pesticides — as such a classic case of products liability — really in general be excluded from liability covers?

The problem lies, on the one hand, in the existing broad scope of products liability cover. On the other hand, it lies in the broad definition of "polluter" in connection with environmental damage. The ambiguity of the term "polluter" is indicated in the United States, where the term is used very broadly. In this context I would mention the trend we witnessed in past years of treating the banks that gave credit to the owners of contaminated land as polluters themselves. The reason for this development was the potential influence that the banks could exert on the owners' policy with regard to cleaning up their property. It follows that even professional indemnity covers for Directors and Officers of banks may be affected.

The Large Number of Potential Claimants

Environmental impairment means that loss or damage is caused by pollution of the water, the soil, or the air. One of these may be impaired by a large number of polluters. And the pollution may also affect a large number of potential claimants. The collection of a large number of individual claims may be undertaken by a public authority. Under the environmental law passed in Italy in 1986, only the state and public authorities are allowed to file suits, a borderline case between private and public law. One of the topics of modern environmental laws (as in the EC Draft Directive on Liability for Damage caused by Waste) is the right of action given to social pressure groups. Popular action, by the way, is not an invention of modern consumer protection legislation but was already a part of

Roman law, which is still found in some classic South American civil law books.[5]

In addition to the state and social groups there is a third group that is capable of channelling a large number of individual losses: namely social and health insurers. The German public health insurance scheme is constantly refining its collection of regional statistics in order to identify individual causes more accurately. These carriers are able to take recourse in accordance with the EC directives on products liability and waste liability and in accordance with the German Environmental Liability Act, although these are all aimed primarily at protecting the individual. It is with these groups that liability insurers will increasingly need to reach agreement on cost sharing. This new risk dimension involving large numbers of small personal injuries — small amounts of damages for pain and suffering in the case of popular action, (hopefully) small amounts of medical expenses in the case of recourse by social insurance carriers — must have an influence on the price of liability insurance.

The Geographical Limits

Easing the proof of causation makes it possible to claim compensation for trans-national pollution. The court cases brought against French potassium mines show how international private law is gradually becoming more important in connection with liability for environmental damage. In the meantime the linkage of tort law to either the law at the place of action or to the law at the place of effect, based on the principle of applying the law that is more favourable for the claimant, has already stood the test.[6] But with the spate of environmental liability laws being passed all over Europe, the question as to which law is the more favourable, both on paper and in practice, is becoming increasingly difficult. For instance, a Portuguese judge may have to apply the strict rules of the 1986 Spanish law on waste though as yet the law is very seldom applied even in Spain itself.

What is in this context the position of liability insurers? Liability insurance traditionally covers "domestic losses" even if these have to be dealt with in accordance with foreign laws. This concept can be extended in two ways: The cover for domestic causes can also include losses resulting from these causes abroad. On the other hand, the cover for domestic consequences can also include causes set abroad. That allows a flexible construction of policies covering trans-national interests of domestic parent companies and its foreign subsidiaries.

[5] Chile, Colombia (Art. 2359 Cod. Civil Colombiano); Alessandri Rodriguez, *De la responsabilidad civil extracontractual en el derecho civil chileno* (Santiago de Chile, 1981), num. 142; Tamayo Jaramillo, *De la responsabilidad civil*, Vol. II (Bogotá, 1986) pp. 80–81.

[6] Rest, *Fortentwicklung des Umwelthaftungsrechts: Völkerrechtliche und international-privatrechtliche Aspekte* (Berlin, 1989).

This gains importance as insurance covers for foreign risks are spreading in line with increasing multinational activities of industrial and commercial enterprises, and this not only with a view to the Single Market in Europe.

Direct insurers' liability specialists, who have concentrated up to now on their own country's laws, have started concerning themselves with foreign environmental liability laws — a complex area because of the structural differences between various environmental laws - unlike the situation with regard to products liability where the laws are largely harmonized. The situation is complicated further by the fact that the concepts of cover adopted by liability insurers vary from one country to the next.

The Temporal Aspects of Insurance Coverage

Environmental losses can take place over many years as in the case of oil pollution, and also in connection with diseases, as with the latency period of cancer.

The temporal aspects are an extremely serious liability problem, as has become apparent in the heavily polluted new states of the Federal Republic of Germany.

In the 1980s, the topic of introducing time-limits into insurance coverage was discussed intensively in connection with the U.S. liability crisis for products liability, professional indemnity and environmental liability. In view of the prevailing occurrence principle, in accordance with which cover is given for loss events occurring during the policy period, even if the policy expired 20 or 30 years ago, there have been various attempts on the part of liability insurers to limit their cover temporally in the case of terminated policies: "claims-made", meaning cover is only given for losses on which claims are made during the policy period or up to a certain deadline afterwards, and the sunset clause, meaning cover is only given for losses occurring during the policy period and reported before a certain deadline. These clauses have often failed to establish themselves in the markets. In addition, the very admissibility of "claims-made" has been questioned, for example, by the French Cour de Cassation. As to the new German insurance model for environmental impairment currently under discussion, manifestation has been chosen as a definition of the insured event. This definition shortens the long tail under occurrence policies but is still more favourable to the insured than the "claims-made" principle. At any rate: pollution risks emanating from normal business operations on an occurrence basis must in the future also in Germany be regarded as uncalculable and uninsurable.

Even so, liability insurers will have to live with the problem of long-term or long-tail losses, making sure at the same time that they do not exceed the limits for their own survival, for instance by cutting out losses that must be foreseen. Insurance cannot be provided against everything. A state monopoly insurer, a social insurer, may speak of a contract between generations and charge the costs produced by one generation to the next one's account — a very questionable method if one looks at the demographic development of most industrialized countries! The liability insurance market with its short-term cycles and competition throughout the EC will not have an easy time in trying to arrive at cost-covering premiums in line with the polluter-pays principle. This principle requires that the overall costs of damage are allocated to the overall costs of production and this can only happen if polluters provide liability insurers with the necessary means — that is with sufficient premiums! — to stand up to their long-term commitments. In this context time-limits are an important precondition for adjusting premiums quickly to new developments in technology and legislation. Of course responsibility for the calculation lies with the liability insurers themselves and their reinsurers, but they will need a fair amount of understanding on the part of their clients and the public to fulfil their difficult task and to give their contribution a chance of continuity.

Several Theories on Liability in the Dutch DES Case

Jan Ekering

I. Short History of DES (Diethylstilbestrol)

In 1937 in England, Dodds et al. invented DES, a synthetic hormone (oestrogen). Its advantages over natural oestrogen — which had already been used in medicine for decades — were that it was considerably cheaper and easier to administer. No patent application was filled for DES.

In 1940 a number of American drug manufacturers applied to the FDA (Food and Drug Administration) for a licence to market DES to treat various illnesses. At that time none of these illnesses was related to pregnancy complications. The licence was granted in 1941.

A supplemental application (supplemental NDA) for use in case of threatened pregnancy, based mainly on research by Smith and Smith, Karnaky and White, was filed in 1947. This application was approved and in 1951 the FDA informed the producers of DES that this medicine was no longer a "new drug", which meant that DES was "generally recognized as safe". Subsequently, it was administered on a large scale to women having pregnancy complications, in particular to those with a history of miscarriages.

In 1971 Herbst et al. found a "statistical association" between the use of DES by pregnant women and the occurrence of clear cell carcinomas in the urogenital system of what came to be called their DES daughters. In the USA, DES was taken off the market for use with threatened pregnancy in 1972, in the Netherlands this happened some years later.

II. DES Litigation in the USA

Michael Harrigan has given you an overview of the many thousands of actions brought by DES daughters in the United States since the mid-seventies against the several hundreds of manufacturers who had marketed DES in that country. The attention which these cases received was largely due to the so-called problem of identification. Because the afflictions of the DES daughters did not manifest themselves until they were 15 years old and because there were so many producers which had marketed the non-patented drug, usually under their own brand name but also under the generic name of "Diethylstilbestrol", many DES daughters were no longer able to identify the producer of the pills taken by their mothers. In the USA, as in the Netherlands, it is a fundamental principle of tort law that the plaintiff has the burden of proving by a preponderance of the evidence that the defendant caused the harm or injury complained-of.

In the DES cases, theories developed in the USA already before 1970 and entailing a relaxation of this requirement of identification (such as civil conspiracy, concert of action, enterprise liability and alternative liability), were rejected by courts throughout the states, on various grounds. In 1980, in the DES case of Sindell V. Abbott, the theory of market share liability was introduced in California and this theory was applied in a number of states, with several variations. However, a considerable number of states have held on to the requirement of identification.

III. DES Litigation in the Netherlands

In April 1986 six Dutch DES daughters, born between 1953 and 1967, instituted proceedings in the Amsterdam District Court against 10 Dutch drug manufacturers and wholesalers and claimed damages for the afflictions from which they alleged to be suffering as a result of the use of DES by their mothers. In the summons it was alleged that insufficient research had been done into the risks presented by DES and that the producers had ignored warnings from scientists. In addition, it was alleged that the mothers had taken DES which had in any case been marketed by one of the defendants. The plaintiffs claimed that each of the defendants was jointly and severally liable.

The four main points of the defence raised by the defendants are the following:

1. It has not been established that the plaintiffs' mothers took DES.
2. It has not been established that the afflictions of the DES daughters were caused by the use of DES.
3. It has not been established that the defendants have acted negligently.
4. It has not been established that the mothers took DES which originated from one of the defendants, let alone from which defendant.

It would take me too far afield to discuss all of these defences. In the opinion of the defendants any one of these defences would, if upheld, be sufficient to dismiss the action.

The District Court could have considered all of these defences simultaneously, but it chose to deal with them in succession. In the first instance the District Court focused its attention on the fourth defence, the problem of identification. By judgement of 15 June 1988, the District Court found that this fourth defence was well-founded and constituted sufficient ground for dismissing the action.

Subsequently, the plaintiffs appealed this judgment to the Court of Appeal of Amsterdam. Again, the debate concentrated mainly on the problem of identification. By judgment of 22 November 1990, the Amsterdam Court of Appeal again dismissed the plaintiffs' action on the basis of this defence.

The case is currently pending in the Supreme Court. The case was argued in court in December of last year.

The opinion of the Attorney General is expected in June of this year and the Supreme Court will not pronounce judgment until several months later. As a result of this fact I must — or at any rate wish to — adopt a more reserved attitude than I would otherwise have done and consequently my discussion of the legal issues which now follows will be descriptive rather than argumentative.

IV. The European Product Liability Directive

The European Product Liability Directive of 25 July 1985 was incorporated into our "old" Civil Code as of 1 November 1990 and taken from the old into our current Civil Code (Book 6, ss. 185–193) but it does not play a part in the proceedings because Article 17 of the Directive provides, briefly stated, that the Directive shall not have a retroactive effect. Even if it had such effect, this would have been of no avail to the plaintiffs, because the DES in question was marketed more than 10 years before the action was brought (Art. 11 Directive, Netherlands Civil Code Book 6:191). Indirectly, the Directive did come into the discussion in connection with Article 4: "The injured person shall be required to prove the damage, the defect and the causal relation between defect and damage." and in connection with Article 13: "This Directive shall not affect any rights which an injured person may have according to the rules of the law of contractual or non-contractual liability or a special liability system existing at the moment when this Directive is notified." I will revert to these points. I must also tell you that the Netherlands has made use of the option to allow the defence of "development risk". (6:185, under e).

V. The Liability Theories Invoked by the Plaintiffs

The liability theories discussed below are all based on the assumption that the three other requirements mentioned above, (i.e.: use of DES by the mothers, causal connection between use of DES and affliction and, finally, culpable behaviour of the producers), are satisfied. No judicial decision whatsoever has been given on these defences, however, and though it may seem superfluous it may still be useful to observe that the defendants expect that in the end the action of the DES daughters will be dismissed on the grounds of one or more of the three other defences as well. Obviously, the DES daughters think differently.

A. *Group Liability*

Book 6, Section 166, Civil Code provides:

> "1. If a member of a group of persons tortiously causes damage and if the risk of causing this damage should have prevented these persons from their collective conduct, they are jointly and severally liable if the conduct can be imputed to them.
> 2. Among themselves, they must contribute to the compensation for damage in equal parts, unless in the circumstances of the case equity requires a different apportionment."

Although the old Civil Code did not have a provision of this kind, it is generally assumed that in 1986 (and also for some considerable time before that year) this principle of group liability was operative in current law. It was applied several times by lower courts.

The provision is one of the rare legal exceptions to the rule that one must identify the tortfeasor who actually caused the damage. This theory has a number of great advantages for the plaintiffs in the DES case:

1. It is not necessary to join all members of the group as defendants.
2. The liability of any member of the group against whom judgment is obtained is joint and several.
3. A member of the group cannot raise the defence that he could not possibly have caused the damage.

The problem for the plaintiffs is of course that there is no question of real group conduct on the part of the producers. The active substance of DES was available to the public and the mere fact that the producers each individually marketed DES over a period of many years does not create a common, mutually attuned awareness. Some producers will have been aware that competitors were also producing and selling DES but even this need not have been the case. The District Court and the Court of Appeal did not want to apply this theory of group liability any more than the courts in the USA — with the exception of the *Bichler* case — wanted to apply the theory of concerted action in DES cases. There are not many authors on this subject who expect that the Supreme Court will give a different ruling on this point.

B. *Alternative Liability*

Around 1960, Professor Meijers, the founding father of our New Civil Code, drafted a section on alternative liability (or, perhaps more correctly, alternative causation). This was eventually included in our New Civil Code without much debate.

Section 6:99 provides:

> "Where the damage may have resulted from two or more events for each of which a different person is liable, and if it is certain that the damage has arisen from at least one of these events, the obligation to repair the damage rests upon each of these

persons, unless he proves that the damage is not the result of the event for which he himself is liable."

(In Dutch: "Kan de schade een gevolg zijn van twee of meer gebeurtenissen voor elk waarvan een andere persoon aansprakelijk is, en staat vast dat de schade door tenminste één van deze gebeurtenissen is ontstaan, dan rust de verplichting om de schade te vergoeden op ieder van deze personen, tenzij hij bewijst dat deze niet het gevolg is van een gebeurtenis waarvoor hij zelf aansprakelijk is.")

The term "event" aims at combining contractual liability and tort liability. In the DES case therefore read "unlawful act" or "tort" may be read instead of "event".

In the USA, alternative liability requires a plaintiff to demonstrate at least three factors:

1. that there are a small number of possibly responsible negligent tortfeasors;
2. that all of them are joined as defendants;
3. that the defendants are in a superior position to offer evidence as to the identification of the responsible party.

In his explanatory notes Meijers does not expressly refer to the case of Summers V. Tyce but he does give the example of the two hunters and also states that in general victims will be in a more difficult position to offer evidence than the tortfeasors. His examples are confined to cases with two possible tortfeasors.

Can this section be of avail to the plaintiffs in the DES case? Just as with group liability it has the attractive feature that the liability of each defendant is joint and several and that the *conditio sine qua non* requirement of causality between tortious act and damage is relaxed (rebuttal is still possible).

But there are quite a few obstacles.

(a) A first obstacle might be the fact that according to some experts the afflictions of the DES daughters occurred in identical form well before the DES period (according to some of them as early as 1903) and in countries where DES was never used. Can the section apply if the affliction also exists as a "natural phenomenon"? The requirements of the section are strict: "where it is *certain* that the damage has arisen from at least one of these (tortious acts)". Such "certainty" seems to require more than a "preponderance of evidence". What happens if in 20% — or 2% — of the cases the affliction is *not* caused by DES?
The District Court and the Court of Appeal have not given any decision on this issue but if the Supreme Court does not simply follow their judgments, some kind of decision will have to be given on this point.

(b) Must all possible tortfeasors be joined as defendants in the proceedings? It has indeed been established that in addition to the 10 defendants, other producers also marketed DES in the Netherlands in the years 1953–67, although the parties disagree about their number. The plaintiffs have alleged, although without providing proof, that the 10 defendants represent 80% of the market. This is contested by the defendants, but let us assume, for the sake of argument, that this is true. Would it not be possible that among the missing 20% of producers — some of whom no longer exist as a legal entity — there are some who did not commit tort, for instance because they did *not* recommend DES, or marketed DES in a form not suitable for the treatment of pregnancy complications but for the treatment of quite different illnesses? Or because in their time the "state of the art" was not the same as in a later period?

In this connection the District Court reasoned as follows:

> "If there is to be question of such a reversal of the burden of proof, it must be established that the tortfeasor is one of the persons held liable. It is impossible to establish this if the damage may also be the consequence of the act of a person who has not been held liable, as in the present case."

The Court of Appeal reasoned:

> "Now that the plaintiffs admit that they cannot state, let alone prove, that the alleged damage was (in any case) caused (in each case) by a party from a group of persons, which must be identified by an exhaustive enumeration, that marketed DES, this means that it cannot be established, in conformity with the requirement of the aforementioned legal rule, at least by which set of 'events' the alleged damage was caused."

These reasons have met with serious criticism from many authors, albeit these authors by no means agree along which line of reasoning a different decision should have been reached.

(c) The defendants have argued that section 99, on alternative liability, did not become operative in current law until the new Civil Code came into effect and that in connection with the transitional law from "old" to "new" Civil Code this section cannot be relied on. The parties admit that so far there is no (published) case law in which the theory of alternative liability has been applied.

In this connection the Court of Appeal reasoned:

> "that the legal rule of 6:99 New Civil Code must be accepted as being operative in current law, since according to the latest views in legal literature (cf. Asser-Hartkamp, 1988) this rule must be deemed to be current law even without a statutory basis. In this regard the Court of Appeal takes the position that a different view would result in the conclusion, which from the point of view of fairness is undesirable, that if the damage of an injured party results from one out of two or more events for each of which by itself another party is liable, such injured party would be unable to recover because it will usually be practically impossible for him to prove to which event his damage is to be attributed."

In the proceedings in the Supreme Court the defendants have contested the proposition that the principle of section 6:99 was already operative before the New Civil Code came into effect (1 January 1992). This issue is not only important in connection with the transitional law but perhaps also in connection with the European Product Liability Directive. I have already said that I would revert to this point. Some authors hold that Article 13 of the Directive prohibits the member states from adopting new legislation on product liability, after July 1985, which imposes a heavier burden on producers than the burden imposed by the Directive. If section 6:99 was not operative in the prevailing law of 1985 and *if* the provision is more burdensome that the Directive, the question arises whether a provision like that of section 6:99 may nevertheless be adopted because it is not restricted to product liability but has a wider scope, viz. all contractual and tort liability. The European Court may, in the future, have to give a ruling on this issue.

C. *Market Share Liability*

In the Netherlands we have of course taken note of the case of Sindell V. Abbott and since then some authors have been arguing that market share liability should also be applied in our country. However, many methods are suggested for doing so.

Some authors wish to stick to the joint and several liability provisions of section 6:99 and to use the concept of market share only in connection with the mutual recourse between the producers. In taking this position they, at least, keep within the text of the section.

Others hold that in the DES case the joint and several liability of section 6:99 must be replaced by liability according to market share towards each of the plaintiffs. Opinions differ as to the question whether producers must also "fill the gap" of the market share of producers who have not been joined as defendants or who have meanwhile ceased to exist.

Some authors hold that this system no longer leaves room for the possibility of exculpation, in conformity with the ruling given in the Hymowitz case.

The Wall Street Journal of 2 November 1989 contains the following statements on the *Hymowitz* case:

> "The limits to legal absurdity stretched another notch this week when the Supreme Court refused to hear an appeal from a case that says corporate defendants must pay damages even after proving that they could not possibly have caused the harm."

A harsh opinion. And possibly incorrect as well. If the liability is not in fact based on causation but on the collective creation of risk *vis-à-vis* the general public, this judgment is not an "absurdity" but a logically thought-out consequence. In that case, however, the crucial question is whether this kind of liability can still be squeezed into our tort liability law in its current, only recently recodified form, or whether separate and new legislation is required before it may be applied — a view that is being propagated in the USA as well.

In the first instance proceedings the plaintiffs did not rely on market share liability nor did they invoke it in the documents in the appeal proceedings. They did invoke such liability when the case was argued in the appeal court but they did not modify their claim for the joint and several liability of the defendants, by bringing an alternative claim for judgment according to market share. This may be one of the reasons why the Court of Appeal did not give a ruling on this point and it is not certain, either, whether the Supreme Court can or will do so.

D. *Multiple Tortfeasors*

Section 6: 102 Civil Code provides: "Two or more persons who are each obliged to compensate for the same damage are jointly and severally liable . . .". In case law the existence of such joint and several liability has been assumed:

1. where two persons jointly commit one tortious act (for instance together they set fire to a house);
2. where the damage is caused by the concurrence of two or more separate torts, committed by different tortfeasors, and where there is a condition *sine qua non* connection between the said torts and the damage as a whole (for instance two separate traffic violations made by two car drivers in respect of a third driver, where each of the violations would not by itself have caused the damage).

In these cases it has been assumed in case law that the injured party is not obliged to sue both (or all, as the case may be) tortfeasors. He may bring an action against one of them and if his action against this one tortfeasor is successful he will receive full compensation for his damage from him. It is up to the tortfeasor who has paid to recover the amount paid from his co-tortfeasor(s). In order to get around the requirement of Section 6:99 that there must be a "closed circle" of possible tortfeasors, the plaintiffs argued in the appeal proceedings that each individual pharmaceutical company which marketed DES in the years 1953–67 (tortiously) failed to do sufficient research on DES or (tortiously) failed to warn against the risks of its use in pregnancy, and that the damage of each individual plaintiff would not have arisen if the defendants had not committed these tortious acts. According to this line of reasoning, the plaintiffs would be free to bring suit against any random selection of all these tortfeasors as defendants and all of these defendant tortfeasors would be jointly and severally liable for the entire damage.

With respect to marketing the Court of Appeal reasoned (actually in connection with Section 6:99, but in my opinion the reasoning holds good for the theory of multiple tortfeasors, as well):

> "Such tort may not be assumed unless the alleged facts also include facts which can constitute proof of a specific act towards these plaintiffs, in which regard one may in particular have in mind the sale of said drug by or through (more than one of) the defendant(s) to the mothers of the plaintiffs individually."

With respect to the allegation of insufficient research or warning the Court of Appeal reasoned:

> "Had there been no omission like the alleged one which from the plaintiffs' point of view might result in liability for other people's products, and if the defendants should have acted entirely in conformity with the legal duty assumed by the plaintiffs, this

would by no means suffice to establish that in such a situation the use of unreliable tablets such as occurred in this case according to the plaintiffs, would not have taken place."

So the plaintiffs' attempts at collectivisation, at achieving the acceptance of "industry-wide liability" towards a collectivity of consumers, have not been successful (so far). We shall have to wait and see whether their effort will be rewarded by the Supreme Court.

VI. Relations with Environmental Liability

There are some obvious parallels with the subject of this seminar. In pollution cases many years may expire between the tortious act and the manifestation of damage.

In pollution cases our insight into the dangers of certain substances has grown over the years. In 1992 we know more about those dangers than we did, say, in 1960. There is a parallel with the concept of development risks. And there could be, of course, more than one possible tortfeasor. If the pollution damage could have been caused by only one of them or if it is impossible to ascertain which polluter caused which part of the damage, or even if the risk that such damage could be caused was created by a number of tortfeasors, the judgment in the DES-case might be highly relevant to future case-law on pollution, even more important for such cases than for products liability, where identification of the tortfeasor generally is no problem.

Post Scriptum

On 5 June 1992, the opinion of the Advocate-General (Hartkamp) was given. Shortly summarised, this opinion rejects for several reasons the application, in this case, of alternative liability as set out in Book 6, Section 99 Civil Code. Instead, the application of a (several) market share liability is recommended. The reasoning is rather similar to that in the Hymowitz case: the total damage, to all DES daughters, must have been caused by the collective producers and liability should be divided according to the risk each of them created. The Hoge Raad (Supreme Court) will pronounce judgment on 18 September 1992.

Environmental Damage Assessment

Colin de la Rue

It will be obvious to everyone that we live today in an age when the cost to industry of pollution has dramatically risen, and seems set to rise even further in future.

This is not so much because the number of pollution incidents is increasing; on the contrary, there has been a step-by-step improvement in preventive standards. There is, however, a *perception* of increase, because the public is much more environmentally aware than before. Incidents which once might have passed unnoticed are today headline news. Claims which once might have been amicably settled for relatively small amounts are today pressed more aggressively for much larger sums. Governments which once had other priorities must today be seen to make the polluter pay.

The issue with which we must now be concerned is the question: how much? The task of quantifying claims often involves intractable problems, and today it is ever more important than before to decide upon the best way of solving these issues.

In order to highlight the problems it may be helpful to focus on experience and developments in the field of oil pollution from ships. This is of course only one relatively narrow area of concern within a wider subject which embraces pollution by all manner of substances, both on land and at sea. But it is an area in which international law is relatively well developed, and in which the ongoing problems are reasonably well defined. The experience of oil pollution cases may foreshadow some of the challenges to be expected in future by environmental lawyers across the board.

It was the *Torrey Canyon* incident in 1967 which first brought home to us all the scale of pollution which a shipping disaster can cause, and which first exposed the inadequacy of most legal systems to provide proper compensation for the resulting damage. This led to the Civil Liability Convention of 1969 ("CLC") coupled with the Fund Convention of 1971. The main feature of CLC is that it imposes strict liability on the shipowner for any pollution damage caused by an escape or discharge of oil from a laden tanker. The effect of this is not just to relieve claimants of the sometimes difficult task of establishing how the incident happened, and of proving negligence on the part of the shipowner or crew. It also means that the shipowner remains liable, even in cases where clearly the incident occurred through no fault of his own. This may happen where, for example, a properly lit tanker is at anchor, but a collision occurs because another vessel is sailing at excessive speed in fog. It is up to the tanker owner to pay the pollution claims, and then later to recover what he can by way of recourse from the owner of the colliding vessel.

In exchange, as it were, for accepting this strict liability, the shipowner is granted the right to limit his liability to an amount based on the tonnage of the ship. In practice, the limitation figure is very frequently irrelevant to claimants, since beyond this figure supplementary compensation is available under the Fund Convention 1971. This established the International Oil Pollution Compensation Fund, an international body which has its headquarters in London. The main aim of the IOPC Fund is to provide compensation for pollution damage in circumstances where CLC proves inadequate, and in practice the most usual situation is where the total of claims exceeds the limit of the shipowner's liability. The aggregate compensation available under both conventions is currently subject to a maximum of some US$82 million, and proposals are being considered for the figures to be significantly increased.

It should be added that contributions to the IOPC Fund are made by levies imposed on oil importers in contracting states. The two conventions therefore strike an apportionment of responsibility for claims between the two sides of the industry, i.e. the owners of the tankers from which the oil escapes, and the owners of the cargoes with the potential to cause pollution damage. The fact that both sides contribute also means, of course, that the total available compensation is greater. One of the reasons why the law is relatively advanced in the field of marine pollution by oil is that the oil industry is a relatively uniform body of commercial interests, concerned with the transport of substantially the same commodity, so that participation is more readily arranged in a compensation system of this sort. It is much more difficult to devise a similar system to govern the transport of other types of hazardous or noxious substances, which may present varying degrees of danger to the environment, and which may be bought and sold by a wide variety of commercial concerns having little in common with each other. This is one reason why it has not so far proved possible to devise an internationally acceptable system for compensating marine pollution by substances other than oil.

The oil pollution conventions have proved highly successful in practice: CLC is now in force in some 70 states, 48 of which have also adopted the Fund Convention; the available compensation has in practice proved sufficient to meet the claims presented in almost every incident dealt with under the conventions; their relatively clear terms leave little scope for argument on questions of liability, and this fosters co-operation amongst interested parties in responding effectively to a spill.

Nevertheless, though liability is seldom an issue, there has in practice been frequent argument on issues of quantum, and as to the types of claim which may be brought within the scope of "pollution damage" as defined in the conventions.

Certainly it has to be accepted that the definition in CLC is expressed in rather imprecise terms, since Article I(6) provides only that it means "loss or damage outside the ship carrying oil by contamination resulting from the escape or discharge of oil... and includes the cost of preventive measures". Preventive measures are "any reasonable measures taken by any person after an incident has occurred to prevent or minimise pollution damage". These definitions leave unanswered the many questions which have arisen on such matters as reasonableness of clean-up or restoration measures, remoteness of claims for pure economic loss, assessment of environmental damage and *locus standi* of claimants.

To a significant extent, the IOPC Fund has succeeded in filling these gaps by formulating and publicising its own practices and policies in the handling of claims. These include, for example, a resolution adopted by its Assembly in 1980 that "the assessment of compensation to be paid by the IOPC Fund is not to be made on the basis of an abstract quantification of damage calculated in accordance with theoretical models". The Fund does not, however, have the last word on the subject, for an aggrieved claimant may always resort to legal proceedings. Jurisdiction is vested in the national courts of the contracting state where the incident occurred or the damage was suffered. In future, national courts may have a little more guidance in the form of a revised definition of "pollution damage", agreed at a Diplomatic Conference in 1984, when Protocols were adopted to amend the Civil Liability and Fund Conventions. The Protocols have not yet entered into force, but there is a prospect that they may do so in the foreseeable future. Even then, there will still be much left for national courts to decide for themselves — and quite properly so, since this is a field in which clearly a balance has to be struck between the need for certainty on the one hand, and the need on the other for sufficient flexibility to deal adequately with the facts of each case. This very flexibility does, however, carry with it the danger that a uniform international system may come under threat, as judges and legislators in different contracting states come under varying degrees of pressure from environmental interests to reject traditional jurisprudence in favour of new and more generous methods of assessing pollution damage.

This danger has been brought into sharper focus by much-publicised developments in recent years in the United States. It was largely to attract the Americans into the international regime that agreement was reached, in 1984, upon substantial increases which ought to be made in the compensation available under CLC and the Fund Convention. This was indeed the main object of the Protocols already mentioned. The United States had plans to ratify the Protocols, but their best intentions were overtaken in March 1989 when *Exxon Valdez* ran aground in Prince William Sound, Alaska. This unleashed public hostility on an unprecedented scale against shipping and oil industry interests, and led only 16 months later to a decision by Congress to reject the Protocols, and to enact instead quite different laws in the form of the Oil Pollution Act 1990.

Much has been said and written elsewhere about the many controversial features of this new legislation. What is of particular interest to us today, in an international body such as the IBA, is the scope which exists for domestic legislation of this sort to influence developments outside its own territorial waters. Environmental damage assessment is one field in which this may possibly happen, for just at the time when this subject is becoming ever more controversial in CLC states, America has been busy developing new ways of compensating claims not normally recognised elsewhere.

The OPA permits a wide range of claims including not only those for the cost of clean-up and restoration, and for loss of earnings from natural resources, but also new categories of claim for loss of damage to natural resources, and loss of use of natural resources, including the cost of assessing the damage. Following a pattern developed under the general environmental laws of the United States, notably the Comprehensive Environmental Response Compensation and Liability Act of 1980 (CERCLA), the OPA provides for so-called natural resource damage assessment (NRDA) regulations to be drawn up, to govern compensation awards for claims of this type. The theoretical calculations involved in these assessments have been known to place an astonishingly high financial value on the environmental damage caused by even a relatively modest incident, but they may nevertheless be seen in some quarters to fill a jurisprudential gap. The question therefore arises whether America's innovations of today will be seen as setting a course to be followed by others tomorrow.

It is against this background that we can now turn to consider some of the specific issues which have arisen in practice.

Clean-up and Restoration

At first it may seem obvious enough that compensation laws must, at the very least, meet the reasonable costs of cleaning up and restoring a damaged site. But whilst it is one thing to state such a principle, it is not always so easy to apply it in practice.

To what extent, for example, is it reasonable for a public authority to incur boundless expense, in an effort to recreate with meticulous precision the exact state of the damaged site before the pollution occurred? Is there a point beyond which further restoration efforts should be considered disproportionately expensive?

This is not an exclusively modern problem. As long ago as 1908 the English Courts had to consider a similar question in the case of *Lodge Holes Colliery*

Co. v. *Mayor of Wednesbury*,[1] where the defendants' mining operations caused a public road to subside. The local authority restored the road to its former level by building an embankment at great cost, when an equally satisfactory road might have been made at lesser expense. The House of Lords held that the principle of *restitutio in integrum* did not entitle the plaintiffs to the cost of precise restoration, regardless of expense; they were entitled to recover from the mine owners only the cost of constructing an equally suitable road.

This precedent was applied more recently in *Dodd Properties (Kent)* v. *Canterbury City Council*,[2] where the Plaintiffs recovered for damage to their building caused by the defendants' pile-driving operations. In assessing damages, the judge said:

> "The plaintiffs are... not bound to accept a shoddy job or put up with an inferior building for the sake of saving expense to the defendants. But I do not consider that they are entitled to insist on complete and meticulous restoration when a reasonable building owner would be content with less extensive work which produces a result which does not diminish to any, or any significant, extent the appearance, life or utility of the building, and when there is also a vast difference in the cost of such work and the cost of meticulous restoration."

Similar questions came up for decision in an environmental context in the *Zoe Colocotroni* case which was heard in 1980 by the first circuit of the US Court of Appeals.[3] The matter concerned an oil tanker which had run aground as a result of her unseaworthy condition, causing pollution on the coast of Puerto Rico. At first instance, the government authorities of Puerto Rico were awarded some US$6 million, of which only $78,000 was needed to compensate them for the cost of cleaning up the spill. The remainder related to the cost of restoring the environment to its former condition, comprising $500,000 as the cost of replanting mangroves, and some $5.5 million as the cost of replacing marine organisms killed by the spill.

In assessing these damages, the judge observed that marine organisms had been killed in an area of about 20 acres. Surveys conducted by the plaintiffs persuaded him that there had been a decline of about 4.6 million organisms per acre as a direct result of the spill, which meant that 92 million marine animals had been killed. He also accepted evidence that there was a ready market with reference to biological supply laboratories, allowing a reliable calculation to be made of the cost of replacing these organisms. Taking the lowest possible replacement cost of $0.06 per organism, the judge arrived at his award at $5.5 million. The same approach led to the further award for the cost involved in a programme of intensive planting of mangrove.

1 [1908] AC 323.
2 [1980] 1 WLR 333.
3 *Commonwealth of Puerto Rico* v. *The S.S. Zoe Coloctroni*, U.S. Court of Appeals, 628 F.2d 652 (1st Cir. 1980).

The Court of Appeals refused to endorse this approach and laid greater emphasis on the need for a sense of proportion in assessing such costs. It held that the recoverable costs were those:

> "... reasonably to be incurred by the sovereign or its designated agency to restore or rehabilitate the environment in the affected area to its pre-existing condition, or as close thereto as is possible without grossly disproportionate expenditures. The focus in determining such a remedy should be the steps a reasonable and prudent sovereign or agency would take to mitigate the harm done by the pollution, with attention to such factors as technical feasibility, harmful side effects, compatibility with or duplication of such regeneration as is naturally to be expected, and the extent to which efforts beyond a certain point would become either redundant or disproportionately expensive".

It remains to be seen how readily the American courts themselves will follow this decision in future, after the advent of the NRDA regulations mentioned earlier. On the face of it, these seem to call for a return to the more rigid methods of calculation favoured at first instance, and rejected by the Court of Appeals. If lawyers outside the United States look to America for a lead in this field, they may care to consider whether the *Zoe* decision should be followed as persuasive authority. Certainly, so far as English law is concerned, it is not inconsistent with earlier decisions on similar questions of principle.

So much for the cost of restoring the damaged site, but what of the possibility of creating an *alternative* site? The Court of Appeals recognised that there might be circumstances where full restoration of the damaged area might be physically impossible or disproportionately expensive. It suggested that an alternative measure of damages might be appropriate if a more reasonable course would be to create a similar environment at an alternative site. As examples, it suggested the possible acquisition of comparable lands for public parks, or reforestation of a similar proximate site, where the presence of oil would not pose the same hazard to ultimate success.

At first glance this is a fairly novel approach. Lawyers in other countries have acknowledged the good sense which lies behind this approach, but some have doubted whether their courts would follow it. It has been said to run counter to normal principle if damage in one location is compensated by ordering the defendant to pay for an alternative site elsewhere. Others may nevertheless consider that this is not really the issue. The real question is whether any reasonable limit should be placed on the costs which the plaintiff may claim for restoring the damaged location. In this context it must surely be relevant for the court to consider whether the cost of fully restoring or reinstating the damaged site is excessive or disproportionate in comparison with the cost of creating a similar environment or amenity at an alternative location. If in all the circumstances this would be a much more reasonable course, then the cost of creating the alternative site provides a yardstick against which to judge the reasonableness or otherwise of the plaintiff's claim.

Financial Loss

Once a spill has been cleared the question arises what claims should be recognised for financial loss, such as loss of earnings, which may have been suffered during the period when the environment was impaired.

One simple point can be quickly established. If the oil causes damage to property owned by the plaintiff, then clearly he is entitled also to recover any financial loss resulting from it. So, for example, if a fisherman's nets are contaminated, or a hotelier's private beach is polluted, there is probably not a court in the world which would deny their claims for consequential loss of earnings.

It is, however, a different matter where, as is more usual, loss of income is suffered without any accompanying damage to property. In many jurisdictions the view is taken that if claims are upheld for all loss or damage attributable to an incident, then this could in some circumstances open the floodgates to an unreasonably wide range of claims for losses which are unduly remote from the defendant's activities. In England this rule of "remoteness" has tended to exclude claims for "pure economic loss". If for example a workman negligently severs a power cable, causing disruption among local businesses, his employers may be liable for any physical damage resulting from the loss of power supply, together with any economic loss consequent thereon, but they will not normally be liable for the potentially wide range of claims for pure business interruption.[4]

Over the last 20 years, the English courts have made various attempts to modify this rule in harsh cases, but this gave rise to some uncertainly as to where the line should be drawn between remote and recoverable claims. In the end, the House of Lords has reaffirmed the original test, so that apart from well recognised exceptions, pure economic loss is in general irrecoverable in English law. It was recognised that this may appear in some cases as unduly arbitrary test, but it was nevertheless favoured as the only rule which could lay down with any certainly the extent of recoverable claims.[5]

The possible application of these principles in an environmental context is illustrated by *Weller and Co* v. *Foot and Mouth Disease Research Institute*,[6] where it was alleged that cattle had been infected with foot and mouth disease following an escape of a virus from the defendants' premises. The U.K. government made an order closing two markets in the area thereby causing a loss of profits to the plaintiff auctioneers. It was held that the defendants owed a duty of care to persons such as cattle owners whose property might foreseeably be injured by their neglect, but they did not owe any duty to the plaintiffs, who

[4] See *Spartan Steel and Alloys Ltd.* v. *Martin & Co* [1973] 1 QB 27.

[5] See *Murphy* v. *Brentwood District Council* [1990] 3 WLR 414; *Dept. of the Environment* v. *Bates* [1990] 3 WLR 457.

[6] [1966] 1 QB 569.

did not have any proprietary interest which could be damaged by the escape of the virus.

Whilst this is the legal theory, it is based very much on policy considerations, and politics can never be very far from the minds of shipowners' P & I Clubs, or other liability insurers concerned with claims for pollution damage. In the field of marine oil pollution, it has not been practical politics to accept claims for lost earnings from hoteliers who own private beaches, but to deny the more typical claims of neighbouring establishments along a public shoreline. Where fishermen have lost earnings through reduced catches, it has not been feasible to invoke the defence that they did not have a proprietary interest in the wild fish killed by the oil. In practice, claims of this nature have invariably been paid, subject only to quite separate issues of proof. This practice is reflected in the amended definition of "pollution damage" in the 1984 Protocol, which recognises the validity of claims for loss of profits.[7]

This does, however, leave us with the question whether some alternative test of remoteness should be devised for environmental incidents, and if so what test? It has, for example, been held by the Courts in Alaska that claims for lost earnings may be made not only by fishermen, but also by seafood processing companies who buy the fish from the fishermen and sell them in canned form. Does one then have to compensate the shops and restaurants which buy the processed food and sell it on to the public? What about airlines who sell fewer seats on flights to the affected area? And what of hotels and restaurants whose trade is adversely affected, even though they are some distance away from the polluted area, because the whole region suffers from a "loss of image" in the minds of tourists? Issues of this sort seem likely increasingly to tax the minds of environmental lawyers, and to determine how far the pockets will be taxed in future of pollution liability insurers.

Non-financial Loss

In reference earlier to the *Zoe Colocotroni* case it was noted that the Court of Appeals had emphasised the need for a sense of proportion in assessing claims for the cost of restoring the environment. If a rehabilitation plan lacks this sense of proportion, a possible explanation is that the claimant in fact has no intention of carrying it out. The *Zoe* spill came ashore on a stretch of the Puerto Rican coastline known as Bahia Sucia. The configuration of the bay, combined with the prevailing winds and currents, made it a natural trap for floating debris, including accumulated quantities of petroleum and tar. It became clear that the government agencies involved had no intention of invigorating this environment by purchasing 92 million marine organisms from biological supply laboratories. Their only reason for presenting these notional costs was to suggest them as a

[7] For the full text of the revised definition of "pollution damage" in the 1984 Protocol, see attached Appendix.

convenient measure of the diminution in value of the affected area. It is of course an inherently controversial question what financial value (if any) should be placed on the environment, and in the *Zoe* case it was doubtless made no easier by the fact that Bahia Sucia translates into English as "Dirty Bay".

Its unfortunate name did not deter the court from finding that the area was a healthy and functioning ecosystem, but it does remind us that pollution incidents have sometimes occurred in close proximity to oil refineries and similar industrial sites, not normally regarded as areas of outstanding natural beauty. It has not been unknown for small amounts of oil to escape from ships in such places, and for their owners then to be made the scapegoats for all manner of pollution which may have accumulated in the area over a period of time from unidentified sources. The injustice is doubled if the damages are calculated on some theoretical basis, which bears no relation to the actual amount of any costs involved in clearing the spill.

This situation is not without its defenders. It is sometimes argued that claims should be accepted for the estimated cost of reinstating the environment, irrespective of whether the supposed measures of reinstatement are actually carried out. In the field of maritime law, supporters of this argument have drawn an analogy with cases where compensation has been awarded for unrepaired damage to ships. This has happened on occasion where, for example, two vessels collide with each other, and the owner of the innocent ship has been able to continue trading the vessel without repairing all of the damage. It may, however, be questioned whether this analogy is valid in an environmental context. So far as the English cases go, the estimated cost of ship repairs has been relevant only as evidence of a reduction in the resale or market value of the vessel. Such a reduction must naturally be shown in order to prove both the fact and the extent of an actual loss to the plaintiff. The environment, however, has no market value and, if measures of reinstatement are not actually carried out, their theoretical cost is no evidence of any actual loss to the claimant. If we look for the essential purpose of pollution compensation laws, it lies surely in protecting the public interest in a healthy, functioning environment, and not in providing windfalls to the public treasury. This policy is reflected in the 1984 Protocols, which make it clear that compensation for impairment of the environment (other than loss of profits) is limited to the cost of reasonable measures of reinstatement actually undertaken or to be undertaken.

This is in contrast to the quite different course charted by the Americans, as exemplified by their complex and controversial methods of Natural Resource Damage Assessment. For example, a category of loss has been developed which not only enables a value to be placed upon the lost use of the damaged environment, but which also requires account to be taken of the so-called "non-user" values of "option", "existence", and "bequest". These values reflect the monetary sums which would willingly be paid by people who are not currently using a resource — such as people living some distance away from a damaged coastline — but who wish to preserve the option to use that resource in the future; it may also include the sums which people would pay just to know that the natural resource remains in existence, and that it will remain available for their children after their death.

This approach has come to be known as "contingent valuation methodology" (or "CVM"), and very recently the US National Oceanic and Atmospheric Administration ("NOAA") has published a Notice of Proposed Rulemaking on this subject. It is expected that this procedure will result later this year in detailed regulations applying to NRDA claims under the Oil Pollution Act.

During the consultation process the American rulemakers will have the opportunity of hearing what industry spokesmen have to say on this subject, and it is to be hoped that in their final form the new rules will avoid the worst excesses to which this methodology could all to readily lead, if pushed to its logical extremes. At first it may seem a harmless proposition if surveys suggest that an average American family would be prepared to pay $50–$100 in order to preserve the natural beauty of Prince William Sound in Alaska. It is, however, quite another matter to conclude that because there are some 100 million families in the United Sates, compensation of $5–$10 billion should be paid for the spill from *Exxon Valdez*. Even one-fifth of these figures, based on a family average of $10–$20, would in theory produce a claim of $1–$2 billion, and this of course is quite apart from the billions paid already for the cost of actual clean-up. The costs actually incurred in cleaning and restoring the environment, together with claims for other financial loss, are compensated in any event.

For ardent opponents of industry this approach may perhaps have some appeal: they may argue that if compensation is awarded to fishermen who depend upon the environment for their livelihoods, then it is not really logical to deny a remedy to sport fishermen whose leisure activities have been adversely affected, merely because their loss cannot readily be measured in financial terms; similarly it may be said to be illogical that a shipowner should escape liability for loss of public amenities, merely because nobody actually owns the damaged coastline, nor derives any income from the birds which are killed by the oil. The courts have indeed found conventional ways of compensating other forms of non-pecuniary loss, such as loss of physical amenity due to personal injuries, and associated pain and suffering.

The difference, of course, is that whilst a physically injured plaintiff has suffered a loss which is real enough, a notional loss of these non-user values is at best somewhat ephemeral. What seems beyond doubt is that damages of this sort are not actually applied in cleaning or restoring the environment affected by the spill, nor in compensating any person for any tangible loss. Inevitably, the damages end up as a windfall to the public treasury.

In these circumstances it may be questioned whether it is right to dignify NRDA damages with the respectability of civil compensation. In reality they are much more akin to a criminal fine. Many would say that strict liability for penalties of this size would be unreasonably harsh, and serve no useful purpose. Certainly there is a need to allay fears that this methodology will produce damages awards which lose sight of the ephemeral nature of these "non-user" values, and which lose the sense of proportion called for by the US Court of Appeals.

Conclusion

In the end it is of course entirely for the American people to decide for itself what laws should apply in its waters. There is, however, danger at hand if lawmakers world-wide conclude too readily that the American regime is a forward-thinking and ready-made model suitable for adoption elsewhere.

If this were to happen in countries subscribing to CLC and the Fund Convention, then the very political foundations of the Conventions could well be in jeopardy. It will be recalled that the funds required to pay compensation are contributed very largely by levies imposed on oil companies in member states, in proportion to their annual imports of oil. The future of the Conventions may well depend on how far national governments are prepared to burden their oil industries with the cost of oil spills, whilst bearing in mind that the spills more often than not will occur in the waters of some other country. The situation cannot persist very long in which the courts of some countries, which may or may not be substantial contributors, award extravagant compensation to their governments and nationals for notional losses, whilst in other countries a more conservative approach is taken to the assessment of claims. The existing consensus could then come under considerable strain.

This must be the very opposite of what we surely all want. If our real priority is to protect a healthy and functioning environment, then what is most in your interest and mine is that the Conventions should continue in force, and that there should be consensus on appropriate increases in the amounts of available compensation from time to time.

Non-marine lawyers may feel that similar considerations apply not just in the field of oil pollution at sea, but indeed throughout the environmental sphere. At the end of the day, the money has to come from somewhere to pay for the rising cost of pollution. The total funds available to compensate global pollution depend very much on the capacity of the insurance and reinsurance markets. If there are extravagant surges in the level of claims, leading to unexpected losses for underwriters, then reinsurers will naturally shy away from this sector, leaving only reduced capacity behind them. This again is surely the very opposite of what is wanted by those with genuine environmental concerns.

Anyone interested in marine pollution is bound to recognise the achievements of those who solved the formidable problems presented by the Torrey Canyon. It was indeed a remarkable success that consensus was achieved between the two quite different sides of the industry, thereby paving the way for the two-tiered compensation Conventions. These Conventions are widely regarded as having operated very successfully in practice.

Some will think that the challenge of today is to preserve and build upon these achievements of the past. No doubt this will involve a process of continuing development, but a balance will always need to be struck between the need for adaptation to changing public opinion, and the need to avoid killing the goose which lays the golden egg.

Appendix

Definition of pollution damage

(A) International convention on civil liability for oil pollution damage, 1969 (CLC 1969)

Article I (6):-

"Pollution Damage" means loss or damage caused outside the ship carrying oil by contamination resulting from the escape or discharge of oil from the ship, wherever such escape or discharge may occur, and includes the costs of preventive measures and further loss or damage caused by preventive measures.

Article I (7):-

"Preventive Measures" means any reasonable measures taken by any person after an incident has occurred to prevent or minimise pollution damage.

(B) 1984 Protocol

Article II (3):-

"Pollution Damage" means:

(a) loss or damage caused outside the ship by contamination resulting from the escape or discharge of oil from the ship, wherever such escape or discharge may occur, provided that compensation for impairment of the environment other than loss of profit from such impairment shall be limited to costs of reasonable measures of reinstatement actually undertaken or to be undertaken;

(b) the costs of preventive measures and further loss or damage caused by preventive measures.

Sea-bird Protection Under Dutch Tort Law: The Judgment of the Rotterdam District Court of 15 March 1991[1]

Fred J. Rutgers

Introduction

The explosive growth of national and international rules for the protection of the environment in the broadest sense, and the sanctions provided by those rules, has not lead in the Netherlands to deactivation of tort law in this field. The government regularly acts on the basis of tort law against threatening environmental pollution — invoking its concern for the environment entrusted to it in the Constitution — and recovers costs incurred by it to prevent environmental damage or to restore the environment to its original state. Environmental organisations and interest groups also act against (imminent) environmental pollution. They do so not only in case "combined" concrete individual rights are at stake, but also in case a more general environmental interest of a diffuse nature threatens to be affected. Does civil tort law protect those interests?

Scope of Tort Law

For an action in tort, Dutch courts introduced in the seventies the requirement that the interest which the plaintiff alleges to be harmed must come under the interests protected by tort law. This requirement entails that the court has to examine whether the plaintiff, irrespective whether it is a public body or a private legal entity, really has a specific interest from a point of view of civil law, traditionally (the threat of) property damage or personal injury. In the negative the claim will not be admitted. Non-admissibility may also follow if

[1] District Court Rotterdam, 15 March 1991, NJ 1992, 92.

another possibility of enforcing legal regulations exists and can be used, e.g. special administrative procedures. The general interest of every governmental body that its regulations be duly observed is not as such an interest which is protected by civil tort law. Simply said, if the government can use the police, it cannot go — in principle — to the civil court to ask a prohibition.

Whether an interest comes under the interests which the rules of tort law aim to protect is far from clear. The test covers, increasingly, more than the interest in property rights and rights of personal integrity. The tendency is that tort law not only protects rights but also reasonable, generally accepted interests. Moreover, if the environment is affected, it is always possible to argue that this will or might finally lead to an infringement of the use of property rights. "Point d'intérêt, point d'action", but is imminent environmental pollution without individual rights, or interests being directly affected, an interest protected by tort law? What is the relationship with the requirement of relativity (New Civil Code 6:163) : the object of the rule which is violated is to protect the injured party from the damage suffered by him. Does environmental pollution constitute an unlawful act against the government? Can it also be an unlawful act against a private organisation whose object it is to defend environmental interests?

The Government

When considering Dutch case law of the past ten years, it seems as if the requirement is used as a sacred formula to confirm a possibility for the government of taking legal action on the basis of tort law, reference being made either to the Constitution (a more general reference is hardly possible) or to imminent damage to goods or persons. Thus the government was found to be entitled to recover the costs of removal of a wreck outside the territorial waters from the vessels which were to blame for the collision, as a consequence of which one of the vessels had sunk, on the basis of the argument that the Kingdom of the Netherlands had taken it on to itself to defend the interests of safe shipping traffic in the area in question.[2] The decision of the District Court in The Hague in the *Vinca Gorthon*[3] is even more far-reaching. The court allowed in principle a claim against owners for removal of a wreck which had sunk outside the territorial waters on the basis of the interest of the government to fight imminent pollution of the Dutch waters and coasts. In this decision the owners were deemed to act unlawfully by not removing the wreck, regardless of the fact whether or not the vessel was to blame for the sinking. The government succeeded in obtaining an order against a German producer to remove polluted waste from a place in the Netherlands where it had been deposited by a Dutch contractor on the ground that the German company had failed to verify sufficiently that Dutch contractor who

[2] Zuidpool/ Gaasterdijk; HR, S&S 1978, 63.
[3] Vinca Gorthon; S&S 1991, 17.

dumped the material, would not act unlawfully.[4] The port authorities in Rotterdam are investigating the possibility of legal action against "upstream" foreign companies who contributed to the presence of polluted mud in the port area.

Interest Groups/Private Organisations

The possibility for an environmental organization of taking legal action with respect to a general environmental interest which threatens to be affected, was accepted by the Dutch Supreme Court[5] in 1987. An injunction claimed by three environmental organisations prohibiting the Municipality of Amsterdam from dumping dredgings in the Nieuwe Meer polder was admitted. The objects of a legal entity described in its articles of association are not sufficient to allow it to institute a court action on the basis of civil tort law in case the interests included in those objects are affected. However, according to the Supreme Court this is possible if the interests can be combined and if the action to prohibit polluting activities can be considered to constitute efficient legal protection for a great number of citizens, in a situation in which it is difficult to estimate the consequences of the pollution for each of them individually. The argument that in case of continuation of the activities of the Municipality public participation, to which those organizations are entitled, would be frustrated, played an important role.

Can private interest groups also claim damages, especially compensation for costs incurred for limitation or repair of damage? This question is answered in the affirmative by some writers:[6] an organization can have a substantive interest of its own in incurring costs for limitation or prevention of damage in accordance with the objects of the organization for a clean environment. And does this apply if costs are incurred for the care for and cleaning up of oil-stained wild sea-birds which do not belong to anybody and whose injuries do not lead to damage or loss of profit? This question is answered in the negative by other writers[7] who apply future Dutch legislation contained in the bill "Liability for Hazardous Substances and Environmental Pollution". This bill, yet to be considered in parliament, imposes a strict liability on the holder of such substances. However, compensation of damage is only possible if it concerns damage consisting of or resulting from damage to goods or persons.

The question is nevertheless answered in the affirmative by the District Court in Rotterdam in its decision referred to above. The court considered that a claim of the "Nederlandse Vereniging tot Bescherming van Vogels" (Dutch Association for the Protection of Birds) for recovery of costs incurred by itself and others for the care of oil-stained birds, can in principle be allowed. The facts of that case were as follows.

[4] Benckiser, HR 14 April 1989, NJ 1990, 712.
[5] Nieuwe Meer case HR, NJ 1987, 743.
[6] Brahms, Grosheide and Messer, "Milieurecht in stelling" (Zwolle, 1990).
[7] Frenk and Messer, "kwartaalbericht NBW" 1991/1.

The "Borcea" Case

On 4 January 1988 the Rumanian bulk carrier *Borcea*, sailing on the North Sea, apparently had a collision, without noticing this. As a result oil leaked out through a crack in a bunker tank, as was established afterwards. A sea pilot who came on board of the vessel drew the attention of the vessel to oil traces and it was established that water had entered the bunker tank. The captain sent a telegram to the owners from Flushing stating that there presumably was a crack in the bunker tank and asking leave for an investigation by divers upon arrival in Ghent, Belgium. The investigation was never carried out.

On 5 January a coastguard aeroplane instituted an investigation on the site further to reports of serious oil pollution, but the investigation did not produce any result, possibly as a consequence of a fresh gale and poor visibility.

The oil subsequently polluted the sea water of the North Sea and the coasts of the Dutch provinces of Zeeland and Zuid-Holland. Several thousands of very seriously oil-stained sea-birds were found on the beaches. The Dutch Association for the Protection of Birds, whose object it is to protect wild bird species, so-called bird shelters and bird centres, started to remove the birds from the beaches, clean them up and look after them, find accommodation for them and subsequently released them again. The bird shelters and bird centres assigned their claims to the Dutch Association for the Protection of Birds and the Association for the Preservation of Monuments of Nature, which was also involved, did the same. The Birds Association instituted an action against the owners of the vessel for recovery of the costs incurred and for a contribution in keeping bird shelters and centres operational.

After having established that Dutch law was applicable to the present case, the District Court first of all considered the admissibility of the claim.

> "Though sea birds are not related to a specific country and cannot be considered to belong to anybody, their maintenance and protection have to be seen as a general interest which deserves to be protected in The Netherlands according to common opinion nowadays. In view of the objects of the plaintiff and the activities which it has been carrying out for the realization thereof during 90 years, as alleged by the plaintiff and not contested by the defendant, that general interest must also be seen as the plaintiff's own interest and in case that interest is affected the plaintiff's claim can be admitted, that is to say not only its claim for stopping that interest from being affected but also its claim for compensation of damage which it sustained for limiting the consequences of that damage. It is only logical that the plaintiff who is entitled to prevent or stop its interests from being harmed, can also claim the damage which it sustained as a consequence thereof or be compensated for the costs which it incurred in order to limit or prevent the consequences thereof by the party who affected its interests. Therefore the plaintiff's claim can be admitted insofar as it is related to the damage sustained by the plaintiff itself. As regards third parties who have assigned their claims to the plaintiff according to the plaintiff, it will have to furnish further information on the basis of which it can be established whether the foregoing also applies to them.... The sole fact that the plaintiff acts as assign of those third parties for compensation of costs like the damage sustained by itself, does not make those third parties entitled to compensation."

It is surprising that the sacred formula — interests which section 1401 of the Civil Code (the general rule of tort) aims to protect — is not used any more.

Subsequently the District Court examined whether the owners, the captain and the crew acted unlawfully towards the Association. The District Court rejected the anticipatory effect of future legislation creating strict liability for hazardous goods invoked by the plaintiff because that would constitute too great a violation of legal security. Nevertheless, in the opinion of the District Court the captain was to blame because upon sending the above-mentioned telegram to the owners he wrongly failed to inform the competent authorities:

> "At that moment he should have realized that the vessel might have lost more oil than he had noticed and what would be the consequences thereof inter alia for the sea birds. Moreover, he could and should have known that the interest to maintain and protect sea birds is considered an interest to be defended by law and that measures are taken to stop the results of oil pollution as much as possible. Consequently, at that moment he should have reported his presumption to a competent authority and his failing to do so constitutes an unlawful act towards the plaintiff."

However, that was not all for the plaintiff, because the owners had furthermore invoked the lack of a causal relationship, within the meaning of the "*conditio sine qua non*" requirement. The warnings which the government had received from others had not led to investigation results and/or governmental measures, so it was not to be expected that a warning to the authorities would have had another result. Therefore, the plaintiff had to adduce evidence of the causal relationship between the fact that no report was made and the damage. Otherwise, it was established that in case of timely reports, thc government would have had the possibility to take measures which prevented or limited the damage to the sea birds.

Implications of the Judgment

These complications about evidence and burden of proof do not change the far-reaching meaning of the judgment. It is the next step after the decision that interest groups can enforce an injunction against polluting action. Cost incurred for the prevention or limitation of harm to the interests which an environmental organization has taken upon itself to protect can be claimed by that organization as its own damage. In the present case the seniority and the respect for the activities of the organization were taken into account as well as the fact that the Association also plays a role in governmental contingency plans.

The question is what would have happened if the owners had observed their duty to report which they had according to the District Court. Could the government have recovered the costs if it had timely neutralised the oil stain? If the vessel is not to blame for the leakage and if fault is required, that is hardly plausible. Another question is whether the costs which the government would have incurred in that case, would have to be deduced from the claim of the Association and the third parties. The District Court has not taken a decision on that point. In the mean time, the Association came to a settlement. The government is involved in similar proceedings in respect of the same event. The government presents evidence on the basis of a similar interlocutory judgement rendered by the Court in those proceedings.

The District Court did not anticipate section 173 of the New Civil Code (defective goods) and/or the section concerning liability for hazardous substances and environmental pollution yet to be inserted in the New Civil Code. Section 173 creates a strict liability of the holder of dangerous goods in case a special danger is created for persons or goods and thus causes damage. The aforementioned bill which creates strict liability for the holder of substances constituting a danger or risk to persons or goods, includes special rules for the recovery of costs for prevention or limitation of damage. If measures are taken by a party other than the party which would have sustained the damage with regard to which the serious and imminent threat is created, the other party can only claim compensation of the costs insofar as those costs could have been claimed by the person who would have sustained the imminent damage. The party against whom an action is instituted can raise the same points of defence he could have raise against the latter. Is compensation of costs of "repair" of the sea-birds which do not belong to anybody, not in conflict with the requirement of (concrete) damage and loss of profit and the requirement of a connection with damage to goods or persons?

In a "Memorandum of Reply" to the bill submitted by the government on 11 June 1991, the government responded to the judgment of the District Court in Rotterdam, which it considered to be in accordance with the future law. The government's view is that sea-birds can be considered "goods" which are damaged and that the claim of the Association is "consequential damage" which qualifies for compensation as if it were a claim for coverage under a liability policy. The government also replied to the question whether the preliminary draft bill pending in parliament about the right of interest groups to institute claims (giving interest groups the right to claim an injunction or order, but not to claim damages) would be opposed to a claim like the one submitted by the Association:

> "It has to be noted that if it is judged in Court that the Association's own interest is affected and that therefore it is established that the Association is entitled to repair of damage such as the costs of cleaning up etc. of the birds — it will also be established that that Association is entitled to compensation of the costs of reasonable measures for the prevention or limitation of such damage. In that case section 6.3.2.11a subsection 2 (measures by another party than the party who would have sustained the damage) is not relevant, nor is the subject a matter dealt with in the preliminary draft concerning the right of interest groups to institute claims, now that according to the District Court it is the Association's own interest which is affected and not an interest of others which is defended by the Association on their behalf."

This stand of the government seems to make the draft bill on the rights of interest groups in this respect superfluous, although it remains to be seen whether and to which extent the courts will follow that stand of the government.

Environmental Liability from the Perspective of an Operator: Council of Europe Draft Convention on Civil Liability for Damage Resulting from Activities Dangerous to the Environment

W. J. Ouwerkerk*

Introduction

The notion of civil liability for damage to the environment is relatively new. About 10 years ago it was still a matter of debate whether the "unowned" environment constituted an interest to be protected by civil law. Is there a general consensus now? Apparently not; the German Environmental Liability Act, for example, which became effective on 1 January 1991, addressess both personal injury and damage to property but not to damage to the "unowned" environment. Nevertheless, civil liability is appealing to lawyers because it draws on a fundamental principle that a person should rectify the damage he causes. Moreover, civil liability is believed to be an instrument entailing greater participation by the public in the guardianship of the environment. However, the imposition of a separate set of civil law rules on the existing structure of regulatory requirements may lead to a body of law with inconsistent legal standards, which is counterproductive to the problem which both systems seek to tackle.

I chose the term "operator" in the title because that person or entity is the focal point in the draft "Convention on Civil Liability for Damage Resulting from Activities Dangerous to the Environment";[1] this draft is being finalised by

* The views expressed herein do not necessarily reflect the views of my company.

[1] See Appendix 1. This draft comprises the text as per the beginning of March 1992. When using the term "the Convention", I refer to this draft.

a group of legal experts working within the framework of the Council of Europe, established at Strasburg. I shall review the defined terms as underlined in the following slightly abbreviated principal provision of Article 6 thereof: "*The operator* in respect of a *dangerous activity* … shall be liable for the *damage* caused by the activity as a result of *incidents* at the time or during the period when he was exercising control of that activity." The Convention addresses personal injury, damage to property and damage to the environment. I intend to focus on "environmental" liability, because as a common good it is conceptually different from the other two traditional subjects addressed by the Convention and comprises "*res quae naturali iure communes sunt omnium*".[2]

Towards a Sustainable Development

Before discussing the civil law consequences on this issue, it may be worth while to look at the existing practical situation. There is a vision of what should generally be achieved to protect the environment but there is no clear sense of direction and priority-setting; this lack of management leads to a confusing array of legal initiatives, which tend to stifle practical solutions.

The current vision world-wide is that a shift towards sustainable development should be achieved, ensuring economic growth without compromising the opportunities for future generations. It encompasses the vision of what needs to be done to broaden the time-horizons, to maximise added-value while minimising wasteful resource use and becoming more "eco-efficient". Industry will continue to play a major role: "Many essential human needs can be met only through goods and services provided by industry, and the shift to sustainable development must be powered by a continuing flow of wealth from industry" (Brundtland report). To this end industry needs an open, competitive market, where the legal instruments set the parameters for a level playing field for industry as the creator of new technologies and products; a level playing field is a prerequisite for an innovative and efficient industry to marshal the necessary human and financial resources. "The irony is that the more a company needs green finance to clean up its act, the less likely it is to get it."[3] Indeed, a sustainable development is possible if investments are justified from a commercial as well as environmental perspective.

Eco-efficiency calls for a comprehensive, well-managed intergovernmental plan of action, agreed at least at the EC level.[4] Legislation and environmental policies should underpin that plan of action, setting priorities and giving direction to activities. Norms and standards to be applied should be common to industry in general; it would be wrong to let modern technology be less competitive

[2] Article 2, para. 11, defines "environment" in more prosaic terms as: "natural resources both abiotic and biotic, such as air, water, soil, fauna and flora and the interaction between the same factors, property which forms part of the cultural heritage and the characteristic aspects of the landscape".

[3] Quote from *Financial Times* in recent interview with U.K. bankers.

[4] In accordance with the requirements of Article 130.R, para. 3 of the EC Treaty.

than old vintage processes. Industry can tune in and use its own creativity and management resources to meet agreed objectives.[5] However, as yet society has relied extensively on compliance with detailed requirements which were not always consistent or predictable for reasons such as:

- incidents (like Love Canal and Seveso) trigger new legislation;
- regulatory requirements are often technology-driven;
- generally worded enabling laws grant wide discretionary powers to the executive branch;
- the trend to delegate to the lower levels of government is being reversed; increasingly new roles are being attributed to the nationalauthorities to regulate the second generation of environmental issues;
- novel instruments are being tested; typical examples are: (1) environmental auditing by outsiders; (2) covenants between industry and authorities; (3) civil liability for environmental damage.

The problems for industry are compounded by insufficient co-operation between the various layers of government. Three layers of government (local, national and the EC) continue to feed an ongoing avalanche of new legislation, each to the full extent of its competence, sometimes adding to what is already there[6] and sometimes overstepping its field of competence, creating overlapping structures and requirements. Each initiative may seem justified from the perspective of the authority concerned, but the lack of co-ordination and the absence of a common set of priorities make it increasingly difficult to predict whether an investment will be justified. Professional lenders are worried about the level of uncertainty. The retrospective liability resulting from judiciary reviews of past operations based on the wisdom of hindsight are illustrative of the impossibility for insurers to predict the magnitude of future environmental claims. Environmental issues have become a lawyers' paradise: more and more lawyers on one side talking to more and more lawyers on the other side.

The various branches and layers of government have not found a management structure capable of addressing managerial questions within government like "who is doing what"? and "what are the priorities"? Moreover, the implementation of government regulation is not reflected on the national budget, but it draws heavily on the resources which industry, or for that matter, a society can marshal.[7] The corporate process to absorb new legislation also draws heavily on industry's available human resources and thus on its capacity to be creative.

[5] Industry's willingness to participate is much more manifest than it was 10 years ago; from a score of declarations of intent from various sectors of the industry I have made the following selection, copies of which are attached hereto: Royal Dutch/Shell Group of Companies, "Policy Guidelines on Health, Safety and the Environment"; CEFIC, "Guidelines for the Protection of the Environment"; ICC, "The Business Charter for Sustainable Development".

[6] See e.g. Article 27, para. 1, of the Convention.

[7] Draft paper "Controlling Regulatory Cost: The Use of Regulatory Budgeting" by John F. Morrall III, prepared for the November 1991 Meetings of the OECD, Public Management Service on Regulation, Reform and Results.

Where does civil liability fit in such an overall context? Are its remedies consistent with the established objectives and priorities? The key word in civil law proceedings is "damage". Can a traditional concept of "damage" also be used in relation to a common good, i.e. the "unowned" environment? At least at this stage of development not all impact from human activities on the environment can be prevented. Not all issues can be tackled at the same time. Under the current circumstances a certain level of environmental impairment should be accepted. Indeed, realistic longer-term environmental objectives are served by sustainable stepwise reductions in the emissions which cause environmental impairment. Accordingly, "damage" should not have a static definition; it should depict a diminishing loss of environmental values correlating with the progress made in achieving the longer-term objectives. A static definition of "damage" under civil law, applied to an individual situation according to a separate rule making process, tends to be out of step with the dynamics of the process in which the longer term objectives and priorities are being tackled. As will be discussed hereafter under the heading "Damage", the Convention fails to recognize this issue. To the contrary, proposed EC legislation provides for a less static approach to determining damage; this approach, when properly applied, will lead to the stepwise emission reductions advocated above.

The Convention

In the 1986 Oslo Conference of European Ministers of Justice the decision was taken to consider options to extend the reach of civil law into promoting environmental protection. The idea was not completely new. Article 11(3) of the Directive 84/631/EEC (OJ, no. L 326, 13.12.84) provides for action by the EC to determine the conditions for civil liability for damage caused by waste together with a system for insurance coverage. So, at the European level, two different initiatives were taken, each following its own track.[8] At least, it seems that until March 1992 the EC did not get a mandate to contribute to the preparation of the Convention on behalf of the EC.

From the point of view of harmonisation of law, the Convention seems a remarkable success. However, the practical implications could be less than had been anticipated previously, because upon analysis of the latest available text it appears that, in the final stage of drafting a provision has been added (Article 27, para. 2) allowing the EC to opt out and decide its own rules. It gives the EC the opportunity to stand back for a while. Discussions in the context of the "Green Paper" which the EC Commission intends to issue, may set the scene for a practical and eco-efficient approach to the matter under consideration.

The EC legislator should abide by the "polluter pays" principle as established in Article 130R of the EC Treaty. Ultimately the Court of Luxembourg has to decide

[8] The EC initiative seems to have come to a standstill; current draft in "Amended Proposal for a Council Directive on Civil Liability for Damage Caused by Waste", OJ, no. C 192, 1991; a new initiative may be taken by the EC Commission by issuing a "green paper" on civil liability.

what in a given situation the meaning of that principle in the Treaty should entail. In my view that principle should inhibit the introduction of legislation which as a matter of convenience seeks to channel liability without fault to an operator as one shackle in a chain of societal activities which cause environmental damage.

Strict liability is often held to be an application of the "polluter pays" principle in that it operates to ensure that the cost of damage caused by an economic activity is paid by the operator of that activity. However, unless skillfully drafted with appropriate checks and corrections, such a liability regime can lead to liability of a presumed polluter. If a third party contribution causes the pollution, the third party is the polluter, and should be considered the person liable pursuant to the "polluter pays" principle. In the discussions on no fault liability one of the recurring themes is that it provides incentives for taking preventive measures to reduce the risk of damage materializing. In my view this is an incorrect presumption. Preventive measures are encouraged in a system which gives recognition to the diligence exercised by the operator and not in a system where the operator is liable no matter what measures were taken to prevent damage from happening. Indeed, a strict liability regime can be counter productive, if the good operators applying high standards withdraw from the market to contain their potential exposure to liability not justified by the diligence with which their operations are conducted. A much more effective liability regime can be established on the basis of the motion accepted in the European Parliament, to govern "fault liability for accidents connected with all chemical and high risk activities ..." (OJ 12.1.87, No. C7/117). The Convention does not justify the choice to opt for strict liability: "Having regard to the desirability of providing for strict liability in this field taking into account the 'Polluter-Pays-Principle''. The meaning of this statement in the preamble is not entirely clear: the "polluter pays" principle which is invoked, applies generally and not only in relation to certain dangerous activities which have been defined in the Convention. The Convention probably intends to justify strict liability by reference to the activities which under the Convention are deemed to pose a particular threat to the environment. However, as indicated hereinabove, the question remains whether a fault-based liability regime would not be more effective in encouraging preventive measures. Moreover, strict liability in relation to dangerous activities must be based on a common understanding about what is particularly dangerous. It is difficult to discern why the activities defined in the Convention, and not other, are considered "dangerous" enough to be subject to strict liability.

Dangerous Activity

Article I sets forth the object and purpose of the Convention: it "aims at ensuring adequate compensation for damage resulting from activities dangerous to the environment and also provides for means of prevention and reinstatement".[9] The

[9] This provision is not entirely correct as the Convention pertains also to compensation for damage to property and injury to persons.

principle reason for establishing a special strict liability regime for "dangerous activities" is that the activity is held to constitute or pose "a significant risk to man, the environment or property". The term "risk" is used in the context of the hazardous properties of defined substances, organisms or radiations. For instance, Article 2, 2(a) reads: "substances or preparations which have properties which constitute a significant risk to man, the environment or property"; this article then provides that certain listed substances or preparations shall "in any event be deemed to constitute such a risk". Article 2, 1 describes the dangerous activities, e.g.

> "Dangerous activity means one or more of the following activities provided that it is performed professionally, including activities conducted by public authorities:
> (a) the handling, storage, production or discharge of one or more dangerous substances or any operation of a similar nature dealing with such substances; etc."

"Risk management" would seem the most sensible response by "operators" to legislation which aims to address "significant risks to the environment". Risk management is the last of four steps which briefly can be described as follows:

(a) *Hazard Identification*: the identification of the hazardous properties inherent in the substance.
(b) *Hazard Assessment*: the assessment in a given situation of the potential of the substance to cause adverse effects on environmental species. To make an assessment one needs information on environmental exposure and effect data related to the species. The assessment is normally expressed by a comparison of the (predicted) environmental concentration of the substance with the (predicted) no effect concentration for the species concerned.
(c) *Risk Assessment*: "Risk" is usually expressed as the probability of the occurrence of an adverse effect. Therefore, a risk assessment cannot be carried out if no probabilities are calculated. Risk assessment is an estimation of the probability that a substance causes adverse effects as a result of the presence (at a given concentration) of that substance in the environment.
(d) *Risk Management*: concerns the decision-making on the measures which should be taken in the light of the first three steps.

In these four steps a clear distinction is made between "hazard" and "risk": a substance can be (potentially) hazardous, but the likelihood that damage will occur depends on a combination of factors. To put it another way: the acceptability of certain concentrations of a (potentially) hazardous substance may depend on the actual situation of the locality, the sensitivity of the species to be protected or the characteristics of the environment where the substance is found.

Different acceptable concentration levels may apply to different environments and situations. This can be briefly illustrated by the following quotes from the summary of a report of November 1990 "Desire for Levels", prepared by the Dutch National Institute of Public Health and Environmental Protection:[10]

> "Maximum acceptable risk levels for water are primarily derived from available chronic toxicity data, following an extrapolation procedure recommended by the Health Council.
>
> ...
>
> For sediment no toxicity data are available. Maximum acceptable risk levels for sediment are derived indirectly from maximum acceptable risk levels for water, using the equilibrium partitioning method.
>
> ...
>
> To derive maximum acceptable risk levels for soil, ecotoxicological extrapolation methods similar to those used for water are used."

The foregoing shows that one cannot relate "significant risk" to the properties of a substance. Therefore, the definition used in Article 2, 2(a) is an obstacle to informed decision-making regarding important health and environmental matters, either by an operator or by a civil law court.

The Convention does not give an indication of the considerations which have been taken into account when designating certain substances as having properties which constitute a "significant risk". In "Premises for Risk Management"[11] some examples are given of the risks run by people in their ordinary walk of life; the examples given in Table 1 are a selection therefrom.

Table 1

Activity/Occurrences	Annual Mortality
Drowning as a result of a dike collapse	1 in 10 million
Flying	1 in 814,000
Walking	1 in 54,000
Cycling	1 in 26,000
Driving a car	1 in 5,700
Riding a moped	1 in 5,000
Riding a motorcycle	1 in 1,000

[10] Report no. 670101002: "Desire for Levels", Background study for the policy document "Setting Environmental Quality Standards for Water and Soil", p. vi. This report does not represent a consensus view and may be reviewed; the quotes given here are nevertheless representative examples of the different situations to be considered individually.

[11] "Premises for Risk Management, Risk Limits in the Context of Environment Policy", Directorate General for Environmental Protection at the Ministry of Housing, Physical Planning and Environment, Second Chamber of the States General, session 1988–1989, 21137, No. 5, p. 7. The premisses in the report will be revised.

Which of these risks should be considered "significant"? Often a distinction is made between "voluntary" and "involuntary" risks; one can also find this distinction in "Premisses for Risk Management":

> "The risks inherent in these activities give some indication of the magnitude of the risk added to natural circumstances by human interference. Environmental risks are largely of an involuntary nature and cannot usually be observed or controlled. As a result, hazards of this type are often regarded as being more serious".

However, I regard the distinction between "voluntary" and "involuntary" risks largely artificial. Granted, mountain climbing may lead to a voluntarily accepted increase in risk, but, when looking to the examples given above, would it not be a fallacy to regard the daily necessary routine of going from A to B, either by foot on the pavement, cycling, by public transport or by whatever other means, as a voluntary acceptance of the risk inherent in that activity? In today's society the daily necessary routine activities are unthinkable without dangerous substances and/or their endproducts for medication, transportation, food preservation, etc.

In a presentation "The myth of 10^6 as a Definition of Acceptable Risk"[12] Kelly and Cardon report on the extensive review they conducted to determine the origin of 10^6 as a (lifetime) criterion of "acceptable risk".

> It is difficult to imagine a criterion in wider use in the US environmental legislation than 10^6. This number guides the use of pesticides and food additives; it defines our allowable exposure to ground water contamination and incinerators. It is the most influential determinant we have in deciding what emissions should be allowed from stacks, how a hazardous waste site should be cleaned up, and how much Alar to leave on apples".

Kelly and Cardon conducted an extensive literature search and when they did not find any written documentation they contacted a "Who's Who" of the environmental industry, e.g. the EPA, the FDA, Greenpeace and environmental divisions of major law firms. Answers varied from "My mind is completely blank" to "It's based on the chance of being hit by lightning, which is one in a million". They found out eventually that the origin is in an article written in 1961 by Mantel and Bryan (though they used a different factor which they just pulled out of a hat for the purposes of discussion) and that the FDA used 10^6 in 1977 in a risk assessment effort concerning a growth promoter in cattle. It was intended to be a "de minimis" rule, a lower regulatory level of "zero risk" below which no consideration would be given as to risk to human health. However, according to this presentation, many federal and state agency decisions came to consider it as a maximum or target level of "acceptable" risk.

[12] Kathryn E. Kelly, and Nanette C. Cardon, "The Myth of 10^6 as a Definition of Acceptable Risk (or, In Hot Pursuit of Superfund's Holy Grail") Environmental Toxicology International, Inc. Seattle, Washington 98101, Presentation 84th Annual Meeting Air & Waste Management Association Vancouver, B.C., Canada 16–21 June, 1991.

The foregoing example highlights that when making a judgement about the acceptability of a risk, one should be aware of the underlying assumptions and the often conservative judgements already made. When making that judgement one should be led by scientific data rather than by mere perception. In their presentation Kelly and Cardon mention that the EPA Science Advisory Board ranks hazardous waste near the bottom of its list of actual risks to the public, but that it was at the top of the Agency's priorities. In response to these findings, according to Kelly and Cardon, US EPA Administrator Reilly has undertaken a major reorganization of the EPA to refocus its efforts on the major sources of actual risk and their reduction.

My conclusion is that "hazardous substances" as such do not form a proper basis for a strict liability system. In order to relate "hazardous substances" to "significant risks" one should first define appropriate "no effect levels" together with a range of acceptable risks to take into account different situations, different kinds of threats, and different kinds of technical remedies. The Convention confuses two important issues. In the first place it designates a group of substances or preparations which "in any event" (*praesumptio iuris et de iure*) shall be deemed to constitute "a significant risk" (Article 2, para. 2(a)) thus disregarding the need for a proper risk assessment in a given situation. In the second place it does not provide a criterion for establishing an acceptable effect level.

The Operator

The Convention designates the "operator" as the party liable, i.e. "the person who exercises the control of a dangerous activity". Conceptually, designating the person in control is acceptable. The question remains, however, who will be deemed to be in control in a given situation. Is it, like in the German Act, the party who holds ("Inhaber") a defined installation? Or is it the occupier of land as under the doctrine of *Rylands* v. *Fletcher* in England, or "le gardien des choses" in French law, or "the professional user" according to proposed legislation in The Netherlands.

Each of the drafters of the Convention representing one of those countries may have found something of his liking in the definition. National preferences of the drafters resulted in a vague, compromised definition, which will be unworkable in practice. The legislation should have been drafted to make that person clearly identifiable.[13] In my opinion, if the significance of the risk or, alternatively, the "polluter pays" principle is seen as justification for imposing strict liability, that liability should lie exclusively with the person in direct operational control. The term "operator", as to be introduced on the European stage, should not remind international bankers of their experience with US Court decisions

[13] Article 13 provides that the Contracting Parties shall ensure that "operators carrying out a dangerous activity ... be required to have and maintain insurance or other financial security up to a certain limit ...". I may also point out that pursuant to Article 18(1) and (2) access to information is granted if the information is in the hands of an "operator".

under CERCLA. Famous by now is the decision by the United States Court of Appeals in United States vs. Fleet Factors[14] where the Court ruled:

> "It is not necessary for the secured creditor actually to involve itself in the day-to-day operations of the facility in order to be liable — although such conduct will certainly lead to the loss of the protection of the statutory exemption. Nor is it necessary for the secured creditor to participate in management decisions relating to hazardous waste. Rather, a secured creditor will be liable if its involvement with the management of the facility is sufficiently broad to support the impression that it could affect hazardous waste disposal decisions if it so chose."

Under the Convention only one person will be deemed to be the "operator", as I understand. One should hope that this will come out more clearly in the explanatory note which is being prepared.

Indeed, further definition of the term "operator" is needed. If a painter decorates a house with paint containing solvents falling under the definition of hazardous substances, he could be the operator under the Convention as the person exercising the control over the dangerous activity of handling hazardous solvents. Will that control change under the Convention if he is painting a tank in a tank farm as a subcontractor to the person who contracted with the tank farm owner/operator? (This example also shows the need to delineate the field of application of the Convention from that of the EC Directive on product liability.[15]

If "control" is the underlying justification for imposing liability, the level of control should also determine the extent of the operator's liability. Unfortunately, this is not the case in the Convention, as indicated by the following examples:

1. It is not an exemption from liability under the Convention if a third party caused the damage and the operator (a) exercised due care with respect to the hazardous substance concerned, taking into consideration the characteristics of such hazardous substance, in light of all relevant facts and circumstances, and (b) took precautions against foreseeable acts or omissions of any such third party and the consequences that could foreseeably result from such acts or omissions.
2. The person suffering damage contributed to the damage. In that situation the liability should be reduced to the extent of the plaintiff's contribution; Article 9, however, leaves that to the discretion of the Court without mentioning the points to be considered when granting compensation.
3. In a *force majeure* situation the operator should be exempt from liability. Such a provision has been taken up in Article 6 of the draft EC Directive on Civil Liability For Damage Caused by Waste and also in Article 4 of the German Act. Article 8(a) of the Convention exempts the operator only in some exceptional *force majeure* situations.

[14] 901 F.2 d 1551 (11th CIR.1990).

[15] OJ no. L 210, 7.8.85.

4. The total damage is inflicted by (1) an incident under the control of an operator and (2) another incident not being a dangerous activity. The drafters did not address this situation, but in that situation the operator should be liable only to the extent of the damage inflicted by the incident under his control.

Damage

"Damage" includes "loss or damage by impairment of the environment ... provided that compensation for impairment of the environment ... shall be limited to the cost of measures of reinstatement undertaken or to be undertaken". This definition in Article 2, para. 8, of the Convention has the effect that virtually any impairment of the environment can be considered "damage". It does not define a threshold nor does it leave room to consider the effects of the impairment. All human activities have an effect on the environment. Even measures taken to protect the environment may have negative effects; the extraction of sulphur from oil products requires much extra energy, which in its turn adds to the production of CO_2. As such, this definition of "damage" is impractical.

According to the definition the amount of compensation shall be limited to the "reasonable" measures of reinstatement. One should not object to what is termed "reasonable", but is it reasonable to leave it completely to the discretion of the judiciary to decide after the event which measures have been appropriate under the circumstances? In the draft EC Directive on Civil Liability for Damage Caused by Waste the wording used in Article 4, para. 2, is more clear and eco-efficient:

> "... the plaintiff may seek such reinstatement or the reimbursement of expenditure incurred to this end except when:
>
> - the costs substantially exceed the benefit arising for the environment from such reinstatement, and
> - other alternative measures to the reinstatement of the environment may be undertaken at a substantially lower cost."

The EC Directive also takes a more practical approach to "impairment of the environment", defining it as "any significant physical, chemical or biological deterioration of the environment ...". This EC definition does not cover every impairment; it should be "significant" and, moreover, "deterioration" in my view refers to a process of impairment from which recovery can only be achieved by means of human interference.

In an indirect way the Convention recognises the need to construe a threshold between acceptable and unacceptable "impairments". According to Article 8 dealing with the exemptions from liability, the operator shall not be liable for damage which he proves "was caused by pollution at tolerable levels to be anticipated under local relevant circumstances". If emissions are not in excess of a permit to operate, the emissions should be considered to comply with this exemption. I understand that the interplay between permits and tolerable levels will be explained in a Note which is being prepared by the Committee of Experts.

Incident

"Incident" is defined as "any sudden occurrence or continuous occurrence or any series of occurrences having the same origin, which causes damage or creates a grave and imminent threat of causing damage".

Potentially the impact of this definition can be substantial, since by including "continuous occurrences" the scope of the Convention extends to normal emissions permitted pursuant to a permit to operate issued by the authorities.

The term "occurrence" is not entirely clear for the purpose of interpreting the meaning of some of the provisions. In a situation where poor maintenance can lead to emissions (whenever pressure in the installation mounts), the question is whether the "poor maintenance" or "the emissions" will be considered the occurrence. Such questions may crop up, for instance, under Article 6, para. 2(a) and (b), according to which operator A or B will be liable depending on the meaning of "continuous occurrences" and "series of occurrences", respectively.

Conclusions

1. The present avalanche of legislative initiatives is not the most effective way of tackling the environmental issues. At this stage of legislative developments a well-managed plan of action should lead to a higher degree of eco-efficiency.
2. In environmental matters the civil law term "damage" cannot easily be reconciled with the dynamics of the process to achieve sustainable stepwise reductions in the emissions which impair the environment.
3. If civil law should play a role in matters of the "unowned" environment, the definition of environmental "damage", needs careful review in order to avoid an inefficient allocation of resources.
4. The legislator should not lose sight of the counter-productive effects of a strict liability regime.
5. The *praesumptio iuris et de iure* that some substances pose a significant risk is in conflict with the law of Paracelsus (1493–1541): "All substances are poisons; there is none which is not poison. The right dose differentiates a poison and a remedy."
6. The impact of the draft Convention may be less than recently anticipated as a result of some changes which indicate that the EC may opt out and review its own options in the light of a green paper to be issued by the EC Commission.

Appendix I

Draft Convention On Civil Liability For Damage Resulting From Activities Dangerous To The Environment

The member States of the Council of Europe, signatory hereto,

Considering that the aim of the Council of Europe is to achieve a greater unity between its members;

Noting that one of the aims of the Council is to contribute to the quality of life of human beings, in particular by promoting a natural, healthy and agreeable environment;

Realising that the public, the environment and property are exposed to specific dangers caused by dangerous activities;

Considering that the emission of pollutants in one country may cause damage in another country and that, therefore, the problems of compensation for such damage are also of an international nature;

Having regard to the desirability of providing for strict liability in this field taking into account the "Polluter-Pays Principle";

Mindful of the work which has already been carried out at an international level, in particular to prevent damage and to deal with damage caused by nuclear substances and the carriage of dangerous goods;

Recognising the need to adopt further measures to deal with grave and imminent threats of damage from dangerous activities and to facilitate the burden of proof for persons requesting compensation for such damage;

Have agreed as follows:

Chapter I: General Provisions

Article 1 (Object and purpose)

This Convention aims at ensuring adequate compensation for damage resulting from activities dangerous to the environment and also provides for means of prevention and reinstatement.

Article 2 (Definitions)

For the purpose of this Convention:

1. *Dangerous activity* means one or more of the following activities provided that it is performed professionally, including activities conducted by public authorities:

a. the handling, storage, production or discharge of one or more dangerous substances or any operation of a similar nature dealing with such substances;
b. the handling, storage, production or discharge of one or more dangerous genetically modified organisms or dangerous micro-organisms or any operation of a similar nature dealing with dangerous genetically modified organisms or dangerous micro-organisms;
c. activities involving technologies producing dangerous radiations [such as those listed in Annex III A] which produce dangerous non-ionising radiations or X-rays;
d. the operation of an installation or site for the incineration, treatment, handling or recycling of waste such as those installations or sites specified in Annex IV, provided that the quantities involved pose a significant risk to man, the environment or property;
e. the operation of a site for the permanent disposal of waste.

2. *Dangerous substances mean*:

a. substances or preparations which have properties which constitute a significant risk to man, the environment or property. A substance or preparation which is explosive, oxydising, extremely flammable, highly flammable, very toxic, toxic, [harmful], corrosive, irritant, [sensitising], carcinogenic, mutogenic, toxic for the reproduction, dangerous for the environment within the meaning of Annex I (A) to this Convention shall in any event be deemed to constitute such a risk.
b. substances specified in Annex I (B) to this Convention. Designation of a substance as dangerous may be restricted to certain quantities or concentrations, certain risks or certain situations in which the substance may be found without prejudice to the application of sub-paragraph (a).

3. *Dangerous genetically modified organism* means a genetically modified organism which has acquired harmful or more harmful properties as a result of genetic modification and which poses a significant risk to man, the environment or property as a result of that modification. Genetically modified organism means an organism in which the genetic material has been altered in a way that does not occur naturally by mating or natural recombination, any descendant of such an organism and any other organism by which the transfer of genetically modified material acquires properties which have a harmful effect. Excluded from techniques of genetic modification referred to in the previous sentence are mutagenesis and cell fusion, including protoplast fusion, or cells from plants, which can be produced by traditional breeding methods.

4. *Dangerous micro-organism* means a micro-organism which poses a significant risk to man, the environment or property such as micro-organisms that are pathogenic or that produce toxins including those which are listed in Annex II to this Convention.

5. *Dangerous non-ionising radiations* mean radiations specified in Annex III [B] which according to their intensity constitute a significant risk to man, the environment or property.

6. *Operator* means the person who exercises the control of a dangerous activity.

7. *Person* means any individual or partnership or any body governed by public or private law, whether corporate or not, including a State or any of its constituent subdivisions.

8. *Damage* means:

a. loss of life or personal injury;
b. loss or damage to property other than to the installation itself or property held in the custody or under the control of the operator, at the site of the dangerous activity;

c. loss or damage by impairment of the environment in so far as this is not considered to be damage within the meaning of sub-paragraphs a or b provided that compensation for impairment of the environment, other than for loss of profit from such impairment, shall be limited to the costs of measures of reinstatement actually undertaken or to be undertaken;
d. the costs of preventive measures and further loss or damage caused by preventive measures;

to the extent that the loss or damage referred to in sub-paragraphs (a) to (c) of this paragraph arises out of or results from the hazardous properties of the dangerous substances, dangerous genetically modified organisms or dangerous micro-organisms or arises or results from radiations or waste.

9. *Measures of reinstatement* mean any reasonable measures aiming to reinstate or restore damaged or destroyed components of the environment or to introduce, where reasonable, the equivalent of these components into the environment.

10. *Preventive measures* mean any reasonable measures taken by any person after an incident has occurred to prevent or minimise loss or damage as referred to in paragraph 8 (a) to (c) of this Article.

11. *Environment* includes natural resources both abiotic and biotic, such as air, water, soil, fauna and flora and the interaction between the same factors, property which forms part of the cultural heritage and the characteristic aspects of the landscape.

12. *Incident* means any sudden occurrence or continuous occurrence or any series of occurrences having the same origin, which causes damage or creates a grave and imminent threat of causing damage.

Article 3 (Geographical scope)

Without prejudice to the provisions of Chapter III this Convention shall apply:

a. when the incident occurs in the territory of a Contracting Party, as determined in accordance with Article 36 regardless of where the damage is suffered; or
b. when the incident occurs outside the territory referred to in sub-paragraph a) and the conflict of laws rules lead to the application of the law in force for the territory referred to in sub-paragraph a).

Article 4 (Exceptions)

This Convention shall not apply:

1. to damage arising from carriage, not being carriage by pipeline, unless such carriage is performed entirely in an installation or on a site inaccessible to the public, is accessory to other activities and is an integral part thereof. Carriage includes the period from the beginning of the process of loading until the end of the process of unloading.

2. to damage caused by a nuclear substance:

   (i) if liability for such damage is regulated either by the Paris Convention of 29 July 1960 on Third Party liability in the field of nuclear energy and its Additional Protocol of 28 January 1964, or by the Vienna Convention of 21 May 1963 on civil liability for nuclear damage or any amendments to those Conventions; or
   (ii) if liability for such damage is regulated by a specific national law provided that such law is in all respects as favourable with regard to compensation for damage as either the Paris or the Vienna Convention referred to under (a) above.

3. to the extent that it is incompatible with the rules of the applicable law relating to workmen's compensation or social security schemes.

Chapter II: Liability

Article 5 (Transitional provisions)
1. This Chapter shall apply to incidents occurring after the entry into force of the Convention with respect to a Contracting Party. When the incident consists of a continuous occurrence or a series of occurrences having the same origin and part of these occurrences took place before the entry into force of this Convention, this Chapter shall only apply to damage caused by occurrences or part of a continuous occurrence taking place after the entry into force.

2. In respect of damage caused by waste disposed of at a site for the permanent disposal of waste this Chapter shall apply to damage which becomes known after the entry into force of the Convention with respect to the Contracting Party on the territory of which the site is situated. However this Chapter shall not apply if:

   a. the site was closed in accordance with the provisions of national law before the entry into force of the Convention;
   b. the operator proves, in the case where the operation of the site continues after that entry into force, that the damage was caused solely by waste disposed of there before that entry into force.

Article 6 (Liability in respect of substances, organisms radiations and certain waste installations or sites)
1. The operator in respect of a dangerous activity mentioned under Article 2, paragraph 1, sub-paragraphs (a) to (d) shall be liable for the damage caused by the activity as a result of incidents at the time or during the period when he was exercising control of that activity.

2. a. if an incident consists of a continuous occurrence, all operators successively exercising control of the dangerous activity shall be jointly and severally liable. However, if the operator proves that the occurrence during the period

when he was exercising control of the dangerous activity could have caused only a part of the damage, he shall only be liable for that part of the damage.

b. If an incident consists of a series of occurrences having the same origin, the operators at the time of any such occurrence shall be jointly and severally liable. However, if the operator proves that the occurrence at the time when he was exercising control of the dangerous activity could have caused only a part of the damage, he shall only be liable for that part of the damage.

3. If the damage resulting from a dangerous activity becomes known after all such dangerous activity at the site or installation has ceased, liability shall rest with the last operator. However, if he or the person who suffered the damage proves that the damage resulted from an incident which occurred at a time when another person was the operator, this operator shall be liable.

4. Nothing in this Convention shall prejudice any right of recourse of the operator against any third party.

Article 7 (Liability in respect of sites for the permanent disposal of waste)
1. The operator of a site for the permanent disposal of waste at the time when damage caused by waste deposited at that site becomes known, shall be liable for this damage. Should the damage caused by waste deposited before the closure of such a site become known after the closure, the last operator shall be liable.

2. Liability under this Article shall apply to the exclusion of any liability of the operator under Article 6, irrespective of the nature of the waste.

3. Liability under this Article shall apply to the exclusion of any liability of the operator under Article 6 if the same operator exercises another dangerous activity on the site for the permanent disposal of waste.

However if this operator or the person who has suffered damage proves that only a part of the damage has been caused by the activity concerning the permanent disposal of waste, this Article shall only apply to that part of the damage.

4. Nothing in this Convention shall prejudice any right of recourse of the operator against any third party.

Article 8 (Exemptions)

According to this Convention, the operator shall not be liable for damage which he proves

(a) was caused by an act of war, hostilities, civil war, insurrection or a natural phenomenon of an exceptional inevitable and irresistible character;
(b) was caused by an act done with the intent to cause damage by a third party, despite safety measures appropriate to the type of dangerous activity in question;

(c) resulted necessarily from compliance with a specific order or compulsory measure of a public authority
(d) was caused by pollution at tolerable levels to be anticipated under local relevant circumstances.
(e) was caused by a dangerous activity taken lawfully in the interests of the person suffering the damage, whereby it was reasonable towards this person to expose him to the risks of the dangerous activity.

Article 9 (Fault of the person who suffered the damage)
If the person who suffered the damage or a person for whom the person who suffered damage is responsible under national law, has by his own fault contributed to the damage, the compensation may be reduced or disallowed having regard to all the circumstances.

Article 10 (Causality)
When considering evidence of the causal link between the incident and the damage or, in the context of a dangerous activity as defined in Article 2 paragraph 1 (e), between the activity and the damage, the court shall take due account of the increased danger of causing such damage inherent in the dangerous activity.

Article 11 (Plurality of installations or sites)
1. When damage results from incidents which have occured in several installations or sites where dangerous activities are conducted or from dangerous activities under Article 2 paragraph 1 (e), the operators of the installations or sites concerned shall be jointly and severally liable for all such damage.

However, if the operator proves that only part of the damage could have been caused by an incident in the installation or site where he carries out the dangerous activity or by a dangerous activity under Article 2 paragraph 1 (e), he shall only be liable for that part of the damage.

2. In case of joint and several liability, each operator shall be entitled to the limitation of liability applicable to him by virtue of provisions of national law pursuant to Article 12.

Article 12 (Limitation of liability)
1. Provisions of internal law may limit the liability of the operator to a maximum amount, [which takes into account the maximum extent of the damage which can be caused by the dangerous activity].

2. The operator shall not be entitled to limit his liability under this Convention if it is proved that the damage resulted from his personal act or omission or an act or omission of his servants or agents, committed with the intent to cause the damage, or recklessly and with knowledge that such damage would probably result, provided that, in the case of such act or omission of a servant or agent, it is also proved that he was acting within the scope of this employment.

Article 13 (Compulsory insurance or other financial security)

A Contracting Party shall ensure that where appropriate, taking due account of the risks of the activity [and] of the financial capacity of the operator, [assurability of the risks of the activity] operators carrying out a dangerous activity on its territory be required to have and maintain insurance or other financial security up to a certain limit and of such type and terms as specified by internal law, to cover the liability under this Convention. [This requirement shall in any case apply to the activities dealing with dangerous substances mentioned in Annex V].

Chapter III: Access to Information

Article 14 (Definition of public authorities)

For the purpose of this chapter "public authorities" means any public administration of a Contracting Party at national, regional or local level with responsibilities, and possessing information relating to the environment with the exception of bodies acting in a judicial or legislative capacity.

Article 15 (Access to information held by public authorities)

1. Any natural or legal person shall, at his request and without his having to prove an interest, have access to information relating to the environment held by public authorities.

The Contracting Parties shall define the practical arrangements under which such information is effectively made available.

2. The right of access may be restricted under national law where it affects:

— the confidentiality of the proceedings of public authorities, international relations and national defence;
— public security;
— matters which are or have been sub judice, or under enquiry (including disciplinary enquiries), or which are the subject of preliminary investigation proceedings;
— commercial and industrial confidentiality, including intellectual property;
— the confidentiality of personal data and/or files;
— material supplied by a third Party without that Party being under a legal obligation to do so;
— material, the disclosure of which would make it morelikely that the environment to which that material related would be damaged.

Information held by public authorities shall be supplied in part where it is possible to separate out information on items concerning the interests referred to above.

3. A request for information may be refused where it would involve the supply of unfinished documents or data or internal communications, or where the request is manifestly unreasonable or formulated in too general a manner.

4. A public authority shall respond to a person requesting information as soon as possible and at the latest within two months. The reasons for a refusal to provide the information requested must be given.

5. A person who considers that his request for information has been unreasonably refused or ignored, or has been inadequately answered by a public authority, may seek a judicial or administrative review of the decision in accordance with the relevant national legal system.

6. The Contracting Parties may make a charge for supplying the information, but such a charge may not exceed a reasonable cost.

[7. These rules may be amended or supplemented by the [Governments of the Parties to this Convention] [the Standing Committee].[1]

Article 16 (Access to information held by bodies with public responsibilities for the environment)

On the same terms and conditions as those set out in Article 15 any natural or legal person shall have access to information relating to the environment held by bodies with public responsibilities for the environment and under the control of a pubic authority. Access shall be given via the competent public administration or directly by the body itself.

Article 17 (Access to information through the intervention of a public law corporate body)

National law may, in addition, provide that the right of access to information under Articles 15 and 16 may be exercised with the assistance of or through a public law corporate body in order to assist the person requesting information to obtain or select relevant information [or in order to remove certain restrictions on the right of access introduced by national law under Article 15 paragraph 2].

Article 18 (Access to specific information held by operators)

1. The person who suffered damage may, at any time, request the court to order an operator to provide him with specific information, in so far as this is necessary to establish the existence of a claim for compensation under the present Convention.

2. Where, under this Convention, a claim for compensation is made to an operator, whether or not in the framework of judicial proceedings, this operator may request the court to order another operator to provide him with specific information, in so far as this is necessary to establish the extent of his possible obligation to compensate the person who has suffered the damage, or of his own right to compensation from the other operator.

3. The information which the operator is required to provide under paragraphs 1 and 2 should concern the elements which are available to him and should deal

[1] This question will be examined once the question of amendments is considered.

essentially with the particulars of the equipment, the machinery used, the technologies producing dangerous radiations, the kind and concentration of the dangerous substances or waste as well as the nature of dangerous genetically modified organisms or dangerous micro-organisms, employed or released.

4. These measures shall not affect measures of investigation which may legally be ordered under internal law.

5. The court may refuse a request which places a disproportionate burden on the operator taking into account all the interests involved.

6. In addition to the restrictions under paragraph 2 of Article 15, which shall apply mutatis mutandis, an operator may refuse to provide information where such information would incriminate him.

7. Any reasonable charge shall be paid by the person requesting the information. The operator may require an appropriate guarantee for such payment. However a court, when allowing a claim for compensation, may establish that this charge shall be borne by the operator, except to the extent that the request resulted in unnecessary cost

Chapter IV: Claims and Actions

Article 19 (Limitation periods)

1. Actions for compensation under this Convention shall be subject to a limitation period of five years from the date on which the claimant knew or ought reasonably to have known of the damage and of the identity of the operator. The laws of the Contracting Parties regulating suspension or interruption of (these) limitation periods shall apply to the limitation period prescribed in this paragraph.

2. However, in no case shall actions be brought after thirty years from the date of the incident which caused the damage. Where the incident consists of a series of occurrences having the same origin the thirty years' period shall run from the date of the last of such occurrences. Where the incident consists of a continuous occurrence the thirty years' period shall run from the end of the occurrence.

3. In respect of a site for the permanent disposal of waste, the thirty years period, as refereed to in paragraph 2 of this Article, shall at the latest run from the date on which the site was closed in accordance with the provisions of national law.

Article 20 (Action by organisations)

1. Any association or foundation which according to its statutes takes care of the protection of the environment and which complies with any further conditions of national law of the State Party where the action is brought, is entitled to bring an action in court or apply to a competent administrative authority requesting:

a. a prohibition of a dangerous activity which is unlawful
   and
   poses a grave threat of damage to the environment; or

b. an order to the operator to take measures to prevent an incident; or
c. an order to the operator to take measures after an incident to prevent damage; or
d. an order to the operator to take measures of reinstatement.

2. National law may stipulate cases where the action is inadmissible.

3. Before deciding upon a request mentioned under paragraph 1 the court may, in view of the general interests involved, hear the competent public authorities with respect to the measures requested.

4. When the national law of a Contracting State referred to in paragraph 1 requires that the association or foundation has its registered seat or the effective centre of its activities in that State, such State may declare at the time of signature, ratification or accession that an association or foundation having its seat or centre of activities in another State Party and complying in that other State with the other conditions mentioned in paragraph 1 of this Article shall have the right to take action in accordance with paragraphs 1 and 2.

The associations or foundations having their seat or centre of activities in a State Party which has made such declaration will have the same right in any other State which has made the same declaration.

Article 21 (Jurisdiction)

1. Actions for compensation under this Convention may only be brought within a State Party at the court of the place:

a. where the damage was suffered; or
b. where the dangerous activity was conducted; or
c. where the defendant has his habitual residence.

2. Requests for access to information held by operators under paragraphs 1 and 2 of Article 18 of this Convention may only be submitted within a State party at the court of the place:

a. where the dangerous activity is conducted; or
b. where the operator who may be required to provide the information has his habitual residence.

3. Actions by organisations under Article 20 paragraph 1 sub-paragraph a of this Convention may only be brought within a State Party at the court or, if national law so provides, before a competent administrative authority of the place where the dangerous activity is or will be conducted.

4. Actions by organisations under Article 20 paragraph 1 sub-paragraphs b and c of this Convention may only be brought within a State Party at the court or, if national law so provides, before a competent administrative authority of the place:

a. where the dangerous activity is or will be conducted;
b. where the measures are to be taken.

Article 22 (Notification)
The court shall stay the proceedings so long as it is not shown that the defendant has been able to receive the document instituting the proceedings or an equivalent document in sufficient time to enable him to arrange for his defence, or that all necessary steps have been taken to this end.

Article 23 (Lis pendens)
1. Where proceedings involving the same cause of action and between the same parties are brought in the courts of different Contracting States, any court other than the court first seised shall of its own motion stay its proceedings until such time as the jurisdiction of the court first seized is established.

2. Where the jurisdiction of the court first seised is established, any court other than the court first seised shall decline jurisdiction in favour of that court.

Article 24 (Related actions)
1. Where related actions are brought in the courts of different Contracting States, any court other than the court first seised may, while the actions are pending at first instance, stay its proceedings.

2. A court other than the court first seised may also, on the application of one of the parties, decline jurisdiction if the law of that court permits the consolidation of related actions and the court first seised has jurisdiction over both actions.

3. For the purposes of this Article, actions are deemed to be related where they are so closely connected that it is expedient to hear and determine them together to avoid the risk of irreconciliable judgments resulting from separate proceedings.

Article 25 (Recognition and enforcement)
1. Any judgment given by a court with jurisdiction in accordance with Article 21 where it is no longer subject to ordinary forms of review, shall be recognised in any Contracting Party, unless:

a. such recognition is contrary to public policy in the State in which recognition is sought;
b. if the defendant was not duly served with the document which instituted the proceedings or with an equivalent document in sufficient time to enable him to arrange for his defence;
c. the judgment is irreconcilable with a judgment given in a dispute between the same parties in the State in which recognition is sought;
d. the judgment is irreconcilable with an earlier judgment given in another State involving the same cause of action and between the same parties, provided

that this latter judgment fulfils the conditions necessary for its recognition in the State addressed.

2. A judgment recognised under paragraph 1 of this article which is enforceable in the State of origin shall be enforceable in each Contracting Party as soon as the formalities required in that State have been compiled with. The formalities shall not permit the merits of the case to be re—opened.

Article 26 (Other Conventions relating to jurisdiction, recognition and enforcement)

Whenever two or more States parties are bound by an international Convention establishing rules of jurisdiction or providing for recognition and enforcement in a State of judgments given in another State, the provisions of those instruments replace the corresponding provisions of Articles 21 to 25 of this Convention.

Chapter VI: Relations between the Convention and other Provisions

Article 27 (Relations between the Convention and the internal law of the Parties or other Conventions)

1. Nothing in this Convention shall be construed as limiting or derogating from any of the rights of the persons suffering damage which may be ensured under the laws of any Contracting Party or under any other agreement to which it is a Party.

2. [In their mutual relations,] Parties which are members of the European Economic Community shall apply Community rules and shall therefore not apply the rules arising from this Convention except in so far as there is no Community rule governing the particular subject concerned.

Chapter VII: The Standing Committee

Article 28 (The Standing Committee)

1. For the purposes of this Convention, a Standing Committee shall be set up after the entry into force of the Convention.

2. Each Contracting Party may be represented on the Standing Committee by one or more delegates.

3. Each delegation shall have one vote. However, within the areas of its competence the European Economic Committee shall exercise its right to vote in the Standing Committee with a number of votes equal to the number of its member States which are Parties to this Convention. It shall not exercise its right to vote in cases where the member States exercise theirs and conversely. As long as no member State of the European Economic Community is a Contracting Party, the Community as a Contracting Party shall have one vote.

4. Any State referred to in Article 34 or in Article 35 which is not a Party to this Convention may be represented on the Standing Committee by an observer. If the European Economic Committee is not a Party it may be represented on the Standing Committee by an observer.

5. Unless, at least one month before the meeting, a Contracting Party has informed the Secretary General of its objection, the Standing Committee may invite the following to attend as observers at all its meetings or one or part of a meeting:

— any non-Contracting State not referred to in paragraph 4;
— any international or national, governmental or non-governmental body technically qualified in the fields covered by this Convention.

6. The Standing Committee may seek the advice of experts in order to discharge its functions.

7. The Standing Committee shall be convened by the Secretary General of the Council of Europe. It shall meet whenever one-third of the Parties or the Committee of Ministers of the Council of Europe so requests.

8. One-third of the parties shall constitute a quorum for holding a meeting of the Standing Committee.

9. Voting may only take place in the Committee if at least one-half of the Contracting Parties shall be present at the time of voting.

10. Subject to Articles 29 and 31 to 33 the decisions of the Standing Committee shall be taken by a majority of the members present.

11. Subject to the provisions of this Convention, the Standing Committee shall draw up its own Rules of Procedure.

Article 29 (Functions of the Standing Committee)

The Standing Committee shall keep under review problems relating to this Convention. It may, in particular:

a. consider any question of a general nature referred to it concerning interpretation or implementation of the Convention. The Committee's conclusions concerning implementation of the Convention may take the form of a recommendation; recommendations shall be adopted by a three quarters majority of the vote cast;
b. propose any necessary amendments to the Convention including its Appendices and examine those proposed in accordance with Articles 31 to 33;

Article 30 (Reports of the Standing Committee)

After each meeting, the Standing Committee shall forward to the Parties and the Committee of Ministers of the Council of Europe a report on its discussions and any decisions taken.

Chapter VII: Amendments to the Convention

Article 31 (Amendments to the Articles)
1. Any amendment to the Articles of this Convention proposed by a Contracting Party or the Standing Committee shall be communicated to the Secretary General of the Council of Europe and forwarded by him at least two months before the meeting of the Standing Committee to the member States of the Council of Europe, to the European Economic Community, to any signatory, to any Contracting Party, to any State invited to sign this Convention in accordance with the provisions of Article 34 and to any State invited to accede to it in accordance with the provisions of Article 35.

2. Any amendment proposed in accordance with the provisions of the preceding paragraph shall be examined by the Standing Committee which:

a. for amendments to Articles [1] to [27] shall submit the text adopted by a three-quarters majority of the votes cast to the Contracting Parties for acceptance;
b. for amendments to Articles [28] to [39] shall submit the text adopted by a three-quarters majority of the votes cast to the Committee of Ministers for approval. After its approval, this text shall be forwarded to the Contracting parties for acceptance.

3. Any amendment to Articles [1] to [27] shall enter into force, on the thirtieth day after three Parties, including at least two member States of the Council of Europe, have informed the Secretary General that they have accepted it.

4. Any amendment to Article [28] to [39] shall enter into force on the thirtieth day after all Parties have informed the Secretary General that they have accepted it.

Article 32 (Amendment of Annexes I-V)
1. Any amendment to the Annexes of this Convention proposed by a Contracting Party or the Standing Committee shall be communicated to the Secretary General of the Council of Europe and forwarded by him at least two months before the meeting of the Standing Committee to the member States of the Council of Europe, to the European Economic Community, to any signatory, to any Contracting Party, to any State invited to sign this Convention in accordance with the provisions of Article 34 and to any State invited to accede to it in accordance with the provisions of Article 35.

2. Any amendment proposed in accordance with the provisions of the preceding paragraph or, where appropriate, of Article 33 shall be examined by the Standing Committee, which may adopt it by a three-quarters majority of the votes cast. The text adopted shall be forwarded to the Contracting Parties.

3. Eighteen months after its adoption by the Standing Committee and unless more than one-third of the Contracting Parties have notified objections, any

amendment shall enter into force for those Contracting Parties which have not notified objections.

Article 33 (Tacit amendments to Annex I.A and I.B)
1. If the European Economic Community adopts an amendment to one of the Appendices to the Directives referred to in Annex I.A and I.B on this Convention, the Secretary General shall communicate it to all the Contracting Parties not later than [four] months after its publication in the Official Journal of the European Communities.

2. Within a time limit of six months after this communication, any Contracting Party may request that the amendment be submitted to the Standing Committee, in which case the procedure under paragraphs 2 and 3 of Article 32 shall be followed. If no Party requests the submission of the amendment to the Standing Committee, the provisions of paragraph 3 below shall apply.

3. Eighteen months after the communication of the amendment to all Contracting Parties and unless more than 1/3 of the Contracting Parties have notified objections, the amendment shall enter into force for those Contracting Parties which have not notified objections.

However the entry into force of the amendment shall be postponed to the date fixed for the member States of the EEC for the compliance of their domestic law with the Directive, if this date is later than the date resulting from the above time limit of 18 months.

Chapter VIII: Final Clauses

Article 34 (Signature, entry into force)
1. This Convention shall be open for signature by the member States of the Council of Europe, the non-member States which have participated in its elaboration and by the European Economic Community. Until the date when the Convention enters into force it shall also be open for signature by any other State so invited by the Committee of Ministers.

2. The Convention is subject to ratification, acceptance or approval. Instruments of ratification, acceptance or approval shall be deposited with the Secretary General of the Council of Europe.

3. This Convention shall enter into force on the first day of the month following the expiration of a period of 3 months after the date on which three States, including at least two member States of the Council of Europe, have expressed their consent to be bound by the Convention in accordance with the provisions of paragraph 2.

4. In respect of any signatory State or the European Economic Community which subsequently expresses its consent to be bound by it, the Convention shall enter into force on the first day of the month following the expiration of a period

of 3 months after the date of the deposit of its instrument of ratification, acceptance or approval.

Article 35 (Non-member States)
1. After the entry into force of the Convention, the Committee of Ministers of the Council of Europe may, on its own initiative or following a proposal from the Standing Committee and after consultation of Contracting Parties, invite any non-member State of the Council of Europe to accede to this Convention.

2. In respect of any acceding State, the Convention shall enter into force on the first day of the month following the expiration of a period of 3 months after the date of deposit of the instrument of accession with the Secretary General of the Council of Europe.

Article 36 (Territories)
1. Any State may at the time of signature or when depositing its instrument of ratification, acceptance, approval or accession, specify the territory or territories to which this Convention shall apply.

2. Any Contracting Party may, at any later date, by a declaration addressed to the Secretary General of the Council of Europe, extend the application of this Convention to any other territory specified in the declaration and for whose international relations it is responsible or on whose behalf it is authorised to give undertakings. In respect of such territory the Convention shall enter into force on the first day of the month following the expiration of a period of 3 months after the date of receipt of such declaration by the Secretary General.

3. Any declaration made under the two preceding paragraphs may, in respect of any territory specified in such declaration, be withdrawn by a notification addressed to the Secretary General. The withdrawal shall become effective on the first day of the month following the expiration of a period of 3 months after the date of receipt of such notification by the Secretary General.

Article 37 (Reservations)
1. Each State or the European Economic Community may declare, at the moment of the signature or at the moment of the deposit of its instrument of ratification, acceptance approval or accession, that it reserves the right:

a. to apply Article 3 (a) to damage suffered in the territory of non-contracting parties only on the basis of reciprocity;
b. to provide in its internal law that, without prejudice to Article 8, the operator shall not be liable if he proves that in the case of damage caused by a dangerous activity mentioned under Article 2, paragraph 1, sub-paragraphs (a), (b) [and (c)], the state of scientific and technical knowledge at the time of the incident was not such as to enable the existence of the dangerous properties of the substance, organism or radiations to be discovered;
c. not to apply Article 20;

[d to replace the liability of the operator, on the basis of Article 7, in a principal or subsidiary way, totally or partially, in a general way, or for certain risks only, by the liability of a guarantee fund or other form of collective guarantee, provided that the victim shall receive protection at least equivalent to the protection he would have had under the liability scheme provided for by this Convention.][2]

2. A State which makes use of a reservation shall notify the Secretary General of the Council of Europe of the relevant contents of its domestic law.

3. Any Contracting Party which extends the application of this Convention to a territory mentioned in the declaration referred to in paragraph 2 of Article 36 may, in respect of the territory concerned, make a reservation in accordance with the provisions of the preceding paragraphs.

4. No reservation shall be made to the provisions of this Convention except those mentioned in this Article.

5. The Contracting Party which has made one of the reservations mentioned in this Article may withdraw it by means of a declaration addressed to the Secretary General of the Council of Europe which shall become effective on the first day of the month following the expiration of a period of one month after the date of its receipt by the Secretary General.

Article 38 (Denunciation)

1. Any Party may at any time denounce this Convention by means of a notification addressed to the Secretary General of the Council of Europe.

2. Such denunciation shall become effective on the first day of the month following the expiration of a period of 3 months after the date of receipt of notification by the Secretary General.

Article 39 (Notifications)

The Secretary General of the Council of Europe shall notify the member States of the Council, any signatory State, the European Economic Community, if a signatory of this Convention, and any Contracting Party of:

a. any signature;
b. the deposit of any instrument of ratification,
   acceptance,
   approval or accession,
c. any date of entry into force of this Convention in accordance with Articles 34 and 35;
d. any other act, notification or communication relating to this Convention.

[2] The Committee has not yet definitively decided on this question.

In witness whereof the undersigned, being duly authorised thereto, have signed this Convention.

Done at… the… in English and French, both texts being equally authentic, in a single copy which shall be deposited in the archives of the Council of Europe. The Secretary General of the Council of Europe shall transmit certified copies to each member State of the Council of Europe and to any State invited to accede to this Convention].

Annex I

Dangerous Substances

A Criteria and methods to be applied to categories of dangerous substances (Article 2, paragraph 2 (a))

The categories referred to in Article 2, paragraph 2 (a), shall be determined by the criteria and methods referred to in or annexed to the Council Directive of 18 September 1979 of the European Community (79/831/EEC) (OJCE Nr. L 259/10) amending for the sixth time Council Directive 67/548/EEC on the approximation of laws, regulations and administrative provisions relating to the classification, packaging and labelling of dangerous substances, and in the Commission Directive of 1 March 1991 of the European Community (91/325/EEC) (OJCE No L 180/1) adapting to technical progress for the twelfth time Council Directive 67/548/EEC, and in the Council Directive of 7 June 1988 of the European Community (88/379/EEC) (OJCE Nr L 187/1) on the approximation of the laws, regulations and administrative provisions of the member States relating to the classification, packaging and labelling of dangerous preparations.

B. List of dangerous substances (Article 2, paragraph 2 (b))

The substances listed in Annex I of Council Directive 67/548/EEC of 27 June 1967 as codified in the twelfth adaptation.]

Annex II

List of dangerous micro-organisms (Article 2, paragraph 4)

[The micro-organisms classified in risk group II, III and IV as adopted by the World Health Organisation.]

Annex III

Dangerous non-ionising radiations

A Technologies producing dangerous non-ionising radiations:

Radiofrequency sealing
Electrochemical plants
Radioemitters
Radar
Arc welding
High power sources
(painting, drying, softening)
Material processing
Cutting and welding equipment][1]

B. Dangerous non-ionising radiations.

Radiofrequency (RF) and microwaves (MW)
Optical radiation (infra-red, visible, ultraviolet)
Laser radiation.

[1] Article 2 (1) (c) gives the possibility to include this list. Activities concerning high voltage lines, electrochemical plants, nuclear fusion, medical diagnosis and therapy and material testing have been excluded subject to the provisions of the draft Directive of the European Economic Community on this matter.

Annex IV

Installations or sites for incineration, treatment, handling or recycling of waste

[See Article 2(i) (d) above]

Designation[1]

Installations for a partial or complete disposal, by incineration, of solid or liquid substances.

Installations for thermal degradation of combustible solid or liquid substances under reduced oxygen supply (pyrolysis installations)[2]

Installations for recovering, by incineration, of individual components from solid substances,
[with the exception of plants recovering precious metals in dross incineration ovens, if less than 200 kg per day of original are used][3]

Installations processing of solid wastes at a rate not lower than 1t per hour,
[with the exception of installations where substances are sorted out from domestic or similar wastes for re—use and recycling]

Installations for handling of solid wastes with an output not lower than 100t per day,
[with the exception of those installations used for handling of evacuated earth or rock originating from the extraction or processing of mineral resources].

Composting installations

Stationary installations for thermal treatment of domestic wastes

Installations for storing or treating discarded cars.

1 This list has been provisionally included following the example of the German Environmental Liability Act (paragraphs 68 to 77 of Appendix I of Federal Law Gazette Part I 1990 page 2642) which came into force on January 1991. This text will be examined in the light of the work of the EEC.

2 Partly covered by Article 2 paragraph 1 (a).

3 A suggestion was made to place these words between brackets and to add additional texts such as a text dealing with deep underground disposal.

Annex V

Specification of the activities referred to in Article 13 [1]

[1] It was suggested that reference should be made either to the Council Directive of 24 June 1982 on the major-accident hazards of certain industrial activities (82/501/EEC — Seveso Directive) or to other criteria which take account of the size of the company.

Appendix II

Royal Dutch/Shell Group of Companies: Policy Guidelines on Health, Safety and the Environment

It is the policy of Shell companies to conduct their activities in such a way as to take foremost account of the health and safety of their employees and of other persons, and to give proper regard to the conservation of the environment. They aim to be among the leaders in their respective industries in these matters.

From the starting point of full compliance with legislative requirements, Shell companies pursue this policy through company strategies and action plans, through visible management commitment and through the individual contributions of their employees, supported by education and training.

1. Health

Shell companies seek to conduct their activities in such a way as to avoid harm to the health of their employees and others; and to promote the health of their employees.

2. Safety

Shell companies work on the principle that all injuries should be prevented, and actively promote amongst all those associated with their activities the high standards of safety consciousness and discipline that this principle demands.

3. Environment

Shell companies pursue in their operations progressive reductions of emissions, effluents and discharges of waste materials that are known to have a negative impact on the environment, with the ultimate aim of eliminating them.

They also aim to provide products and services supported by practical advice which, when used in accordance with this advice, will not cause injury or undue effects on the environment.

Furthermore, Shell companies promote protection of environments which may be affected by the development of their activities and seek continuous improvement in efficiency of use of natural resources and energy.

4. Common Aspects

Shell companies assess health, safety and environmental matters before entering into new activities and reassess them in case of significant change in circumstances.

They require contractors working on their behalf to apply health, safety and environmental standards fully compatible with their own.

They recognise the concerns of shareholders, employees and society on health, safety and environmental matters; provide them with relevant information and discuss with them related company policies and practices.

Shell companies develop and maintain contingency procedures, in co-operation with authorities and emergency services, in order to minimise harm from any accidents.

They work with governments and others in the development of improved regulations and industry standards which relate to health, safety and environmental matters.

They conduct or support research towards the improvement of health, safety and environmental aspects of their products, processes and operations.

They also facilitate the transfer to others, freely or on a commercial basis, of know-how developed by Shell companies in these fields.

Appendix III

The Business Charter for Sustainable Development

Principles for Environmental Management [1]

Foreword

There is widespread recognition today that environmental protection must be among the highest priorities of every business.

In its milestone 1987 report, "Our Common Future", the World Commission on Environment and Development (Brundtland Commission), emphasized the importance of environmental protection in the pursuit of sustainable development.

To help business around the world improve its environmental performance, the International Chamber of Commerce established a task force of business representatives to create this Business Charter for Sustainable Development. It comprises sixteen principles for environmental management which, for business, is a vitally important aspect of sustainable development.

This Charter will assist enterprises in fulfilling their commitment to environmental stewardship in a comprehensive fashion. It was formally launched in April 1991 at the Second World Industry Conference on Environmental Management.

Introduction

Sustainable development involves meeting the needs of the present without compromising the ability of future generations to meet their own needs.

[1] The term "environment" as used in this document also refers to environmentally related aspects of health, safety and product stewardship.

Economic growth provides the conditions in which protection of the environment can best be achieved, and environmental protection, in balance with other human goals, is necessary to achieve growth that is sustainable.

In turn, versatile, dynamic, responsive and profitable businesses are required as the driving force for sustainable economic development and for providing managerial, technical and financial resources to contribute to the resolution of environmental challenges. Market economies, characterised by entrepreneurial initiatives, are essential to achieving this.

Business thus shares the view that there should be a common goal, not a conflict, between economic development and environmental protection, both now and for future generations.

Making market forces work in this way to protect and improve the quality of the environment — with the help of performance-based standards and judicious use of economic instruments in a harmonious regulatory framework — is one of the greatest challenges that the world faces in the next decade.

The 1987 report of the World Commission on Environment and Development. "Our Common Future", expresses the same challenge and calls on the cooperation of business in tackling it. To this end, business leaders have launched actions in their individual enterprises as well as through sectoral and cross-sectoral associations.

In order that more businesses join this effort and that their environmental performance continues to improve, the International Chamber of Commerce hereby calls upon enterprises and their associations to use the following Principles as a basis for pursuing such improvement and to express publicly their support for them.

Individual programmes developed to implement these Principles will reflect the wide diversity among enterprises in size and function.

The objective is that the widest range of enterprises commit themselves to improving their environmental performance in accordance with these Principles, to having in place management practices to effect such improvement, to measuring their progress, and to reporting this progress as appropriate internally and externally.

Principles

1. Corporate Priority

To recognise environmental management as among the highest corporate priorities and as a key determinant to sustainable development; to establish policies, programmes and practices for conducting operations in an environmentally sound manner.

2. Integrated Management

To integrate these policies, programmes and practices fully into each business as an essential element of management in all its functions.

3. Process of Improvement
To continue to improve corporate policies, programmes and environmental performance, taking into account technical developments, scientific understanding, consumer needs and community expectations, with legal regulations as a starting point; and to apply the same environmental criteria internationally.

4. Employee Education
To educate, train and motivate employees to conduct their activities in an environmentally responsible manner.

5. Prior Assessment
To assess environmental impacts before starting a new activity or project and before decommissioning a facility or leaving a site.

6. Products and Services
To develop and provide products or services that have no undue environmental impact and are safe in their intended use, that are efficient in their consumption of energy and natural resources, and that can be recycled, reused, or disposed of safely.

7. Customer Advice
To advise, and where relevant educate, customers, distributors and the public in the safe use, transportation, storage and disposal of products provided; and to apply similar considerations to the provision of services.

8. Facilities and Operations
To develop, design and operate facilities and conduct activities taking into consideration the efficient use of energy and materials, the sustainable use of renewable resources, the minimisation of adverse environmental impact and waste generation, and the safe and responsible disposal of residual wastes.

9. Research
To conduct or support research on the environmental impacts of raw materials, products, processes, emissions and wastes associated with the enterprise and on the means of minimizing such adverse impacts.

10. Precautionary Approach
To modify the manufacture, marketing or use of products or services or the conduct of activities, consistent with scientific and technical understanding, to prevent serious or irreversible environmental degradation.

Appendix IV

CEFIC Guidelines for the Protection of the Environment

All human activity, including that of the chemical industry, affects the environment. CEFIC believes that the protection of the environment is an integral part of good business practice and that the industry has a duty to satisfy itself that its products are manufactured, handled, transported, used and disposed of safely and without unacceptable risks for the environment. This requires that companies not only comply with the law, but also take independent and responsible actions.

In order to assist in translating these principles into management practices, *CEFIC*, in the context of the *Environmental Guidelines for the World Industry* established by the *International Chamber of Commerce*, has prepared the following guidelines for chemical companies:

1. Prepare and regularly review at the highest management level company *environmental policies* and establish procedures for their implementation;
2. Foster among employees at all levels an individual sense of *responsibility* for the environment and the need to be alert to potential sources of pollution associated with the operations;
3. Assess in advance the *environmental implications* of new processes, products and other activities, and monitor the effects of current operations on the local environment;
4. *Minimize* adverse environmental effects of all activities and take steps to minimize waste and to conserve resources;
5. Take the necessary measures to prevent *accidental releases*;
6. In cooperation with public authorities, establish and maintain *contingency procedures* to minimize the effect of accidents that may nevertheless occur;
7. **Provide the public with the information necessary to enable them to understand the potential environmental effects of the companies' operations and be prepared to respond positively to expressions of public concern;**
8. Provide the *public authorities* with relevant information and assist them in establishing well-founded environmental regulations;
9. Provide appropriate advice to *customers* on safe handling, use and disposal of the companies' products;
10. Ensure that *contractors* working on the companies' behalf apply environmental standards equivalent to their own;
11. In *transferring technology* to another party, provide the information necessary to ensure that the environment can be adequatly protected;
12. Promote *research* into the development of environmentally sound processes and products.

Introduction

The seventh Guideline for the protection of the environment states:

> "Provide the public with the information necessary to enable them to understand the potential environmental effects of the companies' operations and be prepared to respond positively to expressions of public concern"

The European Chemical Industry fully understands the public's legitimate interest and the real concerns expressed by the public about the potential effects of industrial operations on their health and safety and on the environment.

Industry has to respond to these concerns by establishing a relationship of openness and trust with the public and especially with the local communities which could be affected by its activities.

Many chemical companies already voluntarily supply information about themselves and the environmental impact of their activities. CEFIC wishes to promote the development and the spread of a more open attitude by encouraging companies to provide information enabling the public to have a better understanding of chemical industry operations and to respond positively to expressions of public concern.

To share the experiences gained by chemical companies — and to foster good management practices —, *CEFIC has produced this document to help responsible managers to establish good procedures for voluntary communication of environmental information to the public.*

Environmental information is understood in widest sense to mean information related to safety and health of the community and environmental protection.

This document lists areas of action that responsible management can take individually — or together with the local authorities or community representatives -, to improve local awareness of the industrial activities concerned, and it suggests some techniques for information exchange and communication.

Its scope is limited to information related to normal daily industrial activities. Emergency or crisis conditions will require more specific actions to be taken.

General Considerations

Industry needs to exist in harmony with those living and working in the communities in which it operates as well as with those which make use of their products. Therefore, community relations are a key element in environmental and product stewardship and an important part of the management function. Active participation in community relation contributes to both the short and long term success of industrial operations.

CEFIC recognizes that various countries and regions differ in their culture, value systems, community infrastructure, response capabilities and resources, and in regulatory requirements. Moreover, different industrial activities present different potential impacts on the environment. These Guidelines, therefore, cannot provide definitive answers to specific situations but they provide the basis for the development of communication plans and activities. It is up to each company to develop the programme most appropriate to their circumstances.

It should be borne in mind that the nature and frequency of communications with the public will vary according to a number of factors such as the nature of the work activities, their effects on local amenities, the level of risk and the level of public interest in information.

Companies may have special commercial or technical information which needs to be kept secret. If information cannot be disclosed, the company should explain why. Circumstances in which it is justifiable to withhold information on the grounds of confidentiality and privacy include:

— information the communication of which would be liable to place company's competitiveness at risk
— information likely to endanger national or company security
— information received in confidence from a third party
— an infringement of the privacy of an individual.

In whatever way companies develop their communication programme, it is essential that top management actively and visibly supports the programme and is involved in its implementation.

General Principles

It is impossible to set down in detail the necessary steps in a local communication programme that will fit every plant at every location. In order to achieve a consistent approach, the following common principles are proposed.

Each company should:

1. **In all circumstances, adopt a positive attitude.**
2. Establish a policy on the voluntary communication of environmental information to the public, make adequate arrangements and provide appropriate resources for implementation of that policy.
3. Designate a person or persons responsible for contact with the public; such person should have knowledge of environmental issues and be trained in communication skills.
4. Handle all requests for information quickly and positively. Moreover, a continuous and dynamic dialogue should be established with local communities in order better to understand their interests, anticipate their concerns and provide them with appropriate information. The impact of such communication programmes on the public should be assessed in order to improve them.
5. Look for any opportunity to publicize good news and be aware of the need rapidly to reveal the facts when problems occur.
6. Provide the local public with the appropriate information to enable them to understand the nature of the operations and their impact on the environment. This information should include measures taken by the company and authorities, in particular:
   — measures to control emission from normal operations
   — safety measures to prevent accidental emissions, and limit their consequences, including actions to be taken in case of an emergency situation*

It should be noted that such information should be in a form which is understandable to a non-specialist and that certain data might require interpretation to assist this understanding.

7. Take into consideration the views of the general public, local authorities, scientific bodies, and other representative organizations when considering the environmental impact of new developments.
8. Pay particular attention to keeping their employees well informed. Not only are they most directly affected by the activities of the company but also they are in close contact with the surrounding community and thus very effective ambassadors.
9. Explain in a positive manner why certain information needs to remain confidential whenever this situation arises
10. Give careful consideration, whenever requested information is not available, to whether such data is relevant and can be reasonably obtained.

A positive attitude is a must in all cases.

Practical Suggestions For Communicating

Communication programmes can only be efficiently established by the companies involved in the light of their special local circumstances. Companies would be well advised to seek the help of communications experts. If this expertise is not available internally, outside help should be considered.

It should be clearly established to whom the programme is addressed, and how communication will take place.

A non exhaustive list of examples of possible measures is given below:

1. Definition of the local community concerned, including:
   — authorities
   — associations
   — special neighbourhood groups
   — media
   — opinion formers
   — elected representatives
   — Trade Union representatives
2. Construction of an inventory of local community contacts
3. Setting up a procedure aimed at understanding the interests and concerns of the local communities
4. Establishment of specific methods for keeping the company employees and pensioners informed

* Specific guidance on communications to the local community about the risks presented by an industrial installation is provided by certain specific programmes such as the CICERO programme developed by CEFIC and the APELL one designed by UNEP for those countries not having a regulatory framework on emergency planning.

5. Coordination of community affairs activities with other industrial operations in the area.
6. Selection of the most appropriate means of communication such as:
   — internal mail and notice boards
   — letters, fact sheets, or brochures sent to neighbouring homes
   — briefings and meetings with local elected representatives
   — public meetings
   — local liaison committees
   — organization of open days and plant tours
   — media announcements and briefing of local journalists
   — educational activities (e.g. school visits, providing seasonal employment for teachers …)
   — advertising
   — environment news releases
   — product information sheets
   — annual reports.

* Reproduced with permission of CEFIC (European Chemical Industry Council).

Limited Insurability of Unlimited Liability: Serial Claims Aggregates and Alternatives: The American View

Charles S. Donovan, Elizabeth M. Miller

Introduction

The United States Environmental Protection Agency ("EPA") estimates that in 1990 alone, the United States spent $115 billion to comply with pollution regulations.[1] The EPA estimates that that figure will increase to as much as $185 billion in the year 2000, equalling 2.6 to 2.8% of the GNP.[2] Not surprisingly, a review by the General Accounting Office[3] of data provided by some of the nation's major insurance companies reached the conclusion that insurers' payments for pollution-related claims are likely to increase in the future.[4]

Liability for environmental pollution is not a new phenomenon. Remedies for environmental pollution damages have been available under the common law since the development of the doctrines of nuisance and trespass. In the last twenty-five years, however, just as the methods of detecting and measuring pollution have expanded, liability has expanded, primarily by the enactment of numerous federal and state statutes.

The straightforward goals in expanding liability are to provide an incentive to act more responsibly to those who cause or contribute to environmental pollution, and to assess the costs of pollution against the persons bearing the most reasonable connection to the pollution. Because the cost of identifying the

1 Gastel, "Environmental Pollution: Insurance Issues," *Ins. Info. Inst. Rep.* (March 1992).

2 Ibid.

3 The General Accounting Office ("GAO") is an independent, non-political agency which assists Congress in carrying out its legislative and oversight responsibility. The GAO audits and evaluates federally funded programmes and operations.

4 Ibid.

persons responsible for causing the pollution may be high, and because it is a cost oftentimes born by the federal or state or local government attempting to enforce the liability rules, almost all environmental pollution liability statutes impose strict liability, that is, liability irrespective of negligent or wilful conduct. And because it is imperative that the pollution be cleaned up or otherwise remedied and the full damages be paid, almost all environmental pollution liability statutes impose joint and several liability on each responsible party, thereby shifting the burden to the responsible party to recover the portion of damages for which it is not responsible against some other responsible party.

Under current federal and state laws in the United States, liability for environmental pollution is risk to be born by nearly every property owner,[5] in some degree. Given the realistic assumption that the majority of property owners is risk-averse — that is, they would prefer to reduce or eliminate uncertainties — a market for insurance or insurance-type devices arises. An insurer will bear the risk that pollution will occur and be detected, and liability imposed, for a price (a premium), and the property owner will achieve the certainty that it will not have to pay the costs of liability, or at least the full costs of liability.

Obtaining insurance is an efficient means of addressing the risk of pollution liability — in the sense that both the property owner and the insurer are better off — only if the risk is assessed accurately, adequate claims reserves are set, and the conditions, exclusions and limits of the policy written accordingly. This is much more easily said than done. The problems in assessing the risk become problems in insuring the risk. These problems arise with particular risks of particular property owners — the more experience insureds and insurers have with particular risks, the better all concerned will become at identifying and overcoming the limitations of insurability.

Where accurate methods of assessing liability are not available, it may be more efficient to address the risk of pollution liability by a means other than insurance. Putting it another way, in the absence of accurate assessment of liability, insurers may be unwilling to offer pollution liability coverage. Voluntarily or involuntarily, property owners bearing risks of pollution liability may turn to insurance alternatives such as self-insurance, group captives, or risk retention groups.

This chapter will provide a broad overview of the risk of pollution liability from the perspective of a lawyer. The reader, it is hoped, will bring the equally essential perspective of an insurer or insured. Combining the two perspectives should allow the reader or identify the limitations of insurability of pollution liability.

Discussion

1. Assessing the Risk of Liability for Environmental Pollution

An examination of the limitations of insurability of liability for environmental pollution must begin with an examination of the risk. The risk of liability for

[5] The term "property owner" refers to owners or operators of real or personal property.

environmental pollution can be broken down into the primary risk that one's act or omission will result in pollution or that pollution will occur or exist on one's property, and the next-order risk that one will be found to be liable for that pollution. Environmental audits will be discussed in the following subsection.

The next-order risk depends upon whether the property owner can be found liable under the applicable statutory and common law rules, as well as upon the probability that the enforcement authority (e.g. the federal, state or local government, or a private party) will in fact enforce the rules against a particular property owner. The liability rules will be discussed in the next subsection.

A. Assessing the Risk of Environmental Pollution — Environmental Audits

To identify and assess the primary risk, the risk of pollution, a property owner should survey the risks of pollution inherent in or resulting from its operations and property, define an acceptable limit of human and environmental exposure to these risks, based on any applicable legal limits and the cost of achieving any limit, and identify the ways in which the operations or property may be modified to reduce or eliminate the risks. This type of risk assessment survey is often called an "environmental audit."[6] Put simply, an auditor inquires into the elements present in the operations or property which create or contribute to a risk of pollution, and, by examining all applicable liability rules, the ways in which these elements expose the owner to liability.

An environmental audit can be broken down into four phases. In the first phase, the auditor[7] should review the records of the operations and property to gather information about the history of the property owner's compliance with environmental regulations and guidelines. If necessary, the auditor should obtain information about compliance from sources other than the property owner's records. This phase is generally the most time-consuming, the most comprehensive, and the most significant. In the second phase, the auditor should propose a programme of self-assessment based on the reviewed information, identifying the risks particular to this property owner, and the means for the property owner to assess these risks. A carefully drawn self-assessment programme will enable the insurer to provide coverage for specific risks it previously avoided or overlooked.

In the third phase, the auditor should gather and analyse information relevant to any areas of risk not subject to adequate self-assessment. Oftentimes these problem areas arise when the property owner lacks meaningful experience due to changes in its operations or modifications to its property; these areas are likely to pose the greatest risks. The sampling and analysis of the third phase is intended to remedy this lack of experience. In the fourth phase, the auditor should develop short-and long-term programmes for minimising and eliminating the risks of pollution, bearing in mind the costs of minimisation or elimination versus the cost of liability and other damages.

A good environmental audit should result in a list of the elements in the property owner's operations or property which cause or contribute to pollution, and an identification of the costs of reducing or eliminating these elements, as well as the costs if the elements are not reduced or eliminated, including the costs of liability. Armed with a good environmental audit, a property owner may be able to reduce or eliminate the risk that the pollution will result.

The property owner may decide to purchase insurance to reduce or eliminate the risk of pollution liability. An insurer who writes pollution liability coverage to reflect the particular risks identified by a thorough environmental audit specific to the insured is most likely to achieve an efficient result. The purchase of insurance, in and of itself, may result in a reduction of the risk of pollution if the insurer requires that the owner take certain steps to eliminate the elements.

Of course, a thorough environmental audit will be costly. The cost may be born solely by the owner, or its insurer may bear some or all of the costs. The amount of time and money spent on the audit must bear a reasonable relation to the potential cost of the potential liability. For this reason, environmental audits may be feasible for the smaller property owner.

Also, at least arguably, a thorough environmental audit may increase the probability that an owner would be found liable for pollution, insofar as the information gathered and generated by the auditor is held to be discoverable, admissible, and relevant in an enforcement action.[8] There is genuine concern that the audit information will not be protected from discovery by the attorney-client privilege or the attorney work product doctrine,[9] which may be mitigated by the EPA's announced policy not to discover the internal environmental audits performed by a potential violator in any enforcement action, for the purpose of not discouraging the performance of environmental audits. Further, there is a genuine concern that notwithstanding the strict liability theory underlying most pollution liability rules, the owner's knowledge of a particular risk of pollution will increase its liability. And finally, there is a genuine concern that the owner's knowledge of a particular risk may eliminate or reduce any insurance coverage.

B. Assessing the Risk of Liability for Environmental Pollution — The Liability Rules

An understanding of the legal rules governing liability for environmental pollution is essential to identifying the limitations of insurability of this risk. Three sources exist for imposing liability: the common law of the states, federal statutes, and state statutes.

1. LIABILITY FOR ENVIRONMENTAL POLLUTION UNDER THE COMMON LAW

Under the common law of most states, damages incurred as a result of environmental pollution may be recovered in tort actions for nuisance, trespass, and

[8] This concern has been raised e.g. in a recent article in *the Financial Times* ("Steps Towards a Pollution Insurance Market" 17 January 1992).

[9] Generally, documents generated in anticipation of litigation or enforcement actions, confidentially, by or for an attorney, are privileged from discovery by other parties. See e.g. Cal. Evid. Code §§ 950–954, Cal. Civ. Proc. Code § 2018; Fed. R.Civ. P. 26(b)(1), 26(b)(3).

strict liability for ultrahazardous activities.[10] In most instances, common law remedies will be available in addition to federal and state statutory remedies. For example, the federal statute governing liability for pollution arising from oil spills (the Oil Pollution Act[11]) states explicitly that state common law is not pre-empted.[12]

The tort of nuisance protests against an interference with the right to the beneficial use and enjoyment of real property.[13] Certain injunctive and damage remedies are available.[14] Air and water pollution, harmful deposits on land, and conditions creating a risk of injury to persons or property fall within the broad definition of nuisance.[15] Generally, liability for nuisance may be imposed upon any and all persons who have created or maintained the nuisance.[16] Defences to nuisance include governmental immunity, statutory authorization (e.g. zoning regulations), statute of limitations, laches, necessity, the plaintiff's consent, comparative fault or failure to mitigate damages.[17]

The tort of trespass, available only to a holder of a possessory interest in real property, protects against an actual physical intrusion on real property arising from tortious activity.[18] Certain injunctive and damage remedies are available.[19] Defences to trespass include privilege and the statute of limitations.[20]

Strict liability in tort may be imposed upon a finding that the defendant engaged in certain inherently dangerous, "ultrahazardous" activities, regardless of the nature of the rights injured by that activity.[21] Defences include the plaintiff's comparative fault or assumption of risk, and the statute of limitations.[22]

There is no federal common law of tort. However, there is a federal common law of maritime tort, under which damages incurred as a result of environmental pollution may be recovered in nuisance or negligence actions.

2. LIABILITY UNDER FEDERAL AND STATE ENVIRONMENTAL POLLUTION LIABILITY STATUTES

There are a number of significant federal statutes imposing liability for environmental pollution, and, depending on the state, parallel state statutes

[10] See generally, *California Environmental Law & Land Use Practice* § 1.01[1](1992).
[11] 33 U.S.C. §§ 2701–2761.
[12] Ibid. § 2718(a)
[13] *California Environmental Law & Land Use Practice* §§ 1.01[2], 1.20[4] (1992).
[14] Ibid. §1.01[2].
[15] Ibid. [3]
[16] Ibid. §1.03[1].
[17] Ibid. §1.07.
[18] Ibid. 1.20.
[19] Ibid. §1.22.
[20] Ibid.1.23.
[21] Ibid.1.30.
[22] Ibid.1.31.

imposing liability for the same incident of pollution. For example, the federal Oil Pollution Act[23] and California's Oil Spill Prevention and Response Act[24] both impose liability for oil spills. The federal Clean Water Act[25] and California's Water Quality Control Act[26] both impose liability for water pollution. The federal Clean Air Act[27] and California's Clean Air Act[28] both impose liability for air pollution.

In most instances, the federal statute states explicitly that states may enact more stringent pollution controls, and oftentimes, the federal statute will require that states enact controls at least as stringent as the federal controls. For example, the federal Oil Pollution Act provides explicitly that any state may impose additional liability and additional requirements.[29] The federal Clean Water Act directs states to adopt water quality standards to protect public health equally or more stringent than the federal standards.[30] The federal Clean Air Act allows states to adopt and enforce air pollution control programmes equally or more stringent than those under the Act.[31]

Many of the federal statutes direct federal agencies (e.g. the EPA, the United States Coast Guard) to work with the parallel state agencies. For example, the federal Oil Pollution Act authorises states to enforce, "on the navigable waters of the State", the requirements for evidence of financial responsibility.[32] The federal Clean Water Act directs states to administer the permit programme.[33]

A number of common issues arise in the enforcement of the federal and state statutes. First, to the extent that the statute retains a requirement of fault, establishing that a violator's actions or omissions caused or contributed to the pollution may be very difficult and costly. A requirement of fault may discourage co-operation from potential violators, in part because of the opportunity to escape liability and in part because of the difficulty in identifying one's obligations.[34] For these reasons, many statutes have eliminated fault as a requirement of a violation, although most have retained it to the extent that they impose greater penalties for intentional, grossly negligent, or knowing violations.

[23] 33 U.S.C. §§ 2701–2761.
[24] Cal. Gov't. Code §§ 8670.1–8670.12 and Cal. Pub. Res.Code §§ 8750–8760.
[25] 33 U.S.C. §§ 1251–1387 (formerly the Federal Water Pollution Control Act).
[26] Cal. Water Code §§ 13300–14076.
[27] 42 U.S.C. § 7401–7671q.
[28] Cal. Health & Safety Code §§ 39000–44384.
[29] 33 U.S.C. §§ 2718(a), 2718(c).
[30] Ibid. § 1313 and 40 C.F.R. § 131.4.
[31] 42 U.S.C. § 7416; Cal. Health & Safety Code §§ 39000–44384.
[32] 33 U.S.C. § 2719.
[33] Ibid. § 1342; 40 C.F.R. §§ 122.4, 123.25(a)(1).
[34] See e.g. Gastel, "Environmental Pollution: Insurance Issues," Ins. Info. Inst. Rep. (April 1992).

Second, to the extent that the strict liability that is imposed is retroactive — that is, liability is imposed upon persons who merely take possession or ownership of some personal or real property which generated pollution at some previous time — fairness concerns arise.[35] For example, hazardous waste statutes (e.g. the Comprehensive Environmental Response, Compensation and Liability Act (and its Superfund amendments),[36] the Resource Conservation and Recovery Act,[37] and the Hazardous Waste Control Act[38]) impose what is often called "cradle-to-grave" liability upon each person in that chain. These fairness concerns may motivate persons taking possession of property with potential pollution liability to attempt to allocate the risk of such liability before the former operator walks away. Walking away will not cut off liability, but it is likely to impose additional transactional costs on the current owner.

Third, where more than one party is potentially responsible, the joint and several liability which is imposed regardless of the inequal contributions, property interests or financial circumstances of the responsible parties, encourages further litigation (in the form of joinders of parties, for example), as well as raising fairness concerns.[39] For example, federal legislation has been proposed which would limit the ability of private responsible parties to join federal, state or local governments or agencies, in actions enforcing hazardous waste liability. Again, the threat of such joint and several liability may motivate potentially responsible parties to allocate the risk of such liability before any party walks away. However, most of the environmental pollution liability statutes provide that no indemnification or hold-harmless agreement will prevent enforcement against a particular party, although they are otherwise enforceable between the agreeing parties.[40]

Finally, even in the absence of disputes concerning the identity of the responsible parties, enforcement of the statutory liability may be hampered by disputes about the appropriate clean-up, remedial or abatement work, and about the reasonableness of the costs incurred by the claimants doing that work. Because this work is likely to take years, the agency or court enforcing the statute will be forced to estimate the cost of future work. A common complaint is that more money is spent on legal fees and costs than on clean-up work. The most recent federal and state statutes, in imposing strict liability and creating pre-litigation administrative claims procedures,[41] have been drafted with this complaint in mind.

[35] Ibid.
[36] 42 U.S.C. §§ 9601–9675.
[37] Ibid. §§ 6901–6992k.
[38] Cal. Health & Safety Code §§ 25100–25250.5.
[39] Ibid.
[40] See e.g. 33 U.S.C. § 2710.
[41] See e.g. ibid. § 2713 (claims procedure).

In the following subsections, the liability rules of the major federal pollution liability statutes — the Oil Pollution Act,[42] the Clean Water Act,[43] the Clean Air Act,[44] the Comprehensive Environmental Response, Compensation and Liability Act (and its Superfund amendments),[45] and the Resource Conservation and Recovery Act[46] — and two parallel state (California) statutes, the Oil Spill Prevention and Response Act[47] and the Hazardous Waste Control Act[48] — are summarised.

a. Liability under the Oil Pollution Act of 1990

Responsible parties

The Oil Pollution Act ("OPA")[49] defines "responsible parties" to mean owners, operators and demise charterers of non-public vessels; owners and operators of privately owned onshore facilities; lessees and permittees of privately owned offshore facilities; licensees of deepwater ports; and, owners and operators of pipelines.[50]

Elements of prima facie case

Each responsible party is liable for the removal costs and damages resulting from a discharge or threat of discharge of oil.[51]

Defences

The responsible party is entitled to a complete defence if it establishes two conditions: that the discharge or threat of discharge and resulting costs and damages were caused solely by an act of God; an act of war; or an act or omission of a third party, where that third party is not the responsible party's employee or agent, or a person in a contractual relationship with the responsible party; and, that the responsible party exercised due care and took precautions against foreseeable acts or omissions of such third party.[52] A showing that the responsible party failed to report the incident, failed to co-operate and assist the public officials, or failed to comply with any applicable order, will preclude a complete defence.[53] The responsible party is entitled to a partial defence against a particular claimant to the extent that the discharge or threat of discharge is caused by the claimant's gross negligence or wilful misconduct.[54] If the

[42] Ibid. §§ 2701–2761.
[43] Ibid. §§ 1251–1387.
[44] 42 U.S.C. §§ 7401–7671q.
[45] Ibid. §§ 9601–9675.
[46] Ibid. §§ 6901–6992k.
[47] Cal. Gov't. Code §§ 8670.1–8670.12 and Cal. Pub. Res. Code §§ 8750–8760.
[48] Cal. Health & Safety Code §§ 25100–25250.5.
[49] 33 U.S.C. §§ 2701–2761.
[50] Ibid. § 2701(32).
[51] Ibid. § 2702(a).
[52] Ibid. § 2703(a).
[53] Ibid. (c).
[54] Ibid. (b).

responsible party establishes that the discharge or threat of discharge and resulting costs and damages were caused solely by an act or omission of a third party, it is entitled to subrogation against that third party.[55]

Costs recoverable as damages

Recoverable removal costs include all removal costs incurred by the United States and any removal costs incurred by a private party for acts taken consistent with the national contingency plan, an outline of general pollution response measures prepared and published by the EPA.[56]

Recoverable damages include damages for injury to, destruction of, loss of, or loss of use of natural resources, including the reasonable costs of assessing such damages; damages for injury to, or economic losses resulting from destruction of, real or personal property; damages for loss of subsistence use of natural resources; damages equal to the net loss of taxes, royalties, rents, fees, or net profit shares due to the injury, destruction, or loss of real property, personal property, or natural resources; damages equal to the loss of profits or impairment of earning capacity due to the injury, destruction, or loss of real property, personal property, or natural resources; and, damages for net costs of providing increased or additional public services during or after removal activities.[57]

Limitation of liability

Liability for removal costs and damages is subject to the following limitations: for tank vessels greater than 3,000 gross tons, the greater of $1,200 per gross ton or $10,000,000; for tank vessels less than 3,000 gross tons, the greater of $1,200 per gross ton or $2,000,000; for all other vessels, the greater of $600 per gross ton or $500,000; for offshore facilities, the total of all removal costs plus $75,000,000; for onshore facilities and deepwater ports, $350,000,000.[58]

However, no limitation of liability applies if the discharge or threat of discharge was caused by the responsible party's gross negligence or wilful misconduct, or violation of an applicable federal safety, construction, or operating regulation.[59] Further, no limitation applies if the responsible party failed to report the incident, failed to co-operate and assist the public officials, or failed to comply with any applicable order.[60]

Financial responsibility requirements

Each responsible party must establish and maintain evidence of financial responsibility in a particular amount.[61] The amount varies from as little as the greater of $600 per gross ton or $500,000 for nontank vessels, to as much as the

[55] Ibid. § 2702(d).
[56] Ibid. §§ 2702(b), 2701(19).
[57] Ibid. § 2702(b).
[58] Ibid. § 2704(a).
[59] Ibid. (c).
[60] Ibid.
[61] Ibid. § 2716(a).

greater of $1,200 per gross ton or $10,000,000 for tank vessels greater than 3,000 gross tons.[62] Financial responsibility may be evidenced by any one or combination of the following methods: insurance, guarantee, surety bond, letter of credit, or qualification as self-insurer.[63] Where one entity owns or operates more than one vessel or facility, evidence of financial responsibility need only be established to meet the maximum liability applicable to the vessel or facility with the maximum liability.[64] Vessels without such evidence of financial responsibility shall be denied clearance and entry into any U.S. port or waters.[65]

By providing evidence of financial responsibility, the guarantor — that is, the insurer, the guarantor, the surety, or the issuer of the letter of credit — becomes subject to direct actions for claims arising from discharges or threats of discharges of oil.[66] The guarantor may invoke the defence that the incident was caused by the wilful misconduct of the responsible party, and the guarantor may invoke any defence available to the responsible party, but the guarantor may not raise any defence otherwise available against the responsible party.[67] The guarantor's liability is limited to the amount of the insurance policy, guarantee, surety bond, letter of credit or other instrument provided in compliance with the requirements for evidence of financial responsibility.[68]

b. *Liability under the Clean Water Act of 1972*

Responsible parties

Any person who discharges and pollutant[69] into navigable waters except in compliance with the water quality related effluent limitations,[70] national standards of performance,[71] toxic and pretreatment effluent standards, and discharge permits which implement these limitations and standards, violates the

[62] Ibid.; 56 Fed. Reg. 49006–49021 (26 September 1991) (proposed regulations implementing section 2716).

[63] 56 Fed. Reg. 49006–49021. § 2716(c).

[64] 33 U.S.C. § 2716.

[65] Ibid. (b).

[66] Ibid. (f).

[67] Ibid.

[68] Ibid.(g).

[69] A "pollutant" is defined as "dredged spoil, solid waste, incinerator residue, sewage, garbage, sewage sludge, munitions, chemical wastes, biological materials, radioactive materials, heat, wrecked or discarded equipment, rock, sand, cellar dirt and industrial, municipal and agricultural waste discharged into water". ibid. § 1362(6).

[70] An "effluent limitation" is any restriction established by a state or the EPA on quantities, rates, and concentrations of chemical, physical, biological, and other constituents which are discharged from point sources into navigable waters. ibid.(11).

[71] A "standard of performance" is a standard for the control of the discharge of pollutants which reflects the greatest degree of effluent reduction which the EPA determines to be achievable through application of the "best available demonstrated control technology, processes, operating methods, or other alternatives, including, where practicable, a standard permitting no discharge of pollutants". ibid § 1316(a). The EPA issues standards by category of source (e.g. pulp and paper mills, dairy product processing, iron and steel manufacturing) ibid. (b).

Clean Water Act ("CWA"),[72] and is subject to enforcement.[73] Generally, any person owning or operating a facility which discharges effluent into navigable waters, at a point or nonpoint source of discharge, must obtain a permit.[74]

In a section revised but not superseded by OPA, the CWA prohibits the discharge of oil or hazardous substances[75] into or on to navigable waters, in harmful quantities, and imposes administrative and civil penalties for such discharges.[76] The CWA states explicitly that any liability imposed under it does not affect any liability imposed under OPA.[77]

Elements of prima facie case

The CWA directs that certain effluent limitations be promulgated for point sources, limitations which require the application of the best practicable control technology currently available, as well as any more stringent limitations required to meet water quality or treatment standards, and, for certain identified categories of pollutants, limitations which require the application of the best available technology economically achievable.[78] Any person who discharges any pollutant not in compliance with these limitations violates the Act.[79] Similarly, any owner, operator, or person in charge of a vessel, onshore or offshore facility which discharges oil or hazardous substance violates the Act.[80]

Defences

There are no defenses as such under the CWA. Issuance of a compliance order, imposition of a civil penalty, and the filing of a civil action are mandatory upon the EPA's finding of a violation.[81] Imposition of an administrative penalty is discretionary.[82] Further, imposition of criminal penalties for negligent and knowing violations including knowing endangerment are mandatory.[83] A showing that the danger and conduct were reasonably foreseeable hazards of an occupation or treatment is an affirmative defence to a "knowing endangerment" charge, that is, a charge that the violation was committed with knowledge that the action put another person in imminent danger of death or serious bodily injury.[84] Private citizens may file civil actions against violators.[85]

[72] Ibid. §§ 1251–1387.
[73] Ibid. § 1311(a)
[74] Ibid. §§ 1342, 1311, 1314.
[75] The CWA directs the EPA to designate substances as "hazardous substances". ibid §§ 1321(a)(14), 1321(b)(2).
[76] Ibid. §§ 1321(b)(3), 1321(b)(6).
[77] Ibid. § 1321(c)(5).
[78] Ibid. § 1311(b).
[79] Ibid. (a).
[80] Ibid. § 1321(b)(3).
[81] Ibid. §§ 1319(a), 1319(d).
[82] Ibid. (g).
[83] Ibid. (c).
[84] Ibid. (3).
[85] Ibid. § 1365(a).

Costs recoverable as damages

While the CWA does not provide explicitly for recovery of costs as damages in a civil action brought against a violator of the Act's water pollution standards, presumably costs would be recoverable under general negligence principles. The CWA does provide explicitly that any costs of removal of discharged oil or hazardous substance are recoverable in a civil action brought to enforce the oil and hazardous substance discharge section of the Act.[86]

The civil penalty for violation is limited to not more than $25,000 per day for each violation (in addition to any injunctive relief).[87] The criteria to be considered in determining the amount of the civil penalty includes the seriousness of the violation, the economic benefit if any resulting from the violation, any history of such violations, any good-faith efforts to comply with the applicable requirements, and the economic impact of the penalty on the violator.[88] The administrative penalty is limited to not more than $25,000 per "single operational upset which leads to simultaneous violations of more than one pollution parameter".[89]

Negligent violations and "knowing" violations may give rise to criminal penalties. The criminal penalty for a negligent violation is limited to a fine of not less than $2,500 nor more than $25,000 per day of violation or imprisonment for not more than one year or both.[90] The criminal penalty for knowing violations are limited to a fine of not less than $5,000 and not more than $50,000 per day or imprisonment for not more than three years or both.[91] The criminal penalty for "knowing endangerment" charges is limited to a fine of not more than $250,000 or imprisonment of not more than fifteen years or both.[92]

Any owner, operator, or person in charge of a vessel, onshore or offshore facility from which oil or hazardous substance is discharged may be subject to an administrative penalty (not more than $10,000 per day for each day during which the violation continues, up to $125,000), and to a civil penalty (not more than $25,000 per day of violation or $1,000 per barrel of oil or substance discharged).[93] If the violation is committed with gross negligence, the civil penalty increases to not less than $100,000 and not more than $3,000 per barrel of oil or substance discharged.[94]

Financial responsibility requirements

The Oil Pollution Act repealed the financial responsibility requirements under the CWA for owners, operators and persons in charge of vessels, onshore and

[86] Ibid. § 1321(b)(1).
[87] Ibid. §§ 1319(d).
[88] Ibid.
[89] Ibid. (g).
[90] Ibid. (c).
[91] Ibid.
[92] Ibid.
[93] Ibid. §§ 1321(b)(6), 1321(b)(7).
[94] Ibid. (b)(7)(D).

offshore facilities relating to potential discharges of oil and hazardous substances[95] Congress indicated that it intended to replace the numerous separate requirements (under the Comprehensive Environmental Response, Compensation and Liability Act as well as the CWA) with unified requirements.[96]

c. *Liability under the Clean Air Act of 1955*

Responsible parties

Any person who violates any requirement of any applicable implementation plan or permit issued pursuant to the Clean Air Act ("CAA")[97] is subject to enforcement.[98] Owners and operators of sources of air pollution ("affected sources", "major emitting facilities" and "major stationary sources") must obtain permits under the Act.[99] "Stationary sources" include any building, structure, facility or installation which emits or may emit any air pollutant.[100] "Owners or operators" include persons who own, lease, operate, control or supervise a stationary source, and any "senior management personnel or a corporate officer."[101]

Elements of prima facie case

The CAA lists the substances to be designated "hazardous air pollutants."[102] The EPA is directed to promulgate emission standards for each category of sources of hazardous air pollutants.[103] Once the EPA has set a specific emission standard for a particular category of source of pollutant, any person who constructs a new major source or continues to operate an existing source in excess of this standard violates the CAA and is subject to enforcement.[104] More specifically, any person who operates an affected source, major source, or other source in the absence of or in violation of a permit issued pursuant to the Act, violates the Act and is subject to enforcement.[105]

Defences

There are no defences as such under the CAA. Insurance of a compliance order, imposition of an administrative penalty and the filing of a civil action are all discretionary.[106] When an owner or operator of an affected source, a major emitting facility, or a major stationary source violates the Act, for example, by

[95] See ibid. (p) (repealed in 1990).
[96] See 56 Fed. Reg. 49006–49021 (26 September 1991) (proposed regulations implementing section 2716 on financial responsibility).
[97] 42 U.S.C. §§ 7401–7671g.
[98] Ibid. §§ 7412(i), 7413(a), 7413(b), 7661a(a).
[99] Ibid. §§ 7413(a), 7413(b).
[100] Ibid. § 7411(a)(3).
[101] Ibid. (5), 7413(h).
[102] Ibid. § 7412(b).
[103] Ibid. (c), 7412(d).
[104] Ibid. (i).
[105] Ibid. § 7661a(a).
[106] Ibid. §§ 7413(a), 7413(d).

failing to comply with emission standards in applicable implementation plans, imposition of a civil penalty is mandatory.[107] Further, imposition of criminal penalties upon conviction for knowing violations including "knowing endangerment" are mandatory.[108] A showing that the danger and conduct were reasonably foreseeable hazards of an occupation or treatment is an affirmative defence to a knowing endangerment charge.[109] Private citizens may file civil actions against violators.[110]

Full or partial exemptions from compliance dates may prevent an imposition of liability. The EPA is authorised to establish compliance dates for particular categories of existing sources, not more than three years after the effective date of the emission standard, before which no violation may arise.[111] Also, the President may exempt any stationary source from compliance with an emission standard for a period of not more than two years if the technology to achieve that standard is unavailable.[112] And, the EPA may issue permits which allow only partial compliance to existing sources which have achieved a 90% reduction in emission.[113] And, where an existing source has installed the best available control technology (as defined by the CAA), or the technology required to meet a lowest achievable emission rate (as defined by the CAA), the compliance date will be no sooner than five years from the date such technology was installed.[114]

Costs recoverable as damages

While the CAA does not provide explicitly for recovery of costs as damages in a civil action brought against a violator of the Act, presumably costs would be recoverable under general negligence principles.

The civil penalty for violation is limited to not more than $25,000 per day for each violation (in addition to any injunctive relief).[115] Criminal penalties for knowing violations are limited, and imprisonment may not exceed five years.[116]

The CAA sets out the criteria to be considered in assessing penalties: the size of the business, the economic impact of the penalty on the business, the violator's full compliance history and good faith efforts to comply the duration of the violation, payment by the violator of penalties previously assessed for the same violation, the economic benefit of non-compliance, and the seriousness of the violation.[117]

[107] Ibid. (b), 7420(a).
[108] Ibid. § 7413(c).
[109] Ibid. (5)(C).
[110] Ibid. § 7604(a).
[111] Ibid. § 7412(i)(3).
[112] Ibid. (4).
[113] Ibid. (5).
[114] Ibid. (6).
[115] Ibid. §§ 7413(b), 7413(d).
[116] Ibid. (c).
[117] Ibid. (e).

Financial responsibility requirements

The CAA does not require permit holders (that is, owners and operators of facilities for the treatment, storage and or disposal of hazardous waste) to establish and maintain evidence of financial responsibility.

d. Liability under the Comprehensive Environmental Response, Compensation and Liability Act of 1980, and the Superfund Amendments and Reauthorization Act of 1986

Responsible parties

The Comprehensive Environmental Response, Compensation and Liability Act, and the Superfund Amendments and Reauthorization Act of 1986 ("CERCLA")[118] holds as responsible all persons connected with a release or threatened release of a hazardous substance[119], including owners and operators of vessels and disposal facilities, and persons arranging for or contracting to transport or treat hazardous substances.[120]

Elements of prima facie case

CERCLA directs the EPA to designate as "hazardous" the types and amounts of substances "which, when released into the environment may present substantial danger to the public health or welfare or the environment".[121] All persons connected with a release or threatened release of a hazardous substance are liable for recoverable costs and damages.[122]

Defences

Persons otherwise liable are excused entirely if thcy cstablish that the release or threat of release of a hazardous substance and the damages resulting therefrom were caused solely by an act of God; an act of war; or, an act or omission of a third party other than their employee or agent, or a person acting in connection with a contractual relationship, but only if they also establish that they exercised due care with respect to the hazardous substance concerned, and that they took precautions against foreseeable acts or omissions of such third party.[123]

118 Ibid. §§ 9601–9675.

119 CERCLA defines "hazardous substance" to include those substances designated as "hazardous" by the EPA pursuant to CERCLA (42 U.S.C. § 9602), the CWA (33 U.C.C. §§ 1321(b)(2)(A), 1317(a) ("toxic pollutant")), the Solid Waste Disposal Act (42 U.S.C. § 6921), the CAA (33 U.S.C. § 7412), the Toxic Substances Control Act (15 U.S.C. § 2606); and, to exclude petroleum, including crude oil, and natural gas. 42 U.S.C. § 9601(14).

120 42 U.S.C. § 9607(a). The breadth of the scope of CERCLA's liability is illustrated by a recent decision holding that parties who arrange for raw materials to be formulated into finished products are responsible parties for purposes of CERCLA liability. See *Jones-Hamilton Co.* v. *Beazer Materials & Serv. Inc.*, 92 C.D.O.S. 2131 (9th Cir. Mar. 12, 1992).

121 42 U.S.C. § 9602(a). See also ibid. § 9601(14) (definition of "hazardous substance").

122 Ibid. § 9607(a).

123 Ibid. (b).

Costs recoverable as damages

Recoverable costs and damages include all costs of removal and remedial actions, and any other necessary costs, incurred by the United States or any other person, which are not inconsistent with the national contingency plan; damages for injury to, destruction of, or loss of natural resources, including the reasonable costs of assessing such injury, destruction or loss; and, the costs of any health assessment or health effects studies carried out pursuant to the Act.[124] Further, CERCLA entitles the United States to an award of punitive damages in an amount at least equal to but not to exceed three times the recoverable costs where the responsible party "fails without sufficient cause to properly provide removal or remedial action".[125] And, CERCLA grants a lien to the United States for the costs and damages it incurs against all real property of the responsible party, and a maritime lien against the vessel where the responsible party is a vessel.[126]

Limitation of liability

For each release of a hazardous substance, or each incident involving such release, the liability of each responsible party shall not exceed $300 per gross ton or $5 million, whichever is greater, for cargo-carrying vessels; $300 per gross ton or $500,000, whichever is greater, for all other non-incineration vessels; between $5 million and $50 million for any motor vehicle, aircraft, pipeline or rolling stock; and, the total of all costs of response plus $50 million for any incineration vessel or facility.[127]

No limitation is available where the release or threat of release of hazardous substance was the result of wilful misconduct or wilful negligence within the privity or knowledge of the responsible party; a violation within the privity or knowledge of the responsible party of an applicable safety, construction or operating standard or regulation; or, the failure to co-operate and assist the public officials with respect to the national contingency plan.[128]

Financial responsibility requirements

Owners and operators of vessels (over 300 gross tons) (excluding non self-propelled barges that do not carry hazardous substances as cargo) must establish and maintain evidence of financial responsibility in the amount of $300 per gross ton or $5 million, which is greater, by any one or combination of the following: insurance, guarantee, surety bond, or qualification as self-insurer.[129] Where one entity owns or operates more than one vessel, evidence of financial responsibility need only be established to meet the maximum liability applicable

[124] Ibid. (a)(4).
[125] Ibid. (c)(3).
[126] Ibid. §§ 9607(1) and 9607(m).
[127] Ibid. (c)(1).
[128] Ibid. (2).
[129] Ibid. § 9608(a).

to the largest vessel.[130] Vessels without such evidence of financial responsibility shall be denied clearance and entry into any U.S. port or waters.[131]

In enacting the Oil Pollution Act, Congress indicated that it intended to replace the numerous separate requirements for financial responsibility for vessels for water pollution (under CERCLA as well as CWA) with unified requirements.[132] Thus, the proposed federal regulations would require vessel owners and operators to obtain a single certificate of financial responsibility for OPA, CERCLA and CWA.[133]

Owners and operators of facilities which produce, transport, treat, store or dispose of hazardous substances must establish and maintain evidence of financial responsibility in an amount set forth in the applicable regulations.[134] When a facility is owned or operated by more than one entity, evidence of financial responsibility may be established by one of the owners or operators, or in consolidated form.[135]

By providing evidence of financial responsibility, the guarantor becomes subject to direct actions for claims arising from releases or threats of releases of hazardous substances.[136] The guarantor may invoke the defence that the incident was caused by the wilful misconduct of the responsible party, but the guarantor may not raise any defence otherwise available against the responsible party.[137] The guarantor's liability is limited to the amount of the insurance policy, guarantee, surety bond, letter of credit or other instrument provided in compliance with the requirements for evidence of financial responsibility.[138]

e. *Liability under the Resource Conservation and Recovery Act of 1976*

Responsible parties

Any person who violates a standard or regulation issued pursuant to the Resource Conservation and Recovery Act ("RCRA")[139] is subject to enforcement.[140] The standards apply to hazardous waste generators, transporters, and owners and operators of facilities for the treatment, storage, and disposal of hazardous waste.[141]

130 Ibid.
131 Ibid.
132 See 56 Fed. Reg. 49006–49021 (26 September 1991) (proposed regulations implementing section 2716 on financial responsibility).
133 Ibid.
134 42 U.S.C. § 9608(b).
135 Ibid.
136 Ibid. (c).
137 Ibid.
138 Ibid. (d).
139 Ibid. §§ 6901–6992k.
140 Ibid. §§ 6928(a), 6928(d), and 6972.
141 Ibid. §§ 6922–6924.

Elements of prima facie case

RCRA's stated objectives include the prohibition of open dumping of solid waste on land; the conversion of existing open dump sites to sites safe for the environment and public health; and, the promulgation of guidelines for solid waste collection, transport, separation, recovery and disposal practices safe for the environment and public health.[142] RCRA directs the EPA to promulgate general guidelines for solid waste management; identify and list the particular "hazardous wastes" subject to the Act; and, establish standards applicable to hazardous waste generators, transporters, and owners and operators of hazardous waste generators, transporters, and owners and operators of hazardous waste treatment, storage and disposal facilities governing record-keeping, labelling, containerisation, composition analyses, manifest systems, and minimisation practices.[143] Owners and operators of facilities for the treatment, storage and or disposal of hazardous waste must obtain RCRA permits, and operate their facilities accordingly.[144]

Defences

No defences are available as such. The issuance of a compliance order and the filing of a civil action is discretionary, but the imposition of a civil penalty for a violation of RCRA or a compliance order is mandatory.[145] The imposition of criminal penalties is mandatory for knowing violations (e.g. transporting hazardous waste "knowingly" to a facility which lacks a permit), including "knowing endangerment" violations.[146] A showing that the danger and conduct were reasonably foreseeable hazards of an occupation or treatment is an affirmative defence to a "knowing endangerment" charge.[147] Private citizens also file civil actions against violators.[148]

Costs recoverable as damages

While RCRA does not provide explicitly for recovery of costs as damages in a civil action brought against a violator of the Act, presumably costs would be recoverable under general negligence principles.

Civil penalties for violations of the Act or a compliance order may not exceed $25,000 for each day of violation or continued non-compliance with the order.[149] Criminal penalties for knowing violations are limited to not more than $50,000 for each day of violation or imprisonment not to exceed five years or both, while the penalties for "knowing endangerment" charges increase to not more than $250,000 or imprisonment of not more than 15 years or both.[150]

[142] Ibid. § 6902(a).
[143] Ibid. §§ 6907(a), 6921(a), 6921(b), 6922–6924.
[144] Ibid. § 6925(a).
[145] Ibid. §§ 6928(a), 6928(g).
[146] Ibid. (d), 6928(e).
[147] Ibid. (f).
[148] Ibid. § 6972.
[149] Ibid. §§ 6928(c), 6928(g).
[150] Ibid. (d), 6928(e).

Financial responsibility requirements

RCRA does not require permit holders (that is, owners and operators of facilities for the treatment, storage and or disposal of hazardous waste) to establish and maintain evidence of financial responsibility.

f. Liability under the California Oil Spill Prevention and Response Act of 1990

Responsible parties

The California Oil Spill Prevention and Response Act ('OSPRA")[151] defines "responsible parties" to include owners and transporters of oil, and any person accepting responsibility for the oil; and, owners, operators, lessees, and demise-charterers of vessels and marine facilities, and any person accepting responsibility for the vessel or marine facilities and any person accepting responsibility for the vessel or marine facility.[152].

Elements of prima facie case

OSPRA states that "[a]ny person who, without regard to intent or negligence, causes or permits any oil to be discharged in or on the marine waters of the state shall immediately contain, cleanup, and remove the oil."[153] More broadly, OSPRA requires those parties merely "potentially" responsible for the discharged oil, to carry out response and clean-up operations at the direction of the state administrator or the United States Coast Guard.[154] Specifically, responsible and potentially responsible parties are required to clean up the oil, abate the effects of the discharge, and take the necessary steps to prevent further discharge.[155]

Defences

OSPRA imposes absolute liability without regard to fault.[156] Where more than one party is responsible, liability is joint and several.[157] Liability for damages, distinct from the costs of removal, is not imposed when the damages arise in the event of war, natural disaster or other act of God, or when caused solely by the negligence or intentional malfeasance of the injured party or a third party's criminal act.[158] Immunity is available to persons undertaking clean-up and response work under limited circumstances.[159]

Costs recoverable as damages

Costs recoverable as damages include all costs of response, containment, clean-up, removal, treatment; economic losses resulting from injury to real or personal

[151] Cal. Gov't Code §§ 8670.1–8670.12 and Cal. Pub. Res. Code §§ 8750–8760.
[152] Cal. Gov't. Code § 8670.3(n).
[153] Ibid. § 8760.25.
[154] Ibid. § 8670.27.
[155] Ibid. 62(a).
[156] Ibid. 56.5.
[157] Ibid. (h).
[158] Ibid. 56.5.
[159] Ibid. 56.

property; injury to or loss of natural resources; loss of taxes, royalties, rents and profit resulting from injury to real or personal property or natural resources; loss of profit or impairment of earning capacity resulting from injury to real or personal property or natural resources; and, loss of use or enjoyment of natural resources.[160]

A civil penalty of not less than $25,000 and not more than $500,000 per intentional or negligent violation may be imposed.[161] Alternatively, a civil administrative penalty of not more than $100,000 for each intentional or negligent violation may be imposed.[162] And, a civil penalty of not more than $10 per gallon of discharged oil may be imposed without regard to intent or negligence, increasing to not more than $30 per gallon in the case of gross negligence or reckless conduct.[163] Criminal penalties may be imposed, not more than a $50,000 fine nor imprisonment for one year or both, where a person knowingly fails to begin clean-up, abatement or removal steps, or otherwise fails to abide directions given in connection with an oil spill, or violates any other provision of OSPRA.[164]

Financial responsibility requirements

Vessels which transport oil, marine terminal operators, and marine facility operators must establish and maintain evidence of financial responsibility, that is, a certificate of financial responsibility.[165] A certificate of financial responsible is conclusive evidence that the holder is a responsible party for that vessel, terminal or facility.[166] Financial responsibility may be demonstrated by evidence of insurance, surety bond, letter of credit, qualifications as a self-insurer, or any combination of the foregoing.[167] Vessel operators must demonstrate the ability to pay at least $500 million for damages that may result during the term of the certificate; marine facility operators must demonstrate the ability to pay for all damages that would be caused by a reasonable worst case oil spill arising from the facility.[168] Owners or operators of more than one vessel, terminal or facility must obtain one certificate for all of the vessels, terminals or facilities.[169]

Significantly, OSPRA provides explicitly that where a spill occurs from one or more of the vessels or facilities, and the potential damages from such spill exceed five % of the financial resources reflected by the certificate, the certificate shall be deemed inapplicable to any other vessel or facility owned or operated

[160] Ibid. 56.5(g).
[161] Ibid. 66.
[162] Ibid. 67.
[163] Ibid. 67.5.
[164] Ibid. §§ 8670.64, 8670.65.
[165] Ibid. § 8670.37.51.
[166] Ibid. 52.
[167] Ibid. 54.
[168] Ibid. 53.
[169] Ibid. 55.

by that party, and the owner or operator will be required to demonstrate "the amount of financial ability required pursuant to this article, as well as the financial ability to pay all damages which arise or have arisen from the spill or spills which have occurred."[170]

g. Liability under the California Hazardous Waste Control Act of 1972

Responsible parties
The California Hazardous Waste Control Act ("HWCA")[171] makes it unlawful for any person to "manage" any hazardous waste except as provided by the Act.[172]

Elements of prima facie case
HWCA directs a state department to adopt standards and regulations for the management of hazardous waste.[173] Further, the department is to issue permits to hazardous waste facilities (facilities for the treatment, transfer, storage, resource recovery, disposal or recycling of hazardous waste).[174] Violations of any standard, regulation issued pursuant to the Act, making false statements in a compliance document, and disposing of hazardous waste at an unauthorized point, may give rise to liability.[175]

"Hazardous waste" is defined as a waste or combination of wastes which because of its quantity, concentration, or physical, chemical, or infectious characteristics may either cause or contribute to an increase in mortality or serious irreversible illness, or pose a substantial hazard to human health or the environment when improperly treated, stored, transported or dispose of, or otherwise managed, including but not limited to "hazardous waste" under RCRA.[176] "Waste" includes discarded, relinquished, and recycled material, and mislabelled and badly packaged material which poses a threat to public health or the environment.[177] "Hazardous waste management" is defined as the transportation, transfer, recycling, recovery, disposal, handling, processing, storage and treatment of hazardous waste.[178]

The state's programme is to be in lieu of a federal programme under RCRA, and thus it must meet the minimum requirements of RCRA.[179] Further, the state's programme is to implement any and all responsibilities imposed by CERCLA.[180]

170 Ibid. (b).
171 Cal. Health & Safety Code §§ 25100–25250.5.
172 Ibid. § 25154.
173 Ibid. § 25150.
174 Ibid. § 25117.1.
175 Ibid. § 25189.2.
176 Ibid. § 25117.
177 Ibid. § 25124.
178 Ibid. § 25117.2.
179 Ibid. §§ 25159, 25159.5.
180 Ibid. § 25159.7.

Defences

There are no defences as such. HWCA authorizes a state department and any state health officer to enforce the standards and regulations issued pursuant to the Act.[181] A civil action for injunctive relief is discretionary.[182] Actions for civil or criminal penalties for intentional, negligent, or knowing violations are mandatory.[183]

Costs recoverable as damages

Civil penalties for intentional or negligent violations are limited to nor more than $25,000 per day of continuing violation, and criminal penalties for knowing violations are limited to not less than $5,000 and not more than $250,000 for each day of violation, or not more than three years' imprisonment or both.[184] Additionally, violation of any standard or regulation constitutes a misdemeanour punishable by a fine of not more than $1,000 or six months' imprisonment or both.[185]

Financial responsibility requirements

HCWA directs the department to adopt standards and regulations specifying the financial assurance to be provided by owners and operators of hazardous waste facilities "that are necessary to respond adequately to damage claims arising out of the operation of that type of facility and to provide for the cost of closure and subsequent maintenance of the facility".[186] This financial assurance may be a trust fund, surety bond, letter of credit, insurance, or other acceptable financial arrangement.[187]

II. Insuring the risk of liability for environmental pollution

Limitations to the insurability of the risk of environmental pollution liability arise from the lack of adequate environmental audits, the lack of claims history, the uncertainty of coverage under existing policies, and the likelihood of resulting litigation, and the sheer magnitude of the potential liability. In the following section, the history of coverage for pollution liability, and the common coverage disputes are reviewed.

A. Coverage for environmental pollution liability under comprehensive general liability policies

Before the advent of coverage written specifically to insure against pollution liability, property owners made claims under their existing comprehensive general liability ("CGL") policies or their existing property policies. CGL

[181] Ibid. § 25180.
[182] Ibid. § 25181.
[183] Ibid. §§ 25189, 25189.6.
[184] Ibid. §§ 25189, 25189.6, 25191.
[185] Ibid. § 25190.
[186] Ibid. § 25245.
[187] Ibid.

coverage is "third party" coverage, covering the liability of the insured to another person, and property coverage is "first party" coverage, covering injury or damage sustained by the insured.

A property owner would make a pollution liability claim under a first-party property policy rather than a third-party CGL policy if the costs it incurred as a result of the liability were sustained by the insured but not as a result of any legal obligations. Just what this means is not clear, as the litigation on the meaning of the "damages" in a CGL policy (discussed below) demonstrates. Generally the costs are incurred as a result of liability imposed by federal or state statutes. Thus, pollution liability claims by their very nature fall within third-party rather than first-party coverage. However, an "owned property" or other exclusion might eliminate coverage under a CGL policy.

Prior to 1966, CGL policies covered bodily injury and damage caused by "accidents," where "accidents" were defined as "unexpected happenings without intention or design." In 1966, the standard CGL policy was changed to replace "accidents" with "occurrences," where "occurrences" are defined as an accidents resulting in damage neither expected nor intended by the insured. In 1973, a pollution exclusion was added to the standard CGL policy, to exclude coverage for all claims other than those arising from "sudden and accidental" discharge of pollutants.

In sum, then, the pre-1986 standard CGL policy obligates the insurer to pay on behalf of the insured all sums which the insured is legally obligated to pay as damages because of bodily injury or property damage to which the policy applies caused by an "occurrence," including property damage arising from "sudden and accidental" releases of pollutant and excluding property damage arising from all other releases of pollutants.

The standard policy was revised again in 1986, this time to bar all coverage for pollution liability claims. Currently, coverage for pollution liability, oftentimes called "environmental impairment liability" ("EIL") coverage, must be purchased separately. When insurers realized that the injury or damage resulting from pollution is often not discoverable until years after the triggering act or omission, many decided to write "claims made" rather than "occurrences made" pollution liability coverage.[188]

For example, coverage for pollution liability may be provided on a "claims-made" policy, where the policy obligates the insurer to indemnify the insured for property damage claims made during the policy period which result from "emission, discharge, release, or escape of any solid, liquid, gaseous, or thermal contaminants, irritants, or pollutants directly from the insured site into or upon the land", and "insured site" refers to listed sites and any site "to which waste materials were legally consigned or delivered by a named insured for storage, disposal, processing, or treatment, provided that the site … was duly authorized

[188] See e.g. Kroll, "'Claims Made' — Industry's Alternative: 'Pay as You Go' Products Liability Insurance," *Ins. L. J.* (February 1976).

for such storage, disposal, processing, or treatment under a permit issued by state or federal authority and in force at the time of all such consignment or delivery."

B. Common Coverage Disputes

Coverage litigation involves the interpretation of policy language where the meaning of language is not clear, in light of the reasonable expectations of the insurer and the insured, and any applicable public policy of the forum state, including the desire for predictability of coverage, and the desire to protect public health and the environment. Oftentimes the litigation reaches the point where the court must determine the extent to which public policy overrides the plain meaning of policy language, or the parties' reasonable expectations.[189] As might be expected, claims for pollution liability made under CGL policies frequently give rise to coverage litigation. The following are common issues in such litigation.

1. ARE GOVERNMENT-MANDATED COSTS "DAMAGES"?

Courts are split over whether government-mandated costs are insurable "damages" within the scope of CGL coverage. The language at issue in the standard CGL policy states that the insurer "will pay on behalf of the insured all sums which the insured shall become legally obligated to pay as damages because of… property damage." Alternative language states that the insurer will provide coverage for "all sums which the insured shall become obligated to pay by reason of the liability ... imposed upon the insured by law ... for damages on account of ... property damage."

Insurers argue that the costs an insured may incur because of government clean-up orders arise from "equitable" rather than "legal" authority; that they constitute "restitution" rather than "damages;"[190] and that the clean-up orders are not predicated on any "wrong" committed by the insured, and thus in the absence of a "wrong," there can be no "damages".[191] Further, the argument goes, if the clean-up order concerns the insured's own property, rather than a third party's property, the costs cannot be "damages".[192]

Many courts hold to the contrary. A recent decision by the California Supreme Court holds that government-mandated costs are "damages" under a CGL policy, reasoning that either such costs are plainly "damages" the insured

[189] In *Summitt Assoc., Inc.* v. *Liberty Mut. Fire Ins. Co.*, 229 N.J. Super. 56, 550 A.2d 1235 (1988), the appellate court reversed the trial court's ruling that the health, safety and welfare of the people of New Jersey outweighed the express provisions of the insurance policy, commenting that no legal principle permits a court to "circumvent what the contract says".

[190] This argument arises from the fact that the statues explicitly authorising the government to issue the clean-up order typically authorise actions for injunctive relief, and injunctive relief is a form of equitable relief.

[191] See generally *AIU Ins. Co.* v *Superior Court*, 51 Cal. 3d 807, 819–821, 274 Cal. Rptr. 826, 829–831 (1990).

[192] Ibid.

is "legally obligated" to pay as a result of property damage, or, the language is ambiguous, and must be construed in favour of the insured.[193] Decisions by courts in Massachusetts, Minnesota, North Carolina, Washington and Iowa reach the same conclusion.[194] On the other hand, courts in Maine and New Hampshire have reached the opposite conclusion. And, very recently, an appellate court in Maryland ruled that an insurer was not obligated to compensate its insured under a CGL policy for the costs the insured incurred in complying voluntarily with a clean-up order issued by the state.[195]

2. DOES THE EXCLUSION FOR POLLUTION UNLESS "SUDDEN AND ACCIDENTAL" EXCLUDE ONLY "EXPECTED OR INTENDED" POLLUTION?

Courts are also split on the construction of pollution exclusion clauses in post-1973 CGL policies. The language at issue states that the insurance does not apply to

> "bodily injury or property damage arising out of the discharge, dispersal, release or escape of smoke, vapors, soot, fumes, acids, alkalis, toxic chemicals, liquids or gases, waste materials or other irritants, contaminants or pollutants into or upon land, the atmosphere or any water course or body of waters, but this exclusion does not apply if such discharge, dispersal, release or escape is sudden and accidental."

Insurers argue that pollution arising from the continuous discharge of hazardous substances over many years cannot be considered a fortuitous, "sudden and accidental" event. However, many courts have construed the pollution exclusion as nothing more than an "occurrence" requirement, holding that it eliminates coverage only where such injury or damage appears to be expected or intended by the insured.[196] Thus, liability for the clean-up of underground hazardous waste would be covered.[197]

The U.S. Court of Appeals for the Fourth Circuit recently disagreed, reasoning that it would violate principles of construction to construe the pollution exclusion as nothing more than an "occurrence" requirement, and that the language clearly states that only "sudden and accidental" discharge of pollutants will give rise to coverage.[198] Thus, liability for the clean-up of a site the insured used to dispose of its processing wastes was not covered, where the dumping of waste at a particular land-fill was "performed as a part of a regular business activity" and thus not "accidental".[199] Courts that have reached the

193 Ibid. 819, 274 Cal. Rptr. 829.
194 See ibid. 819–821, 274 Cal. Rptr. 829–831. See also Gastel, n. 34, *supra*.
195 See Beller, "Pollution Compliance Not Covered, Court Says," *Journal of Commerce* 9 April 1992.
196 See e.g. *Summit Assoc.* v. *Liberty Mut. Fire Ins. Co.*, 229 N.J. Super. 56, 550 A.2d 1235 (1988), *citing Jackson Township* v. *Hartford Accident & Indem. Co.*, 186 N.J. Super. 156 (1982).
197 Ibid.
198 *Liberty Mut. Ins. Co.* v. *Triangle Indus., Inc.*, 1992 U.S. App. LEXIS 3437 (4th Cir. 1992).
199 Ibid.

opposite conclusion have read the "sudden and accidental" language as referring to the damages, rather than to the discharge.[200]

The Fourth Circuit decision also interpreted a "modified" pollution exclusion in later-issued CGL policies, identical to the standard pollution exclusion except that the last clause now reads,

> "but this exclusion does not apply to bodily injury or property damage included within the property hazard or the completed operations hazard if the discharge, dispersal, release, or escape originates away from premises owned by, rented or loaned to a named insured.

"Product hazard" and "completed operations hazard" refer to the protection offered to insureds who produce goods or services which give rise to a risk of injury or loss to persons or property. The court held that disposal of processing waste did not qualify as either a "product hazard" or "completed operations hazard," and thus the exclusion did apply.[201]

Disputes about the enforceability of the pollution exclusion continues. In a case currently pending before a federal district court in Illinois, the court will decide whether liability for the damages caused by contaminated oil allegedly from the insured's leaky transformers is covered, or excluded under the standard pollution exclusion.[202]

Another exclusion in CGL policies which may eliminate coverage for certain pollution liability claims is the exclusion for property damage to "property owned or occupied by or rented to the insured" or "property used by the insured". For example, a recent decision from an appellate court in New Jersey upheld the trial court's ruling that an insurer could not deny coverage for claims arising from the cleanup of hazardous waste buried underneath the insured's property on the basis of the pollution exclusion (or that the discovery of the waste was not an "occurrence"), but reversed the trial court's ruling that the "owned property" exclusion was unenforceable because of public policy.[203]

3. WHEN IS COVERAGE TRIGGERED?

Given that CGL coverage is on an "occurrences" basis, it is often difficult to determine what constitutes the "occurrence" which triggers coverage. Interpretation of the term "occurrence" varies depending upon whether a single event resulted in an immediate injury (e.g. an explosion), a single event resulted in delayed, gradual or continuing injury (e.g. a chemical spill), or a gradual or continuing event resulted in single or multiple injuries (e.g. asbestos or toxic waste exposure). Coverage for a particular instance of pollution liability may turn on when the event causing the pollution occurred, when the injury or

[200] *Broadwell Realty Serv., Inc.* v. *Fidelity & Casualty Co.*, 218 N.J. Super. 516, 528 A.2d 76 (1987).

[201] *Liberty Mut. Ins. Co.*, 1992 U.S. App. LEXIS 3437.

[202] Maxey, "Illinois Judge Dismiss Defenses in Spill Case", *Journal of Commerce* 9 April 1992.

[203] *Summit Assoc.*, 229 N.J. Super. 56, 550 A.2d 1235.

damage resulting from the pollution occurred, when the insured discovered the event causing the pollution, or when the insured discovered the resulting injury or damage.

The language at issue in the standard CGL policy defines an "occurrence" as "accident, including continuous or repeated exposure to conditions, which results in bodily injury or property damage neither expected nor intended from the standpoint of the insured."

Insurers argue that the insurable injury and damage "occurred" prior to the effective date of the policy if the insured discovered or should have discovered the insurable injury and damage prior to that date.[204] Additionally, insurers argue that if the risk of insurable injury and damage was known at the time the policy was purchased, the otherwise insurable injury and damage was "expected" and "intended" and therefore not insurable because not an "occurrence." This latter argument — that there is no "occurrence" because the injury or damage was a "known loss" — may arise when a federal or state agency notifies an insured that it is a responsible or potentially responsible party under a pollution liability statute, or when an environmental audit reveals injury or damage.

A recent decision by a California appellate court illustrates the complexity of trigger of coverage issues. Reviewing in detail arguments involving "continuous injury" versus "manifestation of loss" theories of trigger of coverage, the court adopted the "continuous injury" theory, requiring the insurer to defend the insured on claims arising from the insured's disposal of hazardous wastes at times predating the inception of the CGL coverage.[205] Further, the court ruled that the "known loss" rule would not defeat coverage under a CGL policy, reasoning, "[w]here, as here, there is uncertainty about the imposition of liability and not 'no legal obligation to pay,' there is an insurable risk under a third party policy".[206]

The "continuing injury" theory identifies the date or dates when the injury or damage occurs as the relevant date; the date of the event causing the injury or damage, and the date the injury or damage should have been discovered, are both irrelevant. Thus, under the "continuing injury" theory, coverage under more than one policy may be triggered if the injury or damage continues during the policy periods of more than one policy. By contrast, the "manifestation of loss" theory (which has been followed for pollution claims made on first party policies) identifies the date when appreciable injury or damage first occurs, the date when the insured knew or should have known of such injury or damage; if

[204] Pre-policy "occurrences" are covered under "occurrences made" CGL policies, in contrast to coverage under a "claims made" policy, which cover pre-policy events only to the extent that they include a retroactive date for claims.

[205] *Montrose Chemical Corp. of California* v. *Admiral Ins. Co.*, 1992 Cal. App. LEXIS 238, 5 Cal. Rptr. 2d 938 (1992).

[206] Ibid.

that date is before the effective date of the policy, there is no coverage, despite the fact that the injury or damage may have continued throughout the term of that policy.

C. Writing coverage today

As the evolution of the standard CGL policy illustrates, insurers facing pollution liability claims far exceeding their claims reserves have attempted to narrow the product (e.g. deny coverage, add exclusions) with only limited success. Insurers cannot generate adequate claims reserves in the absence of competent, accurate information about the particular pollution liability risks their insureds face.[207] Only those insurers which perform, or require the insured to perform, adequate environmental audits will have any basis on which to write new coverage.[208] In fact, competent environmental audits have led to the development of insurance products geared to an insured's specific pollution liability risks. For example, the New York-based Commerce and Industry Insurance Co. offers several new insurance products based on environmental audits, including environmental remediation coverage for property transfers; hospital pollution liability coverage; non-owned disposal site coverage; underground storage tank liability coverage; contractor coverage; and asbestos abatement coverage.[209] Competent environmental audits, and a longer claims history will enable insurers to price premiums, set deductibles, and build claims reserves adequate to cover the claims. Coverage written on the basis of competent audits should avoid the coverage issues common on pollution claims under CGL policies.

III. Alternatives to Traditional Commercial Liability Insurance

If traditional commercial liability insurance is not an efficient means of addressing the risks of pollution liability, or if it is not available, property owners facing such risks may elect simply to bear the risks, or they may look for alternatives to traditional insurance. Just what alternatives are available to the owner will depend upon the actions of the commercial insurers, other risk bearers (potential insureds), and state legislatures (and insurance departments). Traditional insurers may respond to the increase in demand for pollution liability coverage by offering new types of coverage, based on competent environmental audits.[210] Individual property owners may self-insure, through the creation of group captives, or, where they band together with other owners facing similar risks, risk retention or risk transfer groups, to the extent permissible under any

[207] McLeod, "Panel Offers Remedies for Industry's Ailments", *Bus. Ins.*, 29 January 1990.

[208] Friedman, S., "Pollution Liability Expanded by Insurers," *Property & Casualty/Risk & Benefits Management* (4 November 1991).

[209] Friedman, n. 8, *supra*.

[210] As mentioned above, commercial insurers are likely to develop new insurance products to meet the new needs created by the risk of pollution liability, products based on environmental audits which identify and assess an insured's specific pollution liability risks. See Friedman, n. 8, *supra*.

applicable state insurance law. State legislatures may create pools or trust funds to insure those persons otherwise unable to obtain insurance.[211]

However, the property owner is not free simply to elect to bear the risk without insurance. Any applicable requirements for maintaining evidence of financial responsibility must be met. For example, vessel owners and operators facing the risk of oil spill liability must obtain one of the following:[212] insurance coverage for an amount specified in the federal regulations (the "applicable amount") not conditioned on any agreement with the owner/insured sufficient to cover any incident giving rise to liability under the Act; a surety bond issued by a surety authorized to do business in the United States, in the applicable amount, not conditioned on any agreement with the owner/insured; a guaranty to discharge the owner/insured's liability under the Act, up to the applicable amount; or, self-insurance, but only where the owner maintains "working capital" (current assets in the United States less all current liabilities) "net worth" (assets in the United States less all liabilities) each in an amount equal to or greater than the applicable amount.[213]

Significantly, the insurance device commonly obtained by vessel owners and operators, membership in a protection and indemnity association ("p & i club"), is unlikely to satisfy these financial responsibility requirements, insofar as the clubs have refused to issue the requisite guaranties.[214] A major impediment, whether for the insurer of the vessel owner or operator, or the guarantor or surety, is the requirement in the proposed regulations that it designate a person in the United States for service of process, and that it consent to be sued directly for any claims for costs or damages brought against the vessel owner or operator.[215]

Most environmental pollution liability statutes provide for instances where no responsible party, or insurer, guarantor, or surety of a responsible party, is available to pay for the costs of remedying the pollution. National and state trust funds, oftentimes funded by a tax on all the persons in the applicable industry, are available as a last resort. For example, OPA creates an Oil Spill Liability Trust Fund for the purpose of paying removal costs incurred by the federal

[211] Some states have created pools to provide liability insurance to insureds which would otherwise have difficulty in obtaining insurance. Typically, these trust funds benefit small businesses. For example, 43 states have pools to provide liability insurance for operators of underground storage tanks, 28 of which have been approved by the EPA as mechanisms by which the operators can satisfy financial responsibility requirements. See Gastel, n. 34, *supra*.

[212] The financial requirements of OPA have been fleshed out by the proposed, but not yet finalised federal regulations promulgated pursuant to the Act. See 56 Fed. Reg. 49006–49021 (26 September 1991). The comment period for the proposed regulations closed at the end of January 1992, but no final rule has been issued yet.

[213] See ibid.

[214] The proposed federal regulations discuss this problem, and in fact request comments answering specific questions about the problem. See ibid.

[215] See ibid.

government and uncompensated damage claims.[216] CERCLA creates the Hazardous Substance Superfund, financed by a tax on chemical feedstocks, crude oil, imported petroleum products, and motor fuels, for the payment of governmental response costs, and costs incurred by private parties which are not recoverable from responsible parties.[217] California's OSPRA creates an Oil Spill Response Trust Fund, financed by fees collected from marine terminal operators, pipeline operators, and refinery operators, for the purpose of paying for clean-up and damages arising from an oil spill where no responsible party is able or willing to pay.[218] Not surprisingly, the trust funds currently in existence are likely grossly inadequate to meet anticipated costs.

Conclusion

In theory, there is no reason why environmental pollution liability should be more difficult to insure than other type of risk. In practice, however, it is. Why? Because the risk was virtually unknown until perhaps twenty-five years ago, and even now remains difficult to assess. At least until recently, insurers did not write liability coverage with environmental risk in mind. Yet judicial decisions have often shifted the risk from the insured to the insurer, on the reasoning that an insured can insure against general risks, which include unknown specific risks, sometimes yielding disastrous consequences for the unprepared insurer. Hopefully, writing coverage will become progressively less difficult as insurers and policy holders use competent environmental audits better to assess the risks, and as experience grows. In the United States, the viability of that hope depends to a great extent on the actions of state and federal legislatures. A stable system of regulation — even a draconian one — would make environmental risks more predictable and, therefore, more insurable.

216 26 U.S.C. § 9509; U.S.C. § 2712(a).
217 42 U.S.C. §§ 9611, 9612.
218 Cal. Gov't. Code §§ 8670.46, 8760.48, 8760.49.

Limited Insurability of Unlimited Liability : Serial Claims Aggregates and Alternatives : The Continental View*

Werner Pfennigstorf

General Observations

"If there were no losses —
There would be no insurance."

This is the Motto of a large American Insurance Company. It is quoted here as a reminder that assuming risks and paying losses is the *raison d'être* of insurance.

Insurance is most needed, and of the greatest benefit, where the risk of loss is great, that is, for the *largest and most infrequent losses*, beyond those which an individual or businessman can provide for in his regular budget. For frequently occurring small losses, insurance is uneconomical. Which risk is so large that it must be insured depends on the business volume, the assets and the financial policy of the owner of the risk.

It is in the nature of economic and technological development for risks to become larger. It is as natural for insurers to make coverage available in response to the increasing demand. It is their business to do this, in the expectation of a reasonable profit.

Unlimited Liability is Nothing New

Unlimited liability did not come into existence with environmental harms and it is not limited to them. Liability under tort law has always been unlimited.

Insurers have had ample time to gather experience with insuring the risk of unlimited liability. They have managed rather well in their efforts to provide

* Paper presented at the International Bar Association's Seminar on Transnational Environmental Liability and Insurance, at Rotterdam, 8–9 May 1992.

coverage matching the risk as closely as possible. In the German-speaking countries, this goal is known as *congruence.*

There are obvious limits to the degree of congruence that can be achieved. For instance, no insurer will, or can, promise to assume the cost of liability for damage caused intentionally.

The fact that liability is unlimited has not been an unsurmountable barrier, however. Unlimited coverage is available for standard liability risks in many countries and in some countries is even required by law for motor vehicles. Some economists and some supervising agencies have had trouble accepting the concept, but insurers know that liability is unlimited in theory only.

In the real world, no liability is unlimited. Claims may reach very large amounts but they are always expressed in figures that can be added up with other claims, statistically analysed and, if the number of cases is sufficiently large and the experience over time is sufficiently stable, become the basis for calculating adequate premiums.

The proviso in the last sentence suggests the answer to the question *why* insurers can provide unlimited cover for motor vehicle liability but *not for most types of commercial liability* and especially not for the risk of environmental damage. These risks lack the elements of stability that are present in motor vehicle insurance, notably a large pool of similar risks, secured against adverse selection by statutory insurance requirements, a large number of claims, moderate deviation from the average, and manageable fluctuation over time.

Incidentally, there are instances where unlimited coverage does in fact exist for environmental liability: in Belgium, the unlimited coverage required by law for motor vehicles includes damage to the environment. Indeed, the largest motor vehicle liability claim in Belgian history is in this category. In 1987 a tank truck carrying 13,000 litres of fuel oil skidded into a canal, rupturing the tank and releasing about 9,000 litres of oil into the water, 27 metres above one of the most important freshwater wells of the country. The claim, which was at first estimated at BF 1 billion, was eventually settled for BF 50 million.

This case proves the point just made: the exceptional risk presented by tank trucks carrying hazardous substances is insurable without limitation because it can be pooled with the much more stable risks of millions of private passenger cars. An unlimited coverage for tank trucks alone would be impossible.

In part, the problems of environmental liability are due to the fact that the risk is new and not yet well known. This is a situation that insurers have faced before, each time they confronted a new type of risk. Satellite launch insurance provides the most impressive demonstration of the odds that insurers are ready to take with new risks. The first years must necessarily be years of experimentation. Over time, the accumulating experience will form a broadening base for assessing the risk although it may never attain a degree of reliability comparable to that of the personal lines.

We may expect that to happen, in due course, with respect to environmental liability as well. In Sweden, the two leading insurers have concluded, on the basis of their experience, that there is no need to exclude pollution from the standard liability policies except for some exceptionally hazardous operations.

In other countries, the prevailing opinion among insurers and reinsurers is that this risk is and will remain more volatile than others. Consequently, the insurers perceive a greater than normal need to limit their own exposure. This is what this chapter is about.

Standard Ways to Limit Coverage

Reinsurance

The oldest method for an insurer to protect itself against unexpected or excessive losses is to pass on a part of the risk to a reinsurer. Indeed, without reinsurance, there would hardly be any liability insurance available at all for commercial risks.

Reinsurance alone, however, apparently does not eliminate the need for limitation of the coverage for commercial liability risks. At least, insurers have not found a way to calculate a premium for unlimited coverage within a range that insureds would be willing to pay.

Limitation by Incident, Causal Connection or Aggregates

LIMIT PER EVENT

Any policy that is not unlimited specifies the amount that the insurer promises to pay, as a maximum, under the contract. The prevailing practice among insurers on the Continent is to specify that the amount shall apply to any one *damaging incident* (Schadenereignis, sinistre), and to specify separate amounts for bodily injuries and property damage (and where applicable, pure economic loss). Some policies (notably automobile policies) also specify separate limits for bodily injury per person and per accident.

As noted, the limits reflect the respective perceptions of insurer and insured of the extent of the risk to be covered and the premium to be charged or paid for the coverage. These perceptions, and the experience on which they are based, include the possibility of more than one person being injured, or more than one person's property being damaged, in the course of the same accident, and the limits reflect that.

Insurers have found it difficult, however, to calculate the risk that one cause, or a series of related causes, may produce an *accumulation* of incidents, each of them calling for the full amount of the policy.

SERIAL CLAIMS CLAUSES

Generally

Serial claims clauses are designed to eliminate the accumulation risk, by providing that several damaging incidents occurring within the policy period shall be deemed one incident if they are somehow related, usually by resulting from the same causal event, variously defined.

In addition to limiting the risk of genuine accumulations, the clauses also serve to protect insurers against fictional accumulations created by courts who may be tempted to declare damages suffered by different persons in one accident to be separate incidents.

Some serial claims clauses currently offered in the German-speaking countries reflect a third purpose: to eliminate the risk of the insurer "cancelling out" of a running series. Even though there is some disagreement on whether such cancellation would survive legal challenge, the concerns did produce clauses providing coverage, subject to the single limit per event, for all claims in the series, including those occurring after expiration of the policy period. Under the German clause, all events of the series are deemed to have occurred at the time of the occurrence of the first event. Thus an insured who opts for this clause would not be covered at all for long-running series that started before the inception of the policy.

Serial claims clauses are most urgently needed in the area of product liability, where one error in design or production may result in a large number of defective products and many different accidents. They have become a standard feature of commercial general liability policies, and they are also commonly used in special environmental liability policies.

Clauses used in environmental liability policies

It should have become apparent that drafting serial claims clauses is not a simple matter, not only because of the different purposes but also because the accumulations for which they are designed are of a different nature in each type of liability insurance. It not surprising, therefore, to find different wordings and approaches in environmental liability policies.

Some of the clauses used in environmental liability policies refer to claims resulting from one polluting incident, or occurrence, or from one environmental impairment (as defined in the policy).

Thus the policy used by the French Environmental Liability Pool (GARPOL / ASSURPOL), defines "sinistre" as "toute réclamation ou série de réclamations, imputable à une meme atteinte à l'environnement fortuitement causée, que cette atteinte ait été isolée, répétée ou continue". Other clauses seek to link claims arising from several polluting events related by a common cause. Thus the policy used by the Italian Environmental Liability Pool provides that the limit specified per event shall also apply: "a) per più danni, anche se verificatisi in tempi diversi, che traggano origine da una stessa causa di inquinamento". The new environmental liability model that was just introduced in Germany contains a more elaborate clause:

> "Several insured events occurring while the insurance is in effect as a result
> — of the same effect on the environment
> — of several effects on the environment resulting directly from the same cause or directly from like causes, if between the like causes there is an intrinsic, especially substantive and temporal, connection,

shall be deemed, regardless of their actual occurrence, one insured event, which is deemed to have occurred at the time of the first of such insured events."

Potential problems

Practical application of serial claims clauses is subject to several problems inherent in their nature. One is the fact that they blur the carefully crafted definitions of the insured event, by contracting several events into one and by referring back to some causal event. Even though it is clear from the context that this is meant only for applying the limit, and that with respect to notices and other details the several events are to be treated separately, some confusion may be created.

An even greater problem is to interpret and apply the definition of the "series", i.e. the link, causal or otherwise, that is meant to justify pulling several insured events together into one. Since the number of causes and the length of the chain of causation for every event are theoretically unlimited, references to the "same cause" or "like causes" of several events invite disagreement. Moreover, any clause relying on causal connection is vulnerable to attack for being vague, and to conscious or innocent misinterpretation for the same reasons that have led courts to find several events in one accident.

The reference in the German clause to the "intrinsic connection" (innerer Zusammenhang) between like causes represents an effort to save the clause from the fate of a similar clause in an architect's liability policy, which was found by the German Supreme Court to be unfairly detrimental to the insured, therefore in violation of the Standard Contract Terms Act and consequently void (Bundesgerichtshof, 28 Nov. 1990, 1991 Versicherungsrecht, 175–176). In that case, the insured architect had made the same mistake (recommending an unsuitable method for waterproofing basements) resulting in defective construction of five homes in the same area.

It is by no means certain that the new clause in the environmental liability model will stand up to corresponding scrutiny, given an appealing set of facts.

AGGREGATE LIMITS

Even the best serial clause cannot connect claims arising from several events that are unrelated by cause or in any other way. The only way for an insurer to limit its exposure in such cases is the aggregate limit per policy period.

Aggregate limits also serve to protect the insurer against the consequences of unfavorable treatment of serial claims clauses by the courts. In the case of the architect and the five flooded basements, the aggregate limit had the effect that the insurer had to pay only two times the limit per event, rather than five times.

The size of the limit is, of course, a matter of risk appreciation and pricing. It may be 2 or 3 times the limit per event in general liability. In environmental liability policies, aggregate limits equal to the limit per event seem to be the rule.

In that case, where the two limits are identical, the question arises whether a serial clause is needed at all. It is certainly not needed for claims arising from events of the same year. Conceivably, if a series of events going back to the same cause is spread out over several years, then a serial clause might make sense by preventing successive annual aggregates from being called up, although in such case it is much more likely that the parties will negotiate special terms for future events in the running series.

DEDUCTIBLES

Deductibles or retentions are quite common in environmental liability policies, though not universal. They appear in Belgian and Norwegian policies, in the Dutch Pool's policy and in the new German coverage model but not in the policies of the French and Italian Pools.

Where they are used, deductibles are specified so that they create an effective incentive for loss prevention.

Conclusion

Insurance coverage that is subject to limitations, whether by event, by series, or by year, is by definition less than full coverage and thus at odds with the purpose and function of insurance, and notably with the goal of congruence in liability insurance.

Doing away with the limits will therefore remain a challenge for the insurance industry and for risk managers. For environmental liability, the challenge is even greater than for other types of liability.

The cure must aim at the causes:

- Much more needs to be known about the dimensions of the risk, technological, medical and legal.
- Effective prevention must be given a chance to become universally accepted industry practice.
- Solutions must be found for handling the claims arising from "old burdens".
- Many more owners of hazardous installations must be persuaded to obtain coverage, to achieve a broader spread of the risk and minimise anti-selection.
- Finally, insurers and insureds must acquaint themselves with the truth that full coverage requires higher premiums.

One way to achieve maximum spread of the risk without anti-selection would be the creation of a compulsory insurance scheme or a government fund. Such schemes hold out the promise of simple, efficient solutions but they must be viewed with caution. Experience suggests that they rarely operate as they were designed, and they might create new problems of their own. They are a remedy of last resort.

Meanwhile, intermediate solutions are emerging, which do not promise unlimited coverage but progress in insuring risks that so far have been considered uninsurable. The Swiss Reinsurance Company has developed coverage models based on the recognition that environmental liability is a long-term risk and should be treated as such, in long-term contracts involving long-term commitments on the parts of both insurer and insured. ("Environmental Impairment Liability Insurance For Enterprises: A Modern Insurance Concept", 1991).

One of the models (for waste deposit facilities) applies structural elements borrowed from life insurance and is consequently referred to as "Liability Life Policy". (Juerg Spuehler, "Major Approaches for Possible Insurance Solutions and their Evaluation", *Geneva Papers*, 14/51. (1989), 178–195.

How these models will be accepted in the market remains to be seen. In any event, it seems safe to predict that coverage limits, both per event and per year, will have to be accepted as an indispensable part of environmental liability policies for the foreseeable future.

Non-Marine Environmental Liability: The Use of Insurance Pools and the European Dimension

Anthony J. E. Fitzsimmons

Introduction

The emergence of pollution claims on liability policies, initially those covering American risks, caused the collapse of the market for the insurance of non-marine pollution risks. The recent burgeoning of pollution claims, particularly on American risks has done nothing to tempt insurers back into this field. Most insurers prepared to cover pollution risks at all will only cover "sudden and accidental" pollution; and many insurers will not even cover that. Blanket exclusions of pollution are becoming widespread in many markets, and it is generally appreciated nowadays that in order to underwrite pollution risks, a combination of careful drafting of policy conditions and very expert underwriting are required, as well as a reasonable "spread" of risks.

From the perspective of potential buyers, the dearth of insurers prepared to cover non-marine pollution risks leaves potential buyers with inadequate or non-existent coverage for such risks. Non-availability of coverage, particularly as regards "gradual" pollution is becoming increasingly unsatisfactory as environmental protection rises higher on political agendas, the trend in the Western World being to impose ever increasing liabilities on polluters, the owners and users of polluted land and those involved in the transport and disposal of waste.

Governments also find the position unsatisfactory. There is little point in having legislation dealing with the financial consequences of pollution if the person made responsible at law has no resources. In the absence of resources from the private sector, it is ultimately the state which has to pick up the consequences of its own pollution legislation, whether by way of social security legislation or because it has initially to pay for clean-up costs.

Even underwriters are not happy. Providing that they can write a reasonable spread of risks, can adequately assess them and cover them on suitable terms, underwriters are not averse to insuring risks. However, previous experience in the pollution field has made underwriters hesitant about re-entering the market. A suitable policy has to be carefully drafted to delimit the areas of risk which underwriters are prepared to insure. Such a new policy may require a major investment in time, and the drafting will involve not only the underwriter, but also his lawyer and at least one of his external environmental experts. The underwriter will need to set up an expert team for assessing proposals. As the market stands at present, all these overheads have to be incurred at a time when the demand for pollution insurance is still remarkably low, partly because potential buyers are unaware of the need for the insurance and partly because those who see the need for it are unaware that anyone is prepared to cover it. All this causes the other difficulty, that of achieving a reasonable *spread* of risks. At present, those who are most keen on buying insurance against pollution are those who already perceive themselves as being seriously at risk of having to face a claim. All these factors conspire to discourage underwriters from putting a toe in this particular pond.

There are, of course, a few very large insurers who can afford the investment and the overheads, and who can by virtue of their global operations, attract a reasonable spread of risks. Such insurers can probably be counted on the fingers of one hand. The problems faced by the less than giant insurer are to achieve a reasonable spread of risk, support the start-up costs and overheads involved, achieve a reasonable volume of premium and, most important, make a profit it not in a short term then certainly in the medium term.

Various solutions have been tried. The U.K. market is in some ways unique in that it is a "broker" market, and this makes it straightforward for brokers to act as a catalyst in bringing together a number of insurers, and thus providing adequate capacity to cover risks. The broker's line slip arrangement does not, however, deal with the problems of start-up costs, underwriting expertise or overheads, at least for the leading underwriter.

Elsewhere in Europe, particularly France, Italy and the Netherlands, underwriters have banded together in "pools". ASSURPOL in France, MAS in the Netherlands and Inquinamento in Italy are the best known in the pollution fields. This is the approach which is the main subject of this chapter.

Insurance pools can take many forms, but in essence they are arrangements under which insurers band together to share common administrative facilities (such as underwriting, collection of premium, reinsurance arrangements and settlement of claims), the risks underwritten being split between the pool members in fixed proportions, overheads usually being split in the same proportions.

Insurance pools are an attractive vehicle by which to solve the problems of less large underwriters who cannot on their own achieve a good spread of risks, or afford the overheads involved in new or difficult areas of the market. Insurance pools are thus in principle an attractive way for less large underwriters to become involved in pollution insurance on a scale with which they feel comfortable, without bearing disproportionate overheads.

Many pools will cover only a very small part of a particular market, and the main problems in setting up most pools are the commercial problems of achieving agreement between the parties and setting up an efficient administration.

Leaving aside national law factors, an additional set of considerations arise if the pool has effects on trade within the EC and is not an *insignificant* element in that trade.

This is because of Article 85(1) of the EEC Treaty, which states:

> "The following shall be prohibited as incompatible with the Common Market: all agreements between undertakings, decisions by associations of undertakings and concerted practices which may affect trade between Member State and which have as their object or effects the prevention, restriction or distortion of competition within the Common Market, and in particular those which:
>
> (a) directly or indirectly fix purchase or selling prices or any other trading conditions;
> (b) limit or control markets...;
> (c) share markets...;
> ..."

Any arrangement which infringes Article 85(1) is automatically void (see Article 85(2), and all the participants are exposed to large fines. The maximum fine is 10% of turnover. For insurance companies this probably means 10% of their premium income in their most recent year. The record (not for an insurer) currently stands at £50m, so this is no minor problem.

Leaving aside the fines that can be levied by the European Commission, the Civil Law consequences can be draconian. Focusing on Insurance Pools, pooling arrangements often contain an agreement whereby one pool member can be put forward as a "fronting" company, backed by reinsurance from other pool members. If the arrangement is void, there is a possibility that the reinsurance arrangements may themselves be void, with the result that the fronting company bears all the risk!

The EEC's anti-trust regime is administered by the European Commission who, as mentioned previously, have the power to examine arrangements and impose fines. Fortunately, the European Commission has a second power, designed to ensure that the baby is not thrown out with the bath water. This comes under Article 85(3) which states:

> "(3) The provisions of [Article 85(1)] may, however, be declared inapplicable in the case of:
>
> - any agreement or category of agreements between undertakings;
> - any decision or category of decisions by associations of undertakings;
> - any concerted practice or category of concerted practices;

which contributes to improving the production or distribution of goods or to promoting technical or economic progress while allowing consumers a fair share of resulting benefit, and which does not:

(a) impose on the undertakings concerned restrictions which are not indispensable to the attainment of these objectives;
(b) Afford such undertakings the possibility of eliminating competition in respect of a substantial part of the products in question"

In summary, the Commission can give its blessing to a particular arrangement if there is an adequate public benefit, without unnecessary restrictions on competition being imposed or competition being eliminated in the market in question. Having won its fight to establish that Article 85 applies to the insurance sector at all, the European Commission takes the view that co-operation between insurers in the following areas is prima facie outlawed by Article 85(1):

(a) establishing common risk premium tariffs;
(b) establishing common standard policy conditions;
(c) arranging for the common coverage of specified types of risks;
(d) the settlement of claims;
(e) registers of and information on aggravated risks.

Many will be surprised to know that such common activities in the insurance market might be illegal. However, from the point of view of establishing a new pooling arrangement (or indeed looking at a non-existing one), at least four of the above types of co-operation are likely, together with a number of others. It is therefore essential that any proposed pooling arrangement which may affect trade between EC Member States be looked at with Article 85 in mind.

The Council of the EC has laid the foundations for what is known in the trade as a "block exemption" for certain types of co-operation between insurers, but the necessary Commission Regulation has not yet been produced. Those involved in operations which may breach Article 85(1) therefore have to go through the full procedure set out in EC Council Regulation No.17 of 6 February 1962. So far as I know, whilst a number of recent insurance pools have been notified to the European Commission, only one has emerged, and that with approval. The pool in question is ASSURPOL, the French pool which specialises in reinsuring pollution risks.

ASSURPOL itself is a French Economic Interest Grouping ("EIG"), established for a period of 20 years. It administers a series of arrangements between insurers and reinsurers in the field of the insurance of damage to the environment, both as a result of "sudden and accidental" events and as a result of non-accidental damage. ASSURPOL and its predecessor were aimed at dealing with the consequences of a specific French environmental liability regime, though the pooling arrangements it administers can be extended to non-French environmental liability risks.

The Functions of ASSURPOL

The key function of ASSURPOL is to administer a reinsurance pool specialising in environmental liabilities. In order to do this, ASSURPOL gathers information about environmental risks and studies statistics, with a view to improving their understanding of the risks involved. It has developed a tariff and standard conditions for the reinsurance of smaller environmental risks. As regards larger or less standard risks, ASSURPOL arranges individual technical examination of proposals and provides quotations. Both the tariff and the individual quotations are of so-called "pure" reinsurance costs, that is the premium charged by reinsurers plus a contribution to pool overheads. Standard policy conditions are used.

The reinsurance pool is able reinsure risks up to limits of FFr 131 million per claim and per contract/year.

Where substantial claims are made, ASSURPOL administers the response to the claim.

Participants in ASSURPOL

ASSURPOL is open to insurers both French and foreign. Participants are divided into two categories.

Insurer members are insurance companies who themselves provide direct insurance of environmental risks. Insurer members undertake to propose for co-reinsurance by the Pool all risks falling within the scope of the pooling agreement. ASSURPOL will provide a quotation, which the insurer member is entitled to decline. If the quotation is rejected, then the insurer member is free to seek reinsurance elsewhere.

If the ASSURPOL reinsurance quotation is accepted, the arrangement will be that the insurer member essentially receives 90% reinsurance. The insurer's 10% retention, must not be protected by other reinsurance.

The insurer members also participate in the reinsurance pool, and to the extent that they assume liability as pool members, they are not entitled individually to reinsure their participation.

Participant members are French or foreign reinsurance enterprises which participate in the reinsurance pool. They must not individually reinsure any liabilities they acquire through participation in the pool.

About 50% of the pool capacity is made up of participant members, the balance being made up of insurer members. The list of Insurer and Participant Members is impressive. Its French members account for about 75% of general liability premium volume in France, and a number of major foreign liability insurers. It is interesting, however, to see that in 1989, ASSURPOL concluded only 200 contracts, with 242 in 1990. Premium incomes were FFr 6.5 million and FFr 10.3 million in 1989 and 1990 respectively. Nonetheless, it has been estimated that the ASSURPOL pool is capable, if demand existed, of accepting reinsurances of more than 70% of environmental damage insurance in France, with a potential to expand abroad. Were the environmental liability insurance market to develop, ASSURPOL could easily become a very dominant player in that market.

Analysis of the ASSURPOL Arrangements by the European Commission: Article 85(1)

It is for the European Commission to consider whether a particular set of arrangements contravene Article 85(1). It is obvious that the ASSURPOL arrangements include decisions by an association of undertakings (e.g. ratings and claims decisions taken by the organs of ASSURPOL); and agreements between undertakings (the matrix of pool reinsurance agreements). The real questions for the Commission were whether there were restrictions on competition and whether those restrictions had an appreciable affect on trade between member states or an insignificant one.

As regards restrictions on competition in insurance markets, the Commission found that the freedom independently to determine general conditions and premium rate for directing insurance policies had been eroded as regards risks within the scope of the ASSURPOL agreements, whether as a result of the tariff for smaller simpler risks or as regards the obligation to seek a quotation for reinsurance from ASSURPOL. Both then set market bench-marks for rating and conditions. It was also considered that the insurer's freedom of action was restricted by the fact that he had to retain, net for his own account, 10% of any risks ceded to the ASSURPOL reinsurance pool.

As regards restrictions regarding reinsurance, the Commission considered that the insurer members restricted their freedom of choice when it came to choosing reinsurance. Whether this restriction is quite as significant as the Commission appears to have thought may be doubted, given that insurer members are not *obliged* to cede reinsurance to the ASSURPOL reinsurance pool, but may, if they wish, cede it elsewhere. However, the obligation to offer relevant environmental risks to ASSURPOL probably does have the effect of informing other participants in ASSURPOL both of the risk's existence and of the fact that another member is seeking the direct insurance and seeking reinsurance, and this probably does amount to a restriction on competition.

It also appears that the participant members may have agreed not to reinsure, outside the Pool, risks which could fall within the Pool's scope. If this is so, it is certainly a restriction on competition.

At the level of retrocession market, the Commission concluded that there were restrictions in the sense that retrocession of risks within ASSURPOL is not allowed except on a common account basis.

In contrast to the above criteria which are more or less objectively ascertainable, the question of an appreciable effect on trade is a value judgment. Whilst the Commission recognised that the market in environmental liability insurance is still "compartmentalised" on a national basis, the Commission took account of the fact that insurers and reinsurers from numerous EC countries participated, and concluded that there would be an appreciable effect on trade between member states at the level of insurance.

As regards reinsurance, the Commission considered that the "exclusive" reinsurance arrangements within the pool, which consisted of reinsurance enterprises in various EC member states, would have an appreciable effect on trade between member states largely because of the size of the insurance and reinsurance companies party to the agreement. Similar criteria applied at the retrocession level.

Could ASSURPOL be Given the Commission's Blessing under Article 85 (3)?

Improving Production or Distribution and Promoting Technical and Economic Progress

The Commission appreciated that environmental damage insurance requires considerable technical knowledge which is not widespread, and that insurance of this type is not readily available even at world level. The Commission also appreciated that the gathering of statistical information and technical knowledge was something to be fostered at least in an immature market. It appreciated that pooling arrangements made it possible for the pool members to obtain a more diversified and balanced portfolio and would make it easier for a direct insurer to make insurance contracts, in the knowledge that he had a relatively "automatic" facility for reinsurance. It would therefore open up the environmental damage market to insurers who would otherwise have had difficulty in gaining access to the market.

Benefit to Consumers

The Commission saw a number of benefits to consumers, not least of which was the *availability* of environmental damage insurance where it was previously much harder to obtain. No mention was made of the Commission's apparent policy of promoting an EC regime under which potential polluters would be *obliged* to carry insurance. This objective will be incapable of achievement if few insurers are prepared to cover environmental risks, which suggests that there may have been a hidden agenda influencing the decision of the European Commission.

Indispensability of the Restrictions

The Commission accepted that any pooling arrangement would involve some restrictions, and accepted that restrictions on the freedom of action of direct insurers were inevitable if the reinsurance pool were to be able to function. Thus, it was acceptable for ASSURPOL to fix reinsurance premiums reflecting the "pure" risk and ASSURPOL overheads and for ASSURPOL to impose standard conditions and joint settlement arrangements. Curiously the restriction on reinsurers accepting from outside the Pool reinsurances of a type that could be ceded through the Pool, was not mentioned.

Non-Elimination of Competition
The Commission appears to have been concerned by the fact that insurer members of ASSURPOL already covered 70-80% of potential customers for other risks. However, the Commission considered that the breaking down of barriers which is being brought about by the Second (and hopefully Third) Non-Life Directives will in any event open up competition not merely to the remaining 20-30% of French insurers but also to liability insurers from elsewhere within the EC.

The European Commission's Blessing
The ASSURPOL arrangements as originally notified to the European Commission seeking approval were in a slightly different form, but they were modified at the suggestion of the Commission, and the Commission's decision reflects the revised arrangements. Overall, the Commission took the view that the ASSURPOL arrangements ought to be exempted from Article 85(1), at least for a minimum period. They gave as their reason:

> "In view of the limited experience gained so far with the insurance of risks in questions owing to their relatively recent character and their susceptibility to internal and external influences, the collaboration between the enterprises must be able to extend over a period which enables knowledge of the risk to improve. Given that a sudden variation in demand for the insurance in question cannot be ruled out, it seems appropriate to grant exemption... for seven years."

Thus the Commission approved the ASSURPOL arrangements in their present form, imposing in addition various conditions to allow them to monitor ASSURPOL's operations.

Lessons to be Learnt

The ASSURPOL decision shows that the European Commission is able to make a realistic assessment of such an esoteric subject as the reinsurance and retrocession of pollution risks. The Commission has understood the serious practical difficulties faced by insurers who wish in principle, to develop a new difficult field of insurance, but without committing a disproportionate amount of their capital to the venture, and has arrived at a sensible result.

There are many other insurers who, in principle, would be prepared to have pollution risks as a small part of their portfolio, but are not prepared to become involved at present because of the problems of disproportionate overheads and a likely inadequate spread of risks. The ASSURPOL decision makes it clear that there is window of opportunity for such insurers to band together and co-operate for a substantial period whilst underwriting experience is gained and the market is developed. It is, however, vital that before embarking on a project of that kind, insurers should take account of the EC's antitrust rules.

Availability of Insurance for Environmental Clean-up Measures in the United States

Robert A. Lewis
Sonia F. Saul

Introduction

In the last two decades, the United States has experienced an eruption of federal, state and regional legislation and regulation in the environmental arena. The reach of that legislation and regulation has been expansive. Applicable to both past and present owners of sites at which hazardous wastes have been discovered, as well as to the generators and transporters of waste deposited there, much of this legislation and regulation seeks to impose clean-up liability that is, simultaneously, strict, joint and several, and retroactive.

According to estimates issued by the United States Environmental Protection Agency, more than 64,000 waste sites were targeted for clean-up and containment by the end of 1990.[1] The decades ahead promise an increase in that figure. More staggering still are the costs of complying with this legislation and regulation; to date, the costs of cleaning up targeted sites has reached into the billions of dollars and have, in many instances, forced companies and individuals into bankruptcy.

Not surprisingly, companies and individuals faced with the massive costs of governmentally mandated clean-up measures in the United States have increasingly turned to their insurance carriers for coverage of clean-up costs, particularly

[1] Gordon, "Practical and Economic Issues Related to Hazardous Waste Cleanup and Insurance Litigation", in *Environmental Coverage: From Interpretation to Litigation* (1991), p. 287.

under commercial liability policies. Equally predictably, insurers have disputed their obligations to indemnify for such costs, citing a host of exclusions and limitations in their policies.

Despite more than a decade of aggressive litigation in American courts over the existence of insurance coverage for such claims, the key coverage issues remain largely unresolved. In the United States, insurance matters are independently regulated by each of the 50 states and policy language is interpreted according to the laws of each state. The consequence has been a veritable patchwork of conflicting decisional authority among the state courts. To make matters worse, only a handful of decisions on issues of coverage for environmental claims have been handed down by the states' highest courts, so that conflict on even the most important coverage questions still exists within the boundaries of most of the states.

This chapter will identify the most important and frequently litigated coverage questions in the environmental field and will examine the leading and most recent decisions coming out of this ongoing controversy in the United States.

Specifically, Sections I and II address how the U.S. court system and the general rules of policy construction have influenced the outcome of environmental coverage disputes. Sections III, IV and V will discuss the most frequently litigated issues arising out of the standard form CGL insuring agreement, including whether the cost of clean-up measures constitute "damages", whether an insured's polluting acts can ever constitute "occurrences", and how policy coverage is triggered in cases of progressive, continuing injury. Sections VI and VII will examine how two of the most significant exclusions in the standard form CGL, the "pollution" and "owned property" exclusions, might affect an insured's claim to pollution coverage. Finally, Section VIII explores alternative sources of coverage outside the standard commercial general liability policy and the issues such alternatives are likely to raise in the coming decade.

I. The Playing Field of Environmental Coverage Disputes

In the United States, regulation of the insurance industry has been left largely to the 50 states and, with certain exceptions not relevant here, is generally outside the reach of federal law. Such regulation has two components. First, before a standard form policy can even be issued in many of the states, it must be filed with and approved by the state's insurance commissioner. Second, when coverage disputes arise, the question is governed by applicable state law — generally the law of that state which has the greatest connection to or interest in the controversy. The same result obtains whether the coverage dispute is filed in a court in one of the 50 state court systems or in a U. S. federal court. Hence, although a large percentage of environmental insurance decisions have been issued by federal courts in the United States, those decisions are based on governing state, not federal, law. While the law of the individual states is quite similar in many ways, it can also be very different. Moreover, the fact that a court in one state has resolved a legal issue in a particular way, while potentially persuasive to a court in another state, is not binding on it in any way. Thus the often conflicting decisional authority emerging from environmental insurance coverage disputes in the United States reflects what is essentially a system of 50 independent court systems interpreting the laws of 50 different states.

II. Standardization and the Canons of Construction

Perhaps the single most important factor in the resolution of environmental insurance coverage disputes in the United States is not found within the terms of any insurance policy. That factor is the rule of policy interpretation.

On the most fundamental level, policies of insurance are written contracts and their interpretation is generally governed by the rules of contract interpretation that have developed in each of the 50 states.[2] But insurance policies differ from commercial contracts in one crucial respect. Unlike most commercial contracts, which are products of extensive negotiations between the parties and are frequently the tailor-made product of painstaking drafting on both sides, insurance policies in the United States have been largely standardised for more than half a century. Standardisation of insurance policies began in the late nineteenth century with the birth of the National Bureau of Casualty Underwriters, which merged with other insurer organisations in 1971 to form the Insurance Services Office ("ISO").[3] ISO, whose membership consists exclusively of insurance companies, is responsible for drafting, promulgating and filing standard policies and endorsements for approval by the insurance commissioners of the various states. While the member companies and subscribers are not obliged to use ISO's standard forms, the majority do. The insurance policy predominantly involved in environmental liability coverage disputes today — the Commercial General Liability Policy or CGL — has been standardised since 1941.[4]

The standardisation of insurance policies in the United State has given rise in the past few decades to a separate set of rules of construction characterised by the maxim "*contra proferentem*". Under universally accepted rules of contract interpretation, if the terms of an insurance policy are clear and unambiguous, they must be strictly applied according to their plain meaning.[5] The doctrine of *contra proferentem* dictates, however, that if the disputed terms of a policy are reasonably susceptible to more than one meaning — i.e. if the terms are ambiguous — they must be read against the drafter insurance company and in favour of

[2] See e.g. *Eagle-Picher Industries, Inc.* v. *Liberty Mut. Ins. Co.*, 682 F. 2d 12, 17 (1st Cir. 1982), *cert. denied*, 460 U. S. 1028 (1983).

[3] K. Abraham, *Environmental Liability Insurance Law* (1991), pp. 33–34.

[4] Ibid. 36.

[5] See e.g. *Reserve Ins. Co.* v. *Pisciotta*, 30 Cal. 3d 800, 807 (1982).

coverage.[6] Its application is automatic and leaves no margin for the insurer. "[S]o long as coverage is available under *any* reasonable interpretation of an ambiguous clause, the insurer cannot escape liability."[7] Moreover, in most states, the burden is on the insurer to show that its interpretation is the only reasonable construction of the policy.[8]

Reminiscent of consumer protection laws, the *contra proferentem* doctrine, as applied in the context of insurance coverage disputes, recognises the unilateral character of standardised policies in the United States and the fact that, apart from questions of premiums and limits of liability, an insured frequently has little power to negotiate the terms of its coverage. The obvious policy behind *contra proferentem* is the theory that because the insurance company has the power to draft unambiguous language favourable to itself, it should also be held responsible when those terms are found ambiguous. In those rare instances where the particular policy in question is truly manuscript and thus the product of joint drafting, the *contra proferentem* rule is inapplicable.

To say that *contra proferentem* rules of construction have had an impact on the resolution of environmental insurance coverage disputes in the United States would be an understatement. Virtually every court in the 50 states faced with an environmental claim has either invoked these rules as part of its coverage analysis or at least recited them as part of its prefatory comments. Indeed, in some instances courts have employed the *contra proferentem* doctrine as a substitute for a more substantive exploration of a policy's meaning, finding coverage where there is even the slightest doubt over a policy's terms.

Contra proferentem has played an important role in the resolution of environmental insurance coverage disputes in at least three respects. First, it has inspired leagues of policyholders to challenge their insurers in court, no matter how unpromising their claims to coverage appear. The pro-insured bent of *contra proferentem* holds out the hope that if an insured can but summon up a "reasonable" alternative meaning to its policy's terms, it will emerge as a victor in the

[6] *Merchants Ins. Group* v. *Warchol*, 560 A. 2d 1162, 1164 (N. H. 1989); *Continental Casualty Co.* v. *Cole*, 809 F. 2d 891, 895 (D. C. Cir. 1987); *Continental Ins. Co.* v. *Paccar, Inc.*, 634 P. 2d 291, 294 (Wash. 1981) (Washington); *Hanover Ins. Co.* v. *21 Mott Street Restaurant Corp.*, 407 N. Y. S. 2d 952, 953 (N. Y. Sup. Ct. 1978); *Ory* v. *Louisiana & Southern Life Ins. Co.*, 352 So. 2d 308, 310 (La. App. 1977); *Caledonia Community Hosp.* v. *St. Paul Fire & Marine Ins. Co.*, 239 N. W. 2d 768, 770 (Minn. 1976); *Steinbach* v. *Continental Western Ins. Co.*, 237 N. W.2d 780, 782 (Iowa 1976); *Rowland* v. *National States Ins. Co.*, 295 So. 2d 335, 337 (Fla. Dist. Ct. App. 1974); *Lincoln Mut. Casualty Co.* v. *American Arbitration Ass'n*, 212 N. W. 2d 765, 767 (Mich. App. 1973); *State Farm Mut. Auto Ins. Co.* v. *Partridge*, 10 Cal.3d 94, 101 (1973). See also Comment, "Insureds Versus Insurers Litigating Comprehensive General Liability Policy Coverage in the CERCLA Arena" (1990) 43 Sw. L. J. 969, 975 n. 45 ("Maryland is the only state that does not follow the ambiguity rule because Maryland courts do not consider insurance policies to be contracts of adhesion").

[7] *State Farm Mutual Auto Ins. Co.* v. *Jacober*, 10 Cal.3d 193, 197 (1973) (emphasis supplied).

[8] *McLaughlin* v. *Connecticut Gen. Life Ins. Co.*, 565 F. Supp. 434, 441 (N. D. Cal. 1983); *Vargas* v. *Ins. Co. of N. America*, 651 F. 2d 838, 840 (2d Cir. 1981).

coverage dispute. That advantage is self-perpetuating. The more frequently insureds challenge the standard terms of their policies in the various jurisdictions, the more likely favourable findings from the courts will emerge. At the very least, inconsistent results from the courts interpreting the same or similar language can be used by insureds as evidence of ambiguity.[9]

Second, the almost rote application of *contra proferentem* principles in environmental insurance coverage disputes has led to the adoption of even more pro-insured rules of policy construction. Under the rules of *contra proferentem*, a court is only required to find in favour of coverage if the insured can establish an objectively reasonable alternative interpretation of *ambiguous* policy language. But in applying this rule, some courts have eliminated the requirement of ambiguity altogether. Hence, in some jurisdictions, courts have found coverage even in the face of clear contrary policy language because the insured was able to show that it nevertheless had an objectively reasonable expectation of coverage.[10] That expectation can be created as a result of statements by the insurer or by language appearing elsewhere in the policy.

Finally, the pre-eminent role of *contra proferentem* has led to an expansion in the scope of admissible evidence in environmental insurance litigation. Under general principles of contract law, courts traditionally have been bound by the "four corners" of the contract they were being asked to interpret; extrinsic or parol evidence was therefore inadmissible in aid of the interpretation of what otherwise appeared to be clear and unambiguous terms.[11] However, in the context of insurance coverage disputes — most notably over environmental claims — these rules have been relaxed. Because a finding of ambiguity is central to the application of *contra proferentem*, many states now at least provisionally allow the introduction of extrinsic evidence in order to assist them in the determination of whether a seemingly clear policy provision is in fact ambiguous.[12] Nowhere is this liberalisation more apparent than in the increasing frequency with which insureds have sought the admission, in environmental coverage litigation, of the drafting and filing history of the standard "sudden and accidental" pollution exclusion. See discussion *infra*.

In light of the foregoing, it is hardly surprising that in the context of environmental claims one of the most hotly contested issues is whether the doctrine of *contra proferentem* should be applied in disputes involving large corporate insureds. According to insurers who have been raised the issue, the factors giving rise to the doctrine — principally unequal bargaining power and the use of standardised policies — are uncharacteristic of the dealings between carriers

[9] See e.g. *Broadwell Realty Services, Inc.* v. *Fidelity & Casualty Co. of N. Y.*, 528 A.2d 76, 86 (N. J. Super, 1987) (split in decisional authority is evidence of ambiguity of "sudden and accidental" pollution exclusion).

[10] See e.g. *Stordahl* v. *Government Employees Ins. Co.*, 564 P. 2d 63, 66 (Alaska 1977).

[11] See generally, *Corbin on Contracts* (3rd edn., 1960), § 559.

[12] See e.g. *Pacific Gas & Electric Co.* v. *G. W. Thomas Drayage & Rigging Co.*, 69 Cal. 2d 33, 37 (1968).

and so-called "sophisticated insureds" who frequently enlist the aid of skilled insurance brokers and knowledgeable risk management teams.[13] In the absence of evidence that the disputed policy language was actively negotiated or jointly drafted by the policyholder, however, the vast majority of courts in the United States have continued to apply *contra proferentem* in favour of even the most sophisticated insureds. For these courts, neither the size of the policyholder,[14] nor the fact that it was assisted by brokers,[15] counsel or risk managers[16] was deemed relevant if the policy was drafted by the insurance company. That rationale was best expressed by the Washington State Supreme Court in *Boeing Co.* v. *Aetna Casualty & Surety Co.*, which wrote:

> "The critical fact remains that the policy in question is a standard form policy prepared by the company's experts, with language selected by the insurer. [If] [t]he specific language in question was not negotiated, therefore, it is irrelevant that some corporations have company counsel. Additionally, this standard form policy has been issued to big and small businesses throughout the state. Therefore, it would be incongruous for the court to apply different rules of construction based on the policyholder because once the court construes the standard form coverage clause as a matter of law, the court's construction will bind policyholders throughout the state regardless of the size of their business."[17]

On the other hand, where there is clear evidence that the policy language was actively negotiated or drafted by the insured — such that it can no longer be considered standardized — the courts have refused to apply *contra proferentem.*[18]

III. The Obligation to "Pay as Damages"

Dispute over whether there is coverage for environmental claims begins with the very first sentence appearing in the insuring agreement to the standard-form Commercial General Liability ("CGL") policy. That sentence provides:

[13] See e.g. *Schering Corp.* v. *Home Ins. Co.*, 712 F. 2d 4 (2d Cir. 1983); *Eagle Leasing Corp.* v. *Hartford Fire Ins. Co.*, 540 F. 2d 1257 (5th Cir. 1976), *rehearing denied*, 546 F. 2d 906, cert. denied, 431 U. S. 967 (1977).

[14] *ACandS, Inc.* v. *Aetna Casualty & Surety Co.* 764 F. 2d 968, 973 (3d Cir. 1985); *Harad* v. *Aetna Casualty & Surety Co.*, 839 F. 2d 979, 986 (3d Cir. 1988).

[15] *Healy Tibbitts Constr. Co.* v. *Employers' Surplus Lines Ins.* Co., 72 Cal. App. 3d 741, 749 (1977); *Clemco Indus.* v. *Commercial Union Ins. Co.*, 665 F. Supp. 816, 819 (N. D. Cal. 1987), *aff'd*, 848 F. 2d 1242 (9th Cir. 1988).

[16] See e.g. *New Castle County* v. *Hartford Accident & Indem. Co.*, 673 F. Supp. 1359, 1364 (D. Del. 1987).

[17] *Boeing Co.* v. *Aetna Casualty & Surety Co.*, 784 P. 2d 507 (Wash. 1990) (en banc). *See also AIU Insurance Co.* v. *Superior Court*, 51 Cal. 3d 807 (1991) (en banc).

[18] *Fireman's Fund Ins. Co.* v. *Fibreboard Corp.*, 182 Cal. App. 3d 462, 466 (1986) (policy language proposed by insured); *Shearson/American Express, Inc.* v. *First Continental Bank & Trust Co.*, 579 F. Supp. 1305, 1311 (W. D. Mo. 1984) (form was joint product of insurer and insured); *Halpern* v. *Lexington Ins. Co.*, 558 F. Supp. 1280, 1283 (E. D. La. 1983), *aff'd*, 715 F. 2d 1991 (5th Cir. 1983) (policy language drafted by insured).

> "We will pay those sums that the insured becomes legally obligated to pay as damages because of "bodily injury" or "property damage" to which this insurance applies."[19]

The principal controversy over this language is whether the costs incurred by an insured because of pollution liability constitute "damages" as that term is employed in the policy.

As a practical matter, claims for coverage of environmental clean-up liability in the United States can arise in three ways: 1. an insured may be found liable in a lawsuit for costs incurred by the government or a third party in conducting a clean-up;[20] 2. the insured may itself incur costs pursuant to an administrative or judicial order directing it to clean up a contaminated area;[21] or 3. the insured may voluntarily undertake the clean-up in anticipation of incurring liability under either of the former approaches. Of the three, cost-recovery actions (example 1) come closest to the classic tort action against which CGL policies were principally designed to insure. While it has been argued that such actions nevertheless seek remedies which are equitable and restitutionary in nature[22] — and therefore fail to meet the "as damages" requirement — the real focus of the controversy has been on whether costs incurred by an insured in complying with a governmentally mandated clean-up order (example 2) constitute "damages".

That controversy has its genesis in a 1954 case often cited by insurers disputing environmental liability claims. *Desrochers* v. *New York Casualty Co.*[23] involved a comprehensive liability policy containing the identical "as damages" language appearing in the modern CGL form. After being sued by an adjoining landowner for flooding on the adjoining property caused by an obstruction on the insureds' premises, the insureds sought coverage for the costs of complying with a subsequent injunction issued by the court directing them to remove the obstruction. On appeal, the New Hampshire Supreme Court ruled that such costs were not "damages" and accordingly that no coverage was afforded by the policy. It reasoned that "damages", as contemplated by the policy, "are remedial rather than preventive", whereas "[the] expense of restoring the plaintiff's property to its former state will not remedy the injury previously done, nor will it be paid to the injured parties".[24]

Since the enactment of exhaustive environmental laws in the United States, *Desrochers* and its progeny have been cited by insurers for the proposition that the "as damages" language of CGL policies was intended to restrict coverage to only monetary judgments awarded in law and was never meant to cover forms of relief awarded in equity, such as the costs of complying with an injunctive

19 J. Robertson, *ISO Commercial Liability Forms: A Side-by-Side Comparison* (1986), p. 7.

20 See e.g. Comprehensive Environmental Response, Compensation, and Liability Act of 1980 ("CERCLA") 107, 42 U. S. C. § 9607.

21 See e.g. CERCLA § 106, 42 U. S. C. 9606.

22 See e.g. *Maryland Cas. Co.* v. *Armco, Inc.*, 822 F. 2d 1348 (4th Cir. 1987), *cert. denied*, 434 U. S. 1008 (1988).

23 106 A. 2d 196 (N. H. 1954).

24 Ibid. 198.

order.[25] Based on such authority, insurers have also taken the position that CGL coverage is intended only to cover "remedial" or backward-looking awards designed to compensate for past harms, and not forward-looking judgments devised to "prevent" future injury.[26] One further argument raised by insurers — and one that is more tied to the specific policy terms — is that the "as damages" clause was intended to serve as limiting language. If the standard form CGL policy were read to cover all forms of relief, including injunctions awarded in equity, the "as damages" limitation would be meaningless.[27]

Although it is sometimes claimed that these arguments are based on technical law versus equity distinctions no longer observed in U.S. jurisprudence, they are often fuelled by more substantive rationales. Insurers have argued, for example, that the costs of compliance with injunctive mandates — such as environmental clean-up orders — often exceed the measure of conventional legal damages that might have been awarded had the insured refused compliance.[28] But, as some commentators have pointed out, this distinction "confuses the nature of the relief granted with the measure of recovery", and does not by itself explain why only compensatory awards should be treated as "damages".[29] The remedial/preventive distinction urged by insurers had also been sharply criticised as based on a shallow conception of the forms of tort recovery. As commentators are quick to point out, many forms of equitable relief are designed to redress or compensate past wrongs and are therefore not wholly "preventive" in nature. Conversely, many classic forms of tort recovery are forward-looking and not wholly remedial in nature.[30]

Although the "as damages" issue is still aggressively litigated in environmental coverage disputes, the vast majority of courts addressing the question — including several state supreme courts — have ruled in favour of policyholders.[31] There are two principal rationales behind those rulings. First, drawing

[25] See e.g. *Continental Insurance Cos.* v. *Northeastern Pharmaceutical & Chemical Co.*, 842 F. 2d 977, 985 (8th Cir.), *cert. denied*, 488 U. S. 821 (1988).

[26] *Armco*, 822 F. 2d at 1352.

[27] Ibid.

[28] Ibid. 1353; *NEPACCO II*, 842 F. 2d at 986; *Patrons Oxford Mut. Ins. Co.* v. *Marois*, 573 A. 2d 16, 18–19 (Me. 1990).

[29] Abraham, n. 3 *supra*, 55. *See also AIU Insurance Co.*, 51 Cal. 3d 807 (1990).

[30] Abraham, n. 3 supra, 64–65.

[31] (California) *AIU Insurance Co.*, 51 Cal. 3d 807; (North Carolina) *C. D. Spangler Constr. Co.* v. *Industrial Crankshaft & Engineering Co., Inc.*, 388 S. E. 2d 557 (N. C. 1990); (Washington) *Boeing Co.*, 784 P. 2d 507 (Wash. 1990) (*en banc*); (Massachusetts) *Hazen Paper Co.* v. *United States Fidelity & Guaranty Co.*, 555 N. E. 2d 576 (Mass. 1990); (Minnesota) *Minnesota Mining & Mfg. Co.* v. *Travelers Indem. Co.*, 457 N. W. 2d 175 (Minn. 1990). See also *Avondale Industries, Inc.* v. *Travelers Indemnity Co.*, 887 F. 2d 1200 (2d Cir. 1989). *rehearing denied*, 894 F. 2d 498 (1990), *cert. denied*, 110 S. Ct. 2588 (1990); *Grisham* v. *Commercial Union Ins. Co.*, 951 F. 2d 872 (8th Cir. 1991), *rehearing denied*, 1992 US App. LEXIS 835 (8th Cir. 1992); (Iowa) *A. Y. McDonald Industries, Inc.* v. *Ins. Co. of North America*, 475 N. W. 2d 607 (Iowa 1991); (Michigan) *United States Aviex Co.* v. *Travelers Ins. Co.*, 336 N. W. 2d 838 (Mich. 1983). *Contra*: *Armco*, 822 F. 2d 1348; *NEPACCO II*, 842 F. 2d 977; *Marois*, 573 A. 2d 16.

on the *contra proferentem* doctrine and similar canons of construction, these courts have reasoned that the law versus equity distinction urged by insurers is beyond the ken of the average layman and contrary to the "reasonable expectations" of ordinary insureds purchasing a "comprehensive" liability policy.[32] To the average layperson, an out-of-pocket loss, whether paid out to a third party or directly incurred for clean-up, is an out-of-pocket loss and, to his mind, constitutes "damages". That argument is reinforced by the fact that the standard form CGL nowhere on its face draws a distinction between legal and equitable forms of relief.

Other courts have reasoned that the availability of coverage for environmental claims should not turn on the mere fortuity of how the government elects to pursue the clean-up of a particular site — *i.e.* whether it will seek monetary compensation from the insured after the clean-up is conducted or whether it will impose the clean-up requirement directly on the insured at the outset. As one court explained: "It would come as an unexpected, if not incomprehensible, shock to the insureds to discover that their insurance coverage was being denied because the plaintiff chose to frame his complaint in equity rather than in law."[33] Moreover, as some commentators have pointed out, a coverage scheme based on the monetary/injunctive relief distinction creates incentives that run completely counter to the scheme of environmental legislation.[34] If insurers refuse to cover anything beyond monetary awards, a policyholder has no incentive to undertake voluntary clean-up measures or even comply with administrative or court clean-up orders. Rather, it will wait until the government or other targeted party seeks indemnification for such expenses, when the prospects of receiving insurance coverage for such "monetary" awards are greater.

IV. Pollution as "Occurrence"

Yet another term of the standard form CGL policy routinely invoked by insurers as a basis for declining coverage for environmental claims is the "occurrence" language also appearing in the Insuring Agreement. That language provides:

> "This insurance applies only to 'bodily injury' and 'property damage' which occurs during the policy period. The 'bodily injury' or 'property damage' must be caused by an 'occurrence'."[35]

The 1973 standard form policy defined "occurrence" as:

> "an accident, including continuous or repeated exposure to conditions, which results in bodily injury or property damage neither expected nor intended from the standpoint of the insured."[36]

[32] See e.g. *Avondale*, 887 F. 2d at 1207; *Aviex*, 336 N. W. 2d at 842–43.
[33] *Aerojet-General Corp.* v. *Superior Court*, 211 Cal. App. 3d 216, 228 (1989).
[34] Abraham, n. 3 *supra*, 59–60.
[35] Robertson, n. 19 *supra*, 7.
[36] Ibid. 38.

In 1986, the definition was amended to read simply:

> "an accident, including continuous or repeated exposure to substantially the same general harmful conditions."[37]

The "expected or intended" language appearing in the pre-1986 "occurrence" definition was not eliminated from the policy, however; it was simply incorporated into a new standard exclusion providing that coverage was unavailable where the "bodily injury" or "property damage" was "expected or intended from the standpoint of the insured".[38]

Both the pre-1986 and the current "occurrence" definitions have been the source of two distinct controversies. The more complicated of the two concerns what constitutes an "occurrence" for purposes of triggering a policy's coverage when gradual or continuous injury has taken place. The trigger of coverage issue is addressed in Section V. But in the context of environmental coverage disputes, insurers have also posed an even more basic question: whether an act of pollution can ever constitute an "occurrence" in light of the expected/intended limitation appearing in both the pre- and post-1986 CGL policies. That question arises most frequently in those cases where the policyholder has routinely discharged polluting waste as part of its everyday business practices.

That question is, itself, composed of two separate issues. First, most insurers have taken the position that if an insured "intends" to discharge waste into the environment, no "occurrence" has taken place.[39] Insureds have, in turn, argued that it is the damage caused, not the discharge itself, which must be expected or intended in order to preclude coverage. Under the insureds' reading of the "occurrence" language, so long as an insured does not desire or know with certainty that damage will result from its intended actions, any consequent liability will be covered under the standard CGL policy. As with most other issues, the courts in the United States are split over the question, with most jurisdictions ruling in favour of policyholders.[40]

[37] Ibid.

[38] Ibid. 9.

[39] *Detrex Chemical Industries, Inc.* v. *Employers Insurance of Wausau*, 681 F. Supp. 438 (N. D. Ohio 1987); *American States Ins. Co.* v. *Maryland Casualty Co.*, 587 F. Supp. 1549 (E. D. Mich. 1984).

[40] Among those courts ruling in favour of policyholders are: *Transamerica Ins. Co.* v. *Sunnes*, 711 P. 2d 212 (1985), *review denied*, 717 P. 2d 631 (1986) (Oregon); *Atlantic Cement Co.* v. *Fidelity & Casualty Co.*, 459 N. Y. S. 2d 425, *aff'd*, 481 N. Y. S. 2d 329 (1983) (New York); *Buckeye Union Ins. Co.* v. *Liberty Solvents & Chemicals Co.*, 477 N. E. 2d 1227 (1984) (Ohio); *City of Johnstown* v. *Bankers Standard Ins. Co.*, 877 F. 2d 1146 (2d Cir. 1989) (New York); *City of Carter Lake* v. *Aetna Casualty & Surety Co.*, 604 F. 2d 1052 (8th Cir. 1979) (Nebraska); *American Universal Ins. Co.* v. *Whitewood Custom Treaters, Inc.*, 707 F. Supp. 1140 (D. S. D. 1989) (South Dakota); *Idaho* v. *Bunker Hill Co.*, 662 F. Supp. 725 (D. Idaho 1987) (Idaho); *Steyer* v. *Westvaco Corp.*, 450 F. Supp. 384 (D. Md. 1978) (Maryland). *Contra*: *Defrex*, 681 F. Supp. 438; *American States*, 587 F. Supp. 1549.

Second, assuming that the resulting damage is the proper focus of the limitation, how far must an insurer go to prove that its insured actually did "intend or expect" the pollution related harm? Subjective intent in any lawsuit is difficult enough to establish, but the obstacles facing an insurer in the environmental context are even greater. The targets of most environmental laws are large corporate entities composed of hundreds of employees, evidence of corporate intent is rare, and — because environmental damage often occurs gradually, as a result of actions taken several decades earlier — any available evidence is likely to be stale. Because practical problems inherent in establishing intent are formidable, both insurers and the courts tend to focus more on the "expectation" prong of the limiting language.

But the question of an insured's expectations has itself bred a hornet's nest of controversy over what degree of probability is necessary to establish an expectation and over whether that expectation should be measured by an objective or subjective standard. The additional phrase "from the standpoint of the insured" is often invoked by insurers as proof that an objective test was intended. Under their formulation of the policy language, if a reasonable person in the insured's shoes *should* have foreseen the harm, then for all practical purposes that harm was "intended or expected".[41] Most courts have rejected this approach for the reason that it effectively precludes recovery for an insured's mere negligence.[42] But apart from this, there is little judicial consensus over the appropriate standard of proof. Some courts adopt an objective standard, while others honour a subjective one.[43] On the issue of probability, both groups waver between requiring, at one extreme, that there be "substantial certainty" of damage[44] and requiring, on the other, only a "high degree of probability".[45]

In conjunction with the "expected or intended" limitation, insurers frequently rely on what is called the "known loss" defence. It is widely recognised, as both a matter of public policy and state statutory proscription, that insurance coverage is unavailable for losses which are known or apparent before a policy is issued.[46]

[41] *Calvert Ins. Co.* v. *Western Ins. Co.*, 874 F. 2d 396 (7th Cir. 1989); *Shell Oil Co.* v. *Accident & Cas. Ins. Co. of Winterthur*, No. 278953, Statement of Decision at 46 (Cal. Super. Ct. San Mateo Cty. Oct. 6, 1988); *Mutual Service Casualty Ins. Co.* v. *Country Life Insurance Co.*, 859 F. 2d 548, 552 (7th Cir. 1988).

[42] *See, e.g., Auto-Owners Insurance Co.* v. *Jensen*, 667 F. 2d 714, 719 (8th Cir. 1981).

[43] *Objective Standard*: See e.g. *Calvert Ins. Co.*, 874 F. 2d 396; *City of Carter Lake*, 604 F. 2d 1052. *Subjective Standard*: See e.g. *City of Johnstown*, 877 F. 2d at 1150; *Ray Indus. Inc.* v. *Liberty Mut. Ins. Co.*, 728 F. Supp. 1310 (E. D. Mich. 1989).

[44] *Claussen* v. *Aetna Casualty & Surety Co.*, 754 F. Supp. 1576 (S. D. Ga. 1990) (Georgia); *City of Johnstown*, 877 F. 2d at 1150; *Honeycomb Systems, Inc.* v. *Admiral Ins. Co*, 567 F. Supp 1400 (D. Me. 1983) (Maine); *Aetna Casualty & Surety Co.* v. *Dichtl*, 398 N. E. 2d 582 (1979) (Illinois); *Quincy Mutual Fire Ins. Co.* v. *Abernathy*, 469 N. E. 2d 797 (1984) (Massachusetts).

[45] *Jensen*, 667 F. 2d at 719, *City of Carter Lake*, 604 F. 2d 1052; *New Castle County* v. *Hartford Acci. and Indem. Co.*, 685 F. Supp. 1321 (D. Del. 1988); *Fischer & Porter Co.* v. *Liberty Mutual Insurance Co.*, 656 F. Supp. 132 (E. D. Pa. 1986).

[46] See e.g. California Insurance Code § 250. See also *Appalachian Ins. Co.* v. *Liberty Mut. Ins. Co.*, 676 F. 2d 56 (3rd Cir. 1982).

Insurers rely on this universal doctrine to argue that an insured who intentionally discharges waste, knowing there is a risk of resulting environmental damage, is precluded from recovery under policies issued during such time periods.[47] This argument has met with less success than similar arguments made under the "expected or intended" limitation. As most courts have been quick to point out, such an argument conflates the very different concepts of "known loss" and "known risk". Insureds routinely purchase and insurers routinely provide insurance coverage for "known risks"; indeed, it is on the basis of such information that insureds buy insurance at all and premiums are set and endorsements are selected. It is only after the "known risk" transpires into an actual loss for the insured that the risk becomes uninsurable. Hence, under the known loss rule, it is not enough for the insurer simply to show that its insured knew there was a risk of environmental damage or that undiscovered environmental damage was actually in progress at the time the policy was purchased. The relevant question is whether the insured knew that it would be subject to a loss through the imposition of legal liability for such damage.[48] Indeed, one court has gone so far as to hold that a policy in effect even after the insured is notified that it is "potentially responsible" for a known contaminated site remains a viable source of coverage.[49]

V. Trigger of Coverage

As the standard form CGL Insuring Agreement cited in Section III makes clear, in order for coverage under a policy to be triggered, the "occurrence" must take place within the policy period. In the classic tort context, the date of an "occurrence" is generally easy to establish. Because environmental damage is often gradual and continuous, however, environmental claims often raise their own unique set of trigger of coverage questions.

The trigger problems raised by environmental claims are best illustrated by example. Suppose a particular site targeted for clean-up is used as a toxic waste dump for a period of 10 years. Each month, beginning in Year 1, hazardous materials are deposited at the site, accumulating over time. One year to the date from each deposit, contaminants begin to leach and are exposed to the soil and underlying groundwater. After two years, the contamination begins to travel to the groundwater underneath each of 10 adjoining properties. Five years from the date of first deposit, the contamination is discovered. Suppose further that, during the 10 years of operation, the owner of the dump site held 10 successive policies of liability insurance with 10 different insurance carriers. Based on the "occurrence" language contained in the standard form CGL policy, which of those ten policies has been triggered?

47 See e.g. *Bartholomew* v. *Appalachian Ins. Co.*, 655 F. 2d 27, 29 (1st Cir. 1981).

48 *Montrose Chemical Corp. of California* v. *Admiral Ins. Co.*, 5 Cal. Rptr. 2d 358, 1992 Cal. App. LEXIS 238 (1992); *City of Johnstown*, 877 F. 2d at 1152–53.

49 *Montrose*, 1992 Cal. App. LEXIS 238.

In the United States, the answer will depend on which state's laws govern, and even then there may be no conclusive authority to guide the court's decision. As one court has noted, there is "no consistent pattern in the myriad trigger cases".[50] Among the jurisdictions, at least four general theories of trigger have emerged, however, each with its own advantages and drawbacks.

Under one approach — the "exposure theory" — the policies in effect during those years in which the subject property was first exposed to the hazardous material would be triggered — i.e. the date of release.[51] Because exposure is the first step in the path toward environmental damage, the earliest policies would be implicated. For an insured faced with a claim of contamination spanning decades, the drawback to the exposure theory is clear, since earlier policies will generally carry lower limits of liability. On the other hand, many older CGL policies do not contain the kinds of exclusions which were later developed in order to limit coverage for pollution liability. Hence, under an exposure theory of trigger, an insured's prospects for coverage may be greater, although the amount of its ultimate recovery may be less.

A second approach — the "manifestation theory" — designates the date the damage was or should have been discovered as the date of "occurrence".[52] The implications of such a theory are the opposite of those under an exposure theory. Manifestation is usually the last step in the contamination process and hence an insured's most current policies will be on the risk. The obvious drawback to such an approach is that discovery of the contamination is only likely to occur once and, therefore, only one policy will be implicated, and it may contain exclusions designed to avoid pollution liability. On the other hand, because that policy will be of more recent vintage, its limits will probably be higher than those on earlier policy periods.

A third approach — the "continuous trigger theory" — is actually a composite of the other two theories because it fixes the date of the "occurrence" as the continuous period from the time of exposure to manifestation.[53] Literally scores of policies might be implicated under this approach, making it an ideal theory for any insured faced with a claim of progressive environmental damage. On the other hand, it poses enormous logistical problems for the courts and insurers who must reach an acceptable resolution as to how the insurance burden should be allocated among the various carriers on the risk.

[50] *Dow Chemical Co.* v. *Associated Indemnity Corp.*, 724 F. Supp. 474, 479 (E. D. Mich. 1989).

[51] See e.g. *Continental Ins. Cos.* v. *Northeastern Pharmaceutical & Chemical Co.*, 811 F. 2d 1180 (8th Cir. 1987), *rev'd on other grounds*, 842 F. 2d 977 (8th Cir.) (*en banc*), cert. denied, 488 U. S. 821 (1988); *Centennial Ins. Co.* v. *Lumbermens Mutual Casualty Co.*, 677 F. Supp. 342 (E. D. Pa. 1987).

[52] See e.g. *Mraz* v. *Canadian Universal Insurance Co.*, 804 F. 2d 1325 (4th Cir. 1986) (Maryland law); *Allstate Insurance Co.* v. *Quinn Construction Co.*, 713 F. Supp. 35 (D. Mass. 1989).

[53] See e.g. *Keene Corp.* v. *Ins. Co. of North America*, 667 F. 2d 1034, 1047 (D. C. Cir. 1981), *cert. denied*, 455 U. S. 1007 (1982); *New Castle Country* v. *Continental Casualty Co.*, 725 F. Supp. 800 (D. Del. 1989) (Delaware); *Gottlieb* v. *Newark Ins. Co.*, 570 A. 2d 443 (N. J. Super. 1990) (New Jersey).

The final approach — commonly referred to as the "injury-in-fact" theory — requires the court to determine on a case-by-case basis when the injury actually occurred.[54] Some commentators have argued that this approach comes closest to reflecting the language of the standard form CGL policy's "occurrence" provision.[55] However, this approach tends to pose the greatest number of problems in application. Determining precisely what the actual injury to a particular site is and when it occurs involves exhaustive case-by-case fact-finding and may require proof of scientific facts and expert testimony. Consequently, for both the insurer and the policyholder, application of the injury-in-fact approach will inevitably result in high litigation costs and uncertain results.

Decisional authority over which trigger approach should be employed literally runs across the board, and no clear trend appears to have emerged. But the expense and practical difficulties associated with the "injury-in-fact" theory suggest that, in all but the most basic environmental claims, its use will not be advocated by either side of the coverage dispute. Of the remaining three, the "continuous trigger" approach is best supported by the nature and terms of the standard form CGL policy. It has been argued, for example, that application of the "manifestation" rule would transform what is, fundamentally, an occurrence-based policy into a claims-made policy because it would tend to restrict coverage to one single policy. While this may have been the intent of the insurance industry when drafting the claims-made form — which restricts coverage to the single policy in effect at the time a claim is asserted against the insured — the drafting history of the CGL policy indicates that its drafters actually contemplated coverage under successive policies.[56] Moreover, because "discovery" based policies, such as claims made forms, permit the insurer more accurately to predict the limits of its exposure, the premiums charged are often less than those paid on occurrence-based policies like the standard form CGL. Hence, as one court recently explained:

[50] *Dow Chemical Co.* v. *Associated Indemnity Corp.*, 724 F. Supp. 474, 479 (E. D. Mich. 1989).

[51] See e.g. *Continental Ins. Cos.* v. *Northeastern Pharmaceutical & Chemical Co.*, 811 F. 2d 1180 (8th Cir. 1987), *rev'd on other grounds*, 842 F. 2d 977 (8th Cir.) (*en banc*), cert. denied, 488 U. S. 821 (1988); *Centennial Ins. Co.* v. *Lumbermens Mutual Casualty Co.*, 677 F. Supp. 342 (E. D. Pa. 1987).

[52] See e.g. *Mraz* v. *Canadian Universal Insurance Co.*, 804 F. 2d 1325 (4th Cir. 1986) (Maryland law); *Allstate Insurance Co.* v. *Quinn Construction Co.*, 713 F. Supp. 35 (D. Mass. 1989).

[53] See e.g. *Keene Corp.* v. *Ins. Co. of North America*, 667 F. 2d 1034, 1047 (D. C. Cir. 1981), *cert. denied*, 455 U. S. 1007 (1982); *New Castle Country* v. *Continental Casualty Co.*, 725 F. Supp. 800 (D. Del. 1989) (Delaware); *Gottlieb* v. *Newark Ins. Co.*, 570 A. 2d 443 (N. J. Super. 1990) (New Jersey).

[54] See e.g. *Independent Petrochemical Corp.* v. *Aetna Casualty & Surety Co.*, 654 F. Supp. 1334 (D. D. C. 1986) (District of Columbia); *United States* v. *Conservation Chemical Company*, 653 F. Supp. 152 (W. D. Mo. 1986) (Missouri).

[55] Abraham, n. 3 *supra*, 102.

[56] *Montrose Chemical*, 1992 Cal. App. LEXIS at 32.

> "To read an occurrence policy to afford coverage only when the injury or damage becomes manifest during the policy period and thus to preclude coverage under successive policies — notwithstanding that the insured has paid a premium higher than that which would have been charged for a "claims made" policy — unfairly transforms the more expensive occurrence policy into a cheaper claims made policy."[57]

Adoption of one theory over others does not end the trigger debate. One question that often arises in cases of continuous environmental damage is whether one or multiple occurrences have taken place. In the hypothetical case set out at the beginning of this section, for example, it could be argued that every time toxic waste was dumped at the site, an "occurrence" took place. Resolution of the question is sometimes critical because deductibles and limits of liability are often tied to the number of "occurrences". Under a policy with a $50,000 per occurrence limit, for example, an insured would be better off claiming multiple, individual occurrences rather than claiming that each dumping event constituted a single progressive harm. Again, no clear trend has emerged over how the calculation should be made, although many courts have rejected the view that there can be only one occurrence in a case of continuous injury.[58]

VI. The Pollution Exclusions

No single issue arising out of the environmental liability context has been more aggressively litigated than the two forms of pollution exclusions appearing in the pre- and post-1986 standard form CGL policies. That outcome hardly comes as a surprise since the pollution exclusion is the only provision in either of the standard forms specifically and expressly deals with environmental liability.

A. *The "Sudden and Accidental" Exclusion*

The first pollution exclusion — commonly known as the "qualified" or "sudden and accidental" exclusion — was included in the 1973 revision of the standard form CGL policy. It provides:

> "This policy does not apply
>
> to bodily injury or property damage arising out of the discharge, dispersal, release or escape of smoke, vapors, soot, fumes, acids, alkalis, toxic chemicals, liquids or gases, waste materials or other irritants or contaminants or pollutants into or upon land, the atmosphere or any water course or body of water, but this exclusion does not apply if such discharge, dispersal, release or escape is sudden and accidental."[59]

[57] Ibid 29.

[58] See e.g. *Industrial Steel Container Co.* v. *Fireman's Fund Insurance Co.*, 399 N. W. 2d 156, 159 (Minn. Ct. App. 1987).

[59] Robertson, n. 19 *supra*, 11.

Virtually every portion of this exclusionary language has been subject to some form of attack. For example, in some cases dispute has arisen over whether the term "atmosphere" was intended to address interior portions of buildings, as well as outdoor air pollution problems, such that claims based on inhalation of asbestos fibres from building materials would be excluded.[60] The vast majority of litigation, however, has revolved around the meaning of the exception for "sudden and accidental" discharges.

That dispute is composed of two distinct issues, although they are generally dealt with together by the courts. First, *what* must be "sudden and accidental" in order for the exception to be triggered — the release of the pollutants or the resulting injury? Second, what do the terms "sudden and accidental" actually mean? Controversy over the latter issue generally focuses on the term "sudden". Does it have a temporal meaning and, if so, what does that imply? Must the "release" be "short in duration" or must it simply "begin abruptly" or both?

It has been the consistent position of insurers throughout the long battle over these terms that 1. it is the actual release of the pollutants that must be sudden and accidental and 2. that the term "sudden" does have a temporal meaning.[61] Insurers have accordingly argued that the qualified exclusion precludes coverage for intentional acts that caused pollution, even if the insured did not intend or expect the resulting environmental damage. Under this reading, the insured who intentionally dumped waste at a site, but who had no idea his actions would create any environmental harm, would not be covered under his CGL policy for any claims arising from the hazard. Because insurers insist on a temporal component, acts of gradual pollution, whether intended or not, would also be excluded from coverage. Insurers argue that any other reading of the term "sudden" — such as an "unexpected" definition — would be redundant in light of the "accidental" language.[62]

Insured, on the other hand, have argued for the broadest possible reading of the "sudden and accidental" exception. Under their construction, the exclusion is intended only to apply to the "intentional polluter" — one who intends the act causing the pollution and expects the resulting injury.[63] The waste dumper in the

[60] *United States Fidelity & Guaranty Co.* v. *Wilkin Insulation Co.*, 578 N. E. 2d 926 (1991) (Illinois).

[61] Among those courts who have applied the clause in favour of insurers are: *Northern Ins. Co.* v. *Aardvark Assoc. Inc.*, 942 F. 2d 189 (3rd Cir. 1991) (Pennsylavnia); *EAD Metallurgical, Inc.*, v. *Aetna Casualty & Surety Co.*, 905 F. 2d 8 (2d Cir. 1990) (New York); *United States Fidelity & Guaranty Co.* v. *Star Fire Coals, Inc.*, 856 F. 2d 31, 35 (6th Cir. 1988) (Kentucky); *Great Lakes Container Corp.* v. *National Union Fire Ins. Co.*, 727 F. 2d 30 (1st Cir. 1984) (New Hampshire); *Outboard Marine Corp.* v. *Liberty Mutual Ins. Co.*, 570 N. E. 2d 1154 (Ill. 1991) (Illinois); *Technicon Electronics Corp.* v. *American Home Assur. Co.*, 544 N. Y. S. 2d 531 (1989) (New York); *Waste Management of Carolinas, Inc.*, v. *Peerless Ins. Co.*, 340 S. E. 2d 374, *rehearing denied*, 346 S. E. 2d 134 (1986) (North Carolina); *Sunnes*, 711 P. 2d 212 (1985) (Oregon).

[62] See e.g. *Powers Chemco Inc.* v. *Federal Ins. Co.*, 549 N. Y. S. 2d 650 (1989).

[63] See e.g. *Avondale Industries*, 887 F. 2d at 1205.

preceding paragraph would therefore be covered because he neither intended nor expected any environmental damage to result. Insureds also routinely dispute a temporal reading of the term "sudden"; under their construction, gradual pollution falls outside the ambit of the exclusion.[64]

In making these arguments, insureds have had an exceptional number of resources at their disposal. For example, given the mandate of applying a plain, everyday meaning to policy terms, it is not uncommon for a court to consult standard dictionaries as a way of resolving the "sudden and accidental" controversy.[65] Insureds have used that to their advantage by selectively citing those dictionaries which supply the most favourable definitions — i.e. those which do not contain a temporal component to the term "sudden" or which, because they supply alternative definitions, raise the spectre of ambiguity. The wealth of inconsistent rulings from the courts on the exclusion's scope has also been enlisted by insureds as additional evidence of that provision's ambiguity— a conclusion that, in light of the *contra proferentem* doctrine, virtually dictates for the policyholder.[66]

Ironically, no single factor has proven to be of more assistance to insureds in their battle over the qualified exclusion than representations made by the insurance industry, itself, at the time the exclusion was being adopted and approved. In many states, regulatory approval by the states' various insurance commissioners was necessary before the exclusion could be included in the standard form CGL policy. In the course of that approval process, one of the standard explanations supplied by ISO's predecessors on the exclusion read as follows:

> "Coverage for pollution or contamination is not provided in most cases under present policies because the damages can be said to be expected or intended and are thus excluded by the definition of occurrence. The above exclusion clarifies this situation so as to avoid any questions of intent. Coverage is continued for pollution or contamination caused injuries when the pollution or contamination results from an accident."[67]

In later proceedings the insurance industry represented that the exclusion merely clarified the meaning of the term "occurrence" of the standard form CGL policy which excluded coverage only if bodily injury or property damage was "expected or intended".[68]

By equating the exclusion with the "expected or intended" "occurrence" definition of the CGL policy (see discussion of "occurrence" above), the insurance industry unwittingly lent credence to the position of policyholders that the

64 See e.g. *Broadwell*, 528 A. 2d 76.

65 See e.g. *New Castle*, 673 F. Supp. 1359, 362–363; *United States Fidelity and Guaranty Co.* v. *Thomas Solvent Co.*, 683 F. Supp 1139 (W. D. Mich. 1988).

66 See e.g. *Thomas Solvent*, 683 F. Supp. at 1156.

67 Insurance Rating Board, Submission to Insurance Commissioner of West Virginia (8 May 1970).

68 In re Pollution and Contamination Filings, West Virginia Insurance Department, Order, at 3 (19 August 1970).

exclusion merely precludes coverage for "intentional polluters". Since then, insureds have routinely sought the admission of these statements in subsequent litigation over environmental claims, arguing that they reflect the collective judgement of the insurance industry and, hence, of their carrier's own intent.[69] At the very least, insureds have argued, those representations show that the exclusion is susceptible to several reasonable alternative interpretations. Controversy over the propriety of admitting such statements in the context of a particular action has often taken on a life of its own.

As is typical of most environmental liability coverage issues, there is a strong split of decisional authority over the scope of the "sudden and accidental" exclusion. At the outset of the controversy, the majority of courts sided with policyholders, finding that the exclusion was indeed co-extensive with the definition of "occurrence" in the standard form policy.[70] In the last few years, however, several courts have held that the exclusion is unambiguous and should be strictly applied to exclude coverage of most forms of environmental pollution.[71] Despite the array of decisional authority available, very few state supreme courts have ruled conclusively on the subject.

B. *The Absolute Pollution Exclusion*

As a response to the controversy generated over the "sudden and accidental" language and what insurers' perceived as the courts' overly generous construction of its meaning, the insurance industry amended the standard form exclusion in 1985. The new version, commonly referred to as the "absolute pollution exclusion" provides:

"This insurance does not apply to

(1) 'Bodily injury' or 'property damage' arising out of the actual, alleged or threatened discharge, dispersal or escape of pollutants:

 (a) At or from premises you own, rent or occupy;
 (b) At or from any site or location used by you or for you or others for the handling, storage, disposal, processing or treatment of waste;
 (c) Which are at any time transported, handled, stored, treated, disposed of, or processed as waste by you or for you or any person or organization for whom you may be legally responsible;

[69] See e.g. *United States Fidelity & Guaranty Co.* v. *Speciality Coatings Co.*, 535 N. E. 2d 1071 (Ill. 1989).

[70] Among the state supreme courts that have sided in favour of policyholders are: *Just* v. *Land Reclamation, Ltd.*, 456 N. W. 2d 570 (Wis. 1990) (Wisconsin); *Claussen* v. *Aetna Casualty & Surety Co.*, 380 S. E. 2d 686 (Ga. 1989) (Georgia); *United States Fidelity & Guaranty Co.* v. *Armstrong*, 479 So. 2d 1164 (Ala. 1985) (Alabama).

[71] Among the state supreme courts that have sided in favour of insurers are: *Lumbermens Mutual Casualty Co., Inc.* v. *Bellerville Industries, Inc.*, 555 N. E. 2d 568 (Mass. 1990) (Massachusetts); *Technicon Electronics*, 544 N. Y. S. 2d 531 (1989) (New York); *Waste Management of Carolinas*, 340 S. E. 2d 374.

(d) At or from any site or location on which you or any contractors or sub-contractors working directly or indirectly on your behalf are performing operations;
  (i) if the pollutants are brought on or to the site or location in connection with such operations; or
  (ii) if the operations are to test for, monitor, clean up, remove, contain, treat, detoxify or neutralize the pollutants.

(2) Any loss, cost, or expense arising out of any governmental direction or request that you monitor, clean up, remove, contain, treat, detoxify or neutralize pollutants.

Pollutants mean any solid, liquid, gaseous or thermal irritant or contaminant, including smoke, vapor, soot, fumes, acids, alkalis, chemicals and waste. Waste includes materials to be recycled, reconditioned or reclaimed."[72]

As its language clearly indicates, the "absolute" exclusion is exhaustive in scope and, by omitting the "sudden and accidental" exception, appears to have eliminated much of the controversy generated by its predecessor. Because of its recent vintage, it has not been the subject of much judicial interpretation. However, where the courts have had occasion to rule on it, the exclusion generally has been found unambiguous in its exclusion of coverage for environmental claims.[73]

The absolute exclusion is not closed to question, however. Some litigation has arisen over whether some products, such as pesticides, paint, sand or mud, actually constitute "pollution".[74] These cases are likely to set a precedent in the coming years for challenges over the extremely broad policy definition of "pollutants". The exclusion is also not free of loopholes. For example, it is conceivable that a spill of chemicals being transported by an insured would not technically be excluded by the policy language if those chemicals were not being handled as waste. Indeed, the absolute exclusion language has since been amended to exclude discharges "anywhere in the world" in order to address such loopholes. One further argument future insureds could raise under the exclusion is that the property damage at issue was not caused by a discharge of pollutants, as required, but by some other force which set the discharge in motion.[75] In short, while amendment to the earlier standard exclusion may curtail litigation over its meaning — and ultimately over the availability of insurance coverage for environmental claims under CGL policies — by no means has it eliminated it.

[72] Robertson, n. 19 Supra, 11.

[73] See e.g. *Guilford Industries, Inc.* v. *Liberty Mutual Ins. Co.*, 688 F. Supp. 792 (D. Me. 1988), *aff'd without op.*, 879 F. 2d 853 (1st Cir. 1989) (Maine law); *Alcolac, Inc.*, v. *St. Paul Fire and Marine Ins. Co.*, 716 F. Supp. 1541 (D. Md. 1989) (Maryland).

[74] *Molton, Allen & Williams* v. *St. Paul Fire & Marine Ins. Co.*, 347 So. 2d 95 (Ala. 1977) (mud and sand not "pollutants"); *A-1 Sandblasting & Steamcleaning Co.* v. *Baiden*, 632 P. 2d 1377 (Ore. App. 1981), *aff'd* 643 P. 2d 1260 (1982) (Oregon) (paint not a "pollutant"); *Westchester Fire Ins. Co.* v. *City of Pittsburgh, Kansas*, 768 F. Supp. 1463 (D. Kan. 1991) (pesticides).

[75] See e.g. *Pepper Industries, Inc.* v. *Home Ins. Co.*, 67 Cal. App. 3d 1012 (1977) (damage caused not by oil spill, but by resulting fire).

VII. The "Owned Property" Exclusion

Yet another exclusion invoked by liability insurers faced with environmental claims in the United States is the "owned property" exclusion. Under the 1973 standard from CGL policy, the exclusion provides:

> "This policy does not apply:
>
> to property damage to:
>
> (1) property owned or occupied by or rented to the insured."[76]

Other CGL policies used by insurers contain a similar standard exclusion which states:

> "This policy does not apply:
> (i) to property damage to:
> (1) property owned or occupied by or rented to the insured,
> (2) property used by the insured, or
> (3) property in the care, custody or control of the insured or as to which the insured is for any purpose exercising physical control."

Although the latter exclusion is broader in scope, the obvious function of both exclusions is to keep insureds fom using their CLG policy as a form of property insurance.

At first blush, both exclusions would therefore appear to preclude coverage where the insured owns or occupies the site targeted for clean-up measures. But, in fact, most environmental claims involve contamination which, while having originated on the insured's property, has migrated or threatened to migrate to off-site locations. The question raised by the "owned property" exclusions, then, is whether measures undertaken by an insured to remediate actual or threatened damage both on and off its property are covered.

The strongest case for coverage is in those situations where property damage has already occurred off-site as a result of contaminant migration from the insured's property. Often in such cases remedial action on the insured's property is necessary to clean up both the owned and non-owned property. But under the 1973 exclusion, insureds have argued that for purposes of coverage it is irrelevant *where* the clean-up occurs so long as non-owned property has been damaged.[77] Were it otherwise, the exclusion would preclude coverage for all property, owned or not, merely because remediation had to take place on the insured's site. This argument has met with varying degrees of success, with some courts favouring full coverage for all clean-up measures and others allocating recovery to that portion of costs attributable solely to the off-site damage.[78]

[76] Robertson, n. 19 *supra*, 12.

[77] See e.g. *Broadwell Realty Services*, 528 A. 2d 76.

[78] See e.g. *Allstate Ins. Co.* v. *Quinn Construction Co.*, 713 F. Supp. at 40; *Conservation Chemical Company*, 653 F. Supp. 152.

The harder case for insureds is where the only actual property damage is to "owned property" and migration to off-site locations is only threatened. As a practical matter, remediation on the insured's property is necessary not simply to clean up that property but also to prevent future property damage from occuring elsewhere. The problem with this scenario is that no property damage to *covered* property (*i.e.* property now owned by the insured) has occured during the policy period, as the Insuring Agreement requires. But insureds have argued that the Insuring Agreement requires nothing more than that liability be incurred because of damage to property, unowned or otherwise. Since in the above scenario clean-up liability surely has been imposed because of damage to property (albeit belonging to the insured), coverage exists.[79]

One further way insureds have succeeded in avoiding the exclusion is simply to dispute what constitutes "owned property". This controversy is almost always raised in the context of groundwater contamination underlying the insured's property for the very simple reason that, in many jurisdictions, groundwater is owned by the state, not the surface landowner.[80] This argument has met with enormous success in the courts, even when the broader "care, custody, or control" exclusion was at issue.[81]

VIII. Other Sources of Coverage Outside the CGL

A. *The Property Policy*

Although the vast majority of environmental claims are made and disputed under CGL policies, in the past few years insureds have been turning in increasing numbers to their first party property policies as a potential source of coverage. Their reasons for doing so are obvious. The "absolute" amendment to the CGL standard form pollution exclusion has made it far more difficult to recover under current liability policies (see Section VI.B. *supra*) and, although the trend in American courts once leaned toward policyholders, some courts are now beginning to show a greater willingness to apply other CGL policy limitations in favour of insurers.

The first-party property policy offers several advantages to insureds faced with an environmental claim. For example, many contain no explicit pollution exclusion and, because its principal function is to insure the policyholder's own property, it also avoids many of the pitfalls of the CGL's "owned property" exclusion. Few environmental claims have actually been litigated under property

[79] Among those cases finding that the owned property exclusion did *not* apply to environmental clean-up on an insured's property if performed to *prevent* damage to a third party's property are: *Hybrid Equip. Corp.* v. *Sphere Drake Ins. Co.*, C. A. No. 14597, 1991 Ohio App. LEXIS 362 (Ohio Ct. App., 9th App. Dist.); *Quinn Constr. Co.*, 713 F. Supp. 35; *Summit Assoc.* v. *Liberty Mutual Fire*, 550 A. 2d q235 (N. J. App. Div. 1988).

[80] See e.g. *AIU Ins. Co.* v. *Superior Court*, 51 Cal. 3d at 817.

[81] *Aviex*, 336 N. W. 2d 838.

policies and hence there is little case law to guide courts in their coverage determinations. The lack of unfavourable authority is an additional benefit for policyholders. On the other hand, as discussed below, the very nature of property policies is at odds with what are essentially environmental *liability* claims and any court versed in the fundamental distinctions between first- and third-party policies is likely to discern that fact. An insured hoping to recover under its property policy will therefore have to be more "creative" in its coverage claim than it would under its CGL policy.

The fundamental question under any property policy is whether damage has occurred to "covered property" caused by a "covered peril". Although there is less uniformity among first-party coverage forms than among CGL forms property policies in the United States can essentially be divided in two camps[82] and the likelihood of recovery will often depend on which category the insured's policy falls into. The "All Risk" policy covers the insured's property against all perils not specifically excluded. Under such a policy, an insured need only prove that it suffered a loss to the insured property; the burden is on the insurer to prove the applicability of any exclusions or limitations. The "Named Perils" policy, by contrast, insures only against specific named risks such as fire, smoke, lightning, explosion, etc. The insured making a claim under such a policy bears the burden of proving that its loss was caused by a named peril.

Both policies are typically limited to cases of "direct loss" which, roughly translated, means that the insured peril must be the "actual cause" of the loss. Actual causation is a legal concept used by courts to distinguish between two or more concurrent causes of an event. For example, assume an employee's negligence causes a fire to break out at the insured's factory which in turn ruptures several tanks of hazardous chemicals which leak into the soil and groundwater. Is the eventual soil and water contamination "caused" by the employee's negligence, the fire or the explosion? The answer will depend upon what state's laws govern the dispute. Actual causation is defined differently in different states, is difficult to apply and often takes on metaphysical proportions.[83] It is therefore beyond the scope of this article. The point here is simply that, especially in the face of complicated environmental claims, proving "direct loss" under a property policy can be fraught with problems.

One way insureds might try to avoid those problems is to insist that, regardless of questions over actual causation, coverage for clean-up costs is available under what is commonly referred to as the "debris removal" clause. Property policies typically contain such clauses which provide that the insurer will pay

[82] Glad and Barnes, "The Final Frontier: First-Party Environmental Claims", in (1990) 12 *Insurance Litigation Reporter* 5

[83] For an illustration of how various courts have dealt with the concurrent causation issue *compare Blaine Richards & Co.* v. *Marine Indem. Ins. Co.*, 635 F. 2d 1051 (2d Cir. 1980) (New York) *with Graham* v. *Public Employees Mut. Ins. Co.*, 656 P. 2d 1077 (Wash. 1983) (Washington) and *Garvey* v. *State Farm & Cas. Co.*, 43 Cal. 3d 395 (1989) (California).

for the removal of debris from the insured's property. Indeed, several cases have found coverage for the clean up of various hazardous wastes, such as oil or PCBs, under such clauses.[84] But the debris removal provision is not, in itself, a coverage provision; it is simply a measure of the insured's recovery. The insured must still show that the "debris" was caused by a named or covered peril.

As suggested earlier, one advantage to property policies is that they avoid the pitfalls of the "owned property" exclusion appearing in the CGL policy. However, the same dilemma confronting liability insureds over how to segregate clean-up costs between on- and off-site damage is still present in the first-party context, although it appears in the reverse. As discussed in the preceding section, remediation measures on insured property may be undertaken not only to clean up the insured site but also to arrest or prevent contaminant migration to adjacent, non-owned property. Indeed, one court has already taken cognizance of this distinction in a first-party context, allocating the clean-up costs accordingly.[85] Hence, even if first-party coverage is available for environmental claims, such policies may not cover the full extent of an insured's loss.

Moreover, even assuming remediation efforts at an insured site are in no measure undertaken for the benefit of adjacent landowners, the coverage question may not be at an end. Typically, property policies cover only the "dwellings or buildings" at an insured site, not the "land" itself or any natural outgrowths such as trees or shrubs.[86] Indeed, more recent policies now contain an explicit exclusion for "land". Although the issue has not been raised directly, some courts have held in *dicta* that the exclusion effectively precludes coverage for clean-up of contamination to soil on the insured's property caused by hazardous waste.[87] Similarly, depending upon the jurisdiction, clean-up of contamination to the groundwater located under the insured property may also be excluded. As discussed in Section VII, in many states, groundwater is owned by the state, not the surface landowner. Hence, the insured would have no "insurable interest" in the water — a necessary prerequisite to coverage under property policies.

Although some property policies contain explicit "pollution" exclusions, many contain an exclusion for "contamination", under which courts have not hesitated to find damage caused by such varied products as pesticides, ammonia gas, and oil vapour excluded from coverage.[88] It is therefore unlikely that indus-

[84] See e.g. *Lexington Ins. Co.* v. *Ryder System, Inc.*, 234 S. E. 2d 839 (Ga. App. 1977) (oil spill); *Daniels, Wedzeb Enterprises, Inc.* v. *Aetna Life & Casualty Co.*, No. JP 81-1413-C (S. D. Ind. 29 June 1983) WL 13684 (PCB contamination).

[85] *Compass Ins. Co.* v. *Cravens, Dargan & Co.*, 748 P. 2d 724 (Wyo. 1988).

[86] Abraham. n. 3 *supra*, 216–217.

[87] *St. Paul Fire & Marine Ins. Co.* v. *Protection Mutual Ins. Co.*, 664 F. Supp. 328, 333–334 n. 8 (N. D. I11. 1987).

[88] *Auten* v. *Employers National Ins. Co.*, 722 S. W. 2d 468 (Tex. Civ. App. 1986) (pesticides); *American Produce & Vegetable* v. *Phoenix Assur. Co.*, 408 S. W. 2d 954 (Tex. Civ. App. 1966) (ammonia gas); *Hi-G, Inc.* v. *St. Paul Fire & Marine Ins. Co.*, 283 F. Supp. 211 (D. Mass 1967), *aff'd* 391 F. 2d 924 (1st Cir. 1968).

trial hazardous waste claims will escape the grip of this exclusion. Some first-party policies, however, do contain a safety hatch of sorts; their contamination exclusions preclude coverage for "contamination [unless] caused by a peril not excluded in this policy". The language virtually invites insureds to assert complicated actual cause arguments as a way to avoid the exclusion's preclusive effect. This was indeed the outcome in one case where the insured successfully argued that the claimed contamination was "caused" by an employee's negligence.[89]

Many first-party policies also contain other exclusions which, for example, preclude coverage for "wear and tear, inherent vice or latent defect" and for increases in hazard knowingly allowed by the insured.[90] Depending on the circumstances, such exclusions are likely to be invoked by first-party insurers seeking to avoid costly environmental claims in the future. For the moment, the slate of first-party environmental coverage disputes is relatively clean. But with more courts turning a sympathetic ear to liability insurers in the environmental arena, that slate will not remain clean long.

B. Environmental Impairment Liability Coverage

One alternative for insureds frustrated with the limited protections of traditional CGL and property policies is coverage under Environmental Impairment Liability policies ("EIL"). EIL policies are marketed under various names including "Environmental Protection Liability" policies and "Pollution Liability" policies. Developed in the mid-1970s when the risk of environmental liability was first recognised, their fundamental if not only function is to provide liability insurance for environmental or pollution-related liabilities.[91]

EIL policies did not emerge as standard forms and, today, there are in fact several competing forms on the market. The principal insuring agreement under many of these forms, however, insures against:

> all sums which the Insured shall be obligated to pay for compensatory but not punitive or exemplary damages by reason of liability imposed upon the Insured by law on account of:
>
> a. Personal Injury, including death at any time resulting therefrom;
> b. Property Damage;
> c. Impairment of diminution of or other interference with any other environmental right or amenity protected by law;
>
> arising within the Territorial Limits designated in the Declarations and caused by Environmental Impairment in connection with the Business of the Insured at the locations designated in the Declarations …

[89] *Raybestos-Manhattan, Inc.* v. *Industrial Risk Insurers*, 433 A. 2d 906 (Pa. Super, 1981).
[90] Glad and Barnes, n. 82 *supra*, 11–12.
[91] Abraham, n. 3 *supra*, 195–196

Environmental Impairment is defined as

(a) the emission, discharge, dispersal, disposal, seepage, release or escape of any liquid, solid, gaseous or thermal irritant, contaminant or pollutant into or upon land, the atmosphere or any watercourse or body of water;
(b) the generation of smell, noises, vibrations, light, electricity, radiation, changes in temperature or any other sensory phenomena but not fire or explosion ...[92]

EIL policies are not a panacea for all environmental risks or for the problems which plague environmental coverage disputes under the standard form CGL policy. In many ways EIL policies may even create more problems than they resolve. First, they are difficult to obtain. Indeed, by the mid-1980s, they became almost completely unavailable.[93] Presently, at best, insurers under EIL policies will agree to cover only a limited set of environmental risks, and then only after extensive risk surveys are conducted. Moreover, as the insuring agreement states, only liability arising out of specifically designated sites is covered. Predictably, the premiums on EIL policies are often prohibitively high.

Second, the insuring agreement of EIL policies may prove to be as much of a breeding ground for litigation as the standard CGL insuring agreement. For example, the agreement promises to pay "all sums which the Insured shall be obligated to pay for *compensatory* ... damages" — a provision which may recall the "as damages" debate under the CGL policy (see Section III). Although few cases under EIL policies have made their way to American courts yet, one court has already ruled that clean-up costs are not incurred on account of the "impairment ... of any other environmental right".[94]

Finally, EIL policies are replete with exclusions which, given many environmental exposures, virtually undermine the promise of coverage for pollution-related liabilities. Among them are exclusions for liability for clean-up of waste disposal sites, exclusions for liability arising out of an insured's failure to comply with statutory regulations, exclusions for the costs of correcting of pre-existing conditions, exclusions for clean-up operations "reasonably considered to be routine and normal", and amazingly — given the tide of litigation over the 1973 standard form pollution exclusion — exclusions for "environmental impairment caused by a sudden and accidental happening".[95]

Both because of their recent vintage and their restricted availability, EIL policies have not been the subject of significant judicial rulings. It is therefore impossible to predict how far they will go in protecting insureds against the onslaught of environmental liability in the U.S. If the foregoing exclusions are any indication, it will not be far.

[92] Ibid 198.
[93] Ibid. 196.
[94] *Detroit Edison Co.* v. *Pacific Ins. Co.*, 742 F. Supp. 287 (M. D. N. C. 1990), *aff'd without op.* 944 F. 2d 901 (1991).
[95] Abraham, n. 3 *supra*, 207–214.

Conclusion

It is probably fair to say that, back in 1973 when it was drafting its standard form CGL policy, the insurance industry never predicted the enormous impact U.S. environmental legislation would have on future coverage claims. The same could also be said for many of its insureds who are now facing liability for actions which, when conducted 15 years earlier, were thought to be legal, proper and safe. Neither side of the current controversy could have contemplated the massive sweep of current environmental liability when their policies were drafted and purchased, and this perhaps explains why the equally massive tide of coverage litigation is so often mired in highly technical, complicated disputes over policy terms in a way that few other coverage disputes are. The crippling costs of environmental liability and the often conflicting authority emerging from the various state and federal courts has only served to fuel those disputes.

Whether insurance coverage for environmental clean-up measures is available in the United States is therefore a question that does not lend itself to a quick and easy resolution. As the foregoing discussion illustrates, the answer will often depend on a variety of factors including the type of terms of the insured's policy, the source, nature and extent of the environmental damage, how liability is being imposed, and what state's law governs the coverage dispute. What is certain is that such disputes will continue to plague American courts for at least another decade.

Cleaning-up Measures on/outside the Insured Site/Insurability

Vianney Bollier

We will devote most of our attention to cleaning-up measures outside of the insured site, since the subject of the present book is centred on Liability, but it is useful to begin by looking at cleaning-up measures within the insured premises or site.

Using the scientific approach of considering first what we believe are the simpler issues, let us start with the hypothesis of a sudden and accidental outburst of polluting liquid. An example could be an short-circuit leading the electric pump of an oil tank generously to spill the contents of the tank as of midnight one Friday evening. If we want the example to be really significant, we have to assume that the safety measures on the plant did not function correctly or at least quickly enough, and that an important quantity of oil had escaped before the leak was stopped. As the cause of the event is a fairly simple misfunctioning and no material damage has been sustained by the pump or by the tank, no insurance cover for the spillage can be triggered from that angle.

The first thing the plant owner will do is to recover the spilt oil. If the tank is surrounded by an appropriate retention basin, the recovery work will by easy: no oil should have escaped from the basin and, except for the fact that we have to insure it will not happen again, we are almost in the presence of a non-event. If, on the other hand, there is no retention basin or its capacity is insufficient, only part of the oil will be recoverable at an economic cost, and for the balance of the oil, the recovery would, when possible, be more expensive than the value of the product itself.

Although the straight comparison between the cost of the recovery efforts and the value of the potentially recovered product is negative, there can be serious reasons to continue those efforts. These efforts will be requalified from recovery costs to cleaning-up costs, and will correspond to a situation where what you spend is geared by the need to restore your property to its original shape and productive potential.

Let us now assume that an adjoining building has been polluted by the spilt oil. Under an All Risks Property Damage policy, and considering that the cause of the event is not a normal part of the operations, the exposure to a polluting liquid is considered a damage, and the policy should respond not only for the cleaning-up costs, but also for, say, the repainting of the walls and, if necessary, the replacement of damaged computer equipment. On the other hand, if the Insurance policy covers only Fire, Explosion and Allied Perils, a careful reading of the Allied Perils clause would be necessary in order to ascertain the application of the cover, but most modern wordings do provide the cover.

There are several variations to our basic example which may have an influence on insurance coverage. You can, for instance, assume that the leak of liquid was caused by an accident to a factory-owned and manned fork-lift truck puncturing the tank: in that case, there could be insurance cover for the tank itself, but the cleaning-up situation is the same as before.

Another variation is that there is a small leak in the underground section of a pipe, which is discovered on the occasion of an excavation or because the spilt oil has spread sufficiently to alter the surface of the ground in the area of the leak. Although there is damage to the pipe, the fact that the leak is neither sudden nor accidental but results from wear and tear and lack of maintenance, will bar the application of the insurance policy for cleaning-up costs, unless the wear and tear exclusion is limited to the equipment and allows coverage for the consequences.

If the leak has been caused not by lack of maintenance but by an accidental phenomenon (for instance, a vagrant electrical shock caused by lightning), the application of the policy would be much easier even if some period of time has elapsed between the occurrence and the discovery of its consequences, but provided the causal relation can still be established with acceptable certainty.

As a last variation, we will consider an example where the original cause, whatever it was, resulted in a fire or explosion: in those circumstances, insurance cover will apply fairly broadly to the damage sustained by the premises, and to the expenses exposed for its cleaning-up.

It is clear then, that it is difficult to theorize on the insurability of cleaning-up expenses. But before we turn to the question of what happens outside the premises involved, I would like to volunteer a few comments on the theory of insurability.

A distinction which is generally made by legal experts suggests that Mediterranean countries have a different approach from those in the broadly speaking Anglo-Saxon culture. As you know, Mediterranean countries have a tendency to be wary of insurers as a potential aggravator of the risk factor.

An extreme example of that attitude can be found in France, where life insurance on the head of another person was long considered immoral because of its possible encouragement to murder an insured person for your own benefit!

Even today, there remains in France the belief that, for example, to allow somebody to insure in the area of Directors' Liability, the facilitation of the condemnable behaviour more than outweights the advantages of protecting the interests of the victim, should the tortfeasor be insolvent.

As a Frenchman with a Cartesian education, it has taken a great effort for me to realize why such apparent reasoning is self-destructive and how it is the victim of a boomerang effect resulting from the confusion between the causes and the consequences of a phenomenon. But I am now convinced that the areas where insurance does facilitate the manifestation of claims are in fact very narrow.

Whilst we can all observe with amazement the situation in the United States, I believe that one of the interesting consequences of the unifying European economic environment therefore appears to be the necessity of a synthesis between the too simplistic moral approach used in some countries, and the pragmatic approach seen in some others.

What then happens to cleaning-up costs incurred outside of the premises? To put it in simple terms, the best you can hope if you have not taken very specific insurance measures, is a big battle with your insurance company. To have a clean and operative factory was enough of a motivation inside your premises to justify exposing cleaning-up efforts but, as far as Third Parties are concerned, why should you spend so much money?

I was faced a few years ago with a situation where a nice green meadow, where cows used to graze and their milk was turned to cheese, was converted into an oil pond. Economically sound — that is low cost — recovery expenses were first exposed to pump the oil and put it back into the system: the Third Party Liability insurers considered that since their insured was only recovering his own property, no indemnity was due in this respect. Although an American insured would object to this interpretation, we Europeans continue to think that there is nothing fundamentally wrong at this stage, and we can turn to the next step which was the real cleaning-up. Because he was a believer of the good will of Mother Nature, the polluter thought that Mother Nature would do the trick, and the Mayor of the township was therefore advised that the owner of the meadow should only wait for the next rainfall.

As you can imagine, the owner of the meadow did not agree, and the polluter turned again to his Third Party Liability insurer. That insurer of course agreed with the Mother Nature theory, and the polluter turned back to the mayor and said that he would have been delighted to use detergents for the cleaning-up of the meadow, at the risk of killing all the fishstock of the river, but that his uncooperative Third Party insurer did not want to pay, either for the detergents or for the fish.

At this stage, we, as broker for the polluter, were called in and asked to provide a solution. In order to convince the insurer to pay, we had to create scenarios based on the necessity for "good conduct" as opposed to "laissez faire", and on the unavoidability of aggravated damage if not only cleaning-up, but intelligent cleaning-up, could be devised and effected.

Our insurers reluctantly agreed, a *modus operandi* was elaborated and, at the end of the cleaning-up operations, we thought that we could close our file. The following year, however, the oil that had seeped into the soil, seeped again upwards out of the soil, so that the meadow was again of an interesting brownish colour, the cows somewhat sick and the cheese inedible.

So, we had to reopen our file, and explain to the Third Party insurers that, although necessary, a second round of the same simple cleaning-up measures would not be sufficient because the soil itself had been "damaged". The eradication of the problem consisted in boring one hundred holes on an area covering about two acres, using a square grid of about nine feet. Each hole was three inches in diameter and had a depth of twelve feet, and the idea was that the oil which had impregnated the soil would become concentrated and could therefore be pumped.

Because this was the first claim of that nature in the twenty years' experience of our client, the Third Party Liability insurers finally agreed to reimburse most of the expenses, although since they had been rendered compulsory by the authorities, their indemnification nature had in their view become questionable.

However, a further consequence was that a beautiful exclusion would be incorporated in the policy for the future unless the premium be multiplied by five, and a deductible equal to the amount of that claim be imposed upon the insured. Although this was of little comfort to our insured, I believe that, even multiplied by five, the premium in question remained many times smaller than any premium of the same nature in the United States of America.

Reverting to a more general approach, we observe that, at least in Europe, insurers are still willing to make a distinction between those industries for which pollution is a significant element of risk because of the nature of their operations, and those where pollution is peripheral. In this latter case, it remains possible to extend the wording of Third Party Liability insurance so that cleaning-up and restoration expenses are indemnified up to a sublimit, and independently from physical damage and financial loss to Third Parties.

In these areas where the potential consequences of the pollution have had an impact on the general public and on the political authorities, insurance has become compulsory by law and, often, within the frame of international treaties.

This is especially true for the nuclear industry, in respect of which the insurance profession has organized itself world-wide by a network of national pools who cross-reinsure each other. More recently, the nuclear power plant operators in the U.S.A. have set up mutual insurance companies which in some instances compete with the pools and in others supplement them, but those mutuals are limited to Property and Business Interruption and do not address Third Party Liability insurance.

For those industries where pollution is a central preoccupation even if insurance is not compulsory, it is necessary to buy separate pollution insurance from specialised markets, and frequently from pools such as the GARPOL in France (now ASSURPOL). These insurances apply when the pollution does not result from a wilful decision of the management of the insured or from a passive acceptance of an operational risk.

There is of course a natural tendency on the part of industrial companies and their brokers narrowly to define the intrinsic potential polluters, and broadly to define the peripheral potential polluters. In other words, the industrial companies who buy insurance from the specialized pollution pools are the victims of a vigorous anti-selection.

As the insurers members of the pools become aware of that situation, the limits provided by the pools tend to diminish, and the premiums asked by the pools tend to increase, so that the anti-selection is self-increasing.

In the absence of the recent legal changes which took place within the E.C. and of their consequences on the laws of each country such as, for instance, Germany, it is likely that the insurability of cleaning-up and assimilated costs would have remained hazardous, limited and expensive.There is now, however, a much wider need for insurance, and since the spread of the risk will improve, we can hope that the insurability of cleaning-up and assimilated costs will also improve.

The CRTD Convention on Civil Liability and Compensation

Robert Cleton

1. Introduction

On 10 October 1989 a *Convention on Civil Liability for Damage Caused during Carriage of Dangerous Goods by Road, Rail and Inland Navigation Vessel (CRTD)*, hereinafter referred to as **CRTD Convention**,[1] was established by the Economic Commission for Europe of the United Nations (ECE) in Geneva. The CRTD Convention was open for signature until 31 December 1990 and thereafter it was open for accession by states who have not signed the Convention. The CRTD Convention has not yet entered into force; for its entry into force at least five states must have become a Party to the Convention.

The CRTD Convention is a milestone in a long history. This Convention dates back to 1972, when the Dutch government requested Unidroit[2] to undertake a preliminary study on civil liability for damage caused during the carriage of dangerous goods by road, rail and inland navigation vessel. A parallel initiative was undertaken by the same government with the Inland Transport Committee of ECE. The ECE decided only in 1976 to approach Unidroit with a similar request for a preliminary study with respect to road carriage. Unidroit established a Committee of Governmental Experts to take up the subject and this Committee started its deliberations in 1981. Unidroit's report, with a draft text for a Convention, applying to carriage by road, rail and inland navigation vessel,[3] was presented to the Inland Transport Committee in 1986. The ITC formed a

[1] The text of this Convention has been added as an annex to this chapter.
[2] International Institute for the Unification of Private Law, Rome.
[3] At the first session of the Group of experts there was a debate whether transport by pipeline and, as was suggested by an Arab delegation, transport by camel should be covered as well.

special working group which finished its work in 1989. The working group amended the Unidroit text on a number of points, but it left the underlying principles of the draft untouched.

It has taken several years before governments understood that the increasing carriage of dangerous goods creates a new and ever greater risk of injury to persons and of damage to property and to the environment. However, after the disaster which occurred in Los Alfaquès in July 1978 most governments started to realise that damage on such a massive scale as was caused during that catastrophe is likely to occur in the future, notwithstanding the taking of the most stringent precautions, and that the existing mechanism in most states to deal with claims arising from such massive damage is not capable of ensuring adequate compensation for victims. The Los Alfaquès disaster was a turning-point in the attitude of many governments taking part in the work of the ECE. In 1988 another major accident occurred in Herrborn in the former Federal Republic of Germany.

It should be noted that a similar project was undertaken in the early seventies by the International Maritime Organization (IMO) in London with respect to the transport of hazardous and noxious substances (usually reffered to as HNS) by sea. However, a draft Convention prepared by the Legal Committee of IMO failed to receive the approval of a Diplomatic Conference held in 1984 in London, and it was referred back to the IMO for further consideration. The HNS Convention is still a priority item on the agenda of the Legal Committee and it will probably take some more years before a new text is agreed upon.

The principal aims of the CRTD Convention are:

1. to ensure the provision of adequate and speedy compensation of victims, and
2. to facilitate the international carriage of goods by providing uniform international rules on civil liability for damage which may be caused by dangerous goods during their carriage. Adequate compensation should be guaranteed by imposing an obligation to insure this liability risk.

2. The Main Features of the CRTD Convention

Before discussing the Convention in detail I would like to mention its main features. These are the following:

(a) strict liability for damage caused by the dangerous goods during their carriage;[4]
(b) this liability is imposed on the carrier only;

[4] This implies that other damage caused by a vehicle carrying dangerous goods will not be compensated under the CRTD Convention, but under the applicable national law. Where, however, in one incident damage is caused both by dangerous goods and by other factors and such damage is not reasonably separable, all such damage shall be deemed to have been caused by the dangerous goods (Art. 1 para. 10, closing sentence).

(c) the carrier's liability is limited to a certain amount per event;[5]
(d) compulsory insurance of the above-mentioned liability.

3. The Scope of Application of the CRTD Convention

Modes of Transport Covered by the Convention

The Convention applies to transport of dangerous goods by road, by rail and by inland navigation vessel. The CRTD Convention is perhaps the only Convention which deals with the transport of three different modes of transport. The reason for including these three modes was that there is a close connection between these modes of transport and there is no reason to leave one particular form of inland transport out of this compensation scheme. Moreover, the regulation of maritime and air transport does not fall under the competence of the ECE but under that of the IMO and ICAO respectively. This approach has been heavily criticised by the professional organisations of inland navigation carriers, which pointed out that in particular on the Rhine many seagoing vessels (mainly coasters) are involved in the transport of dangerous goods. Since the CRTD Convention does not apply to such vessels, this would mean that the burden of strict liability, combined with compulsory insurance, would only be imposed on inland navigation carriers and that the inland navigation industry is being discriminated against.

"Carriage by road", "carriage by rail" and "carriage by inland navigation vessel" have been defined in Article 1 of the Convention. With respect to carriage by road it should be noted that only carriage on board a motor vehicle, articulated vehicle or semi-trailer, as defined in Article 1 of the Convention on Road Traffic of 8 November 1968, is covered by the Convention. As has been pointed out, the carriage of dangerous goods on board a seagoing ship, even if a seagoing ship is navigating inland waters, falls outside the scope of the CRTD Convention. It is the intention that all carriage by seagoing ships will be covered by the future HNS Convention of IMO.

In cases of "piggy-back" transport, where dangerous goods are transported in one vehicle, for instance, a road vehicle or railway wagon, and that vehicle is being carried part of the journey on board another vehicle, without the goods being unloaded,[6] the goods are deemed to be carried on board that other vehicle (Article 3, para 4). Another choice would have been possible, i.e. to apply the Convention rules to the vehicle on which the dangerous goods had been loaded, but most delegations were of the opinion that during that part of the journey the actual control of the transport operation is exercised by the operator of the underlying vehicle. However, the CRTD Convention does not apply when the vehicle is carried on board a seagoing ship or aircraft.

[5] See, however, Art. 24, para. 1a (reservation clause), which allows a State Party to apply higher limits than those prescribed under Art. 9 or no limit at all.

[6] For instance a road vehicle carried on board a ferryboat crossing a river or estuary.

Carriage on Privately owned Grounds

Dangerous goods may be moved in a factory or a wharehouse in the course of a manufacturing process or during storage operations. In those cases the carriage may be only accessory to such activities and form in fact an integral part thereof. In such cases there is no question of genuine carriage and for this reason such "carriage" has been excluded from the sphere of application of the Convention provided, however, that the carriage has been performed entirely on privately owned grounds (Article 4, para. 1(a)).

Damage to be Compensated

As to the nature of the damage which may be compensated under the Convention, Article 1, paragraph 10 contains a definition of "damage". "Damage" includes:

(a) loss of life and personal injury caused on board or outside the vehicle carrying the dangerous goods;
(b) loss or damage to property *outside* the vehicle carrying the dangerous goods; in this respect a train of vehicles, for instance, barges coupled in a train, or a railway train, the train of vehicles is treated as one vehicle and damage to goods loaded in one vehicle caused by dangerous goods in another vehicle of the same train will not be compensated under the Convention, the reason for this exception being that the owner of the damaged goods will have a claim under the contract of carriage concluded with the carrier and the Convention should not interfere with that contract of carriage;
(c) loss or damage by contamination to the environment caused by the dangerous goods, provided that compensation for impairment of the environment other than for loss of profit from such impairment shall be limited to costs of reasonable measures of reinstatement actually undertaken or to be undertaken;
(d) the costs of preventive measures and further loss caused by preventive measures.

"Preventive measures" have been defined in paragraph 11 of Article 1 as "any reasonable measures taken by any person after the incident has occurred to prevent or minimize damage", and "incident" (see para. 12) as "any occurrence or series of occurrences having the same origin, which causes damage or creates a grave and imminent threat of causing damage".

The question as to what extent environmental damage should be compensated gave rise to an extensive discussion. It was decided to adopt for subparagraph (c) the definition of "pollution damage", included in the Civil Liability Convention for oil pollution damage of 1969 (CLC), as amended by the 1984 Protocol to that Convention. This definition restricts to a certain extent the compensation which can be claimed for impairment of the environment by limiting such compensation to costs of reasonable measures of reinstatement actually undertaken or to be undertaken, thus ruling out any claims based on abstract calculations with respect to the loss of natural resources. By referring in the definition to loss of profit, subparagraph (c) allows compensation for pure economic loss, provided of course that there is a sufficient causal relationship between the accident and the damage suffered.

The concept of "preventive measures", as a type of damage for which compensation can be claimed, has been adopted from the CLC Convention. It is not unlikely that after an incident has occurred which could give rise to massive damage, the authorities involved will have to take extensive precautionary measures, including possibly the evacuation of the population of a certain area.

Dangerous Goods

The CRTD Convention does not contain a general definition of "dangerous goods". It will apply to any substance or article which is either listed in the classes, or covered by a collective heading of the classes, of the European Agreement Concerning International Carriage of Dangerous Goods by Road (ADR) or is subject to the provisions of that Agreement (Article 1, para. 9 CRTD). Article 4(c), however, excludes carriage of certain minimum quantities as specified in ADR. The ADR has not been formally included in the CRTD Convention, but is merely used as a reference list. The advantage of referring to the ADR list is that the ADR Agreement is wellknown to carriers and the chemical industry and that each updating of the ADR list will have an automatic effect on the CRTD Convention. The Convention applies to both bulk carriage and carriage of dangerous goods in packaged form.

Exclusion of Contractual Claims

One of the concerns of the Committee of Experts was to avoid possible conflicts between the CRTD Convention and existing international Conventions relating to the transport of passengers or goods. Such conflicts could arise if a carrier could be held liable both under the CRTD Convention on the basis of extra-contractual liability and under a contract of carriage governed by another Convention (such as the CMR Convention relating to international carriage of goods by road or the COTIF Convention on international rail transport). However, it was felt that the exception must even be extended further and that the CRTD Convention should not interfere with existing contractual relationships between carriers and claimants at all, but only with the compensation of complete outsiders to the transport operation. There was an agreement on the basic idea of the exception (which has been included in Article 3, para. 1), but it proved to be very difficult to express in proper legal wording. The final result may not be entirely satisfactory.

It should be pointed out, however, that most contractual claims for property damage will not be covered by the Convention due to the fact that all claims with respect to damage to property carried in the same vehicle or train of vehicles have been excluded as a consequence of the definition of "property damage" in Article 1, para. 10(b). In view of the fact that claims in respect of death or injury caused to persons on board the vehicle will fall under the Convention (unless their claims arise out of a contract of carriage concluded with the carrier) and such claims could include claims relating to members of the crew, Article 3, para. 2 provides that the CRTD Convention shall not apply to the extent that its provisions are incompatible with those of the applicable law relating to workmen's compensation or social security schemes.

Geographical Scope of Application

There may be cases where as a consequence of a serious accident damage is caused in more than one state. Such an accident happened, for instance, many years ago in Martelanges on the Belgo-Luxemburg border. Another example of such transfrontier damage could be a collision occurring on the German part of the Rhine and causing pollution damage in Germany and Holland. If damage is caused by an incident occurring in a state party to CRTD both on the territory of that state party and on the territory of another state which is not a party to the Convention, the question may arise whether the victims in the last-mentioned state should benefit from the compensation regime of the Convention. They shall of course be entitled to invoke their own national law but that law may not be sufficiently strict to entitle them to compensation for their damage. The same question may arise when the incident occurs in the territory of a non-state party but has caused damage in the territory of a state party. Article 2 CRTD takes a restrictive approach in this respect: the Convention only applies to damage sustained in the territory of a state party *and* caused by an incident occurring in a state party. However, if preventive measures have been taken in the territory of a state which is not a party to CRTD such measures to prevent or minimise damage caused in the territory of another state which is a state party, such preventive measures will be compensated under the Convention.

4. The CRTD Liability System

The Basis of Liability

The CRTD Convention has departed from the traditional system of fault liability and imposes a strict liability on the carrier for all damage caused by the dangerous goods carried by him. It proved to be easier to reach consensus among governments on the issue of strict liability than on the question on whom the strict liability should be imposed. The latter question is a difficult and controversial one. The following options were discussed:

1. channelling of liability to the carrier;
2. channelling of liability to the owner, producer or shipper of the dangerous goods;
3 joint and several liability of the carrier and of one of the persons mentioned under 2;

4. liability imposed on the carrier to a certain reasonable limit and a supplementary liability on the shipper of the goods to cover possible catastrophe cases;
5. an international compensation fund.

Both carriers and the chemical industry have argued that it would be unfair to impose on them any additional liability in respect of the transport of dangerous goods. They maintained that the other party would be the most suitable one to bear this new financial burden or that it would even be wiser to establish an international compensation fund to which national governments could make contributions. The Committee of governmental experts had to make a choice between the various options and in this respect it took into account the principal aim of the new Convention, i.e. to provide the victim with an easy recourse action for compensation. Such a system also requires that the person liable should be easy to identify. The carrier is undoubtedly in general the person who will be easily identifiable after an incident has happened. On the contrary, in most cases it will much more difficult for the victim, being an outsider to the transport operation, to establish the identity of the producer, owner or shipper of the dangerous goods. There was an additional reason to choose the carrier as the person liable. Since compulsory liability is attached to the strict liability the entire system should be practicable and not give rise to unnecessarily high insurance costs. According to the insurance industry a system of carrier's liability could be fitted into existing liability insurance schemes; to cover a shipper's liability a new type of insurance would have to be created. Another consideration has been that, in view of the intended inclusion of packaged goods into the Convention, for each consignment of dangerous goods an insurance certificate would have to be issued and checked upon delivery for transportation. A carrier's liability insurance can be checked much more easily.

With respect to the option to establish an international compensation fund, reference could be made to the *International Compensation Fund for Oil Pollution Damage*, established under the Oil Pollution Fund Convention of 1971. This Fund has already operated for several years and has proven to be effective. The IOPC Fund is financed by contributions from persons who receive crude oil and/or fuel oil in the territories of member states of the Fund. This Fund operates on the basis of two types of oil only and is applicable to a restricted number of contributors so that the administration of the Fund is relatively simple. With respect to a Convention on dangerous goods applicable to a wide range of chemical products and other dangerous substances, such as natural gas, the situation is quite different. The oil industry is more or less a homogeneous branch of industry and the number of contributors is restricted. Contributions for a compensation fund with respect to dangerous goods would have to be levied from a large number of contributors and would therefore be much more complicated. Also the degree of risks posed by the various contributing substances would vary considerably. A Compensation Fund financed by the participating states is not acceptable. Why should the taxpayer contribute to compensation for damage caused by industry?

The Committee considered that the most practicable and economical solution would be to channel liability under the Convention to the carrier. This does not exclude the possibility that the carrier would for his part would be entitled to bring a recourse action against any person liable for the damage under the applicable national law, for instance because of negligence on the part of such person or his servants.

However, there are two exceptions to this rule.

1. According to Article 6 the carrier shall be relieved of liability if he proves that the dangerous goods have been loaded on to or unloaded from the vehicle under the sole responsibility of person other than the carrier or his servants or agents, such as the consignor or consignee. In such case that other person shall be liable under the Convention. Where the operations of loading or unloading have been carried out under the joint responsibility of the carrier and the other person referred to in the preceding sentence, the carrier and that other person are jointly and severally liable and the damage shall be divided among them according to the degree of fault attaching to each of them. When the other person cannot prove that the carrier is to blame, the other person has to bear the entire damage. These provisions could imply in certain cases that the chemical industry will have to meet claims made under the Convention.

2. Article 5, para. 4(c) provides that the carrier shall be relieved from liability if he proves that the consignor or any other person failed to meet his obligation to inform him of the dangerous nature of the goods, and that neither he nor his servants or agents knew or ought to have known of their dangerous nature. In such case the consignor or such other person shall be liable as if he were the carrier (Article 7).

It should be noted that in first instance the burden of proof that these exceptions are applicable rests upon the carrier.

The carrier may invoke only a limited number of defences:[7]

(a) act of war, hostilities, civil war, insurrection or a natural phenomenon of an exceptional, inevitable and irresistible character;
(b) damage wholly caused by an act or omission with the intent to cause damage by a third party (for instance acts by terrorists);
(c) misinformation by the consignor or another person on the dangerous nature of the goods (see above);
(d) an intentional or negligent act by the person who suffered the damage.[8]

Who is the Carrier?

Since the liability under the Convention has been imposed mainly on the carrier, who is obliged to take out insurance to cover his liability, it is important to know

[7] See Art. 5, para. 4.
[8] See for this exception Art. 5, para. 5.

who shall be considered as "carrier". Article 1, para. 8 contains the definitions of 'carrier". Paragraph 8 makes a distinction between a carrier by road or by inland navigation and a rail carrier.

With respect to carriage by road and by inland navigation vessel "carrier" means: the person who at the time of the incident controls the use of the vehicle on board the dangerous goods are carried. However, it will not always be easy for a victim to find out who was actually in control of the vehicle at the time of the incident and since one of the principles of the Convention is that the person liable should be easily identifiable, para. 8 contains a presumption that the person in whose name the vehicle is registered in a public register is the carrier. If the vehicle is not registered, the owner shall be presumed to control its use. The person registered or the owner will only escape liability if they prove that another person was in control of the vehicle (for instance in the case of leasing or bareboat charter) and they are able to disclose the identity of that other person or, if they are unable to do so, they prove that such other person has taken control of the vehicle without their consent and in such circumstances that they could not reasonably have prevented such use. When a truck loaded with dangerous goods has been stolen and has caused an accident, they must prove that the truck has been sufficiently protected against theft.

The drafters of the Convention had to solve one further problem in respect of the definition of road and inland navigation carriers: which carrier should be liable when one vehicle is towed or pushed by another vehicle, for example, a semi-trailer by a truck or a barge by a pushing boat? One can stick to the carrier as the vehicle on board which the dangerous goods have been loaded, or one can consider the owner of the truck, the tugboat or pusher as the carrier, since the latter is the person who is in control of the transport operation. Arguments have been put forward in favour of both solutions, but in the end it was decided that the person in control of the moving vehicle should be deemed to be the carrier (see Article 1, para. 8(a), final sentence). This solution has in my view the disadvantage that, for instance, with respect to a semi-trailer, the carrier liable will be a different person every time the semi-trailer is being attached to another lorry or has been disconnected and parked pending its attachment to a lorry for the next leg of the voyage. For every leg another carrier must take out insurance, assuming that he is aware of the nature of the goods loaded in the semi-trailer. This solution could have an undesirable effect with respect to salvage operations rendered to inland navigation vessels. Inland navigation vessels in danger are often towed or pushed by the salving ship to a place of safety and also when preventive measures are taken in respect of a truck loaded with dangerous goods that truck has to be towed away to a safer place. It would be unreasonable and also quite discouraging to make the salvor or the person taking the preventive measures liable as a carrier under the Convention. Therefore Article 5, para. 8 provides that these persons are not deemed to be a carrier.

With respect to rail carriage it was not considered appropriate to impose the liability on the owners of railway wagons who are not in control of the transport operation. The railway carrier has been defined in Article 1, para. 8(b) as the person or persons operating the railway line on which the incident occurred. Where a railway line is operated jointly by more than one company the operators are jointly and severally liable.

Period of Liability

A much debated question was also whether the carrier should only be liable for an incident occurring during the time that the goods are actually on board the vehicle for carriage or whether his liability should extend to operations of loading and unloading. Finally the majority of the governmental delegations argued in favour of the inclusion of such operations into the period of the carrier's liability on the ground that many incidents occurred during loading and unloading and that such incidents could give rise to serious damage (see Article 3, para. 3). However, this extension raised objections on the part of the carriers who pointed out that in many cases it is not the carrier who is in control of these operations of loading and unloading, but the shipper and consignee respectively. For this reason Article 6 makes exception to the rule that the carrier can be held liable for the damage caused. This exception has been discussed above in sub-paragraph 4.1 (basis of liability).

Channelling of Liability

Paragraphs 6 and 7 of Article 5 contain provisions dealing with the channelling of liability. Paragraph 6 contains a rule that has been provided for in other conventions as well. Its purpose is to avoid that an action is being brought against the carrier on the basis of national law rather than in accordance with the Convention, for instance to circumvent the limitation of liability rule of the convention (Article 9). The second sentence of paragraph 6 makes an exception with respect to cases where the carrier is not liable under paragraph 4c of Article 5 on the ground that he has not been properly informed about the dangerous nature of the goods. It is quite possible that the accident was caused by the negligence of the carrier or by the negligence of his servant or agent and that for this reason he could be held liable under general tort rules of the applicable national law. There is no reason why the carrier should in such case escape liability, provided that he remains entitled to invoke the limitation of liability under Article 9 of the Convention.

In paragraph 7 a number of persons have been specified against whom no claim under the Convention or otherwise (i.e. national law) may be made, unless they have caused the damage intentionally or recklessly. This provision has been based on Article 4, para. 2 of the 1984 Protocol to the CLC Convention. This provision has in the first place a social function in protecting the servants and agents of the carrier and members of the crew against possible huge claims for which they cannot obtain insurance cover. It also is meant to encourage persons to undertake salvage operations in respect of a ship in danger and other preventive measures (in any case not to discourage them). Last but not least the intention of this channelling of liability is to avoid as much as possible double insurance.

However, this channelling of liability is not absolute since para. 9 or Article 5 maintains the right of recourse of the carrier against the consignor or the consignee or against any other third party.

5. Limitation of Liability

Articles 9–12 of the CRTD Convention deal with the limitation of the carrier's liability. The limitation amounts included in Article 9 have been agreed upon only in the final stage of the negotiations in the ECE working group. These amounts are also essential with a view of the obligation imposed on the carrier under Article 13 to insure his liability. The insurance must cover the carrier's liability under the Convention in sums fixed by applying the limits provided for by Article 9 (Article 13, para. 2). The question of to what amounts such insurance cover can be obtained under present market conditions has been the subject of a long debate. Presently there is little experience in the insurance markets with respect to the coverage of such massive damage.

Article 9 makes a distinction between the liability of the road and rail carrier on the one hand and the liability of the carrier by inland navigation vessel on the other. For road and rail carriage the limits have been fixed per incident at 18 million units of account with respect to claims for loss of life or personal injury and at 12 million units of account with respect to any other claims (mainly with respect to property claims). For inland navigation the amounts have been set per incident at 8 and 7 million units of accounts respectively.[9] It was felt that such distinction was justified because the insurance market for inland navigation would provide an insufficient broad basis to cover the same high amounts as had been set for road and rail carriers. According to paragraph 3 or Article 9 any unpaid balance of personal claims resulting from exhaustion of the fund for such claims shall rank ratebly with the other claims in the fund destined for those claims.

According to Article 10, para. 1, the carrier is not entitled to limitation of his liability, if the damage was caused by his intentional or reckless act or by a similar act of his servant or agent, provided that the servant or agent acted within the scope of his employment. The carrier may constitute a limitation fund but is not obliged to do so. A limitation fund is constituted by depositing the sum of his limited liability or by producing a bank or other guarantee. Such a fund may (and will often) be constituted by the insurer of the carrier (Art. 11). Once a fund has been constituted and has been made available for the payments of claims no claimant is allowed to exercise any rights against any other assets of the carrier in respect of his claim and any arrests or attachments made or any bail or security furnished to avoid such arrest or attachment shall be released.

[9] The "unit of account" has been defined in Article 12 as the Special Drawing Right defined by the International Monetary Fund.

The main function of the limitation fund is to make an orderly distribution of the amount available for compensation among several claimants possible. It will also prevent many claimants from making arrests on the assets of the carrier. Such arrests may cause much litigation about a possible release of the assets.

Article 29 (see the final clauses of the Convention) contains a special procedure for a speedy amendment of the limitation amounts laid down in Article 9. The normal procedure for amendment of an international convention is to convene a diplomatic conference which will establish a protocol which has to be ratified or acceded to according to the traditional rules for the entry into force of conventions. Such procedure may cause a considerable delay in the entering into force of the protocol.

Unfortunately several governments have insisted on the inclusion of a reservation clause with respect to the limitation amount of Article 9 (see Article 24, para. 1a). It may be expected that several states will make use of this reservation clause and will introduce higher limits or even unlimited liability (for instance France) with respect to claims under the CRTD Convention. This goes contrary to one of the principal aims of the Convention which is to introduce uniformity of liability rules in Europe in this field. However, it must be admitted that states who have already introduced in their national law a system of strict liability to higher limitation amounts or even combined with unlimited liability are not prepared to make a step backward by accepting an international regime which would give less legal protection to their citizens. With respect to the compulsory insurance Article 24 provides that a state which has made a reservation is only allowed to impose on its national carriers an obligation to take out insurance for any higher amounts than those required by the CRTD Convention.

6. Compulsory Insurance

Articles 13–17 provide for a compulsory insurance scheme. These articles follow in general the pattern of similar provisions in other conventions. The carrier's liability under the Convention must be covered by insurance or other financial guarantee, if the goods are carried in the territory of a state party to the Convention. The insurance or other financial guarantee must cover the carrier's liability for the entire period of the carriage in the sums fixed by applying the limits prescribed in Article 9 (see for an exception with respect to carriers of a state which has made a reservation to Article 9 above under paragraph 5). According to Article 15 a claim for compensation under the Convention may be brought directly against the insurer. The carrier must be in possession of an insurance certificate issued or approved by a competent authority designated by the state party concerned. In order not to interfere with the existing international compulsory insurance scheme for motor vehicles of the European Communities and the green card system a state party may declare that it will not apply the provisions of the convention on the insurance certificate to carriage of dangerous goods in its territory in respect of which an international scheme is in force covering the liability of the carrier under the Convention. However, it is not quite clear whether the requirements of the CRTD Convention are in conformity with the procedures applied under the green card system.

A controversial issue dealt with in Article 16, para. 4, relates to the dispensation from the compulsory insurance which may be given to railway companies which are fully owned or financially controlled by a state party or a constituent part of such state. Some delegations and the representatives of the road and inland navigation carriers saw in such dispensation a discrimination which could give rise to a possible distortion of competition among the modes of transport concerned.

7. Claims and Actions

Articles 18–21 contain provisions with regard to certain procedural matters. Article 18 contains a prescription period of 3 years.[10] This period starts to run from the date at which the person suffering the damage knew or ought reasonably to have known of the damage and of the identity of the carrier. This period may be extended by the parties involved, but only after the accident. Often the claimant and defendant, or rather their lawyers, need in the course of negotiating a settlement of the claim more time to reach a final agreement. It would be undesirable to have to start a court action in the mean time, only because the prescription period would be running out. However, an action shall be extinguished after a period of 10 years after the accident. Carriers and their insurers must be able to close their accounts after a certain period.

Article 19 provides which courts are exclusively competent to receive claims under the Convention. Only courts of a state party to the CRTD Convention are competent, since courts of a state which is not a party to the Convention are not bound to apply the Convention. Paragraph 4 provides that after a limitation fund has been constituted only the courts of the state where the fund is constituted shall be competent with regard to the apportionment and distribution of the fund. It is possible that after an accident actions are brought before the courts of different states parties. Since the carrier or his insurer is obliged to constitute one limitation fund only, one court should be competent to deal with the distribution of the fund.

Articles 20 and 21 deal with the recognition and enforcement of judgements obtained under the Convention. Article 21 has been included in particular with regard to the EEC Convention of 1968 on recognition and enforcement of judgements, but it can be applied to other conventions as well.

[10] This period conforms with the prescription periods in other international conventions, such as CLC.

8. Final clauses

The CRTD Convention contains the usual final clauses. I have already mentioned Articles 24 (reservations to the Convention) and 29 (special amendment procedure regarding the limits of liability). The Convention is open for signature until 31 December 1990,[11] thereafter it is open for accession by states only. This is only a formality. The CRTD Convention will enter into force after five states will have become a party to the convention.

9. Concluding Remarks

The increased transport of dangerous goods by all modes of transport creates special risks for damage to human life, property and the environment and this justifies that special international arrangements are being made to guarantee a fair and speedy compensation of victims. Experience has shown that the number of accidents causing damage of a catastrophic magnitude is relatively small. But accidents such as have occurred in Martelanges, Los Alfaquès, and Herrborn prove that such accidents may happen notwithstanding all precautionary measures having been taken. The success of the CRTD Convention will depend largely on the possibility to find adequate insurance cover for the liabilities which will be introduced by the Convention.

The CRTD Convention deals with a very complex legal matter. A further complication is caused by the fact that the Convention is applicable to transport of dangerous goods by three different modes of inland transport.

So far only Germany and Morocco have signed the CRTD Convention. It is not very likely that the Convention will enter into force within the forseeable future. The main problem is posed by the insurability of the risk, in particular for the inland navigation industry.[12] Germany and the Netherlands have the intention to use the substantial provisions of the CRTD as a model for their national legislations. The Dutch government has presented to Parliament a Bill to supplement the Civil Code with provisions on liability for damage caused by dangerous goods and this Bill also applies to transport of dangerous goods by sea, inland navigation vessel, road and rail. With respect to limitation of liability and compulsory insurance the Bill deviates from the CRTD provisions.[13]

[11] States which have signed the Convention must ratify, accept or approve it before they become a Party.

[12] Although transport by inland navigation vessel is considered to be the safest way of transportation of dangerous goods and such transportation should not be discouraged by imposing new liability risks which could not be accepted from a commercial point of view.

[13] Limitation of liability of the owner of a seagoing vessel is regulated by the London Convention on limitation of liability for maritime claims, 1976. With respect to the limitation of liability of the owner of an inland navigation vessel, of a road carrier and railway carrier separate legal provisions on limitation of liability will be introduced, taking into account the insurability of the risk with respect to each mode of transport.

Appendix I

Convention on Civil Liability for Damage Caused During Carriage of Dangerous Goods by Road, Rail and Inland Navigation Vessels, (CRTD)

THE STATES PARTIES TO THIS CONVENTION,

NOTING the continuous increase in the carriage of dangerous goods,

CONSCIOUS of the existence at international level of technical standards aimed at securing safety during such carriage,

DESIRING to establish uniform rules ensuring adequate and speedy compensation for damage caused during carriage of dangerous goods by road, rail and inland navigation vessels,

HAVE AGREED as follows:

Definitions

Article 1

For the purpose of this Convention:

1. *Carriage by road* means carriage of dangerous goods on board a road vehicle;

2. *Road vehicle* means any motor vehicle, articulated vehicle, trailer or semi-trailer, as defined in article 1 of the Convention on Road Traffic of 8 November 1968;

3. *Carriage by rail* means carriage of dangerous goods on board a railway wagon, including a rail motor-coach unit or railcar;

4. *Carriage by inland navigation vessel* means carriage of dangerous goods on board a ship;

5. *Ship* means any vessel or craft, not being a sea-going ship or sea-borne craft, of any type whatsoever;

6. *Vehicle* means a road vehicle, a railway wagon or a ship. Where several vehicles are coupled together to form a train, such a train shall be regarded as a single vehicle;

7. *Person* means any individual or partnership or any public or private body, whether corporate or not, including a State or any of its constituent subdivisions;

8. *Carrier* means:

(a) with respect to carriage by road and by inland navigation vessel:
the person who at the time of the incident controls the use of the vehicle on board which the dangerous goods are carried.
The person in whose name the vehicle is registered in a public register or, in the absence of such registration, the owner of the vehicle shall be

presumed to control the use of the vehicle unless he proves that another person controls the use of the vehicle and he discloses the identity of that person or, if he is unable to disclose the identify of such person, he proves that such other person has taken control of the vehicle without his consent and in such circumstances that he could not reasonably have prevented such use.

Where the vehicle on board which the dangerous goods have been loaded is moved by another vehicle, the person who controls the use of that other vehicle shall be deemed to be the carrier.

(b) with respect to carriage by rail: the person or persons operating the railway line on which the incident occurred; if there is joint operation each of the joint operators shall be considered as carriers;

9. *Dangerous goods* means, with respect to carriage by road, rail or inland navigation vessel, any substance or article which is either listed in the classes, or covered by a collective heading of the classes of the European Agreement concerning the International Carriage of Dangerous Goods by Road (ADR) or is subject to the provisions of that Agreement.

10. *Damage* means:

(a) loss of life or personal injury on board or outside the vehicle carrying the dangerous goods caused by those goods;
(b) loss or damage to property outside the vehicle carrying the dangerous goods caused by those goods, to the exclusion of any loss of or damage to other vehicles in the same train of vehicles or any loss of or damage to property on board such vehicles;
(c) loss or damage by contamination to the environment caused by the dangerous goods, provided that compensation for impairment of the environment other than for loss of profit from such impairment shall be limited to costs of reasonable measures of reinstatement actually undertaken or to be undertaken;
(d) the costs of preventive measures and further loss caused by preventive measures.

Where it is not reasonably possible to separate damage caused by the dangerous goods from that caused by other factors, all such damage shall be deemed to be caused by the dangerous goods;

11. Preventive measures means any reasonable measures taken by any person after an incident has occurred to prevent or minimize damage;

12. Incident means any occurrence or series of occurrences having the same origin, which causes damage or creates a grave and imminent threat of causing damage;

13. Green card system means the international motor insurance system described in annex 2 to the Consolidated Resolution on the facilitation of road

transport (R.E.4) of the Economic Commission for Europe of the United Nations.

Sphere of Application

Article 2
This Convention shall apply:

(a) to damage sustained in the territory of a State Party and caused by an incident occurring in a State Party;
(b) to preventive measures, wherever taken, to prevent or minimize such damage.

Article 3
1. This Convention shall apply to claims, other than claims arising out of any contract for the carriage of goods or passengers, for damage caused during carriage of dangerous goods by road, rail or inland navigation vessel.

2. This Convention shall not apply to the extent that its provisions are incompatible with those of the applicable law relating to workmen's compensation or social security schemes.

3. Carriage of dangerous goods by road, rail or inland navigation vessel includes the period from the beginning of the process of loading the goods onto the vehicle for carriage until the end of the process of unloading the goods.

4. Where the vehicle on board which the dangerous goods have been loaded is carried over part of the journey by another vehiclc without the goods being unloaded, such goods shall be deemed, during the part of the journey, to be carried on board that other vehicle.

5. This Convention shall not apply when the vehicle on board which the dangerous goods have been loaded is carried by a sea-going ship, sea-borne craft or aircraft.

Article 4
This Convention shall not apply:

(a) to damage arising from the carriage performed entirely in a place to which members of the public do not have access, provided that such carriage is accessory to other activities and is an integral part thereof;
(b) to damage caused by a nuclear substance
   (i) if the operator of a nuclear installation is liable for such damage under either the Paris Convention of 29 July 1960 on Third Party Liability in the field of Nuclear Energy and its additional Protocol of 28 January 1964 or the Vienna Convention of 21 May 1963 on Civil Liability for Nuclear Damage or any amendments to those Conventions, or
   (ii) 0f the operator of a nuclear installation is liable for such damage by virue of national law governing the liability for such damage, provided

that such law is in all respects as favourable to persons who may suffer damage as either the Paris or Vienna Conventions as referred to under (i);

(c) to carriage of dangerous goods by road, rail or inland navigation vessel which complies with conditions of marginal 10 010 or which does not exceed the quantities of marginal 10 011 of ADR.

Liability Provisions

Article 5

1. Except as provided in paragraphs 4 and 5 of this article and in article 6, the carrier at the time of an incident shall be liable for damage caused by any dangerous goods during their carriage by road, rail or inland navigation vessel.

2. If an incident consists of a series of occurrences having the same origin, the liability shall attach to the carrier at the time of the first of such occurrences.

3. If two or more persons referred to in article 1, paragraph 8(b) are liable as a carrier under this Convention, they shall be jointly and severally liable.

4. No liability shall attach to the carrier if he proves that:

(a) the damage resulted from an act of war, hostilities, civil war, insurrection or a natural phenomenon of an exceptional, inevitable and irrestistible character; or
(b) the damage was wholly caused by an act or omission with the intent to cause damage by a third party; or
(c) the consignor or any other person failed to meet his obligation to inform him of the dangerous nature of the goods, and that neither he nor his servants or agents knew or ought to have known of their nature.

5. If the carrier proves that the damage resulted wholly or partially either from an act or omission with the intent to cause damage by the person who suffered the damage or from the negligence of that person, the carrier may be exonerated wholly or partially from his liability to such person.

6. No claim for compensation for damage shall be made against the carrier otherwise than in accordance with this Convention. However, in the case referred to in paragraph 4(c) of this article, any liability for damage which may be incurred by the carrier according to the applicable law shall not be affected, provided that the limits of his liability shall not exceed the limits stipulated in article 9.

7. Subject to paragraph 9 of this article and to articles 6 and 7, no claim for compensation for damage under this Convention or otherwise may be made against:

(a) the servants or agents of the carrier or the members of the crew;
(b) the pilot of the ship or any other person who, without being a member of the crew, performs services to the vehicle;

(c) the owner, hirer, charterer, user, manager or operator of the vehicle, provided that he is not the carrier;
(d) with the consent of the owner of the ship;
(e) any person performing salvage operations on instruction of a competent public authority;
(f) any person other than the carrier taking preventive measures for damage caused by those measures;
(g) any servant or agents or the persons mentioned under (b), (c), (d), (e) and (f),

unless the damage resulted from their personal act or omission, committed with the intent to cause such damage or recklessly and with knowledge that such damage would probably result.

8. For the purpose of article 1, paragraph 8, and article 3, paragraph 4, no person performing operations under paragraph 7 (d), (e) or (f) of this article, nor his servants or agents, shall be deemed to be a carrier.

In such cases the person who was the carrier at the time of the incident giving rise to such operations shall remain the carrier for the purpose of this Convention.

9. Nothing in this Convention shall prejudice any right of recourse of the carrier against the consignor or the consignee of the goods causing the damage or against any other third party.

Article 6

1. If the carrier proves that the dangerous goods have been loaded on or unloaded from the vehicle under the sole responsability of a person other than the carrier or his servants or agents, such as the consignor or the consignee, and he discloses the identity of such person, he shall be relieved of his liability for damage caused by such goods during that period of loading or unloading and such other person shall be liable for that damage under this Convention.

Where, however, the operations of loading or unloading have been carried out under the joint responsability of the carrier and the other person referred to in this paragraph, the carrier and the other person shall be jointly and severally liable under this Convention for damage caused during the period of loading or unloading.

For the purpose of this paragraph a person shall not be deemed to be responsible for the process of loading or unloading, if he has carried out such process on behalf of the carrier or of another person such as the consignor or the consignee. In such a case the carrier or the other person shall remain liable.

2. The provisions of this Convention shall apply in respect of such other person as referred to in paragraph 1 correspondingly provided that:

(a) article 5, paragraph 6 shall not apply in respect of claims for compensation for damage made against such other person, nor shall articles 13 to 17 apply to the liability of that person;

(b) the limits of article 9 shall apply to the aggregate of all claims arising from any one incident against the carrier and such other person;
(c) a fund constituted by the carrier or by such other person in accordance with article 11 shall be deemed to be constituted by both.

3. In the relation between the carrier and any other person liable under paragraph 1 of this article, liability shall be borne by that other person unless the damage was caused by the fault of the carrier or of his servants or agents.

When both the carrier or his servants or agents and the other person or his servants or agents have contributed to the damage by their fault, the carrier and that other person shall each bear such part of the liability as corresponds to the degree of fault attaching to each of them.

4. This article does not apply if the process of loading or unloading has been carried out under the sole or joint responsability of a person performing operations mentioned in article 5, paragraph 7(d), (e) or (f).

Article 7
Where no liability attaches to the carrier in accordance with article 5, paragraph 4(c), the consignor or the other person referred to therein shall be deemed to be the carrier for the purposes of this Convention. However, article 5, paragraph 6 shall not apply in respect of claims for compensation for damage made against the consignor or the other person, nor shall articles 13 to 17 apply to their liability under this Convention.

Article 8
1. Whenever damage has resulted from an incident involving two or more vehicles each of which is carrying dangerous goods, each carrier, unless exonerated under article 5, paragraphs 4 and 5 or article 6, shall be liable for the damage. The carriers shall be jointly and severally liable for all such damage which is not reasonably separable.

2. However, the carrier shall in respect of each vehicle, be entitled to the limits of liability applicable to him by virtue of article 9.

3. Nothing in this Convention shall prejudice any right of recourse of a carrier against any other carrier.

Limitation of Liability

Article 9
1. The liability of the road carrier and of the rail carrier under this Convention for claims arising from any one incident shall be limited as follows:

(a) with respect to claims for loss of life or personal injury: 18 million units of account;
(b) with respect to any other claim: 12 million units of account.

2. The liability of the carrier by inland navigation vessel under this Convention for claims arising from any one incident shall be limited as follows:

(a) with respect to claims for loss of life or personal injury: 8 million units of account;
(b) with respect to any other claim: 7 million units of account.

3. Where the sums provided for in paragraph 1(a) and paragraph 2(a) of this article are insufficient to pay the claims mentioned therein in full, the sums provided for in paragraph 1(b) and paragraph 2(b) shall be available for payment of the unpaid balance of claims under paragraph 1(a) and paragraph 2(a). Such unpaid balance shall rank rateably with claims mentioned under paragraph 1(b) and paragraph 2(b).

Article 10
1. The carrier shall not be entitled to limit his liability under this Convention if it is proved that the damage resulted from his personal act or omission or an act or omission of his servants or agents, committed with the intent to cause such damage or recklessly and with knowledge that such damage would probably result, provided that, in the case of such act or omission of a servant or agent, it is also proved that he was acting within the scope of his employment.

2. Where the carrier has a claim against the claimant arising out of the same incident, their respective claims shall be set off against each other and the provisions of this Convention shall apply to the balance, if any.

3. The carrier may invoke the right to limit his liability notwithstanding that a limitation fund as mentioned in article 11 has not been constituted.

4. If limitation of liability is invoked without the constitution of a limitation fund, the provisions of article 11, paragraphs 4 to 7 shall apply correspondingly.

5. Questions of procedure arising under the rules of this article shall be decided in accordance with the law of the State Party in which action is brought.

Article 11
1. The carrier may constitute a fund with the court or other competetent authority of any one of the States Parties in which an action is brought under article 19. If such action under article 19 has not been brought in a State Party, then the carrier may constitute his fund with the court or other competent authority of any one of the States Parties referred to in article 19, paragraphs 1(a), (b) or (c), or in subparagraph (d) provided that the carrier and all the victims have their habitual residence in the territory of the same State Party. The fund shall be constituted in the sum of the amounts set out in article 9 as applicable to him, together with interest thereon from the date of the incident until the date of the constitution of the fund. Any fund thus constituted shall be available only for payment of claims in respect of which limitation of liability may be invoked under this Convention.

2. A fund may be constituted either by depositing the sum or by producing a bank guarantee or other guarantee, admitted by the legislation of the State Party where the fund is constituted and considered to be adequate by the court or another competent authority.

3. Any person providing the carrier with insurance or other financial security under this Convention shall be entitled to constitute a fund in accordance with this article on the same conditions and having the same effect as if it were constituted by the carrier. Such fund may be constituted even in the event that according to article 10, paragraph 1 the carrier shall not be entitled to limit his liability, but its constitution shall in that case not prejudice the rights of any claimant against the carrier. The fund shall be deemed to be constituted by the carrier.

4. Subject to the provisions of article 9, paragraph 3, the fund shall be distributed among the claimants in proportion to their established claims against the fund.

5. If, before the fund is distributed, the carrier or any person providing him with insurance or other financial security has as a result of the incident paid compensation for damage, such person shall, up to the amount he has paid, acquire by subrogation the rights which the person so compensated would have enjoyed under this Convention.

6. The right of subrogation provided for in paragraph 5 of this article may also be exercised by a person other than those mentioned therein in respect of any amount of compensation for damage which he may have paid but only to the extent that such subrogation is permitted under the applicable law.

7. Where the carrier or any other person establishes that he may be compelled to pay at a later date in whole or in part any such amount of compensation with regard to which such person would have enjoyed a right of subrogation pursuant to paragraphs 5 and 6 of this article had the compensation been paid before the fund was distributed, the court or other competent authority of the State where the fund has been constituted may order that a sufficient sum shall be provisionnally set aside to enable such person at such later date to enforce his claim against the fund.

8. Where the carrier, after an incident, has constituted a fund in accordance with this article, and is entitled to limit his liability:

(a) no person having a claim for damage arising out of that incident shall be entitled to exercise any right against any other assets of the carrier in respect of such claim;
(b) the court or other competent authority of any State Party shall order the release of any property belonging to the carrier which has been arrested or attached in respect of a claim for damage arising out of that incident, and shall similarly release any bail or other security furnished to avoid such arrest or attachment.

9. Paragraph 8 of this article shall only apply if the claimant has access to the court administering the fund and if the fund is actually available and freely transferable in respect of his claim.

10. Subject to the provisions of this article, the rules relating to the constitution and distribution of a limitation fund, and all rules of procedure in connection

therewith, shall be governed by the law of the State Party in which the fund is constituted.

Article 12

1. The "unit of account" referred to in article 9 is the Special Drawing Right as defined by the International Monetary Fund. The amounts mentioned in article 9 shall be converted into national currency on the basis of the value of that currency on the date of the constitution of the limitation fund or, if no fund has been constituted, on the date when payment is made or equivalent security is given. The value of the national currency, in terms of the Special Drawing Right, of a State party which is a member of the International Monetary Fund shall be calculated in accordance with the method of valuation applied by the International Monetary Fund in effect on the date in question for its operations and transactions. The value of the national currency, in terms of the Special Drawing Right, of a State Party which is not a member of the International Monetary Fund shall be calculated in a manner determined by that State.

2. Nevertheless a Contracting State which is not a member of the International Monetary Fund and whose law does not permit the application of the provisions of paragraph 1 of this article may, at the time of ratification, acceptance, approval or accession, or at any time thereafter, declare that the unit of account referred to in that paragraph shall be equal to 15 gold francs. The gold franc referred to in this paragraph corresponds to sixty-five and a half milligrammes of gold of millesimal fineness nine hundred. The conversion of the gold franc into the national currency shall be made according to the law of the State concerned.

3. The calculation mentioned in the last sentence of paragraph 1 of this article and the conversion mentioned in paragraph 2 shall be made in such a manner as to express in the national currency of the State Party as far as possible the same real value for the amounts in article 9 as would result from the application of the first three sentences of paragraph 1 of this article. Contracting States shall communicate to the depositary the manner of calculation pursuant to paragraph 1 of this article or the result of the conversion in paragraph 2 as the case may be, when depositing an instrument of ratification, acceptance, approval of or accession to, this Convention and whenever there is a change in either.

Compulsory Insurance

Article 13

1. The carrier's liability shall be covered by insurance or other financial security, such as a bank guarantee, if the dangerous goods are carried in the territory of a State Party.

2. The insurance or other financial security shall cover the entire period of the carrier's liability under this Convention in the sums fixed by applying the limits of liability prescribed in article 9 and shall cover the liability of the person named in the certificate as carrier or, if that person is not the carrier as defined in article 1, paragraph 8, of such person as does incur liability under this Convention.

3. Any sums provided by insurance or by other financial security maintained in accordance with paragraph 1 of this article shall be available only for the sarisfaction of claims under this Convention.

Article 14

1. Each State Party shall designate one or several competent authorities to issue or approve certificates attesting that carriers falling within the definition of article 1 paragraph 8(a) have a valid insurance or other financial security in accordance with the provisions of this Convention.

2. The certificate shall be issued or approved by the competent authority:

(a) of the State or registration in respect of a carrier whose vehicle is registered in a State Party; or
(b) of the State Party where the carrier has his principal place of business or, if he has none, his habitual residence, if the vehicle is not registered.

With respect to a carrier not mentioned under (a) or (b) of the first sentence of this paragraph the certificate shall be issued or approved by the competent authority of a State Party in the territory of which the dangerous goods are carried.

3. The certificate shall contain the following particulars:

(a) the number of the certificate;
(b) the type of, and the particulars identifying, the road vehicle or ship;
(c) the name of the carrier and his principal place of business or, if he has none, his habitual residence;
(d) the type of security;
(e) the name and principal place of business of the insurer or other person providing security;
(f) the period of validity of the certificate which shall not be longer than the period of validity of the insurance or other security.

4. The certificate shall be produced for inspection on demand by the competent authorities.

5. The certificate shall be issued in English or in French or shall, if issued in any other language, include a translation into one at least of those languages.

6. The State where the certificate is issued or approved shall, subject to the provisions of this Convention, determine the conditions of issue and validity of the certificate.

7. Certificates issued in a State Party shall be accepted in all States parties for all purposes covered by this Convention. Nevertheless a State Party, should it consider that an insurer or other person providing security named in the certificate may not be financially capable of meeting his obligations imposed by this Convention, may be any time request consultation with the State which has issued the certificate.

Each State shall designate the authority competent to make or receive any communication relating to the compulsory insurance or any other financial security.

Any State Party may accept certificates issued by the competent authorities, or by bodies recognized, for the purpose of this Convention, by the competent authorities of States not party to it.

8. Insurance or other financial security shall not satisfy the requirements of this Convention if it can cease, for reasons other than the expiry of the period of its validity specified in the certificate, before three months have elapsed from the date on which the notice of its termination is given to the authority referred to in paragraph 2 of this article, unless the certificate has been surrendered to those authorities or a new certificate has been issued within the said period. The foregoing provisions shall similarly apply to any modification which results in the insurance or security no longer satisfying the requirements of this Convention.

9. This article shall not apply in the case of carriage by a road vehicle in the territory of a State party which is a party to the green card system if there is in force in respect of the vehicle and produced for inspection on demand by the competent authorities a green card certifying coverage of carrier's liability under this Convention.

10. Two or more States Parties may agree to dispense with the requirements of this article for the certificate or green card referred to in paragraph 9 of this article in respect of road vehicles registered in their territories, for the carriage, within their territories, of goods by road covered by this Convention.

Article 15

1. Any claim for compensation under articles 5 or 6 may be brought directly against the insurer or other person providing financial security for the carrier's liability or, in the case of a road vehicle to which the green card system applies, against the insurer or the green card bureau of the State where the incident occurred.

2. In the case referred to in paragraph 1 of this article the defendant may avail himself of:

(a) the limit of liability under article 9 applicable to the carrier, irrespective of whether the carrier is entitled to limit his liability, and
(b) the defence, other than bankruptcy or winding up of the carrier, which the carrier would have been entitled to invoke.

The defendant shall not avail himself of any other defence which he might have been entitled to invoke in proceedings brought by the carrier against him nor may be dispute any clause of the insurance contract or other financial security.

3. The defendant shall in any event have the right to require that the carrier be joined in the proceedings.

Article 16

1. With respect to carriage by road and by inland navigation vessel: where the carrier is a State Party or any constituent part of such State Party and the carriage is performed on non-commercial governmental service, that State may provide that the carrier shall be dispensed from the obligation to cover his liability by insurance or other financial security.

2. If, according to paragraph 1 of this article, insurance or other financial security is not maintained in respect of such a vehicle, the provisions of this Convention relating to compulsory insurance shall not apply to such vehicle. However, a certificate issued by the competent authorities stating that the carrier is a State Party or a constituent part of such State and that the carrier's liability is covered within the limits prescribed by this Convention shall be produced for inspection on demand by the authorities referred to in article 14, paragraph 4.

3. The certificate referred to in paragraph 2 of this article shall be in conformity with the provisions of article 14, paragraph 3.

4. With respect to carriage by rail: where the carrier is a State Party or any constituent part of such State, or where he is a body fully owned or financially controlled by a State Party, that State may provide that the carrier shall be dispensed form the obligation to cover his liability by insurance or other financial security.

Whenever a rail transport enterprise owned or financially controlled by two or more States Parties is concerned, the same right to dispensation is granted to the State where the enterprise is located.

Article 17

A Contracting State shall take the appropriate legislative measures to ensure that the provisions of this Convention relating to compulsory insurance have been complied with.

Claims and Actions

Article 18

1. Rights of compensation under this Convention shall be extinguished unless an action is brought within three years from the date at which the person suffering the damage knew or ought reasonably to have known of the damage and of the identity of the carrier. The period may be extended if the parties so agree after the incident.

2. In no case, however, shall an action be brought after ten years from the date of the incident which caused the damage.

3. Where the incident consists of a series of occurrences, the periods mentioned in paragraphs 1 and 2 of this article shall run from the date of the last of such occurrences.

Article 19

1. Actions for compensation under any provision of this Convention may only be brought in the courts of any State Party:

(a) where the damage was sustained as a result of the incident; or
(b) where the incident occurred; or
(c) where preventive measures were taken to prevent or minimize damage; or
(d) where the carrier has his habitual residence.

Reasonable notice of the commencement of such an action shall be given to the defendant.

2. If the road vehicle or ship involved in the incident is subject to registration, the State of registration of the road vehicle or ship shall be deemed to be that of the habitual residence of the carrier.

3. Each Contracting State shall ensure that its course possess the necessary jurisdiction to entertain such actions for compensation.

4. After a fund has been constituted, the courts of the State in which the fund is constituted shall be exclusively competent to determine all matters relating to the apportionment and distribution of the fund.

Article 20

1. Any judgment given by a court with jurisdiction in accordance with article 19 which is enforceable in the State of origin where it is no longer subject to ordinary forms of review, shall be recognized in any State Party, except:

(a) where the judgment was obtained by fraud; or
(b) where the defendant was not given reasonable notice and a fair opportunity to present his case; or
(c) where the judgment is irreconcilable with an earlier judgment given in the State where the recognition is sought, or given in another State Party with jurisdiction in accordance with article 19 and already recognized in the State where the recognition is sought, involving the same cause of action and between the same parties.

2. A judgment recognized under paragraph 1 of this article shall be enforceable in each State Party as soon as the formalities required in that State have been complied with. The formalities shall not permit the merits of the case to be re-opened.

Article 21
Whenever two or more States Parties are bound by an international Convention establishing rules of jurisdiction or providing for recognition and execution in a State of judgments given by a court of another State, the provisions of those instruments replace the corresponding provisions of article 19, paragraphs 1, 2 and 3 and of article 20 of this Convention.

Final Provisions

Article 22
1. This Convention is open for signature by all States at Geneva from 1 February 1990 until 31 December 1990 inclusive.

2. This Convention is subject to ratification, acceptance or approval by States which have signed it.

3. This Convention is open for accession by all States which are not signatory States as from 1 January 1991.

4. Ratification, acceptance approval or accession is effected by the deposit of a formal instrument to that effect with the depositary.

Article 23
1. The Convention enters into force on the first day of the month following the expiration of twelve months after the date of deposit of the fifth instrument of ratification, acceptance approval or accession.

2. For each State that ratifies, accepts, approves, or accedes to this Convention after the deposit of the fifth instrument of ratification, acceptance, approval or accession, this Convention enters into force in respect of that State on the first day of the month following the expiration of twelve months after the date of the deposit of its instrument of ratification, acceptance, approval or accession.

3. Any instrument of ratification, acceptance, approval or accession deposited after the entry into force of any Protocol amending the Convention shall be deemed to apply to this Convention as amended.

Article 24
1. A State may declare at the time of signature, ratification, acceptance, approval or accession that:

(a) in respect of claims for damage under any or all of the heads of damage defined in article 1, paragraph 10, it will apply higher limits of liability than those specified in article 9 or no limit of liability for damage arising out of an incident occurring in its territory, provided that in that State the regime of liability governing compensation for such damage is of a similar nature to that under this Convention.

Such a State may oblige carriers whose vehicles are registered in its territory or, in the case of unregistered vehicles, having their principal place of business or habitual residence in its territory, to cover their liability by insurance or other financial security to amounts higher than those required by in article 13, paragraph 2 of this Convention.

(b) it will not apply the provisions of article 5, paragraph 4(a) or (b);

(c) it will apply its national law in place of the provisions of article 5, paragraph 5, in so far as such law provides that compensation for loss of life or personal injury may be reduced or disallowed only in cases of intentional conduct or gross negligence by the injured person or the person entitled to claim compensation.

2. The right of a State to make the declarations provided for in paragraph 1 is subject to its national law being in conformity with the conditions set out in the relevant sub-paragraphs of that paragraph at the time of entry into force of this Convention, and, in any event, not later than five years after this Convention has been opened for signature.

3. A State which makes use of any of the options provided for under paragraph 1 shall notify the Depository of the contents of its national law.

4. No other reservations are permitted to this Convention.

Article 25

1. Reservations made under this Convention at the time of signature are subject to confirmation upon ratification, acceptance or approval.

2. Reservations and confirmations of reservations are to be in writing and to be formally notified of the Depository.

3. A reservation takes effect simultaneously with the entry into force of this Convention in respect of the State concerned.

4. Any State which makes a reservation under this Convention may withdraw it at any time by a formal notification in writing addressed to the Depository. Such withdrawal is to take effect on the first day of the month following the expiration of six months after the date of the receipt of the notification by the Depository.

Article 26

Each State, at the time of signature, ratification, acceptance, approval or accession, shall notify the Depository of the competent authority or authorities designated by it under article 14, paragraphs 1 and 7.

Article 27

This Convention applies to any incident as defined in article 1, paragraph 12 occurring after its entry into force.

Article 28

1. A Conference for the purpose or revising or amending this Convention may be convened by the Inland Transport Committee of the Economic Commission for Europe of the United Nations.

2. Upon the request of not less than one-third of the States-Parties, with a minimum of three, the Inland Transport Committee shall convene a Conference of the Contracting States for revising or amending this Convention.

Article 29

1. Upon request of at least one-quarter of the States Parties, with a minimum of three, any proposal to amend the limits of liability laid down in article 9 shall be circulated by the Depository to all Contracting States.

2. Any amendment proposed and circulated as above shall be submitted to a Committee, convened by the Inland Transport Committee of the Economic Commission for Europe of the United Nations and composed of a representative of each Contracting State, for consideration at a date at least six months after the date of its circulation.

3. Amendments shall be adopted by a two-thirds majority of the Contracting States present and voting in the committee on condition that at least one-half of the Contracting States shall be present at the time of voting.

4. When acting on a proposal to amend the limits, the committee shall take into account the experience of incidents and in particular the amount of damage resulting therefrom, changes in the monetary values and the effect of the proposed amendment on the cost of insurance.

5. (a) No amendment of the limits of liability under this article may be considered less than five years from the date on which this Convention was opened for signature nor less than five years from the date of entry into force of a previous amendment under this article. No amendment under this article shall be considered before this Convention has entered into force.
   (b) No limit may be increased so as to exceed an amount which corresponds to the limit laid down in this Convention increased by six per cent per year calculated on a compound basis from the date on which this Convention was opened for signature.
   (c) No limit may be increased so as to exceed an amount which corresponds to the limit laid down in this Convention multiplied by three.

6. Any amendment adopted in accordance with paragraph 3 of this article shall be notified by the Depository to all Contracting States. The amendment shall be deemed to have been accepted at the end of a period of eighteen months after the date of notification, unless within that period not less than one-quarter of the States that were Contracting States at the time of the adoption of the amendment by the committee have communicated to the Depository that they do not accept the amendment in which case the amendment is rejected and shall have no effect.

7. An amendment deemed to have been accepted in accordance with paragraph 6 of this article shall enter into force eighteen months after its acceptance.

8. Alle Contracting States shall be bound by the amendment, unless they denounce this Convention in accordance with article 30, paragraph 1 at least six months before the amendment enters into force. Such denunciations shall take effect when the amendment enters into force.

9. When an amendment under this article has been adopted by the committee but the eighteen month period for its acceptance has not yet expired, a State which becomes a Contracting State during that period shall be bound by the amendment if it enters into force. A State which becomes a Contracting State after that period shall be bound by an amendment which has been accepted in accordance with paragraph 6 of this article. In the cases referred to in this paragraph a State becomes bound by an amendment when that amendment enters into force, or when this Convention enters into force for that State if later.

Article 30

1. This Convention may be denounced by any Contracting State at any time.

2. Denunciation is effected by the deposit of an instrument to that effect with the Depository.

3. A denunciation takes effect on the first day of the month following the expiration of six months after the deposit of the instrument of denunciation with the Depository. Where a longer period of the denunciation to take effect is specified in the instrument of denunciation it takes effect upon expiration of such longer period after its deposit with the Depository.

Article 31

1. The Secretary-General of the Untied Nations shall be the Depository of this Convention.

2. The Depository shall:

(a) inform all States which have signed or acceded to this Convention of:

(i) each new signature or deposit of an instrument of ratification, acceptance, approval or accession, together with the date thereof;
(ii) each declaration made under article 12, paragraph 2;
(iii) each reservation made under article 24, including each notification under paragraph 3 of that article;
(iv) the withdrawal of any reservation under article 25, paragraph 4;
(v) each notification received under article 26;
(vi) each request received under article 28, paragraph 2 and article 29, paragraph 1;
(vii) the date of entry into force of this Convention and of any amendment thereto under articles 28 and 29;
(viii) the deposit of an instrument of denunciation of this Convention together with the date of its deposit and the date on which it takes effect;

(b) transmit certified true copies of this Convention to all signatory States and to all States acceding to the Convention.

IN WITNESS WHEREOF the undersigned, being duly authorized thereto, have signed this Convention.

DONE at Geneva, this tenth day of October, one thousand nine hundred and eighty-nine, in a single original, of which the English, French and Russian texts are equally authentic.

A Maritime View

Gerd Jan van der Ziel

U.S. Oil Pollution Act, 1990

The United States do not intend to adhere to the international regime on oil pollution liability, as laid down in the International Convention on Civil Liability for Oil Pollution Damage, Brussels, of 29 November 1969, ratified by some 67 countries, and the International Convention on the Establishment of an International Fund for Compensation for Oil Pollution Damage, Brussels, of 18 December 1971, ratified by 45 countries. Both conventions were amended by Protocols of which the most important ones, concluded 25 May 1984, are not yet in force. (It is intended to hold a Diplomatic Conference in November 1992 to discus and adopt an amendment to these Protocols with the effect of accelerating their entry into force.)

After the *Exxon Valdez* accident the United States have set their own course by enacting new national legislation dealing with oil pollution. This Oil Pollution Act 1990, which substantially amends the earlier Federal Water Pollution Control Act, contains three issues which are particularly worrying the shipping industry.

The first one is the limitation of liability. These limits, which are substantially higher than under the CLC 1984 Protocols, are not available if the incident is caused *inter alia* by gross negligence of the responsible party or if it is caused by any violation of an applicable federal safety, construction or operating regulation by the responsible party. Given the likelihood of establishing a breach of some applicable federal regulation and the unknown and highly flexible nature of the test for "gross negligence" at shipboard level, denial of the shipowner's right to limit liability is a probability in any spill.

For shipowners a cover for such unlimited liability is not available in the market. The present standard cover from any P&I-Club is limited to $500 million and an additional $200 million is, at least for the time being, still obtainable in the market. It is, however, by no means certain that in the future such a fairly high cover of $700 million remains obtainable. The capacity of an insurance market is not a given fact, but it used to fluctuate. Anyway, any tankowner will have to pay a surcharge of $0.41 per ton for each U.S. voyage on top of his normal premium. That means for a large tanker an additional $40,000 to $50,000 per voyage.

A second item under OPA '90 is the requirement to maintain evidence of financial responsibility sufficient to meet the applicable limits of liability. Such evidence can be maintained through "insurance, surety bond, guarantee, letter of credit, qualification of a self-insurer, or other evidence of financial responsibility". A notice of proposed rulemaking, prepared by the U.S. Coast Guard, was published on 26 September 1991. From this notice it may be concluded that it is difficult, if not impossible in most cases, to meet any of the proposed criteria. U.S. insurers provide insurance up to a limit of $5 million, which is only adequate for very small vessels. Surety bonds and guarantees for this purpose are not available at all. The requirements for self-insurance are so stringent that from the shipping and oil companies who trade to U.S. ports only one could theoretically and possibly meet all but one of the requirements. And under the heading "other evidence of financial responsibility" the USCG, unlike some state governments, is not prepared to accept the cover provided by the P&I-Clubs. The notice provoked some 300 commentaries from interested parties. It is evident that, without some rethinking by U.S. authorities, U.S. seaborne trade must shortly come to a halt.

A third issue, however, is even more onerous. Under OPA '90 a whole new range of liabilities is introduced both in respect of economic and non-economic losses and available for federal, state and local governments, and for any person who uses the affected natural resource for subsistence. Furthermore, under OPA '90 a procedure for Natural Resource Damage Assessment will become applicable, which uses intricate and controversial methods of calculating damages caused by an oil spill. In particular, the contingent valuation of a damaged natural resource, such as the option value, the existence value or the bequest value to citizens who do not use or plan to use the resource in question, could add billions of dollars to the final bill. Recently, on 13 March 1992, the National Oceanographic and Atmospheric Administration (NOAA) published an Advance Notice of Proposed Rulemaking, which provides guidance as to how NOAA expects to carry out such contingent valuation under OPA '90.

It is clear that under OPA '90 the way is opened for speculative damages which are potentially recoverable by an exceptional wide range of plaintiffs.

It is also clear that when in the future, in case of a substantial spill, the risk of going bankrupt will turn into a probability of going bankrupt, the appetite of trading to and from the U.S. will diminish greatly, in particular for the larger and more responsible maritime carriers.

Draft HNS Convention

My second subject is the draft Convention on Liability and Compensation for Damage in connection with the Carriage of Hazardous and Noxious Substances by Sea, or, abbreviated, the draft HNS Convention. You may find the latest text as Appendix I to this chapter.

When concluding the CLC Convention on Oil Pollution Liability in 1969, governments realised that the carriage of hazardous goods other than oil could also cause damage to persons, property and the environment, but that the drafting of one international instrument covering both oil and other hazardous goods was too complex a task at one and the same time. In the early eighties the discussions on HNS substances started. However, a Diplomatic Conference on the subject, held in 1984, failed due to views being too diverging. Later, compromises were sought and found, but the subject remains an extremely knotty one. A new Diplomatic Conference is foreseen in 1994/5.

The present draft entails a two-tier system. Under the first tier the shipowner assumes a strict liability for damages caused by HNS substances up to certain limits for which he has to take out a compulsory insurance cover. A second tier provides supplementary compensation for claims which remained unpaid under the first tier. This supplementary compensation was to be paid by a Scheme or Fund, and financed by a levy paid by the shippers of HNS substances. An ingenious collection system is provided for: each state party appoints one or more issuing agents who collect the levy against the sale of a dangerous goods certificate to a shipper who has to transfer its contributions to the Scheme on a quarterly basis.

The draft as it stands at present, leaves quite important things open, while on other matters views are still very diverse. The main item still open is the amount of the limits. Suggestions have been put forward for a limit of SDR 15 million for small ships and up to SDR 100 million for bigger ones. Additionally, the second tier should provide for SDR 200–300 million available compensation for claimants. These limits are extremely high. For small ships it is even three times as high as the limit under CERCLA, the U.S. national law relating to this subject. It will become extremely difficult for the P&I-Clubs to find coverage on the reinsurance market against a reasonable premium.

A further major discussion item is the question of to which substances the new regime should be applicable. Initially it was the intention to limit the special regime to the carriage of extremely dangerous goods, carried in bulk and in reasonably large quantities. The list is now extended to small packages, bunkerfuel in ships carrying no dangerous goods at all, and even empty ships which carried a dangerous cargo during a previous voyage. However, it might be possible that the compulsory insurance need not be taken out for all these substances and it is already certain that some of them will not have to contribute to the Scheme. These discussions may end up with three different lists.

Another point of discussion is the legal relation to limits of liability as laid down in other conventions, such as the 1976 Convention on Limitation for Maritime Claims and the 1974 Athens Convention relating to the Carriage of Passengers and their Luggage by Sea. Furthermore, a lot of more or less technical points in respect of the working of the Scheme, which may have important financial consequences, still have to be solved.

I am, indeed, not optimistic about ever having a workable and effective liability regime for the carriage of dangerous goods as long as governments (who in many cases are amongst the largest claimants) maintain their political desire for full compensation for victims of damage caused by the carriage of hazardous goods. Certain risks are inherent to a modern society, in which we all drive our cars, wear nylon sweaters and use plastic products. In my view, governments could and should pay still more attention to the prevention of damage than trying to impose on carriers "after-the-event" liabilities which go beyond what is reasonably insurable.

Prevention

With regard to prevention, attention has to be focused on the role that IMO plays. IMO stands for International Maritime Organization — the specialised agency of the United Nations dealing with maritime matters. Under the auspices of IMO many international instruments have been developed, greatly enhancing the safety of maritime transport. In Appendix II you will find a list of the most important ones.

In March 1992, IMO's Marine Environmental Protection Committee (MEPC) adopted further and more stringent regulations relating to oil tankers. New tankers have to be built with either double hulls, a mid-deck construction or any other method of design ensuring at least the same level of protection in the event of collision or stranding. In respect of existing tankers it provides for an enhanced programme of inspections during special, intermediate and annual surveys. Existing vessels of 5 years of age and over shall have on board a complete file of the survey results for scrutiny by the competent authority of any government of a state party to MARPOL 73/78. Furthermore, existing vessels will have to be upgraded 25 to 30 years after their delivery in such a way that, in effect, it will lead to their being phased out.

All these IMO safety regulations had their effects. According to the statistics of Lloyd's Maritime Information Services in the period 1 January 1981 to 31 December 1990, a clear overall decline of about 25% in serious casualties occurred despite an increase in the size of the world fleet of about 6%.

A comparison of the frequency of specific incident types at the beginning and the end of the reference period reveals a dramatic reduction in the occurrence of collision, contact, stranding, fire and explosion events. One may conclude that safety at sea improved considerably over the period.

Of all casualties, reportedly only 5% resulted in pollution. The International Tanker Owners Pollution Federation (ITOPF) database statistics (which, unlike Lloyd's, exclude Gulf War losses) show 252 oil spills greater than 5,000 barrels

(700 tons) in the period 1970–9 and 91 in the 10 years ending 1989, a reduction of almost two-thirds. In terms of total oil lost the same picture can be seen: oil spilt between 1970 and 1979 totalled about 3.5 million tonnes, as against some 1.2 million tonnes between 1980 and 1989. Again, about a two-thirds reduction.

However, despite the general trend in safety and prevention being promising, two caveats have to be made. The casualty event category of hull/machinery damage, which is often related to inadequate maintenance and repair routines and accounts for nearly one-third of all serious casualties, increased in the 1981–90 period. In combination with an expected further increase in the average age of the world fleet during the nineties, this increase causes concern. Another reason for concern is that in the group of vessels younger than 10 years, the collision, contact and stranding events represented over half the total number of casualties, with hull/machinery damage representing a further third. This raises questions about the standards of training and qualification of those responsible for sophisticated navigation equipment and highly automated machinery systems. This reverse side of low-cost crews is now generally recognised. The maritime community is working hard to enhance standards of shore-based management, training and operational procedures. However, it will take time for these efforts to bear fruit in terms of a reduction in human error.

I hope that these two caveats do not indicate a future reversion of the present positive trend. I do not yet dispose of the full 1991 figures. However, the latest total loss figure provided by the Institute of London Underwriters showed for 1991 an 30% increase on 1990. This increase, measured against the average in the 1987–90 period amounts to nearly 20%.

Decline of International Salvage Resources

A week ago a report was published, drawn up by Bureau Veritas, a Classification Society, in this event, however, acting as an independent consultant. This report was made at the request of the Salvage Working Group, a joint maritime industry body representing salvors, shipowners, insurers and other interested parties. This Salvage Working Group was established to review the future of marine salvage response capability. I will not bother you further with figures and statistics, but the conclusions of the report are clear:

- The global availability of salvage resources has declined dramatically over the past decade, together with a parallel deterioration of the professionalism in salvage services rendered to shipping casualties. In particular, the larger world-wide operating salvage firms, mainly based in Western Europe, have reduced their capacities to, in some cases, no more than a fraction of their previous levels. These gaps were not filled by Chinese or Korean firms, like in other segments of maritime industry.

- Regionally, the situation differs enormously: East of Aden, in particular in the Far East, the situation is still reasonably satisfactory, whereas in the U.S. only one dedicated ocean-going salvage tug is available any more. In Europe the situation is different per country: in those countries where a flourishing tourist and fishing industry exists along its coasts like Spain, France and Italy, governments have stepped in and made arrangements with private salvors which enable them to keep salvage tugs and equipment available to protect the coastline. In other European countries the situation is less satisfactory.

In this respect there is a remarkable difference in policy (again!) between the United States and many other governments. The United States, as a result of Exxon Valdez, have established an impressive framework for combating marine pollution. I already mentioned the Oil Pollution Act, which also calls for design regulations for tankers and the availability of on board contingency plans. The U.S. were the initiator and promoter of the IMO - International Convention on Oil Pollution Preparedness, Response and Cooperation, 1990, (text attached as Appendix III). Sixteen large oil spill response vessels will be deployed at strategic locations around the U.S. Coasts, all without, quite remarkably, rescue towage or salvage capability. It seems that the United States is concentrated almost entirely on post-spill actions, while many other governments believe that marine salvage is the first line of defence against marine pollution: try to keep the pollutant in the ship!

The loophole in the anti-pollution defence of the non-availability of vessels with sufficient salvage and rescue capabilities should be filled as soon as possible, both in the U.S. and, where it exists, in Europe.

Concluding Remarks

- Provisions relating prevention really help in avoiding environmental damage.
- Prevention requires continuous and dedicated attention both from the industry and from governments. It is a process which never can be considered accomplished.
- Imposing liabilities which are not reasonably insurable may eventually prove to be counter-productive. In such cases risks tend to be thrown back on other ways and means than on proper insurance cover.
- When better prevention leads to fewer casualties, the insurance thereof may become more attractive to insurers and the capacity of the insurance market may extend. (Other factors will have their impact on market capacity fluctuations as well.)
- Governments do better to dedicate their efforts primarily to rule-making relating to prevention and, secondarily, both in time and nature, to legislation-relating liabilities.

Appendix I

Draft International Convention on Liability and Compensation for Damage in Connection with the Carriage of Hazardous and Noxious Substances by Sea dated 3 December 1991

Chapter I: General Provisions

Article 1 Definitions

For the purposes of this Convention:

CLC(1) CRTD 1(5) 1. "Ship" means by seagoing vessel and seaborne craft, of any type whatsoever.

CLC I(2) CRTD 1(7) 2. "Person" means any individual or partnership or any public or private body, whether corporate or not, including a State or any of its constituent subdivisions.

CLC I(3) 3. "Owner" means the person or persons registered as the owner of the ship or, in the absence of registration, the person or persons owning the ship. However, in the case of a ship owned by a State and operated by a company which in that State is registered as the ship's operator, "owner" shall mean such company.

4. "Shipper" means the person on whose behalf, or by whom as a principal, the *hazardous and noxious substances* are delivered for carriage.

CRTD 1(9) 5. "*Hazardous and Noxious Substances*" means any substance [carried as cargo][1] included in the categories below which is carried on board a ship or loaded on a vehicle [carried as cargo][2] on board a ship.

(a) oils carried in bulk as listed in appendix I of Annex I to the Protocol of 1978 relating to the International Convention for the Prevention of Pollution from Ships, 1973, [other than oils covered by the Protocol of 1984 to amend the International Convention on Civil Liability for Oil Pollution Damage, 1969;][2]

[1] The addition of the text in brackets is suggested by the Working Group of Technical Experts on Hazardous and Noxious Substances.

[2] The deletion of the text in brackets is suggested by the Working Group of Technical Experts on Hazardous and Noxious Substances.

(b) noxious liquid substances listed in appendix II of Annex II to the Protocol of 1978 relating to the International Convention for the Prevention of Pollution from Ships, 1973, [as amended and those substances and mixtures provisionally categorized as falling in pollution category A, B, C or D in accordance with the provisions of regulation 3(4) of Annex II;][1]

(c) dangerous liquefied substances to be carried in bulk by type I or type II as specified in the International Code for the Construction and Equipment of Ships Carrying Dangerous Chemicals in Bulk;

[(c) dangerous liquid substances carried in bulk listed in chapter 17 of the International Code for the Construction of Equipment of Ships Carrying Dangerous Chemicals in Bulk, 1983, as amended, and the products for which the preliminary suitable conditions for the carriage have been prescribed by the Administration and port Administrations involved in accordance with paragraph 1.1.3 of the Code;][3]

(d) *hazardous and noxious substances* included in the International Maritime Dangerous Goods Code, as amended, with the exception of nuclear substances;

[(d) dangerous, hazardous and harmful substances, materials and articles carried as cargo in packaged form covered by the International Maritime Dangerous Goods Code, as amended;][1]

(e) liquefied gases as listed in article 1.2 and chapter XIX of the International Code for the Construction and Equipment of Ships Carrying Liquefied Gases in Bulk, [as amended and the products for which preliminary suitable conditions for the carriage have been prescribed by the Administration and port Administration involved in accordance with paragraph 1.1.6 of the Code;][1]

(f) substances with explosion risks arising during the unloading of the substance in bulk if the flashpoint is less than 60 centirades (measured by a closed cup test); and

[(f) substances carried in bulk with a flashpoint less than 60°C (measured by a closed cup test);][1]

(g) substances with explosion risks arising from the previous carriage in bulk of:

[1] The addition of the text in brackets is suggested by the Working Group of Technical Experts on Hazardous and Noxious Substances.

[3] The texts in brackets are suggested by the Working Group of Technical Experts on Hazardous and Noxious Substances, as addition to the existing text in the case of subparagraphs (b) and (e),

(i) oil within the meaning of appendix I of Annex I to the Protocol of 1978 relating to the International Convention for the Prevention of Pollution from Ships, 1973;
(ii) liquefied gases referred to in (f) above; and
(iii) substances capable of giving off gas with a flashpoint of less than 60 centigrades (measured by a closed cup test).

[(g) residues from the previous carriage in bulk of substances with a flashpoint of less than 60°C (measured by a closed cup test); and][4]

[(h) solid bulk materials pressing chemical hazards covered by appendix B of the Code of Safe Practice for Solid Bulk Cargoes, as amended.][5]

6. "Damage" means:

CRTD 1(10[a]) (a) loss of life or personal injury on board or outside the ship carrying the *hazardous and noxious substances* caused by those [substances];

CRTD 1(10[b]) (b) loss of or damage to property outside the ship carrying the *hazardous and noxious substances* caused by those [substances], to the exclusion of any loss of or damage to other ships in the same [train of ships] or any loss of or damage to property on board such ships;

CRTD 1(10[c]) CLC I(6[a]) (c) loss or damage by contamination of the environment caused by the *hazardous and noxious substances*, provided that compensation for impairment of the environment other than loss of profit from such impairment shall be limited to costs of reasonable measures of reinstatement actually undertaken or to be undertaken; and

CRTD 1(10[d]) CLC I(6[b]) (d) the costs of preventive measures and further loss or damage caused by preventive measures.

CRTD 1(10) Where it is not reasonably possible to separate damage caused by the *hazardous and noxious substances* from that caused by other factors, all such damage shall be deemed to be caused by the *hazardous and noxious substances*.

CLC I(7) CRTD 1(11) 7. "Preventive measures" means any reasonable measures taken by any person after an incident has occurred to prevent or minimize damage.

[5] New subparagraph suggested by the Working Group of Technical Experts on Hazardous and Noxious Substances.

[6] See article 17 and footnote.

CLC I(8) CRTD 1(12) 8. "Incident" means any occurrence of series of occurrences having the same origin, which causes damage or creates a grave and imminent threat of causing damage.

CRTD 3(3) 9. "Carriage by sea" means the period from the time when the *hazardous and noxious substances* enters any part of the ship's equipment, on loading, to the time they cease to be present in any part of the ship's equipment, on discharge. If no ship's equipment is used, the period begins and ends respectively when the *hazardous and noxious substances* cross the ship's rail.

10. "Contributing cargo" means any substance included in Annex I to this convention which is:

(a) to be carried by sea as cargo [from] [or to] [a port within] [the territory of] a Contracting State; and
(b) to be loaded on a vehicle to be carried by sea as cargo [from] [or to] [a port within] [the territory of] a Contracting State.

[11. "Contributing ship" means any ship, entering the territory of, and calling at a port within, a Contracting State, on which no *hazardous and noxious substances* are carried as cargo, but which is subject to explosion risk arising from the previous carriage in bulk [of those substance referred to in subsection (g) of the definition of "*Hazardous and Noxious Substances*"].][6]

12. "The Scheme" means the International *Hazardous and Noxious Substances* Scheme established under article 11.

13. "Issuing agent" means a person performing the tasks referred to in article 14, paragraph 1.

14. "Compulsory insurance certificate" means a certificate indicate that a shipowner carrying *hazardous and noxious substances* has insurance cover or financial securities to meet his liabilities under this convention in respect of damage resulting from an incident involving *hazardous and noxious substances.*

15. "*Hazardous and Noxious Substances* certificate" means a certificate issued by an issuing agent in respect of contributing cargo or a contributing ship.

CLC I(4) 16. "State of the ship's registry" means in relation to registered ships the State of registration of the ship, and in relation to unregistered ships the States whose flag the ship is entitled to fly.

[6] See article 17 and footnote.

17. "Organization" means the International Maritime Organization.

18. "Secretary-General" means the Secretary-General of the Organization.

Article 2 Scope of application

This Convention shall apply exclusively:

CLC II(a) FUND 3(a) (a) to any damage caused in the territory, including the territorial sea, of a State Party:

CLC II(a[ii]) FUND 3(a[ii]) (b) to damage by contamination of the environment caused in the exclusive economic zone of a State Party, established in accordance with international law, or, if a State Party has not established such a zone, in an area beyond and adjacent to the territorial sea of that State determined by that State in accordance with international law and extending not more than 200 nautical miles from the baselines from which the breadth of its territorial sea is measured;

(c) to damage, other than damage by contamination of the environment, caused outside the territory, including the territorial sea, of any State, if this damage has been caused by a ship registered in a State Party or, in the case of an unregistered ship, by a ship entitled to fly the flag of a State Party; and

CLC II(b) FUND 3(b) (d) to preventive measures, wherever taken, to prevent or minimize such damage.

Article 3

CRTD 3(1) 1. This Convention shall apply to claims, other than claims arising out of any contract for the carriage of goods and passengers, for damage arising from the carriage of *hazardous and noxious substances* by sea.

CRTD 3(2) 2. This Convention shall not apply to the extent that its provision are incompatible with those of the applicable law relating to workmen's compensation or social security schemes.

3. This Convention shall not apply:

LLMC 3(b) (a) to pollution damage covered by the International Convention on Civil Liability for Oil Pollution Damage, 1969 (or any amendments); and

CRTD 4(b) (b) to damage caused by a nuclear substance:

(i) if the operator of a nuclear installation is liable for such damage under either the Paris Convention of 29 July 1960 on Third party Liability in the Field of Nuclear Energy and its additional Protocols of 28

January 1964 and 16 November 1982 or the Vienna Convention of 21 May 1963 on Civil Liability for Nuclear Damage or under any amendments to those Conventions, or

(ii) if the operator of a nuclear installation is liable for such damage by virtue of a national law governing the liability for such damage, provided that such law is in all respects as favourable to persons who may suffer damage as either the Paris or Vienna Conventions as referred to under (i).

CLC XI(1) 4. The provisions of this Convention shall not apply to warships or other ships owned or operated by a State and used, for the time being, only on Government non-commercial service.

CLC XI(2) 5. With respect to ships owned by a State Party and used for commercial purposes, each State shall be subject to suit in the jurisdictions set forth in article 33 and shall waive all defences based on its status as a sovereign State.

Chapter II: Liability

Article 4 Liability of the Owner

CLC III(1)
CRTD 5(1+2) 1. Except as provided in paragraphs 2 and 3 the owner at the time of an incident shall be liable for damage caused by any *hazardous and noxious substances* in connection with their carriage by sea, provided that if an incident consists of a series of occurrences having the same origin the liability shall attach to the owner at the time of the first of such occurrences.

CLC III(2)
CRTD 5(4) 2. No liability shall attach to the owner if the proves that:

(a) the damage resulted from an act of war, hostilities, civil war, insurrection or a natural phenomenon of an exceptional, inevitable and irresistible character; or

(b) the damage was wholly caused by an act or omission done with the intent to cause damage by a third party; or

CLC III(2[c]) (c) the damage was wholly caused by the negligence or other wrongful act of any Government or other authority responsible for the maintenance of lights or other navigational aids in the exercise of that function; or

CRTD 5(4[c]) [(d) the consignor or any other person failed to meet his obligation to inform him of the hazardous or noxious nature of the substances, and that neither he nor a person mentioned in paragraph 5, subparagraph (a), of this article either knew or ought to have known of their nature.]

CLC III(3)
CRTD 5(5)

3. If the owner proves that the damage resulted wholly or partially either from an act or omission done with intent to cause damage by the person who suffered the damage or from the negligence of that person, the owner may be exonerated wholly or partially from his liability to such person.

CLC III(4)
CRTD 5(6)

4. No claim for compensation for damage shall be made against the owner otherwise than in accordance with this Convention [provided, however, that in the case referred to in paragraph 2(d) of this article, any liability for damage which may be incurred by the owner according to the applicable law shall not be affected.]

CLC III(4)
CRTD 5(7)

5. Subject to paragraph 6 of this article, no claim for compensation for damage under this Convention or otherwise may be made against:

(a) the servants or agents of the owner or the members of the crew;
(b) the pilot or any other person who, without being a member of the crew, performs services for the ship;
(c) any charterer (howsoever described, including a bareboat charterer), manager or operator of the ship;
(d) any person performing salvage operations with the consent of the owner or on the instructions of a competent public authority;
(e) any person taking preventive measures; and
(f) all servants or agents of persons mentioned in subparagraphs (c), (d) and (e);

unless the damage resulted from their personal act or omission, committed with the intent to cause such damage, or recklessly and with knowledge that such damage would probably result.

CLC III(5)
CRTD 5(9)

6. Nothing in this Convention shall prejudice any right of recourse of the owner against the consignor or the consignee of the substance causing the damage or against any other third party.

Article 5 Incidents Involving Two or More Ships

CRTD 8

1. Whenever damage has resulted from an incident involving two or more ships each of which is carrying *hazardous and noxious substances*, each owner, unless exonerated under article 4, paragraphs 2 and 3, shall be liable for the damage. The owners shall be jointly and severally liable for all such damage which is not reasonably separable.

2. However, each owner shall be entitled to the limits of liability applicable to him.

3. Nothing in this Convention shall prejudice any right of recourse of an owner against any other owner.

Article 6 Limitation of Liability

CLC V(1) 1. The owner of a ship shall be entitled to limit his liability under this Convention in respect of any one incident to an aggregate amount calculated as follows:

(a) [7] units of account for a ship not exceeding [...] units of tonnage; and
(b) for a ship with a tonnage in excess thereof, for each additional unit of tonnage, [...] units of account in addition to the amount mentioned in subparagraph (a);

provided, however, that this aggregate amount shall not in any event exceed [...] units of account.

CLC V(2) 2. The owner shall not be entitled to limit his liability under this Convention if it is proved that the damage resulted from his personal act or omission, committed with the intent to cause such damage, or recklessly and with knowledge that such damage would probably result.

CLC V(3) 3. Subject to article 7, the owner shall, for the purpose of availing himself of the benefit of limitation provided for in paragraph 1 of this article, constitute a fund for the total sum representing the limit of his liability with the court or other competent authority of any one of the States Parties in which action is brought under article 33 or, if no action is brought, with any court or other competent authority in any one of the States parties in which an action can be brought under article 33. The fund can be constituted either by depositing the sum or by producing a bank guarantee or other guarantee, acceptable under the legislation of the State Party where the fund is constituted, and considered to be adequate by the court or other competent authority.

CLC V(4) 4. The fund shall be distributed among the claimants in proportion to the amounts of their established claims.

CLC V(5) 5. If before the fund is distributed the owner or any of his servants or agents or any person providing him insurance or other financial security has as a result of the incident in question, paid compensation for damage, such person shall, up to the amount he has paid, acquire by subrogation the rights which the person so compensated would have enjoyed under this Convention.

CLC V(6) 6. The right of subrogation provided for in paragraph 5 of this article may also be exercised by a person other than those mentioned therein in respect of any amount of compensation for damage which he may have paid but only to the extent that such subrogation is permitted under the applicable national law.

CLC V(7) 7. Where the owner or any other person establishes that he may be compelled to pay at a later date in whole or in part any such amount of compensation, with regard to which such person would have enjoyed a right of subrogation under paragraphs 5 or 6 of this article, had the compensation been paid before the fund was distributed, the court or other competent authority of the State where the fund has been constituted may order that a sufficient sum shall be provisionally set aside to enable such person at such later date to enforce his claim against the fund.

CLC V(8) [8. Claims in respect of expenses reasonably incurred or sacrifices reasonably made by the owner voluntarily to prevent or minimize damage shall rank equally with other claims against the fund.][8]

CLC V(9) 9. (a) The "unit of account" referred to in paragraph 1 of this article is the Special Drawing Right as defined by the International Monetary Fund. The amounts mentioned in paragraph 1 shall be converted into national currency on the basis of the value of that currency by reference to the Special Drawing Right on the date of the constitution of the fund referred to in paragraph 3. The value of the national currency, in terms of the Special Drawing Right, of a State Party which is a member of the International Monetary Fund, shall be calculated in accordance with the method of valuation applied by the International Monetary Fund in effect on the date in question for its operations and transactions. The value of the national currency, in terms of the Special Drawing Right, of a State Party which is not a member of the International Monetary Fund, shall be calculated in a manner determined by that State.

(b) Nevertheless, a State party which is not a member of the International Monetary Fund and whose law does not permit the application of the provisions of paragraph 9(a) may, at the time of ratification, acceptance, approval of or accession to this Convention or at any time thereafter,

[8] See document LEG 64/10, paragraph 55.

declare that the unit of account referred to in paragraph 9(a) shall be equal to 15 gold francs. The gold franc referred to in this paragraph corresponds to sixty-five-and-a-half milligrammes of gold of millesimal fineness nine hundred. The conversion of the gold franc into the national currency shall be made according to the law of the State concerned.

(c) The calculation mentioned in the last sentence of paragraph 9(a) and the conversion mentioned in paragraph 9(b) shall be made in such manner as to express in the national currency of the State Party as far as possible the same real value for the amounts in paragraph 1 as would result from the application of the first three sentences of paragraph 9(a). States Parties shall communicate to the depository the manner of calculation pursuant to paragraph 9(a), or the result of the conversion in paragraph 9(b) as the case may be, when depositing an instrument of ratification, acceptance, approval of or accession to this Convention and whenever there is a change in either.

CLC V(10) 10. For the purpose of this article the ship's tonnage shall be the gross tonnage calculated in accordance with the tonnage measurement regulations contained in Annex I of the International Convention on Tonnage Measurement of Ships, 1969.

CLC V(11) 11. The insurer or other person providing financial security shall be entitled to constitute a fund in accordance with this article on the same conditions and having the same effect as if it were constituted by the owner. Such a fund may be constituted even if, under the provisions of paragraph 2, the owner is not entitled to limit his liability, but its constitution shall in that case not prejudice the rights of any claimant against the owner.

Article 7

1. A State party may, at the time of ratification, acceptance, approval of or accession to this Convention [or at any time thereafter], declare that the limitation of the liability of the owner under this Convention shall wholly or partly be determined by [either] the provisions of:

[(a)] the Convention on Limitation of Liability for Maritime Claims, done at London on 19 November 1976, or any amended or revised version thereof;

[(b) the International Convention relating to the Limitation of the Liability of Owners of Sea-going ships, done at Brussels on 10 October 1957, or any subsequent amendment to that Convention;]

[(c) the International Convention for the Unification of certain Rules relating to the Limitation of the Liability of Owners of Sea-going Vessels, done at Brussels on 25 August 1924;]

[(d) provisions on limitation of liability in national law.]

2. A State Party which makes use of the option provided for in paragraph 1 shall apply the provisions of such convention or national law with respect to all claims against the owner arising on any distinct incident which are subject to limitation thereunder, including claims not covered by the present Convention.

3. Where in accordance with paragraph 1 the owner is entitled to limit his liability for damage and the limits are insufficient to pay all claimants for such damage in full, he shall constitute a supplementary fund to compensate any unpaid balance of claims for damage made under this Convention. It shall be constituted in the sum of such unpaid balance but it shall not exceed the difference between the limits established in accordance with article 6, paragraph 1, and paragraph 1 of this article.

4. A fund constituted under the conventions or national law as referred to in paragraph 1 and a supplementary fund shall be constituted before one and the same court, being the court or other competent authority of a State Party referred to in article 6, paragraph 3, and in the form prescribed by that paragraph.

5. A supplementary fund thus constituted shall only be available for the payment of claims for damage under this Convention in respect of which limitation of liability may be invoked.

6. Article 6, paragraphs 4, 5, 6, 7 and 11 shall apply *mutatis mutandis* in respect of the supplementary fund.

7. Where the claims exceed the limits provided for in a convention or under national law referred to in paragraph 1, the courts or other competent authorities of a State Party which make use of the option provided for in that paragraph shall order the release of the ship or of other property belonging to the owner and of any security furnished to avoid the arrest, in accordance with the provisions of the convention or national law referred to in that

paragraph, only if a supplementary fund has been constituted pursuant to paragraph 3.

Article 8

CLC VI(1) 1. Where the owner, after an incident, has constituted a fund in accordance with article 6 or 7 and is entitled to limit his liability:

(a) no person having a claim for damage arising out of that incident shall be entitled to exercise any right against any other assets of the owner in respect of such claim; and
(b) the court or other competent authority of any State Party shall order the release of any ship or other property belonging to the owner which has been arrested in respect of a claim for damage arising out of that incident, and shall similarly release any bail or other security furnished to avoid such arrest.

CLC VI(2) 2. The foregoing shall, however, only apply if the claimant has access to the court administering the fund and the fund is actually available in respect of his claim.

Article 9 Death and Injury

1. Claims in respect of death or personal injury have priority over other claims save to the extent that the aggregate of such claims exceeds two thirds of the total amount established in accordance with article 6, paragraph 1.

2. When a supplementary fund has been established under article 7, paragraph 3, claims in respect of death or personal injury shall have priority over other claims save tot he extent that the aggregate of such claims exceed two thirds of the total amount referred to in that provision.

Article 10 Compulsory Insurance of the Owner

CLC VII(1) 1. The owner of a ship registered in a State Party and (actually) carrying *hazardous and noxious substances* shall be required to maintain insurance or other financial security, such as the guarantee of a bank or similar financial institution in the sums fixed by applying the limits of liability prescribed in article 6, paragraph 1, to cover his liability for damage under this Convention.

CLC VII(2) 2. A compulsory insurance certificate attesting that insurance or other financial security is in force in accordance with the provisions of this Convention shall be issued to each ship after the appropriate authority of a State Party has determined that the requirements of paragraph 1 have been complied with. With respect to a ship registered in a State Party such compulsory insurance certificate shall be issued or certified by the appropriate authority of the State of the ship's registry; with respect to a ship not registered in a State Party it may be issued or certified by the appropriate authority of any State Party. This compulsory insurance certificate shall be in the form of the annexed model and shall contain the following particulars:

(a) name of the ship and port of registration;
(b) name and principal place of business of owner;
(c) type of security;
(d) name and principal place of business of insurer or other person giving security and, where appropriate, place of business where the insurance or security is established; and
(e) period of validity of certificate, which shall not be longer than the period of validity of the insurance or other security.

CLC VII(3)

3. The compulsory insurance certificate shall be in the official language or languages of the issuing State. If the language used is neither English nor French, the text shall include a translation into one of these languages.

CLC VII(4)

4. The compulsory insurance certificate shall be carried on board the ship and a copy shall be deposited with the authorities who keep the record of the ship's registry or, if the ship is not registered in a State Party, with the authority of the State issuing or certifying the certificate.

CLC VII(5)

5. An insurance or other financial security shall not satisfy the requirements of the article if it can cease, for reasons other than the expiry of the period of validity of the insurance or security specified in the certificate under paragraph 2 of this article, before three months have elapsed from the date on which notice of its termination is given to the authorities referred to in paragraph 4 of this article, unless the compulsory insurance certificate has been issued within the said period. The foregoing provisions shall similarly apply to any modification which results in the insurance or security no longer satisfying the requirements of this article.

CLC VII(6) 6. The State of registry shall, subject to the provisions of this article, determine the conditions of issue and validity of the compulsory insurance certificate.

CLC VII(7) 7. Compulsory insurance certificates issued or certified under the authority of a State Party in accordance with paragraph 2 shall be accepted by other States Parties for the purposes of this Convention and shall be regarded by other States Parties as having the same force as compulsory insurance certificates issued or certified by them even if issued or certified in respect of a ship not registered in a State Party. A State Party may at any time request consultation with the issuing or certifying State should it believe that the insurer or guarantor named in the compulsory insurance certificate is not financially capable of meeting the obligations imposed by the Convention.

CLC VII(8) 8. Any claim for compensation for damage may be brought directly against the insurer or other person providing financial security for the owner's liability for damage. In such case the defendant may, irrespective of the fact whether or not the owner be entitled to limit his liability, avail himself of the limit of liability prescribed in accordance with paragraph 1 of this article. He may further avail himself of the defences (other than the bankruptcy or winding up of the owner) which the owner himself would have been entitled to invoke. Furthermore, the defendant may avail himself of the defence that the damage resulted from the wilful misconduct of the owner himself, but the defendant shall not avail himself of any other defence which he might have been entitled to invoke in proceedings brought by the owner against him. The defendant shall in any event have the right to require the owner to be joined in the proceedings.

CLC VII(9) 9. Any sums provided by insurance or by other financial security maintained in accordance with paragraph 1 of this article shall be available exclusively for the satisfaction of claims under this Convention.

CLC VII(10) 10. A State Party shall not permit a ship under its flag to which this article applies to trade unless a certificate had been issued under paragraph 2 or 12 of this article.

CLC VII(11) 11. Subject to the provisions of this article, each State Party shall ensure, under its national legislation, that insurance or other security to the extent specified in paragraph 1 of this article is in force in respect of any ship, wherever registered, entering or leaving a port in its territory, or arriving at or leaving an offshore terminal in its territorial sea.

CLC VII(12)

12. If insurance or other financial security is not maintained in respect of a ship owned by a State Party, the provisions of this article relating thereto shall not be applicable to such ship, but the ship shall carry a compulsory insurance certificate issued by the appropriate authorities of the State of the ship's registry stating that the ship is owned by that State and that the ship's liability is covered within the limit prescribed in accordance with paragraph 1 of this article. Such a compulsory insurance certificate shall follow as closely as possible the model prescribed by paragraph 2 of this article.

[13. The owner of any contributing shall maintain insurance or other financial security to meet his liability under this Convention.]

Chapter III: Compensation by the International Hazardous and Noxious Substances Scheme

Article 11 Establishment of the Scheme

1. An International Hazardous and Noxious Substances Scheme is hereby established with the following aims:

(a) to provide compensation for damage in connection with the carriage of *hazardous and noxious substances* by sea, to the extent that the protection afforded by chapter II after the application of article 7 of this Convention is inadequate or not available; and
(b) to give effect to the related tasks set out in article 13.

FUND 2(2)

2. The scheme shall in each State Party be recognized as a legal person capable under the laws of that State of assuming rights and obligations and of being a party in legal proceedings before the courts of that State. Each State Party shall recognize the director of the Scheme (hereinafter referred to as "The Director") as the legal representative of the Scheme.

Article 12 Compensation

FUND 4(1)

1. For the purpose of fulfilling its function under article 11, paragraph 1(a), the Scheme shall pay compensation to any person suffering damage if such person has been

unable to obtain full and adequate compensation for the damage under the terms of chapter 11 of this Convention:

(a) because no liability for the damage arises under chapter II of this Convention:
(b) because the owner liable for the damage under chapter II of this Convention is financially incapable of meeting his obligations in full and any financial security that may be provided under chapter II of this Convention does not cover or is insufficient to satisfy the claims for compensation for damage; an owner being treated as financially incapable of meeting his obligations and a financial security being treated as insufficient if the person suffering the damage has been unable to obtain full satisfaction of the amount of compensation due under chapter II of this Convention after having taken all reasonable steps to pursue the legal remedies available to him; and
(c) because the damage exceeds the owner's liability under the terms of chapter II of this Convention, or under the terms of any other international convention in force or open for signature, ratification or accession at the date of this Convention.

FUND 4(1) [2. Expenses reasonably incurred or sacrifices reasonably made by the owner voluntarily to prevent or minimize damage shall be treated as damage for the purposes of this article.]

FUND 4(2) 3. The Scheme shall incur no obligation under the preceding paragraph if:

(a) it proves that the damage resulted from an act of war, hostilities, civil war or insurrection or was caused by *hazardous or/and noxious* substances which have escaped or been discharged from a warship or other ship owned or operated by a State and used at the time of the incident, only on government non-commercial service; or
(b) it proves that the damage did not result from an incident involving a ship.

FUND 4(3) (4) If the Scheme proves that the damage resulted wholly or partially either from an act or omission done with intent to cause damage by the person who suffered the damage or from the negligence of that person, the Scheme may be exonerated wholly or partially from its obligation to pay compensation to such person. The Scheme shall in any event be exonerated if the owner proves that the damage resulted wholly or partially either from an act or omission done with intent to cause damage by the person who suffered the damage or from the negligence of that person, and is exonerated wholly or partially from his liability to such person. However, there shall be no such exoneration of the Scheme with regard to preventive measures.

FUND 4(4)

5. (a) Except as otherwise provided in subparagraph (b) of this paragraph, the aggregate amount of compensation payable by the Scheme under this article shall in respect of any one incident be limited, so that the total sum of that amount and any amount of compensation actually paid under chapter II of this Convention for damage within the scope of application of this Convention as defined in article 2 shall not exceed [......] units of account.
(b) The aggregate amount of compensation payable by the Scheme under this article for damage resulting from a natural phenomenon of an exceptional, inevitable and irresistible character shall not exceed [......] units of account.
(c) Interest accrued on a fund constituted in accordance with this Convention, if any, shall not be taken into account for the computation of the maximum compensation payable by the Scheme under this article.
(d) The amounts mentioned in this article shall be converted into national currency on the basis of the value of that currency with reference to the Special Drawing Right on the date of the decision of the Assembly of the Scheme as to the first date of payment of compensation.

6. Claims in respect of death or personal injury shall have priority over other claims save to the extent that the aggregate of such claims exceeds two-thirds of the total amount established in accordance with paragraph 5.

FUND 4(6)

7. The Assembly of the Scheme may decide that, in exceptional cases, compensation in accordance with this Convention can be paid even if the owner of the ship has not constituted a fund in accordance with [chapter II of]

this Convention. In such cases paragraph 5(d) of this article applies accordingly.

Article 13 Related tasks of this Scheme

For the purpose of fulfilling its function under article 11, paragraph 1(a), the Scheme shall have the following tasks:

(a) to consider claims made against the Scheme;

FUND 12(1) (b) to prepare an estimate in the form of a budget of:

EXPENDITURE:

FUND 12(1)(i)(a) (i) costs and expenses of the administration of the Scheme in the relevant year and any deficit from operations in the preceding years; and

(ii) payments to be made by the Scheme in the relevant year;

INCOME:

FUND 12(1)(ii)(a) (iii) surplus funds from operations in preceding years, including any interest;

FUND 12(1)(ii)(b) (iv) initial contributions to be paid in the course of the year;

(v) contributions to be received from the issuing agents in the course of the forthcoming year, if required to balance the budget; and

FUND 12(1)(ii)(d) (vi) any other income;

(c) to calculate [annually] [quarterly] the value [per unit] of a *hazardous and noxious substances* certificate, having regard to the budgetary requirements as established in accordance with subparagraph (b) and the statistical information received in accordance with subparagraph (g);

(d) to establish and keep up to date a list of issuing agents;

(e) to supply *hazardous and noxious substances* certificates to issuing agents;

(f) to receive funds quarterly from issuing agents;

(g) to receive statistics from issuing agents and, on request, from other sources;

(h) to [establish and] review in the light of experience the requirements for appointment of issuing agents;

(i) to review the scope of definition of contributing cargo in the light of claims experience and trading patterns;

FUND 4(7) (j) to use at the request of a State Party its good offices as necessary to assist that State to secure promptly such personnel, material and services as are necessary to enable the State to take measures to prevent or mitigate damage arising from an incident in respect of which the Scheme may be called upon to pay compensation under this Convention; and

FUND 4(8) (k) to provide where appropriate credit facilities with a view to the taking of preventive measures against damage arising from a particular incident in respect of which the Scheme may be called upon to pay compensation under this Convention.

Article 14 Tasks of the Issuing Agents

1. Issuing agents shall:

(a) obtain *hazardous and noxious substances* certificates from the Scheme;
(b) sell *hazardous and noxious substances* certificates [at a price determined by the individual issuing agent] to shippers of contributing cargoes [and owners of contributing ships];
(c) make quarterly contributions to the Scheme being the sum of the [units of] *hazardous and noxious substances* certificates sold by them in the preceding quarter multiplied by the value of each [unit of] *hazardous and noxious substances* certificate as set by the Scheme; and
(d) provide statistics to the Scheme as requested by the Scheme.

2. Issuing agents shall be required to be of adequate financial standing to meet any financial obligation to the Scheme.

Article 15[9] [Initial contributions by States Parties

FUND 71 11(1) 1. In respect of each State Party, an initial contribution shall be made of an amount which shall for each State be calculated on the basis of a fixed sum for each [unit] of contributing cargo exported from that State during the calendar year preceding that in which this Convention enters into force for that State.

FUND 71 11(2) 2. The fixed sum referred to in paragraph 1 shall be determined by the Assembly within [..] months after the entry into force of this Convention.

[9] The provisions under this Article should be deleted if Articles 38 and 39 remain in the draft.

3. In performing this function, the Assembly shall take account of the budgetary provisions in article 13, subparagraph (b).

FUND 71 11(3) 4. The initial contributions shall, in respect of each State Party, be paid within [..] months following the date at which the Convention entered into force for that State.]

Article 16 Non-payment of Contributions

FUND 13(1) 1. The amount of any contribution due under article 14, paragraph 1(c), and which is in arrear shall bear interest at a rate which shall be determined in accordance with the Internal Regulations of the Scheme, provided that different rates shall be fixed for different circumstances.

FUND 13(3) 2. Where a person who is liable in accordance with the provisions of article[s] 14 [and 15][10] to make contributions or initial contributions to the Scheme does not fulfill his obligations in respect of any such contribution or any part thereof and is in arrears the Director shall take all appropriate action against such person on behalf of the Scheme with a view to the recovery of the amount due. However, where the defaulting contributor is manifestly insolvent or the circumstances otherwise so warrant, the Assembly may, upon recommendation of the Director, decide that no action shall be taken or continued against the contributor.

Article 17 Purchase of *Hazardous and Noxious Substances* Certificates

1. A *hazardous and noxious substances* certificate shall be purchased by:

(a) the shipper of any contributing cargo; and
[(b) the owner of any contributing ship.][11]

[2. An issuing agent may issue a dangerous goods certificate,
(a) for an individual shipment, or
(b) quarterly (or on a longer term but not exceeding one year). This certificate shall cover all shipments effected in each quarter (or during such a longer term to be agreed upon).][12]

[10] See footnote to Article 15.
[11] See document LEG 64/10, paragraph 89.
[12] Proposal submitted by Japan. See document LEG 65/10, paragraph 89.

3. *A hazardous and noxious substances* certificate shall contain information:

(a) as to the [nature and amount] of the contributing cargo in respect of which that certificate has been issued and the voyage to which the certificate relates; and

[(b) as to the name of the contributing ship in respect of which that certificate has been issued and the voyage to which the certificate relates.][13]

[4. "Notwithstanding the provisions of paragraph 3, a dangerous goods certificate referred to in paragraph 2(b) is not required to contain information on the voyage to which it relates."][14]

Article 18 Duties of States Parties

1. States Parties shall under their national law enact appropriate provisions:

(a) to enable the licensing establishment and operation of issuing agents within their jurisdiction in accordance with the requirements [adopted by the scheme under article 13, subparagraph (h)]; and

(b) relating to the collection of statistics on *hazardous and noxious substances* [exported] [carried by sea][15] from their [ports] [territory] from sources other than issuing agents.

2. States Parties shall ensure that any issuing agent licensed to operate within its jurisdiction appears on a list to be established and kept up to date by the Director in accordance with paragraphs 3, 4 and 5 of this article.

FUND 15(2) 3. For the purposes set out in paragraph 2, each State Party shall communicate, at a time and in the manner to be prescribed in the Internal Regulations of the Scheme, to the Director the name and address of any issuing agent licensed to operate within its jurisdiction.

FUND 15(3) 4. For the purposes of ascertaining who are, at any given time, issuing agents the list shall be *prima facie* evidence of the facts stated therein.

[13] See document LEG 64/10, paragraph 89.
[14] Proposal submitted by Japan. See document LEG 65/10, paragraph 89.
[15] See document LEG 65/8, paragraph 54.

FUND 15(4)

5. Where a State Party does not fulfill its obligations to submit to the Director the communication referred to in paragraph 3 and this results in a financial loss for the Scheme, that State Party shall be liable to compensate the Scheme for such loss. The Assembly shall, on the recommendation of the Director, decide whether such compensation shall be payable by a State Party.

6. Each State Party shall take any appropriate measures under its law, including the imposing of such sanctions as it may deem necessary, with a view to the effective execution of any obligation:

(a) to purchase a *hazardous and noxious substances* certificate in respect of contributing cargo [exported] [carried by sea] [from] [imported] [into] [to] 1/ a port within the territory of that State;
[(b) to purchase a *hazardous and noxious substances* certificate in respect of a contributing ship [departing from] [arriving at] a port within the territory of that state;]
(c) on an issuing agent domiciled within that State to make a quarterly contribution to the Scheme;
(d) on an owner to have a compulsory insurance certificate on board a ship if that ship is carrying *hazardous and noxious substances* [or is a contributing ship]; and
(e) on a shipper to present a *hazardous and noxious substances* certificate on delivery of a contributing cargo for carriage by sea.

Article 19

FUND 14(1)

1. Each State Party may at the time when it deposits its instrument of ratification or accession or at any time thereafter declare that it assumes itself obligations that are incumbent under this Convention on any person who is liable to contribute to the Scheme in accordance with article 14, paragraph 1(c), in respect of *hazardous and noxious substances* dispatched by sea from the territory of that State. Such declaration shall be made in writing and shall specify which obligations are assumed.

FUND 14(2)

2. Where a declaration under paragraph 1 is made prior to the entry into force of this Convention in accordance with article 42, it shall be deposited with the Secretary-General

who shall after the entry into force of the Convention communicate the declaration to the Director.

FUND 14(3) 3. A declaration under paragraph 1 which is made after the entry into force of this Convention shall be deposited with the Director.

FUND 14(4) 4. A declaration made in accordance with this article may be withdrawn by the relevant State giving notice thereof in writing to the Director. Such notification shall take effect three months after the Director's receipt thereof.

FUND 14(5) 5. Any State which is bound by a declaration made under this article shall, in any proceedings brought against it before a competent court in respect of any obligation specified in the declaration, waive any immunity that it would otherwise be entitled to invoke.

Article 20 Organization and Administration

FUND 16 The Scheme shall have an Assembly and a Secretariat headed by a Director.

Article 21 Assembly

FUND 17 The Assembly shall consist of all States Parties to this Convention.

Article 22

FUND 18 The functions of the Assembly shall be:

FUND 18(1) (a) to elect at each regular session its Chairman and two Vice-Chairmen who shall hold office until the next regular session;

FUND 18(2) (b) to determine its own rules of procedure, subject to the provisions of this Convention;

(c) to develop, apply and keep under review Internal and Financial Regulations relating to the aim of the Scheme as described in article 11, paragraph 1(a), and the related tasks of the Scheme listed in article 13;

FUND 18(4) (d) to appoint the Director and make provisions for the appointment of such other personnel as may be necessary and determine the terms and conditions of service of the Director and other personnel;

(e) to adopt the annual budget prepared in accordance with article 13, subparagraph (b), and agree the value [per unit] of a *hazardous and noxious substances* certificate calculated in accordance with article 13, subparagraph (c);

(f) to consider and approve as necessary any recommendation of the Scheme regarding:
(i) the requirements for appointment of issuing agents; and
(ii) the scope of definition of contributing cargo;

FUND 18(6) (g) to appoint auditors and approve the accounts of the Scheme;

FUND 18(7) (h) to approve settlements of claims against the Scheme, to take decisions in respect of the distribution among claimants of the available amount of compensation in accordance with article 12 and to determine the terms and conditions according to which provisional payments in respect of claims shall be made with a view to ensuring that victims of damage are compensated as promptly as possible;

FUND 18(9) (i) to establish any temporary or permanent subsidiary body it may consider to be necessary to define its terms of reference and to give it the authority needed to perform the functions entrusted to it; when appointing the members of such body, the Assembly shall endeavour to secure an equitable geographical distribution of members and to ensure that the States Parties are appropriately represented; the Rules of Procedure of the Assembly may be applied, *mutatis mutandis*, for the work of such subsidiary body;

FUND 18(10) (j) to determine which States not party to the Convention and which intergovernmental and international non-governmental organizations shall be admitted to take part, without voting rights, in meetings of the Assembly and subsidiary bodies;

FUND 18(11) (k) to give instructions concerning the administration of the Scheme to the Director and subsidiary bodies;

FUND 18(13) (l) to supervise the proper execution of the Convention and of its own decisions; and

FUND 18(14) (m) to perform such other functions as are allocated to it under the Convention or are otherwise necessary for the proper operation of the Scheme.

Article 23

FUND 19(1) 1. Regular sessions of the Assembly shall take place once every calendar year upon convocation by the Director.

FUND 19(2) 2. Extraordinary sessions of the Assembly shall be convened by the Director at the request of at least one third of the members of the Assembly and may be convened on the Director's own initiative after consultation with the Chairman of the Assembly. The Director shall give members at least thirty days' notice of such sessions.

Article 24

FUND 20 A majority of the members of the Assembly shall constitute a quorum for its meetings.

Article 25 Secretariat

FUND 28(1) 1. The Secretariat shall comprise the Director and such staff as the administration of the Scheme may require.

FUND 28(2) 2. The Director shall be the legal representative of the Scheme.

Article 26

FUND 29(1) 1. The Director shall be the chief administrative officer of the Scheme. Subject to the instructions given to him by the Assembly, he shall perform those functions which are assigned to him by this Convention, the Internal Regulations of the Scheme and the Assembly.

FUND 29(2) 2. The Director shall in particular:

(a) appoint the personnel required for the administration of the Scheme;
(b) take all appropriate measures with a view to the proper administration of the Scheme's assets;
(c) collect the contributions due under this Convention while observing in particular the provisions of article 16, paragraph 2;
(d) to the extent necessary to deal with claims against the Scheme and carry out the other functions of the Scheme, employ the services of legal, financial and other experts;
(e) take all appropriate measures for dealing with claims against the Scheme, within the limits and on conditions to be laid down in the Internal Regulations of the Scheme, including the final settlement of claims without the prior approval of the Assembly where these regulations so provide;
(f) prepare and submit to the Assembly the financial statements and budget estimates for each calendar year;
(g) prepare, in consultation with the Chairman of the Assembly, and publish a report on the activities of the Scheme during the previous calendar year; and

(h) prepare, collect and circulate the papers, documents, agenda, minutes and information that may be required for the work of the Assembly and subsidiary bodies.

Article 27

FUND 30

In the performance of their duties the Director and the staff and experts appointed by him shall not seek or receive instructions from any Government or from any authority external to the Scheme. They shall refrain from any action which might reflect on their position as international officials. Each State Party on its part undertakes to respect the exclusively international character of the responsibilities of the Director and the staff and experts appointed by him, and not to seek to influence them in the discharge of their duties.

Article 28 Finances

FUND 31(1)

1. Each State Party shall bear the salary, travel and other expenses of its own delegation to the Assembly and of its representatives on subsidiary bodies.

FUND 31(2)

2. Any other expenses incurred in the operation of the Scheme shall be borne by the Scheme.

Article 29 Voting

FUND 32

The following provisions shall apply to voting in the Assembly:

(a) each member shall have one vote;
(b) except as otherwise provided in article 30, decisions of the Assembly shall be made by a majority vote of the members present and voting;
(c) decisions where a two-thirds majority is required shall be a two-thirds majority vote of those present; and
(d) for the purpose of this article the phrase "members present" means "members present at the meeting at the time of the vote", and the phrase "members present and voting" means "members present and casting an affirmative or negative vote". Members who abstain from voting shall be considered as not voting.

Article 30

FUND 33

The following decisions of the Assembly shall require a two-thirds majority:

FUND 33(a)

(a) a decision under article 16, paragraph 2, not to take or continue action against a contributor;

(b) a decision under article 18, paragraph 5, regarding compensation payable by a State Party;

FUND 33(b) (c) the appointment of the Director under article 22, paragraph 4; and

FUND 33(c) (d) the establishment of subsidiary bodies, under article 22, paragraph 9, and matters relating to such establishment.

Article 31

FUND 34(1) 1. The Scheme, its assets, income, including contributions, and other property shall enjoy in all States Parties exemption from all direct taxation.

FUND 34(2) 2. When the Scheme makes substantial purchases of movable or immovable property, or has important work carried out which is necessary for the exercise of its official activities and the cost which includes indirect taxes or sales taxes, the Government of States Parties shall take, whenever possible, appropriate measures for the remission or refund of the amount of such duties and taxes.

FUND 34(3) 3. No exemption shall be accorded in the case of duties, taxes or dues which merely constitute payment for public utility services.

FUND 34(4) 4. The Scheme shall enjoy exemption from all customs duties, taxes and other related taxes on articles imported or exported by it or on its behalf for its official use. Articles thus imported shall not be transferred either for consideration or gratis on the territory of the country into which they have been imported except on conditions agreed by the Government of that country.

FUND 34(5) 5. Persons contributing to the Scheme and victims and owners of ships receiving compensation from the Scheme shall be subject to the fiscal legislation of the State where they are taxable, no special exemption or other benefit being conferred on them in this respect.

FUND 34(6) 6. Information relating to individual contributors supplied for the purpose of the Convention shall not be divulged outside the Scheme except in so far as it may be strictly necessary to enable the Scheme to carry out its functions including the bringing and defending of legal proceedings.

FUND 34(7) 7. Independently of existing or future regulations concerning currency or transfers, States Parties shall authorize the transfer and payment of any contribution to the Scheme and of any compensation paid by the Scheme without any restriction.

Chapter IV: Claims and Actions

Article 32 Time Bar

CLC VIII
CRTD18(1)

1. Rights to compensation under chapter II of this Convention shall be extinguished unless an action is brought thereunder within three years from the date at which the person suffering the damage knew or ought reasonably to have known of the damage and of the identity of the owner. The period may be extended if the parties so agree after the incident.

FUND 6

2. Rights to compensation under chapter III shall be extinguished unless an action is brought thereunder or a notification has been made pursuant to article 34, paragraph 6, within three years from the date when the damage occurred.

[1 *Any action for compensation* under Chapter II of this Convention shall be *time-barred* unless such action is brought thereunder within three years from the date at which the person suffering the damage knew or ought to have reasonably known of the damage and of the identity of the owner. The period may be extended if the parties so agree after the incident.

2. Any action for compensation under Chapter III of this Convention shall be time-barred unless such action is brought thereunder or a notification has been made pursuant to Article 34, paragraph 6, within three years from the date at which the person suffering the damage knew or ought reasonably to have known of the damage and of the identity of the owner. The period may be extended if the parties so agree after the incident.][16]

[CLC VIII]
CRTD 18(2)

3. In no case, however, shall an action be brought after ten years from the date of the incident which caused the damage.

CLC VIII
CRTD 18(3)

4. Where the incident consists of a series of occurrences, the ten-years period mentioned in paragraph 3 of this article shall run from the date of the last of such occurrences.

Article 33 Jurisdiction in Respect of Action against the Shipowner

CLC IX(1)
CRTD 19(1)

1. Where an incident has caused damage in the territory, including the territorial sea or an area referred to in article 2(b), of one or more States Parties, or preventive measures have been taken to prevent or minimize damage in such territory including the territorial sea or area, actions for compensation for damage may only be brought in the courts of any such State Party or States.

2. Where an incident has caused damage exclusively outside the territory, including the territorial sea, of any State and the conditions for application of this Convention set out in article 2(c) have been fulfilled or preventive measures to prevent or minimize such damage have been taken, actions for compensation for damage may only be brought in the courts of:

(a) the State Party where the ship is registered or, in the case of an unregistered ship the State Party, whose flag the ship is entitled to fly;
(b) the State Party where the owner of the ship has his habitual residence or his principal place of business; and
(c) the State Party where a fund has been constituted in accordance with article 6, paragraph 3 and article 7, paragraph 3.

3. Reasonable notice of any action taken under paragraph 1 or 2 shall be given to the defendant.

CLC IX 2
CRTD 18(3)

4. Each State Party shall ensure that its courts possess the necessary jurisdiction to entertain actions for compensation under this Convention.

CLC IX(3)

5. After a fund under article 6 or a supplementary fund under article 7 has been constituted by the owner or by the insurer or other person providing financial security in accordance with article 10, the courts of the State in which such fund is constituted shall be exclusively competent to determine all matters relating to the apportionment and distribution of the fund.

Article 34 Jurisdiction in Respect of Action against the Scheme

FUND 7(1)

1. Subject to the subsequent provisions of this article, any action against the Scheme for compensation under article 12 of this Convention shall be brought only before a court

competent under article 33 in respect of actions against the owner who is liable for damage caused by the relevant incident or before a court in a State Party which would have been competent if an owner had been liable.

FUND 7(2) 2. Each State Party shall ensure that its courts possess the necessary jurisdiction to entertain such actions against the Scheme as are referred to in paragraph 1.

FUND 7(3) 3. Where an action for compensation for damage has been brought before a court against the owner of a ship, or his guarantor, such court shall have exclusive jurisdictional competence over any action against the Scheme for compensation under the provisions of article 12 of this Convention in respect of the same damage.

FUND 7(4) 4. Each State Party shall ensure that the Scheme shall have the right to intervene as a party to any legal proceedings instituted in accordance with this Convention before a competent court of that State against the owner of a ship or his guarantor.

FUND 7(5) 5. Except as otherwise provided in paragraph 6, the Scheme shall not be bound by any judgement or decision in proceedings to which it has not been a party or by any settlement to which it is not a party.

FUND 7(6) 6. Without prejudice to the provisions of paragraph 4, where an action under this Convention for compensation for damage has been brought against an owner or his guarantor before a competent court in a State Party, each party to the proceedings shall be entitled under the national law of that State to notify the Scheme of the proceedings. Where such notification has been made in accordance with the formalities required by the law of the court seized and in such time and in such a manner that the Scheme has in fact been in a position effectively to intervene as a party to the proceedings, any judgement rendered by the court in such proceedings shall, after it has become final and enforceable in the State where the judgement was given, become binding upon the Scheme in the sense that the facts and findings in that judgement may not be disputed by the Scheme even if the Scheme has not actually intervened in the proceedings.

Article 35 Recognition and Enforcement

CLC X(1)
CRTD 20(1)

1. Any judgement given by a court with jurisdiction in accordance with article 33 where it is no longer subject to ordinary forms of review, shall be recognized in any State Party, except:

(a) where the judgement was obtained by fraud; or
(b) where the defendant was not given reasonable notice and a fair opportunity to present his case.

CLC X(2)
CRTD 20(2)

2. A judgement recognized under paragraph 1 which is enforceable in the State of origin shall be enforceable in each State Party as soon as the formalities required in that State have been complied with. The formalities shall not permit the merits of the case to be re-opened.

FUND 8

3. Subject to any decision concerning the distribution referred to in article 12, paragraph 6, any judgement given against the Scheme by a court having jurisdiction in accordance with article 34, paragraphs 1 and 3 shall, when it has become enforceable in the State of origin and is in that State no longer subject to ordinary forms of review, be recognized and enforceable in each State Party.

Article 36 Subrogation and Recourse

FUND 9(1)

1. The Scheme shall, in respect of any amount of compensation for damage paid by the Scheme in accordance with article 12, paragraph 1, of this Convention, acquire by subrogation the rights that the person so compensated may enjoy against the owner or his guarantor.

FUND 9(2)

2. Nothing in this Convention shall prejudice any rights of recourse or subrogation of the Scheme against any person [including persons referred to in article 4, paragraph 2(d)]. In any event the right of the Scheme to subrogation against such persons shall not be less favourable than that of an insurer of the person to whom compensation has been paid.

FUND 9(3)

3. Without prejudice to any other rights of subrogation or recourse against the Scheme which may exist, a State Party or agency thereof which has paid compensation for damage in accordance with provisions of national law shall acquire by subrogation the rights which the person so compensated would have enjoyed under this Convention.

Article 37 Supersession Clause

CLC XII

This Convention shall supersede any convention in force or open for signature, ratification or accession at the date on which this Convention is opened for signature, but only to the extent that such conventions would be in conflict with it: however, nothing in this article shall affect the obligations of States Parties to States not party to this Convention arising under such conventions.

Chapter V: Transitional Provisions

Article 38 Preliminary Meetings

1. The Secretary-General shall convene a preliminary meeting of the States that have deposited instruments of ratification, acceptance, approval or accession under article 41 after the [...] State has deposited its instrument of ratification, acceptance, approval or accession. This meeting shall take place as soon as possible and, in any case, not more than 60 days after the [...] State has deposited its instrument of ratification, acceptance, approval or accession.

2. Further preliminary meetings shall be convened by the Secretary-General at the request of a simple majority of the States referred to in paragraph 1.

3. The preliminary meeting shall agree and the Secretary-General shall communicate to the States referred to in paragraph 1, States that have signed this Convention and Members of the Organization not later than [three] calendar months after the [...] State has deposited its instrument of ratification, acceptance, approval or accession:

(a) preliminary requirements regarding the appointment of issuing agents as required under article 13, subparagraph (h); and
(b) the *hazardous and noxious substances* being contributing cargo requiring a *hazardous and noxious substances* certificate under article 17 for the first six months after this Convention enters into force.

4. No later than [two] months before this Convention enters into force the preliminary meeting shall agree and the Secretary-General shall communicate to the States referred to in paragraph 1, States that have signed the Convention and Members of the Organization the cost [per

unit] of a *hazardous and noxious substances* certificate in respect of a contributing cargo or contributing voyage to be paid by issuing agents to the Scheme in respect of the first two quarters after this Convention has entered into force.

5. Any decision taken by a preliminary meeting in respect of the matters referred to in paragraphs 3 and 4 shall be on the basis of a simple majority of the States referred to in paragraph 1 present and voting at a preliminary meeting.

6. Two thirds of the States referred to in paragraph 1 shall constitute a quorum for a preliminary meeting.

7. Any decision taken at a preliminary meeting shall be subject to review by the Assembly save for the cost [per unit] of a *hazardous and noxious substances certificate* referred to in paragraph 4.

8. Any costs incurred by the Organization in respect of a preliminary meeting shall be reimbursed to the Organization by the Scheme within [eighteen] months of the date this Convention enters into force.

Article 39 Information on Contributing Cargo, Contributing Voyages and Issuing Agents

1. A State which has deposited an instrument of ratification, acceptance, approval or accession prior to the date on which the [...] State deposits its instrument of ratification, acceptance, approval or accession and the [...] State shall submit to the Secretary-General information on:

(a) the quantity of contributing cargo as defined by the preliminary meeting referred to in article 38, paragraph 3(b) carried by sea as cargo from a [port within] [the territory of] the State in the twelve months prior to the meeting referred to in article 38, paragraph 4;
(b) the number of ships on contributing voyages that arrived or departed from a port within the State in the twelve months prior to the meeting referred to in article 38, paragraph 4; and
(c) information on issuing agents licensed within the State in accordance with the preliminary requirements referred to in article 38, paragraph 3(a).

2. A State which deposits an instrument of ratification, acceptance, approval or accession after the date the [........] State deposited its instrument of ratification, acceptance, approval or accession shall submit to the Secretary-

General, or as the case may be, the Scheme, the information required in paragraph 1, or the equivalent information decided by the Assembly, for the twelve-month period prior to this Convention entering into force for that State.

3. When the Convention enters into force for a State subsequent:

(a) to the Convention itself entering into force; and
(b) to the first session of the Assembly referred to in article 40, the information requested in paragraph 2 shall be submitted to the Scheme.

Article 40 First Session of the Assembly

FUND 36 The Secretary-General shall convene the first session of the Assembly. This session shall take place as soon as possible after entry into force of this Convention and, in any case, not more than thirty days after such entry into force.

Chapter VI: Final Clauses

Article 41 Signature, ratification, Acceptance, Approval and Accession

SAL 28(1) 1. This Convention shall be open for signature at the Headquarters of the Organization from [........] to [........] and shall thereafter remain open for accession.

SAL 28(2) 2. States may express their consent to be bound by this Convention by:

(a) signature without reservation as to ratification, acceptance or approval; or
(b) signature subject to ratification, acceptance or approval, followed by ratification, acceptance or approval; or
(c) accession.

SAL 28(3) 3. Ratification, acceptance, approval or accession shall be effected by the deposit of an instrument to that effect with the Secretary-General.

Article 42 Entry into Force

SAL 29(1) 1. This Convention shall enter into force [eighteen months] after the date on which [...] States have expressed their consent to be bound by it.

SAL 29(2) 2. For a State which expresses its consent to be bound by this Convention after the conditions for entry into force have been met, such consent shall take effect [eighteen months] after the date of expression of such consent.

Article 43 Revision and Amendment

SAL 32(1) 1. A conference for the purpose of revising or amending this Convention may be convened by the Organization.

SAL 32(2) 2. The Secretary-General shall convene a conference of the States Parties to this Convention for revising or amending the Convention, at the request of [...] States Parties or [...] of the States Parties, whichever is the higher figure.

SAL 32(3) 3. Any consent to be bound by this Convention expressed after the date of entry into force of an amendment to this Convention shall be deemed to apply to the Convention as amended.

Article 44 Amendment of Limits

PAL VIII(1) 1. Upon the request of at least [...] [, but in no case less than...] of the States Parties to this Convention, any proposal to amend the limits specified in article 6, paragraph 1, and article 12, paragraph 5, shall be circulated by the Secretary-General to all Members of the Organization and to all Contracting States.

PAL VIII(2) 2....Any amendment proposed and circulated as above shall be submitted to the Legal Committee of the Organization (hereinafter referred to as "the Legal Committee") for consideration at a date at least six months after the date of its circulation.

PAL VIII(3) 3. All Contracting States to this Convention, whether or not Members of the Organization, shall be entitled to participate in the proceedings of the Legal Committee for the consideration and adoption of amendments.

PAL VIII(4) 4. Amendments shall be adopted by a two-thirds majority of the Contracting States to this Convention present and voting in the Legal Committee, expanded as provided in paragraph 3, on condition that at least one half of the Contracting States shall be present at the time of voting.

PAL VIII(5) 5. When acting on a proposal to amend the limits, the Legal Committee shall take into account the experience of incidents and, in particular the amount of damage resulting therefrom, changes in the monetary values and the effect of the proposed amendment on the cost of insurance. It shall also take into account the relationship between the limits established in article 6, paragraph 1, and those in article 12, paragraph 5.

PAL VIII(6) 6.(a) No amendment of the limits under this article may be considered less than five years from the date this Convention was opened for signature nor less than five years from the date of entry into force of a previous amendment under this article.

(b) No limit may be increased so as to exceed an amount which corresponds to a limit laid down in this Convention increased by [...] per cent per year calculated on a compound basis from the date on which this Convention was opened for signature.

(c) No limit may be increased so as to exceed an amount which corresponds to a limit laid down in this Convention multiplied by [...].

PAL VIII(7) 7. Any amendment adopted in accordance with paragraph 4 shall be notified by the Organization to all Contracting States. The amendment shall be deemed to have been accepted at the end of a period of [...] months after the date of notification, unless within that period no less than one-fourth of the States that were Contracting States at the time of the adoption of the amendment have communicated to the Secretary-General that they do not accept the amendment, in which case the amendment is rejected and shall have no effect.

PAL VIII(8) 8. An amendment deemed to have been accepted in accordance with paragraph 7 shall enter into force [...] months after its acceptance.

PAL VIII(9) 9. All Contracting States shall be bound by the amendment, unless they denounce this Convention in accordance with paragraphs 1 and 2 of article 45 at least six months before the amendment enters into force. Such denunciation shall take effect when the amendment enters into force.

PAL VIII(10) 10. When an amendment has been adopted but the [...] month period for its acceptance has not yet expired, a State which becomes a Contracting State during that period shall be bound by the amendment if it enters into force. A State which becomes a Contracting State after that period shall be bound by an amendment which has been accepted in accordance with paragraph 7. In the cases referred to in this paragraph, a State becomes bound by an amendment when that amendment enters into force, or when this Convention enters into force for that State, if later.

Article 45 Denunciation

PAL VI(1) 1. This Convention may be denounced by any State Party at any time after the date on which it enters into force for that State Party.

PAL VI(2) 2. Denunciation shall be effected by the deposit of an instrument of denunciation with the Secretary-General.

PAL VI(3) 3. Denunciation shall take effect twelve months, or such longer period as may be specified in the instrument of denunciation, after its deposit with the Secretary-General.

Article 46 Extraordinary Sessions of the Assembly

FUND P 35(1) 1. Any State Party may, within ninety days after the deposit of an instrument of denunciation the result of which it considers will significantly increase the level of contributions from the remaining States Parties, request the Director to convene an extraordinary session of the Assembly. The Director shall convene the Assembly to meet not less than sixty days after receipt of the request.

FUND P 35(2) 2. The Director may convene, on his initiative, an extraordinary session of the Assembly to meet within sixty days after the deposit of any instrument of denunciation, if he considers that such denunciation will result in a significant increase in the level of contributions of the remaining States Parties.

FUND P 35(3) 3. If the Assembly, at an extraordinary session, convened in accordance with paragraph 1 or 2 decides that the denunciation will result in a significant increase in the level of contributions for the remaining States Parties, any such State may, not later than one hundred and twenty days before the date on which the denunciation takes effect, denounce this Convention with effect from the same date.

Article 47 Cessation

FUND P 36(1) 1. This Convention shall cease to be in force on the date when the number of States Parties falls below [...].

FUND P 36(2) 2. States which are bound by this Convention on the day before the date it ceases to be in force shall enable the Scheme to exercise its functions as described under article 48 and shall, for that purpose only, remain bound by this Convention.

Article 48 Winding up of the Scheme

FUND P 37(1) 1. If this Convention ceases to be in force, the Scheme shall nevertheless:

(a) meet its obligations in respect of any incident occurring before the Convention ceased to be in force; and
(b) be entitled to exercise its rights to contributions to the extent that these contributions are necessary to meet the obligations under subparagraph (a), including expenses for the administration of the Scheme necessary for this purpose.

FUND P 37(2) 2. The Assembly shall take all appropriate measures to complete the winding up of the Scheme including the distribution in an equitable manner of any remaining assets among those persons who have contributed to the Scheme.

FUND P 37(3) 3. For the purposes of this article the Scheme shall remain a legal person.

Article 49 Depositary

PAL IX(1) 1. This Convention and any amendment adopted under article 44 shall be deposited with the Secretary-General.

PAL IX(2) 2. The Secretary-General shall:

(a) inform all States which have signed this Convention or acceded thereto, and all Members of the Organization, of:

OPRC 18(2)(a)(i) (i) each new signature or deposit of an instrument of ratification, acceptance, approval or accession together with the date thereof;
PAL IX(2)(iii) (ii) the date of entry into force of this Convention;
PAL IX(2)(iv) (vii) any proposal to amend limits of amounts of compensation which have been made in accordance with article 44, paragraph 1;
PAL IX(2)(v) (iv) any amendment which has been adopted in accordance with article 44, paragraph 4;
PAL IX(2)(vi) (v) any amendment deemed to have been accepted under article 44, paragraph 7, together with the date on which that amendment shall enter into force in accordance with paragraphs 8 and 9 of that article;
OPRC 18(2)(a)(iii) (vi) the deposit of any instrument of denunciation of this Convention together with the date on which it is received and the date on which the denunciation takes effect; and

FUND P 38(2)(b) (vii) any communication called for by any article in this Convention; and

OPRC 18(2)(b) (b) transmit certified true copies of this Convention to all States which have signed this Convention or acceded thereto.

OPRC 18(3) 3. As soon as this Convention enters into force, a certified true copy thereof shall be transmitted by the depositary to the Secretary-General of the United Nations for registration and publication in accordance with article 102 of the Charter of the United Nations.

Article 50 Languages

PAL X This Convention is established in a single original in the Arabic, Chinese, English, French, Russian and Spanish languages, each text being equally authentic.

DONE AT [LONDON] this [......................................].

IN WITNESS WHEREOF the undersigned, being duly authorized by their respective Governments for that purpose, have signed this Convention.

Appendix II

Major International Shipping Conventions and Recommendations

Dealing with the Ship

SOLAS 74 (International Convention for the Safety of Life at Sea, 1974) as amended, lays down a comprehensive range of minimum standards for the safe construction of ships and for the basic safety equipment (e.g. fire prevention, navigational, life-saving and radio) to be carried on board. SOLAS also contains operational instructions, particularly on emergency procedures, and provides for regular surveys and for the issue of certificates of compliance.

The International Bulk Chemical (IBC) and International Gas Carrier (IGC) Codes are mandatory requirements under SOLAS 74.

MARPOL 73/78 (International Convention for the Prevention of Pollution from Ships, 1973, as modified by the Protocol of 1978 relating thereto) as amended, contains measures designed to prevent pollution caused both accidentally and in the course of routine operations. Five annexes in the Convention cover, respectively, pollution by oil, noxious liquid substances in bulk, harmful substances carried in packaged forms, sewage and garbage. The International Bulk Chemical (IBC) and the Bulk Chemical (BCH) Codes are mandatory under MARPOL 73/78.

COLREG (Convention on the International Regulations for Preventing Collisions at Sea, 1972), as amended, lays down the basic "rules of the road", such as rights of way, safe speed, action to avoid collision, procedures to observe in narrow channels and in restricted visibility.

International Convention on Load Lines, 1966 sets the minimum permissible freeboard, according to the season of the year and the trading area of the ship; special ship construction standards are laid down in regard to watertightness.

Dealing with the Shipowner

IMO resolution A.441(XI). IMO invited every State to take the necessary steps to ensure that the owner of a ship which flies the flag of that State provides such State with the current information necessary to enable it to identify and contact the person contracted or otherwise entrusted by the owner to discharge his responsibilities for that ship in regard to matters relating to maritime safety and the protection of the marine environment.

Dealing with the Seafarer and the Ship

ILO Convention 147 (Merchant Shipping (Minimum Standards) Convention 1976) requires Administrations to have effective legislation on safe manning standards, hours of work, seafarers' competency, and social security. It also sets employment standards equivalent to those contained in a range of ILO instruments (covering e.g., minimum age, medical care and examination, social security, training).

Dealing with the Seafarer

STCW (International Convention on Standards of Training, Certification and Watchkeeping for Seafarers, 1978) lays down training, certification and qualification requirements (including syllabuses and sea time) for senior officers; all officers in charge of watches in the deck, engine and radio departments; and ratings forming part of a watch. All such seafarers are required to have a certificate, endorsed in a uniform manner. It also specifies basic principles to be observed in keeping deck and engine watches and special qualification requirements for personnel on oil, chemical and liquefied gas tankers.

IMO resolution A.481 (XII) (on principles of safe manning) recommended that all Administrations provide each of their registered ships with a document specifying the minimum number and grades of qualified seafaring personnel required to be carried from the safety standpoint. It gives basic principles and detailed guidance to be observed by Administrations when assessing the safe manning of ships.

IMO resolution A.443(XI). IMO invited Governments to take the necessary steps to safeguard the shipmaster in the proper discharge of his responsibilities in regard to maritime safety and the protection of the marine environment by ensuring that:

(a) the shipmaster is not constrained by the shipowner, charterer or any other person from taking in this respect any decision which, in the professional judgement of the shipmaster, is necessary;

(b) the shipmaster is protected by the appropriate provisions, including the right of appeal, contained in, *inter alia*, national legislation, collective agreements or contracts of employment, from unjustifiable dismissal or other unjustifiable action by the shipowner, charterer or any other person as a consequence of the proper exercise of his professional judgement.

Appendix III

International Maritime Organization Conference on International Co-operation on Oil Pollution Preparedness and Response

International Convention on Oil Pollution Preparedness, Response and Co-operation, 1990

Text Adopted by the Conference

THE PARTIES TO THE PRESENT CONVENTION,

CONSCIOUS of the need to preserve the human environment in general and the marine environment in particular,

RECOGNIZING the serious threat posed to the marine environment by oil pollution incidents involving ships, offshore units, sea ports and oil handling facilities,

MINDFUL of the importance of precautionary measures and prevention in avoiding oil pollution in the first instance, and the need for strict application of existing international instruments dealing with maritime safety and marine pollution prevention, particularly the International Convention for the Safety of Life at Sea, 1974, as amended, and the International Convention for the Prevention of Pollution from Ships, 1973, as modified by the Protocol of 1978 relating thereto, as amended, and also the speedy development of enhanced standards for the design, operation and maintenance of ships carrying oil, and of offshore units,

MINDFUL ALSO that, in the event of an oil pollution incident, prompt and effective action is essential in order to minimize the damage which may result from such an incident,

EMPHASIZING the importance of effective preparation for combating oil pollution incidents and the important role which the oil and shipping industries have in this regard,

RECOGNIZING FURTHER the importance of mutual assistance and international co-operation relating to matters including the exchange of information respecting the capabilities of States to respond to oil pollution incidents, the preparation of oil pollution contingency plans, the exchange of reports of incidents of significance which may affect the marine environment or the coastline and related interests of States, and research and development respecting means of combating oil pollution in the marine environment,

TAKING ACCOUNT of the "polluter pays" principle as a general principle of international environmental law,

TAKING ACCOUNT ALSO of the importance of international instruments on liability and compensation for oil pollution damage, including the 1969 International Convention on Civil Liability for Oil Pollution Damage (CLC); and the 1971 International Convention on the Establishment of an International Fund for Compensation for Oil Pollution Damage (FUND); and the compelling need for early entry into force of the 1984 Protocols to the CLC and FUND Conventions,

TAKING ACCOUNT FURTHER of the importance of bilateral and multilateral agreements and arrangements including regional conventions and agreements,

BEARING IN MIND the relevant provisions of the United Nations Convention on the Law of the Sea, in particular of its part XII,

BEING AWARE of the need to promote international co-operation and to enhance existing national, regional and global capabilities concerning oil pollution preparedness and response, taking into account the special needs of the developing countries and particularly small island States,

CONSIDERING that these objectives may best be achieved by the conclusion of an International Convention on Oil Pollution Preparedness, Response and Co-operation,

HAVE AGREED as follows:

Article 1 General Provisions

(1) Parties undertake, individually or jointly, to take all appropriate measures in accordance with the provisions of this Convention and the Annex thereto to prepare for and respond to an oil pollution incident.

(2) The Annex to this Convention shall constitute an integral part of the Convention and a reference to this Convention constitutes at the same time a reference to the Annex.

(3) This Convention shall not apply to any warship, naval auxiliary or other ship owned or operated by a State and used, for the time being, only on government non-commercial service. However, each Party shall ensure by the adoption of appropriate measures not impairing the operations or operational capabilities of such ships owned or operated by it, that such ships act in a manner consistent, so far as is reasonable and practicable, with this Convention.

Article 2 Definitions

For the purposes of this Convention:

(1) "Oil" means petroleum in any form including crude oil, fuel oil, sludge, oil refuse and refined products.

(2) "Oil pollution incident" means an occurrence or series of occurrences having the same origin, which results or may result in a discharge of oil and which poses or may pose a threat to the marine environment, or to the coastline or related interests of one or more States, and which requires emergency action or other immediate response.

(3) "Ship" means a vessel of any type whatsoever operating in the marine environment and includes hydrofoil boats, air-cushion vehicles, submersibles, and floating craft of any type.

(4) "Offshore unit" means any fixed or floating offshore installation or structure engaged in gas or oil exploration, exploitation or production activities, or loading or unloading of oil.

(5) "Sea ports and oil handling facilities" means those facilities which present a risk of an oil pollution incident and includes, *inter alia*, sea ports, oil terminals, pipelines and other oil handling facilities.

(6) "Organization" means the International Maritime Organization.

(7) "Secretary-General" means the Secretary-General of the Organization.

Article 3 Oil Pollution Emergency Plans

(1) (a) Each Party shall require that ships entitled to fly its flag have on board a shipboard oil pollution emergency plan as required by and in accordance with the provisions adopted by the Organization for this purpose.

(b) A ship required to have on board an oil pollution emergency plan in accordance with subparagraph (a) is subject, while in a port or at an offshore terminal under the jurisdiction of a Party, to inspection by officers duly authorized by that Party, in accordance with the practices provided for in existing international agreements or its national legislation.

(2) Each party shall require that operators of offshore units under its jurisdiction have oil pollution emergency plans, which are co-ordinated with the national system established in accordance with article 6 and approved in accordance with procedures established by the competent national authority.

(3) Each Party shall require that authorities or operators in charge of such sea ports and oil handling facilities under its jurisdiction as it deems appropriate have oil pollution emergency plans or similar arrangements which are co-

ordinated with the national system established in accordance with article 6 and approved in accordance with procedures established by the competent national authority.

Article 4 Oil Pollution Reporting Procedures

(1) Each party shall:

(a) require masters or other persons having charge of ships flying its flag and persons having charge of offshore units under its jurisdiction to report without delay any event on their ship or offshore unit involving a discharge or probable discharge of oil:

(i) in the case of a ship, to the nearest coastal State;

(ii) in the case of an offshore unit, to the coastal State to whose jurisdiction the unit is subject;

(b) require masters or other persons having charge of ships flying its flag and persons having charge of offshore units under its jurisdiction to report without delay any observed event at sea involving a discharge of oil or the presence of oil:

(i) in the case of a ship, to the nearest coastal State;

(ii) in the case of an offshore unit, to the coastal State to whose jurisdiction the unit is subject;

(c) require persons having charge of sea ports and oil handling facilities under its jurisdiction to report without delay any event involving a discharge or probable discharge of oil or the presence of oil to the competent national authority;

(d) instruct its maritime inspection vessels or aircraft and other appropriate services or officials to report without delay any observed event at sea or at a sea port or oil handling facility involving a discharge of oil or the presence of oil to the competent national authority or, as the case may be, to the nearest coastal State;

(e) request the pilots of civil aircraft to report without delay any observed event at sea involving a discharge of oil or the presence of oil to the nearest coastal State.

(2) Reports under paragraph (1)(a)(i) shall be made in accordance with the requirements developed by the Organization and based on the guidelines and general principles adopted by the Organization. Reports under paragraph (1)(a)(ii), (b), (c) and (d) shall be made in accordance with the guidelines and general principles adopted by the Organization to the extent applicable.

Article 5 Action on Receiving an Oil Pollution Report

(1) Whenever a Party receives a report referred to in article 4 or pollution information provided by other sources, it shall:

(a) assess the event to determine whether it is an oil pollution incident;
(b) assess the nature, extent and possible consequences of the oil pollution incident; and
(c) then, without delay, inform all States whose interests are affected or likely to be affected by such oil pollution incident, together with

(i) details of its assessments and any action it has taken, or intends to take, to deal with the incident, and
(ii) further information as appropriate,

until the action taken to respond to the incident has been concluded or until joint action has been decided by such States.

(2) When the severity of such oil pollution incident so justifies, the Party shall provide the Organization directly or, as appropriate, through the relevant regional organization or arrangements with the information referred to in paragraph (1)(b) and (c).

(3) When the severity of such oil pollution incident so justifies, other States affected by it are urged to inform the Organization directly or, as appropriate, through the relevant regional organizations or arrangements of their assessment of the extent of the threat to their interests and any action taken or intended.

(4) Parties should use, in so far as practicable, the oil pollution reporting system developed by the Organization when exchanging information and communicating with other States and with the Organization.

Article 6 National and Regional Systems for Preparedness and Response
(1) Each Party shall establish a national system for responding promptly and effectively to oil pollution incidents. This system shall include as a minimum:

(a) the designation of:

(i) the competent national authority or authorities with responsibility for oil pollution preparedness and response;
(ii) the national operational contact point or points, which shall be responsible for the receipt and transmission of oil pollution reports as referred to in article 4; and
(iii) an authority which is entitled to act on behalf of the State to request assistance or to decide to render the assistance requested;

(b) a national contingency plan for preparedness and response which includes the organizational relationship of the various bodies involved, whether public or private, taking into account guidelines developed by the Organization.

(2) In addition, each Party, within its capabilities either individually or through bilateral or multilateral co-operation and, as appropriate, in co-operation with

the oil and shipping industries, port authorities and other relevant entities, shall establish:

(a) a minimum level of pre-positioned oil spill combating equipment, commensurate with the risk involved, and programmes for its use;
(b) a programme of exercises for oil pollution response organizations and training of relevant personnel;
(c) detailed plans and communication capabilities for responding to an oil pollution incident. Such capabilities should be continuously available; and
(d) a mechanism or arrangement to co-ordinate the response to an oil pollution incident with, if appropriate, the capabilities to mobilize the necessary resources.

(3) Each Party shall ensure that current information is provided to the Organization, directly or through the relevant regional organization or arrangements, concerning:

(a) the location, telecommunication data and, if applicable, areas of responsibility of authorities and entities referred to in paragraph (1)(a);
(b) information concerning pollution response equipment and expertise in disciplines related to oil pollution response and marine salvage which may be made available to other States, upon request; and
(c) its national contingency plan.

Article 7 International Co-operation in Pollution Response

(1) Parties agree that, subject to their capabilities and the availability of relevant resources, they will co-operate and provide advisory services, technical support and equipment for the purpose of responding to an oil pollution incident, when the severity of such incident so justifies, upon the request of any Party affected or likely to be affected. The financing of the costs for such assistance shall be based on the provisions set out in the Annex to this Convention.

(2) A Party which has requested assistance may ask the Organization to assist in identifying sources of provisional financing of the costs referred to in paragraph (1).

(3) In accordance with applicable international agreements, each Party shall take necessary legal or administrative measures to facilitate:

(a) the arrival and utilization in and departure from its territory of ships, aircraft and other modes of transport engaged in responding to an oil pollution incident or transporting personnel, cargoes, materials and equipment required to deal with such an incident; and
(b) the expeditious movement into, through, and out of its territory of personnel, cargoes, materials and equipment referred to in subparagraph (a).

Article 8 Research and Development

(1) Parties agree to co-operate directly or, as appropriate, through the Organization or relevant regional organizations or arrangements in the promo-

tion and exchange of results of research and development programmes relating to the enhancement of the state-of-the-art of oil pollution preparedness and response, including technologies and techniques for surveillance, containment, recovery, dispersion, clean-up and otherwise minimizing or mitigating the effects of oil pollution, and for restoration.

(2) To this end, Parties undertake to establish directly or, as appropriate, through the Organization or relevant regional organizations or arrangements, the necessary links between Parties' research institutions.

(3) Parties agree to co-operate directly or through the Organization or relevant regional organizations or arrangements to promote, as appropriate, the holding on a regular basis of international symposia on relevant subjects, including technological advances in oil pollution combating techniques and equipment.

(4) Parties agree to encourage, through the Organization or other competent international organizations, the development of standards for compatible oil pollution combating techniques and equipment.

Article 9 Technical Co-operation

(1) Parties undertake directly or through the Organization and other international bodies, as appropriate, in respect of oil pollution preparedness and response, to provide support for those Parties which request technical assistance:

- (a) to train personnel;
- (b) to ensure the availability of relevant technology, equipment and facilities;
- (c) to facilitate other measures and arrangements to prepare for and respond to oil pollution incidents; and
- (d) to initiate joint research and development programmes.

(2) Parties undertake to co-operate actively, subject to their national laws, regulations and policies, in the transfer of technology in respect of oil pollution preparedness and response.

Article 10 Promotion of Bilateral and Multilateral Co-operation in Preparedness and Response

Parties shall endeavour to conclude bilateral or multilateral agreements for oil pollution preparedness and response. Copies of such agreements shall be communicated to the Organization which should make them available on request to Parties.

Article 11 Relation to other conventions and international agreements

Nothing in this Convention shall be construed as altering the rights or obligations of any Party under any other convention or international agreement.

Article 12 Institutional Arrangements

(1) Parties designate the Organization, subject to its agreement and the availability of adequate resources to sustain the activity, to perform the following functions and activities:

(a) information services:

- (i) to receive, collate and disseminate on request the information provided by Parties (see, for example, articles 5(2) and (3), 6(3) and 10) and relevant information provided by other sources; and
- (ii) to provide assistance in identifying sources of provisional financing of costs (see, for example, article 7(2);

(b) education and training:

- (i) to promote training in the field of oil pollution preparedness and response (see, for example, article 9); and
- (ii) to promote the holding of international symposia (see, for example, article 8(3));

(c) technical services:

- (i) to facilitate co-operation in research and development (see, for example, articles 8(1), (2) and (4) and 9(1)(d));
- (ii) to provide advice to States establishing national or regional response capabilities; and
- (iii) to analyse the information provided by Parties (see, for example, articles 5(2) and (3), 6(3) and 8(1)) and relevant information provided by other sources and provide advice or information to States;

(d)technical assistance:

- (i) to facilitate the provision of technical assistance to States establishing national or regional response capabilities; and
- (ii) to facilitate the provision of technical assistance and advice, upon the request of States faced with major oil pollution incidents.

(2) In carrying out the activities specified in this article, the Organization shall endeavour to strengthen the ability of States individually or through regional arrangements to prepare for and combat oil pollution incidents, drawing upon the experience of States, regional agreements and industry arrangements and paying particular attention to the needs of developing countries.

(3) The provisions of this article shall be implemented in accordance with a programme developed and kept under review by the Organization.

Article 13 Evaluation of the Convention

Parties shall evaluate within the Organization the effectiveness of the Convention in the light of its objectives, particularly with respect to the principles underlying co-operation and assistance.

Article 14 Amendments

(1) This Convention may be amended by one of the procedures specified in the following paragraphs.

(2) Amendment after consideration by the Organization:

(a) Any amendment proposed by a Party to the Convention shall be submitted to the Organization and circulated by the Secretary-General to all Members of the Organization and all Parties at least six months prior to its consideration.
(b) Any amendment proposed and circulated as above shall be submitted to the Marine Environment Protection Committee of the Organization for consideration.
(c) Parties to the Convention, whether or not Members of the Organization, shall be entitled to participate in the proceedings of the Marine Environment Protection Committee.
(d) Amendments shall be adopted by a two-thirds majority of only the Parties to the Convention present and voting.
(e) If adopted in accordance with subparagraph (d), amendments shall be communicated by the Secretary-General to all Parties to the Convention for acceptance.
(f) (i) An amendment to an article or the Annex of the Convention shall be deemed to have been accepted on the date on which it is accepted by two thirds of the Parties.
(ii) An amendment to an appendix shall be deemed to have been accepted at the end of a period to be determined by the Marine Environment Protection Committee at the time of its adoption, which period shall not be less than ten months, unless within that period an objection is communicated to the Secretary-General by not less than one third of the Parties.
(g) (i) An amendment to an article or the Annex of the Convention accepted in conformity with subparagraph (f)(i) shall enter into force six months after the date on which it is deemed to have been accepted with respect to the Parties which have notified the Secretary-General that they have accepted it.
(ii) An amendment to an appendix accepted in conformity with subparagraph (f)(ii) shall enter into force six months after the date on which it is deemed to have been accepted with respect to all Parties with the exception of those which, before that date, have objected to it. A Party may at any time withdraw a previously communicated objection by submitting a notification to that effect to the Secretary-General.

(3) Amendment by a Conference:

(a) Upon the request of a Party, concurred with by at least one third of the Parties, the Secretary-General shall convene a Conference of Parties to the Convention to consider amendments to the Convention.
(b) An amendment adopted by such a Conference by a two-thirds majority of those Parties present and voting shall be communicated by the Secretary-General to all Parties for their acceptance.

(c) Unless the Conference decides otherwise, the amendment shall be deemed to have been accepted and shall enter into force in accordance with the procedures specified in paragraph (2)(f) and (g).

(4) The adoption and entry into force of an amendment constituting an addition of an Annex or an appendix shall be subject to the procedure applicable to an amendment to the Annex.

(5) Any Party which has not accepted an amendment to an article or the Annex under paragraph (2)(f)(i) or an amendment constituting an addition of an Annex or an appendix under paragraph (4) or has communicated an objection to an amendment to an appendix under paragraph (2)(f)(ii) shall be treated as a non-Party only for the purpose of the application of such amendment. Such treatment shall terminate upon the submission of a notification of acceptance under paragraph (2)(f)(i) or withdrawal of the objection under paragraph (2)(g)(ii).

(6) The Secretary-General shall inform all Parties of any amendment which enters into force under this article, together with the date on which the amendment enters into force.

(7) Any notification of acceptance of, objection to, or withdrawal of objection to, an amendment under this article shall be communicated in writing to the Secretary-General who shall inform Parties of such notification and the date of its receipt.

(8) An appendix to the Convention shall contain only provisions of a technical nature.

Article 15 Signature, Ratification, Acceptance, Approval and Accession

(1) This Convention shall remain open for signature at the Headquarters of the Organization from 30 November 1990 until 29 November 1991 and shall thereafter remain open for accession. Any State may become Party to this Convention by:

(a) signature without reservation as to ratification, acceptance or approval; or
(b) signature subject to ratification, acceptance or approval, followed by ratification, acceptance or approval; or
(c) accession.

(2) Ratification, acceptance, approval or accession shall be effected by the deposit of an instrument to that effect with the Secretary-General.

Article 16 Entry into Force

(1) This Convention shall enter into force twelve months after the date on which not less than fifteen States have either signed it without reservation as to ratifi-

cation, acceptance or approval or have deposited the requisite instruments of ratification, acceptance, approval or accession in accordance with article 15.

(2) For States which have deposited an instrument of ratification, acceptance, approval or accession in respect of this Convention after the requirements for entry into force thereof have been met but prior to the date of entry into force, the ratification, acceptance, approval or accession shall take effect on the date of entry into force of this Convention or three months after the date of deposit of the instrument, whichever is the later date.

(3) For States which have deposited an instrument of ratification, acceptance, approval or accession after the date on which this Convention entered into force, this Convention shall become effective three months after the date of deposit of the instrument.

(4) After the date on which an amendment to this Convention is deemed to have been accepted under article 14, any instrument of ratification, acceptance, approval or accession deposited shall apply to this Convention as amended.

Article 17 Denunciation

(1) This Convention may be denounced by any Party at any time after the expiry of five years from the date on which this Convention enters into force for that Party.

(2) Denunciation shall be effected by notification in writing to the Secretary-General.

(3) A denunciation shall take effect twelve months after receipt of the notification of denunciation by the Secretary-General or after the expiry of any longer period which may be indicated in the notification.

Article 18 Depositary

(1) This Convention shall be deposited with the Secretary-General.

(2) The Secretary-General shall:

- (a) inform all States which have signed this Convention or acceded thereto of:
  - (i) each new signature or deposit of an instrument of ratification, acceptance, approval or accession, together with the date thereof;
  - (ii) the date of entry into force of this Convention; and
  - (iii) the deposit of any instrument of denunciation of this Convention together with the date on which it was received and the date on which the denunciation takes effect;
- (b) transmit certified true copies of this Convention to the Governments of all States which have signed this Convention or acceded thereto.

(3) As soon as this Convention enters into force, a certified true copy thereof shall be transmitted by the depositary to the Secretary-General of the United Nations for registration and publication in accordance with Article 102 of the Charter of the United Nations.

Article 19 Languages

This Convention is established in a single original in the Arabic, Chinese, English, French, Russian and Spanish languages, each text being equally authentic.

IN WITNESS WHEREOF the undersigned, being duly authorized by their respective Governments for that purpose, have signed this Convention.

DONE AT London this thirtieth day of November one thousand nine hundred and ninety.

Annex: Reimbursement of Costs of Assistance

(1) (a) Unless an agreement concerning the financial arrangements governing actions of Parties to deal with oil pollution incidents has been concluded on a bilateral or multilateral basis prior to the oil pollution incident, Parties shall bear the costs of their respective actions in dealing with pollution in accordance with subparagraph (i) or subparagraph (ii).

(i) If the action was taken by one Party at the express request of another Party, the requesting Party shall reimburse to the assisting Party the cost of its action. The requesting Party may cancel its request at any time, but in that case it shall bear the costs already incurred or committed by the assisting Party.

(ii) If the action was taken by a Party on its own initiative, this Party shall bear the costs of its action.

(b) The Principles laid down in subparagraph (a) shall apply unless the Parties concerned otherwise agree in any individual case.

(2) Unless otherwise agreed, the costs of action taken by a Party at the request of another Party shall be fairly calculated according to the law and current practice of the assisting Party concerning the reimbursement of such costs.

(3) The Party requesting assistance and the assisting Party shall, where appropriate, co-operate in concluding any action in response to a compensation claim. To that end, they shall give due consideration to existing legal regimes. Where the action thus concluded does not permit full compensation for expenses incurred in the assistance operation, the Party requesting assistance may ask the assisting Party to waive reimbursement of the expenses exceeding the sums compensated or to reduce the costs which have been calculated in accordance with paragraph (2). It may also request a postponement of the reimbursement of

such costs. In considering such a request, assisting Parties shall give due consideration to the needs of the developing countries.

(4) The provisions of this Convention shall not be interpreted as in any way prejudicing the rights of Parties to recover from third parties the costs of actions to deal with pollution or the threat of pollution under other applicable provisions and rules of national and international law. Special attention shall be paid to the 1969 International Convention on Civil Liability for Oil Pollution Damage and the 1971 International Convention on the Establishment of an International Fund for Compensation for Oil Pollution Damage or any subsequent amendment to those Conventions.

The Green Card System and the E.C.E. Convention on Civil Liability for Damage Caused During Carriage of Dangerous Goods by Road, Rail and Inland Navigation Vessels (C.R.T.D.)

Peter F. Morgan

The International Motor Insurance Card System — commonly known as the "Green Card System" — is based upon a Recommendation which was issued in 1949 by the Economic Commission for Europe to the member governments and it came into operation with effect from the 1 January 1953. The Green Card System, proposed by European insurers, was designed as a system which could adapt to changes at the levels of national and international laws whilst at the same fulfilling fundamental requirements, namely that:

(i) it should facilitate the movement of traffic without impediment across international frontiers; and most importantly,

(ii) it should provide a guarantee for the protection of Third Party victims in the visited country within the ambit of the "local" compulsory Third Party insurance legislation.

The Green Card System has, to date, been in operation for 39 years and, away from internal problems, it has at the general level operated very successfully, for which credit has to be given to the insurance markets of the 31 member countries, and essentially this has been due to the performance of the Green Card Bureaux established in these various countries, which now include five countries outside of Europe.

According to its objectives the Green Card System has adapted over these 39 years to the various international and national developments. Indeed, at certain national levels, the Green Card as a document has become superfluous, because of the relationships between the Nordic countries and because of bilateral relationships established by Germany with certain Eastern and Middle European countries, together with Austria and Switzerland, and arrangements which have emerged between the Benelux countries. In 1959 the Council of Bureaux decided upon a model form of Agreement whereby obligations were no longer dependent upon the presence of a "Green Card" but were judged to be on the basis of the nationality of the registration plate of the vehicles concerned. It was this arrangement in particular which attracted the Commission of the European Communities to adopt the Green Card System as a basis for its 1972 Directive on Motor Insurance.

Having described above, albeit in a superficial way, the origin and nature of the Green Card System I now turn to the E.C.E. Convention of 1989 concerning civil liabilities arising from the transportation of dangerous goods.

There can be no doubt that the studies on this subject, which were initially conducted within UNIDROIT, were of importance and consistent with the perpetual trend to improve and extend the protection of victims. Evidently discussions on this subject were difficult and complex, more especially as the objective was for a Convention which covered the transportation of dangerous goods by three modes of transport — road, rail and inland navigation vessels. Eventually, nevertheless, a draft of the Convention emerged and tribute for this has to be paid to those concerned with its drafting and in no small measure due to Mr. Cleton of the Dutch Ministry of Justice.

There was at the initial stage some disappointment in the Council of Bureaux with the draft, so far as road transport was concerned, since it provided no recognition of the Green Card System in relation to the cross-frontier movement of motor vehicles. Also at the general insurance level there was concern amongst insurers at the application of the prospective Convention to environmental damage which was considered to be somewhat remote from the basic traditionally available cover under motor insurance policies.

In the early discussions within the E.C.E., following the preparation of the draft of the Convention, the Council of Bureaux endeavoured to persuade governments to accept the Green Card System into the Convention, **for the purposes of Road Transport**, in two particular respects:

(a) a recognition of the Green Card (or as appropriate of the nationality of the registration plate) instead of the alternative form of insurance certificate which was prescribed;

(b) adoption of the inter-Bureaux System for the handling and settlement of Third Party claims whereby the victim in the country of accident had a central and legally constituted entity to which the claim could be addressed. Such entities it was stressed were the subject of specific provisions in the compulsory insurance laws of the majority of the participating countries and had, in all of those countries, the recognition of the respective Governments on the basis foreseen in the Geneva Recommendation of 1949 (later succeeded by Annex 2 of the E.C.E. Consolidated Resolution on the Facilitation of Road Transport).

The fundamental concern of the Council of Bureaux was that the Convention should not create obstacles for the operation of the Green Card System. Furthermore there was a very genuine belief that the different regimes of insurance documentation, liability rules and claims handling and settlement practices, could well give rise to confusion and conflict, more especially as regards incidents whereby certain of the Third Party injuries or damage were the consequence of a conventional road traffic accident, and other injuries or damage, from the same event, which were directly related to the dangerous goods being transported at the time by the motor vehicle concerned. It therefore appeared logical, practical and sensible, that all Third Party liabilities arising from the particular event which were required to be covered within the relevant compulsory insurance laws, or under these laws in conjunction with the Convention, should be dealt with under one common insurance system. In this connection it was strongly felt by the Council of Bureaux and by insurers that the Green Card System would be the most appropriate arrangement in as much as it had been tried and tested over so many years.
The endeavours by the Council did in the event meet with success as the Governments decided to retain the Green Card System and agreed to bring into the Convention the following references:

(a) A definition of the Green Card System in **Article 1.13**.
(b) **Article 14.9** of the Convention which stipulates that the provisions of Article 14 shall not apply:

> "in the case of carriage by a road vehicle in the territory of a State party to the Green Card System if there is in force in respect of a vehicle and produced for inspection on demand by the competent authorities a Green Card certifying coverage of carrier's liability under this Convention".

Also there is **Article 14.10** which allows that:

> "Two or more States Parties may agree to dispense with the requirements of this Article for the certificate or Green Card referred to in paragraph 9 of this Article in respect of road vehicles registered in their territories for the carriage, within their territories, of goods by road covered by this Convention".

(c) There is, finally, **Article 15.1** of the Convention which declares that:

> "Any claim for compensation under Articles 5 or 6 may be brought directly against the Insurer or other person providing financial security for the carrier's liability or, in the case of a road vehicle to which the green card System applies, against the Insurer or the Green Card Bureau of the State where the incident occurred".

The Members of the Council of Bureaux were relieved at the above references in the Convention and indeed were grateful to the governments for the demonstration of their support for the Green Card System. Only one possible difficulty was foreseen, possibly more theoretical than real, this being the inference which could be drawn from Article 14.9 that the Green Card, as an evidentiary document, should certify insurance coverage of the carrier's liability under the Convention. The point here is that the format of the Green Card, which is a uniform document, is under control of the Principal Working Party on Road Transport of the Inland Transport Committee of the E.C.E. in Geneva. Under that control, the format of the Green Card cannot specify the scope of the insurance coverage in question. In regard to Third Party (or civil liabilities), it is historically and fundamentally related to the requirements of the Compulsory Third Party insurance laws in the countries of accident or to other forms of legislation (such as that prescribed in the Convention) which either amend or supplement the compulsory Third Party insurance laws. This represents an academic, or theoretical point, but it is one to which the Council of Bureaux has to adhere. This apart, there is now a compatibility between the Convention and the Green Card System and in this respect the Council of Bureaux is very content.

The Council of Bureaux is not competent to express views on the underwriting aspects of motor insurance cover although it has obviously an understanding of the concerns which were expressed by insurers regarding the prospective application of the Convention to environmental damage with particular regard to the fact that such damage was not a regular part of normal motor insurance coverage, for which other classes of insurance could be involved. Above all it was considered that governments should have regard to the fact that insurers could only provide cover insofar as it was within their financial and technical means — with due regard to the reinsurance capacity for which reinsurers had their own financial and technical limits. Such views were advanced by the C.E.A. (European Insurance Committee — Comité Européen des Assurances), which the Council of Bureaux supported, but silently, for the reasons which were expressed.

Essentially the C.E.A. requested that cover for loss or damage to the environment should be strictly limited so that there would be an ability to offer more cover to the carrier for bodily injury which had a greater social priority. Therefore the C.E.A., on behalf of Insurers, requested an acceptable compromise on the limits of liability as between the legislative provisions and the economic and technical means available to different countries, taking into account the fact that in some instances the size of the market and the difficulties and cost of reinsurance could represent a barrier which would be difficult for the small or medium-sized Insurers to overcome.

Any Convention or Directive or initiative has to have regard to the capacity of the insurance markets to provide the required insurance cover. This was a reasonable and important issue to be raised on behalf of the insurance markets, bearing in mind that the Convention provides for insurance coverage in respect of the liability provisions which were foreseen in that Convention.

In the event limits of liability were inserted in the Convention, at a level which was higher than the Insurers wished to see, but at a level which in the opinion of the C.E.A. could just about be managed.

The general summary is that the Convention was produced on a basis which the Council of Bureaux (for road transport only) could support and Insurers through the C.E.A. (for general liabilities) could live with.

There is now an acceptable all-round compromise result which can allow for the Council of Bureaux and Insurance markets to accept the Convention, in particular as regards injuries or damage sustained by actual victims arising from accidents due to the dangerous goods which are transported. The conclusions of the Council of Bureaux and the insurance markets have been promoted, these have in large measure been appreciated, and the future will determine upon whether in the final analysis the compulsory Third Party insurance laws, or supplementary laws based upon the Convention, will receive the necessary support.

Marine Pollution: Prevention, Punishment, Compensation and Reward

Geoffrey Brice, Q.C.

The last thirty years has seen the development of the large oil tanker from a vessel of less than 100,000 tons deadweight to some, constructed in recent years, of over 500,000 tons deadweight. In the event of a casualty such as occurred to the tankers *Torrey Canyon*, *Amoco Cadiz*, *Exxon Valdez* and the *Haven* massive pollution could result and did result. The same applies to ships carrying chemicals and other hazardous cargoes.

The public has become increasingly aware of the threat from oil cargoes. International Conventions beginning with Prevention of Oil Pollution Convention, 1954 have been concluded to regulate the carriage of oil. The first Convention to impose strict liability for pollution damage was the Brussels Civil Liability Convention, 1969 (CLC) and the Fund Convention, 1971. Voluntary compensation schemes such as TOVALOP and CRISTAL have likewise been concluded. States have been permitted to intervene in marine casualties involving oil pollution by the Brussels Prevention Convention 1969. Efforts are being made to arrange compensation for damage by chemicals in the preparation at the International Maritime Organisation of a new Convention on hazardous and noxious substances (HNS).

However, regulation, compensation and punishment are not enough if the marine environment is to be protected. What is needed is a system of reward to prevent pollution occurring when it is threatened. This is to be found in developments in the law of salvage.

The origins of the law of salvage extend back very many centuries and principles of salvage law are to be found throughout the maritime world. If a ship or her cargo were in peril at sea and were preserved from that peril by salvors then an award of salvage remuneration was due restricted only by the value of the property salved. The level of remuneration awarded by a Court or

Arbitrator reflected the benefit which the salvor had conferred upon the owner of the salved property. The public interest lay in encouraging the salvors to perform salvage services by awarding them generous salvage remuneration for meritorious services. The Brussels Convention on Salvage 1910 reflects this concept. However more than 50 years after that Convention was concluded, new technical developments changed the perception of danger to ship or cargo: for if they were in danger then, in certain circumstances, the property of others or the environment generally could also be in danger.

It was rapidly realised by the maritime community and governmental authorities that awarding compensation under voluntary and compulsory schemes was not enough. What had to be done was to encourage those who were usually first on the scene, namely the professional salvors, to render a service immediately with a view not only to saving the ship and cargo but also protecting the environment. Other casualties involving dangerous chemicals or even nuclear cargo brought an increased sense of urgency to this problem.

The first legal action that was taken in the field of maritime salvage, following the *Amoco Cadiz* casualty in 1978, was a redrafting of the most commonly used form of salvage contract, Lloyd's Standard Form of Salvage Agreement "No Cure — No Pay". An exception was made to the traditional principle of "No Cure — No Pay" by providing a "safety net" for salvors guaranteeing them their expenses together with a possible increment or mark up of 15%. The expenses were generously defined to include a fair rate for their craft and equipment. The new form was known as "LOF 1980".

Prior to the conclusion of "LOF 1980" in its final form action was already being taken by the Comité Maritime International (CMI) and by the International Maritime Organization (IMO) and its predecessor. What was needed was a new Convention covering both threats to the environment from oil and from other substances such as dangerous chemicals. In short there was an international effort to conclude a new International Convention replacing the Brussels Convention of 1910.

After 10 years' work and debate a new Convention, the London Convention on Salvage, 1989, was concluded at a Diplomatic Conference attended by 66 states in April 1989. This Convention brought into existence entirely new provisions providing "Special Compensation" to a salvor in cases involving a threat to the environment. The salvor could still (the fund permitting) recover a traditional salvage award; but the shipowner would be liable for the "Special Compensation" which was based upon the salvor's expenses. The key article in the London Convention is Article 14, which provides -

"Special compensation

1. If the salvor has carried out salvage operations in respect of a vessel which by itself or its cargo threatened damage to the environment and has failed to earn a reward under article 13 at least equivalent to the special compensation assessable in accordance with this article, he shall be entitled to special compensation from the owner of that vessel equivalent to his expenses as herein defined.

2. If, in the circumstances set out in paragraph 1, the salvor by his salvage operations has prevented or minimized damage to the environment, the special compensation payable by the owner to the salvor under paragraph 1 may be increased up to a maximum of 30% of the expenses incurred by the salvor. However, the tribunal, if it deems it fair and just to do so and bearing in mind the relevant criteria set out in article 13, paragraph 1, may increase such special compensation further, but in no event shall the total increase be more than 100% of the expenses incurred by the salvor.

3. Salvor's expenses for the purpose of paragraphs 1 and 2 means the out-of-pocket expenses reasonably incurred by the salvor in the salvage operation and a fair rate for equipment and personnel actually and reasonably used in the salvage operation, taking into consideration the criteria set out in article 13, paragraph 1(h), (i) and (j).

4. The total special compensation under this article shall be paid only if and to the extent that such compensation is greater than any reward recoverable by the salvor under article 13.

5. If the salvor has been negligent and has thereby failed to prevent or minimize damage to the environment, he may be deprived of the whole or part of any special compensation due under this article.

6. Nothing in this article shall affect any right or recourse on the part of the owner of the vessel.

It will be seen that in certain circumstances, if the salvor has by his services prevented or minimised damage to the environment, he may receive an increment on his expenses of up to 100% under the provisions of Article 14.2.

By Article 1(d) *Damage to the environment* means substantial physical damage to human health or to marine life or resources in coastal or inland waters or areas adjacent thereto, caused by pollution, contamination, fire, explosion or similar major incidents.

The new Convention is not yet law in most states although it has been approved by the United States Congress; and it has already be incorporated into a new form of a widely used salvage agreement, Lloyd's Standard Form, "No cure — No Pay" (LOF 1990). This development of the law of salvage is of great benefit to the maritime community, to coastal states and to all those who wish to see the preservation of clean oceans, shorelines and waterways.